RSCCD

S0-AWF-927

Santiago Canyon College
Library

THE MAKING OF A TERRORIST

PRAEGER SECURITY INTERNATIONAL ADVISORY BOARD

Board Cochairs

Loch K. Johnson, Regents Professor of Public and International Affairs, School of Public and International Affairs, University of Georgia (U.S.A.)

Paul Wilkinson, Professor of International Relations and Chairman of the Advisory Board, Centre for the Study of Terrorism and Political Violence, University of St. Andrews (U.K.)

Members

Vice Admiral Arthur K. Cebrowski, USN (Ret.), former Director of Force Transformation, Office of the Secretary of Defense (U.S.A.)

Eliot A. Cohen, Robert E. Osgood Professor of Strategic Studies and Director, Philip Merrill Center for Strategic Studies, Paul H. Nitze School of Advanced International Studies, The Johns Hopkins University (U.S.A.)

Anthony H. Cordesman, Arleigh A. Burke Chair in Strategy, Center for Strategic and International Studies (U.S.A)

Thérèse Delpech, Senior Research Fellow, CERI (Atomic Energy Commission), Paris (France)

Sir Michael Howard, former Professor of History of War, Oxford University, and Professor of Military and Naval History, Yale University (U.K.)

Lieutenant General Claudia J. Kennedy, USA (Ret.), former Deputy Chief of Staff for Intelligence, Headquarters, Department of the Army (U.S.A.)

Paul M. Kennedy, J. Richardson Dilworth Professor of History and Director, International Security Studies, Yale University (U.S.A.)

Robert J. O'Neill, former Chichele Professor of the History of War, All Souls College, Oxford University (Australia)

Shibley Telhami, Anwar Sadat Chair for Peace and Development, Department of Government and Politics, University of Maryland (U.S.A.)

Jusuf Wanandi, co-founder and member, Board of Trustees, Centre for Strategic and International Studies (Indonesia)

Fareed Zakaria, Editor, Newsweek International (U.S.A.)

HV
6431
. M353
2006

THE MAKING OF A TERRORIST

RECRUITMENT, TRAINING, AND ROOT CAUSES

Volume II: Training

Edited by James J. F. Forest

PRAEGER SECURITY INTERNATIONAL
Westport, Connecticut · London

OCM60741966

Santiago Canyon College
Library

Library of Congress Cataloging-in-Publication Data

The making of a terrorist : recruitment, training, and root causes / edited by
James J. F. Forest.
     p.   cm.
  Includes bibliographical references and index.
  ISBN 0–275–98543–1 ((set) : alk. paper)—ISBN 0–275–98544–X ((vol.
i) : alk. paper)—ISBN 0–275–98545–8 ((vol. ii) : alk. paper)—ISBN
0–275–98546–6 ((vol. iii) : alk. paper)   1. Terrorism.   2. Terrorists.   I. Forest,
James J. F.
  HV6431.M353   2006
  303.6'25—dc22   2005016849

British Library Cataloguing in Publication Data is available.

Copyright © 2006 by James J. F. Forest

All rights reserved. No portion of this book may be
reproduced, by any process or technique, without the
express written consent of the publisher.

Library of Congress Catalog Card Number: 2005016849
ISBN: 0-275-98543-1 (set)
       0-275-98544-X (vol. I)
       0-275-98545-8 (vol. II)
       0-275-98546-6 (vol. III)

First published in 2006

Praeger Security International, 88 Post Road West, Westport, CT 06881
An imprint of Greenwood Publishing Group, Inc.
www.praeger.com

Printed in the United States of America

The paper used in this book complies with the
Permanent Paper Standard issued by the National
Information Standards Organization (Z39.48-1984).

10 9 8 7 6 5 4 3 2 1

Contents

Preface

The chapters assembled for this volume contribute to our knowledge of both ideological and operational learning in the world of terrorism. Several authors explore terrorist training camps and activities in certain parts of the world—including Afghanistan, Bosnia, Colombia, Indonesia, Ireland, the Philippines, and the United States—while others address some of the psychological and sociological forces that help develop the new recruit's will and skill to kill.

Part I: Teaching Tools and Developmental Experiences

The first four chapters of the volume bring us into the realm of psychological research, beginning with Jerrold Post's discussion of interviews he and his colleagues conducted with Middle Eastern terrorists incarcerated in Israeli and Palestinian prisons. As a whole, these interviews illuminated how the lives of individuals were shaped by powerful sociopsychological forces that led them onto the path of terrorism. As highlighted by the direct quotes presented in this chapter, an understanding of these forces reveals how "hatred is bred in the bone." Professor Post, Director of the Political Psychology Program at the George Washington University and a former member of the Central Intelligence Agency, illustrates how the individual comes to subordinate his individuality to the group, which becomes the central pillar of his identity. The need of individuals to belong and to exercise control in their own lives is paramount for every individual, but it is intensified in communities where segments of the population are ostracized or persecuted based on ethnic, religious, or social background. By belonging to a radical group, otherwise powerless individuals become powerful. Group identity provides a foundation of relative stability upon which disenfranchised or isolated members of a society build a base of commonality and join together.

In the next chapter, Stanford University Professor Albert Bandura explores the role of moral disengagement in the terrorist world. A social psychologist who has studied terrorism for many years, Bandura notes how humans typically have an internal collection of self-sanctions that play a central role in the regulation of our conduct. However, there are many psychological processes by which these moral self-sanctions can be disengaged from inhumane conduct.[1] Further, the removal of one's inhibitions is accelerated if violent courses of action are presented as serving a moral imperative, and the targeted people are divested of human qualities.[2] In so doing, otherwise considerate individuals can commit atrocities of appalling proportions. Terrorism can thus be seen as the product of a complex network of influences that enable and motivate people to perpetrate terrorist acts rather than stemming mainly from a pernicious nature.

This is followed with a chapter (co-authored by Professors Marc Galanter of New York University and James Forest of the Combating Terrorism Center at West Point) on the social systems found within charismatic groups and how the characteristics of these systems compel their members to behave in certain ways. In essence, the charismatic group can be viewed as a close-knit community defined by the following primary characteristics: It has a strongly-held belief system and a high level of social cohesiveness; its members are deeply influenced by the group's behavioral norms and impute a transcendent (or divine) role to their leader. These groups may differ among themselves in the particulars of their ideology and ritual behavior, but they do have several traits in common, including: 1) an attraction to joining the group; 2) the transformative experience of membership; and 3) the social system forces that surround the group's members, giving meaning and structure. These traits of charismatic groups help explain the behavioral transformations described in many of the chapters of this volume. Through a mix of psychological and social dimensions observed in this discussion, the charismatic group and the individual form a symbiotic relationship, serving each other's needs. When joining a charismatic group, an individual is transformed by powerful forces into a personal extension of the group's identity, which compels them to carry out activities that were unthinkable prior to group membership. Even when a suicide terrorist attack is the goal, this act can be justified as serving the needs of the group, needs which take primacy over the individual's basic desire for a longer life.

The next chapter of this section, by noted psychologist and cult expert Arthur Deikman of the University of California, San Francisco, explores the psychological dimension of power held by charismatic leaders and focuses on what this can tell us about the dynamics of terrorist groups. He notes that cult thinking is most prominently evident when members of a group devalue outsiders while ignoring the faults of the leader and fellow believers. Outsiders are declared to be inferior, bad, or damned, while those in the cult group view themselves as superior, good, or saved. We see this in its most extreme form in the mind of the terrorist. Cult leaders, tyrants, and terrorists invariably defend immoral and violent actions as serving God, truth, or country. This analysis thus suggests that it is often not deprivation or injustice that is the decisive motivation for terror, but the need to see oneself as good and heroic, esteemed by the community, and blessed by God.

The next two chapters of this section review a variety of print and online resources that provide the types of operational learning necessary for conducting terrorism. Professor James Forest of West Point begins with a description of training manuals that have been authored and made available by several organizations, from the Christian Identity movement to al Qaeda. Advanced multimedia websites and online discussion forums facilitate the sort of teacher-learner interaction that takes place in terrorist training camps. Further, while the Internet plays an important role in developing the new terrorist recruit's will and ability to kill others, it brings a whole new set of tools for terror, enabling the development of technology-oriented terrorism, or "cyberterrorism." Overall, this chapter suggests that the globalization of information and technology are helping facilitate the spread of old and new forms of terrorism.

Similarly, as Columbia University Professor Brigitte Nacos observes in her chapter on the media, terrorists learn much about each other through daily news reports, video clips, and websites. Further, the media serve a vital role in facilitating the spread of the terrorist's propaganda, helping individuals and groups gain attention, recognition, legitimacy, and respect. When terrorists uses the media effectively—for example, as seen in the cases of Osama bin Laden and Abu Musab al-Zarqawi—other terrorists learn from and follow their example. Recently, a proliferation of videotaped beheadings—which began in Iraq but spread to Saudi Arabia and other parts of the world—is but one of many examples of this phenomenon of mediated terrorism.

Part II: Case Studies of Terrorist Learning

The next section of the volume begins with a chapter by RAND terrorism specialist Brian Jackson, in which he examines the terrorist training regimen of the Provisional Irish Republican Army. His discussion provides a unique account of how the PIRA inducted new recruits to support its military activities, taught volunteers new skills to support and improve the group's operational capability, and provided members with the intelligence and counterintelligence skills needed both to collect the information required for operations and to prevent security force penetration or disruption of group activities. Jackson's assessment of the PIRA's efforts in these areas leads to several lessons that can be drawn relevant to training by terrorist groups: a sufficient amount of sanctuary provides better opportunities for realistic and more thorough training, especially for sophisticated weaponry and tactics; terrorist groups need specialists to provide the expertise necessary for specific advanced operations and tasks; and connections with outside groups or experts can be useful to a terrorist organization—but only if those links are close enough to provide current and useful knowledge support and if the assistance provided to the group is relevant to its operational context.

Next, Carnegie Endowment researcher Martha Brill Olcott partners with Bakhtiyar Babajanov, a Senior Research Fellow at the Academy of Sciences of Uzbekistan, in an analysis of personal study notebooks of young men who were recruited for jihad and attended terrorist training camps in Uzbekistan during the 1990s.[3] They describe how students learned cartography (map making), the use of small firearms (mainly Soviet-era rifles and the occasional Egyptian rocket-propelled grenade launcher), tactics for targeting the enemy (both on the ground and in the air), explosive device construction (including antipersonnel mines), and how to make poison using corn, flour, beef, yak dung, alcohol, and water. While the motivational/ideological knowledge represented in these students' notebooks reflects a clear Islamic radicalist influence, it is equally interesting to note that, according to Olcott and Babajanov, "the teachers who used Russian terminology clearly had experience with the Red Army and Soviet system of military instruction, and those who used Arabic likely passed through terrorist camps in Afghanistan and maybe even those of the Middle East."[4] Their exploration of these training materials provides a unique window into the world of teaching and learning in the terrorist world.

In the following chapter, Professor Adam Dolnik, of the Institute of Defense and Strategic Studies (IDSS) in Singapore, describes the process of becoming a suicide bomber, noting that this process differs considerably depending on the given cultural, regional, and ideological context. In the Middle East, Palestinian recruits for suicide bombing are put through a testing period and then asked to prepare a videotape of their last will. In Sri Lanka, most of the perpetrators of suicide bombing attacks are experienced members of the Tamil Tigers who have already established their credibility. Since members of this group are routinely issued potassium cyanide capsules (to be consumed when on the verge of capture), the preparedness to die at any given moment is a baseline attribute for all potential volunteers. He concludes that suicide bombings represent the ultimate terrorist tactic. Besides their tactical advantages, they also have the capability of satisfying many terrorist objectives in a single attack: demonstration of dedication and capability, attracting attention and media coverage, producing a high number of casualties, and instigating general feelings of vulnerability. Finding recruits for suicide missions is never difficult once a precedent has been established. Suicide attacks can be justified on any religious or ideological grounds in the appropriate historical and cultural context. It is therefore very likely that the use of this tactic will become increasingly frequent in areas where it has already been established and will be introduced to many other struggles around the world.

The next chapter, co-authored by Professor Rohan Gunaratna and fellow IDSS researcher Arabinda Acharya, explores the role of training—particularly the training camps established by al Qaeda—in facilitating the spread of the global Islamic militant terrorist threat. The training camps set up by al Qaeda and its associates became the lifeblood for the groups, providing indoctrination and training for foot soldiers, go-betweens, planners, document forgers, communications specialists, scouts, technicians, bombers, and even hijackers. According to some estimates, many militant Muslims from more than fifty countries have passed through the camps, spending from two weeks to more than six months learning the general and specific skills that modern terrorism requires. Many veterans of the camp remain unaccounted for. From their analysis, Gunaratna and Arabinda conclude that given the importance of these facilities to terrorist organizations, the necessity of locating and disrupting terrorist camps can hardly be overemphasized.

In a similar vein, as international terrorism consultant Evan Kohlmann observes in the following chapter, participation in the Bosnian conflict also allowed mujahideen to develop terrorist-related tactical skills as well as common bonds of loyalty and friendship between *jihadists* of various nationalities. Indeed, he notes, many of al Qaeda's most important military and leadership figures were catapulted forward on the world stage as a result of their early involvement with the mujahideen in Bosnia. He cites several reasons why the Bosnian experience provides a critical chapter in the story of contemporary militant Islam. First, the deployment of Arab fighters to Bosnia, who were generally loyal to the jihadi leadership in Afghanistan, exploded during the mid-1990s into numbers sometimes estimated even to exceed 5,000. Second, this massive and significant migration of Arab-Afghans to Bosnia occurred at an early stage of the al Qaeda movement, meaning that the experience had long-lasting effects—both practically and ideologically—on the terrorist group. Third, Bosnia's unique geographic position directly between Western Europe and the Middle East was the ideal jumping-off point for organizational expansion of the movement into Italy, France, Germany, Austria, Canada, and the United Kingdom. It provided an environment where trained foreign Muslim fighters arriving from Afghanistan could mingle with (and help teach) unsophisticated but eager terrorist recruits from Western Europe and could form new plans for the future of the jihad. No such contact had ever occurred before in the short history of al Qaeda, and it provided the organization and its radical membership limitless possibilities for development and growth—as well as a geographic step in the ladder towards its enemies in Western Europe and North America.

Jemaah Islamiyah (JI), a terrorist group in Indonesia affiliated with al Qaeda, is the focus of the next chapter. IDSS Professor Kumar Ramakrishna examines the processes by which JI indoctrinates new militants. In this respect, it can be argued that against the necessary wider historical, sociocultural and political backdrop of indigenous militant strains of Islam in Indonesia, the key to JI indoctrination involves three intersecting factors: first, the deliberate exposure of recruits to the radical Islamist ideology of Qaedaism; second, intensive psychological programming aimed at engendering hatred for Westerners in particular; and third, the existence of an isolated "ingroup space" within which both ideological and psychological programming can be carried out with maximum efficiency. His analysis suggests a number of problems that are in need of closer analysis and engagement. First and foremost, one cannot ignore the wider communities of religious prejudice from which JI terrorists ultimately emerge. Second, ostensibly nonviolent leaders like Bashir—who nonetheless preach polarized, absolutist ideologies that nudge impressionable individuals along the continuum toward hate obsession and potential terrorist recruitment—are clearly a cause for concern. Third, certain educational environments that deliberately limit contact with the outside world and appear to propagate alternate constructions of reality should be spotlighted and their managements urged to expose their student populations to wider informational and intellectual vistas. And of particular salience, the continuing inability of either liberal Muslims or Islamic modernists to devise and propagate modern interpretations of the faith that trump the simplistic, "us-versus-them" radical story lines in the estimation of the Muslim ground is a problem that urgently needs redressing.

The religious-based "us-versus-them" mentality seen among JI members is also found among members of Christian militia groups in the United States, as described in the next chapter, co-authored by University of North Carolina–Charlotte Professor Cindy Combs and her research colleagues Elizabeth Combs and Lydia Marsh. Their analysis illuminates three important aspects of the relationship that continue to shape the training of the Christian militia today: the Biblically-based theology that seeks to rationalize the preparation for violence by members of militia groups; a fervent belief in the Bill of Rights, particularly the right to bear arms and the right to generate an "unorganized militia"; and a commitment to a loose, virtually leaderless membership structure, with members trained to act alone or in small groups to "take back" the government, through force if necessary. They note how members of militia groups are often well-trained in the use of arms and explosives. Some militia groups even have skilled armorers and bomb makers, and members with outdoor survival skills who are adept at guerrilla-warfare techniques. Among their conclusions, the authors note that militia groups, while not directly responsible for the actions of their members, may offer social and psychological support that will enable individuals to carry out lethal acts on their own. Thus, the danger from these groups may lie in the ability of individuals, motivated by militia propaganda, to launch unilateral attacks on disparate targets, coordinated only by timing—and that danger remains clear and not yet preventable.

The next chapter, by Professor Magnus Ranstorp, Director of the Center for the Study of Terrorism and Political Violence (CSTPV) at the University of St. Andrews, Scotland, explores the Hizballah training camps of Lebanon. Since its foundation in 1982, Hizballah has developed a highly complex and multifaceted terrorist infrastructure under Iranian guidance and support and with Syrian patronage. Hizballah's training camps have served multiple political and operational purposes over time, extending from solidifying its structure in the early 1980s to providing very advanced guerrilla and terrorist training to its own and other selected fighters from Palestinian factions. Over time, the group acquired an impressive weaponry arsenal and a high degree of interoperability between its military and terrorist wing, especially with the expert assistance of Iranian military advisers and instructors. In his view, there are few organizations as capable, precise and dangerous as Hizballah.

Next, Professor Román Ortiz of Los Andes University (Bogotá) provides an insightful analysis of terrorist training activities employed by the FARC, Colombia's most lethal band of guerillas. He notes how the content of FARC training courses have changed over time, in order to meet the strategic needs of the organization. For example, in the beginning of the 1990s FARC's leadership established a broad training program to develop skills for major mobile warfare operations such as extensive ambushes or attacks against fortified bases. However, by the end of the decade the group abandoned mobile warfare and gradually returned to guerilla warfare, and thus refocused its training courses on tactics such as mine warfare, sniping, and anti-aircraft defense. This analysis underscores how a terrorist group's training is influenced by its strategic environment in addition to its ideological or political objectives.

A growing concern worldwide over the possible terrorist use of weapons of mass destruction provides the context for the next chapter, in which RAND policy analyst John Parachini examines Aum Shinrikyō's development of a chemical weapons program. Parachini describes the evolution of this program, the types of knowledge and materials that were acquired, and the key players involved—such as the group's chief chemist Masami Tsuchiya, who joined Aum after receiving his master's degree in organic chemistry from Tsukuba University, and Tomomasa Nakagawa, who was trained as a medical doctor at Kyoto Prefectural University of Medicine. Overall, Aum's experience with chemical agents illustrates the opportunities and limitations nonstate actors encounter when they attempt to develop an unconventional weapons capability on their own from scratch. While Aum killed far fewer people with toxic chemicals than a host of major bombings in the last twenty years, the very fact that they acquired the knowledge and materials to successfully conduct terrorist attacks is alarming. Even a small group of people, if they have sufficient resources and are able to maintain tight security, can pose a catastrophic danger.

Finally, the last chapter of this volume (by James Forest) provides a summary of terrorist training camps around the world—the most common and important places where indoctrination and operational teaching for terrorism (on strategic and tactical levels) takes place. In addition to strategic and tactical learning, terrorist training camps incorporate a number of psychological development processes—as described in the earlier chapters of this volume—which advance the ideological motivations that brought the students to the camps in the first place. The physical isolation of the training camps is an important aspect to this process, in part because members come to rely on each other (and thus build bonds of mutual trust within the organization) for success and survival. In short, training camps for terrorism are obviously places of great concern for the civilized world, because they bring enthusiastic learners (with a willingness to kill) together with experts who teach them how to kill.

Conclusion

This second volume in the *Making of a Terrorist* series is meant to provide a general overview of the most important places of terrorist learning and the developmental processes that take place within them. As a collection, the chapters address the problem of global terrorism from a central lens of knowledge—specifically, the role of teaching and learning in helping a terrorist organization maintain its capacity to carry out its deadly operations. Our ability to combat the global terrorist threat requires a better understanding of how and where activities such as ideological indoctrination and operational learning take place, before devising ways to disrupt or degrade the terrorists' organizational capabilities. Thus, these chapters provide an important contribution to the study of terrorism, offering policy implications for counterterrorism professionals, scholars, and policymakers around the world.

Acknowledgments

The views expressed herein are those of the author and do not purport to reflect the position of the United States Military Academy, the Department of the Army, or the Department of Defense.

Acknowledgments

A massive endeavor such as this requires a great deal of support from one's colleagues, family and friends, as well as generous amounts of caffeine and hubris. Thankfully, I have not suffered for lack of any of these. For their continued support, I extend my sincere gratitude foremost to the faculty and staff of the Combating Terrorism Center (CTC) at West Point (Jarret, Kip, Bill, Brian, Lianne, Daniella, Thalia, Jeff, Janice, Jude, and Reid), from whom I continue to learn much every day. Two men in particular—General (R) Wayne Downing, Chair of the CTC, and Brigadier General (R) Russell Howard, former Head of the Department of Social Sciences at West Point and founding Director of the CTC—have inspired countless others with their leadership, counterterrorism expertise, and commitment to improving our nation's security, and I am grateful for the opportunity to learn from them. Guidance and suggestions from USMA Academy Professor (and Colonel) Cindy Jebb and Dr. Rohan Gunaratna (Senior Fellow at the CTC) were also very helpful in identifying themes and authors for this project. And my faculty colleagues throughout West Point—and particularly the Department of Social Sciences—have been a continual source of support and assistance.

Over the last few years, I have been intrigued and inspired by colleagues and friends who study terrorism and counterterrorism—many of whose words are represented in the pages of these volumes. Each of the chapters in these volumes is the product of thoughtful research and analysis, and I offer my heartfelt thanks to the authors for their hard work and commitment to excellence. It is my sincere hope that all the collective effort put into this project will inspire a new generation to pursue further research in the field of terrorism and counterterrorism studies.

Finally, and of course most importantly, I owe a great debt of gratitude to my wife Alicia, who provided an incredible amount of patience and understanding through long nights and weekends while I disappeared into the solitary world of editing. Her support during this process was particularly phenomenal given that while I was working to produce the final manuscript of these volumes, she was working on the final term of a demanding pregnancy. Book and baby are now being introduced to the world at roughly the same time; thus, with the appropriately optimistic and hopeful energy the newborns bring, I dedicate this book to my new daughter, Chloe Lynn. I pray that she and all those of her generation will grow up in a world where the scourge of terrorism is better understood, prevented, and defeated.

CHAPTER 1

Exploring the Training of Terrorists: An Introduction

JAMES J. F. FOREST

On 21 May 1991, former Prime Minister of India Rajiv Gandhi stood smiling among a throng of supporters and well-wishers in the peaceful village of Sriperumbudur (in the province of Tamil Nadu, India) when a young Tamil woman by the name of Dhanu stepped forward, bent down to touch his feet in a customary sign of reverence, and detonated the explosive belt she was wearing (a harness of six grenades). Gandhi and seventeen others were killed instantly, while others were injured or maimed for life.[1] On 15 August 1998, a car bomb packed with 500 pounds of explosives detonated in the popular shopping district of Omagh, a small town in county Tyrone, Northern Ireland (about seventy miles west of Belfast).[2] The entire front wall of SD Kells clothes shop was blasted into the building, and the roof collapsed onto the top floor. At the Pine Emporium, a furniture shop, the blast was such that furniture could later be seen sticking out the windows at the back of the building. A water main under the road was exposed by the blast, and this began pouring gallons of water over the wreckage, washing bodies down the hill. All in all, twenty-eight people were killed by the blast, and hundreds more were injured.

On 28 October 2001, six members of the Islamist Sipah-e-Sihaba group entered St. Dominic's Church in Behawalpur, Pakistan, during Protestant services and opened fire on the congregation. Sixteen people were killed, including the minister and a Muslim guard posted outside the church.[3] A few months later, on 27 January 2002, a young woman by the name of Wafa Idris, a paramedic who lived in Ramallah, entered a shopping district in Jerusalem and detonated a 22-pound bomb filled with nails and metal objects, killing an eighty-one-year-old man and injuring more than 100 bystanders. Idris, a member of the al-Aqsa Martyr's Brigade, was the first known *istish-hadiyat* (female martyr) of the Islamic fundamentalist movement in the Middle East—but others soon followed, including Dareen Abu Aisheh, who wounded two Israeli policeman when she detonated her bomb at a roadblock near Maccabim on 27 February 2002; Aayat al-Akhras, who strolled into a supermarket in the neighborhood of Kiryat Yovel in Jerusalem and killed two Israeli civilians and wounded twenty-two more on 29 March 2002; and Hanadi Jaradat, a twenty-nine-year-old lawyer who calmly entered a highly popular restaurant on 4 October 2003 and killed nineteen Israeli and Arab men, women, and children.[4]

And on 7 January 2005 a group of suspected Islamic militants were arrested in Manila, the capital of the Philippines. The group was discovered in the process of assembling bombs for what was intended to be an attack on the Christian festival of the Black Nazarene, an annual event which attracts tens of thousands of devotees. When police examined the improvised explosive devices and bomb components, including timing gadgets and cables, they realized that the death toll of the explosions, had they occurred, would have been considerable.[5]

News stories similar to these can be found today, any day, somewhere in the world—a group or individual with the motivation to kill innocents need only act upon that motivation, and the world bears witness to yet another terrorist attack. These events can take many forms, including arson, assassination or targeted murders, bombing, commercial and industrial sabotage, hijacking, hostage-taking, kidnapping, mass rape and mutilation (such as the attrocities that took place in Uganda and Rwanda during the 1990s), and the use (or threatened use) of weapons of mass destruction. While terrorist attacks have been a continual nightmare for places like Israel, Pakistan, and Sri Lanka, concern about terrorism in the United States grew sharply during the 1990s—and for good reason. This was the decade in which America felt the sting of both domestic terrorists—with periodic abortion clinic attacks, the bombing of the Murrah Federal Building in Oklahoma City in 1995, and the bombing of the Centennial Olympic Park in Atlanta in 1996—as well as foreign terrorists, including the bombing of the World Trade Center in 1993, the attack on U.S. soldiers as they slept in the Khobar Towers in Saudi Arabia, and the destruction of the U.S. Embassies in Kenya and Tanzania in 1998. Of the 392 international attacks in 1999, 186 of them utilized bombs, and of these, 111 were directed at U.S.-related targets.[6]

Each of the terrorist events described thus far in this chapter required specialized knowledge of explosives, covert movement and communication, and automatic weapons. From decades of research, we know that successful terrorist attacks require careful planning and training, in addition to intense personal motivation on the part of the attackers. However, the type of knowledge required for such activities is not typically found in your local library, public school, or in other traditional places where formal learning takes place. Thus, the question arises, where and how does learning take place in the terrorist world? The use of terrorism in pursuit of political objectives, as explored in the previous volume of this publication, can encompass a variety of ideological, social, political, and other factors which helps to foster a willingness to kill. But where does one learn *how* to kill? How does one develop the ability to assemble bombs and shoot weapons, particularly without hurting yourself in the process? In exploring the answers to such questions, this second volume in the *Making of a Terrorist* series addresses an array of developmental processes and places related to terrorist training.

Collectively, the chapters in this volume cover a diverse set of topics which help us better understand how an ordinary individual can be molded into an effective member of a terrorist organization. The first half of the volume focuses on training tools and developmental experiences in the world of terrorism and illuminates the types of strategic and tactical learning, the psychological and group socialization processes, and the overall individual transformation that takes place in training for terrorism. The second half of the volume provides case studies that explore these terrorist training issues within various locations throughout the world. But first, this introductory chapter provides a brief overview of research and concepts to illuminate some of what is known about locations and methods of terrorist training.

Training and Learning in the World of Terrorism

In 2004, U.S. authorities discovered a thirty-nine-page document titled "Rough Presentation for Gas Limo Project," which lays out a scenario for using limousines to deliver bombs equipped with cylinders of a flammable gas.[7] The document is believed to have been written by Issa al-Hindi, an al Qaeda operative captured in Britain last year. It recommends concealing bombs in limos because the vehicles "blend in" and "can transport larger payloads than sedans . . . and do not require special driving skills." The limos can "access underground parking structures that do not accommodate trucks" and "have tinted windows that can hide an improvised explosive device from outside." The document calls for the deployment of three limos, each carrying twelve or more compressed-gas cylinders to create a "full fuel-air explosion by venting flammable gas into a confined space and then igniting it." It also suggests painting the cylinders yellow to falsely "signify toxic gases to spread terror and chaos when emergency and hazmat teams arrive." Al Qaeda used similar devices in the truck bomb that blew up the U.S. Embassy in Dar es Salaam, Tanzania in 1998 and in a 2002 attack on a Tunisian synagogue.[8]

This document offers a dramatic example of training (or operational knowledge transfer) in the terrorist world. To sustain their capacity for conducting attacks, terrorist groups must facilitate the documentation and dissemination of such knowledge, and they do so through a variety of manuals, handbooks, and other documents. Examples include *The Green Book* of the Irish Republican Army, *The Turner Diaries* and the *Field Manual for Free Militia* used by members of Christian militias in the United States, *The Mujahideen Poisons Handbook* produced by Hamas, and the multivolume *Encyclopedia of the Afghan Jihad* produced by al Qaeda. Through the globalization of access to information technology, publications such as these offer valuable learning tools for would-be terrorists. As Bruce Hoffman aptly observed, "Using commercially published or otherwise readily accessible bomb-making manuals and operational guides to poisons, assassinations and chemical and biological weapons fabrication, . . . the 'amateur' terrorist can be just as deadly and destructive as his more 'professional' counterpart."[9]

One online training manual recommends that Muslim holy warriors should use lax firearms laws in the United States to get sniper and military assault rifle training.[10] This document informs jihad trainees that "in some countries of the world, especially in the U.S.A., firearms training is available to the general public," and that "it is perfectly legal to obtain weapons such as AK-47 assault rifles."[11] It urges would-be warriors to take advantage of these environments to learn firearm fighting skills, especially sniping and assault rifle use.[12] A six-page document titled *How Can I Train Myself for Jihad* advises that "military training is an obligation in Islam upon every sane, male, mature Muslim, whether rich or poor, whether studying or working and whether living in a Muslim or non-Muslim country." It offers tips on various ways to make "suitable preparations for battle" including physical training, martial arts, survival and outdoors training, firearms training, and military training.[13] Al Qaeda's *Encyclopedia of the Afghan Jihad* includes "lessons" on a variety of topics, including qualifications and characteristics for members, counterfeit currency and forged documents, apartments and hiding places, means of communication and transportation, training, weapons purchasing and transportation, member safety and security, surveillance and information gathering, espionage, and sabotage.

Publications such as these, in turn, help frame a type of "Terrorism 101" curriculum provided at training camps and other centers of terrorist learning. As described in several chapters of this volume, the typical training camp requires a combination of resources, geographic isolation, and individuals with specific abilities. Throughout history, they have served as perhaps the most important places where the transformation from individual to terrorist has taken place. One account of the combat training and conditioning of the recruit's mindset that occurs in the al Qaeda camps of Afghanistan is provided by the biography of Zacarias Moussaoui, the so-called 20th member of the cell that conducted the September 11, 2001 attacks:

Once in the camp, it is easy, as in any sect to make him lose his bearings. First of all, he is put through athletic training, and then into weapons handling. These are intensive exercises. He is always being set challenges that are increasingly difficult to meet. The young recruit is not well fed. He gradually becomes exhausted. He never manages to completely come up with what is being asked of him. After several weeks or months, he gets the feeling that he's not capable of doing what is expected of him. He experiences a feeling of embarrassment and malaise. In his own eyes, he is completely belittled: he feels guilty because he is incompetent. And yet he is told over and over again that others before him have succeeded and gone on to "great things." . . . And if he carries on, it is to the bitter end. Because the only thing he can do to help the cause is to give his life to it. And this will also prove to others that, at the end, he met their expectations.[14]

Al Qaeda's training camps in places like Afghanistan and Bosnia are perhaps the most commonly cited locations where terrorist training is known to have taken place. Vivid descriptions of these camps are provided in recently-published books like Rohan Gunaratna's *Inside Al Qaeda*, Peter Bergen's *Holy War Inc.*, Marc Sageman's *Understanding Terror Networks*, Gilles Kepel's *Jihad: The Trail of Political Islam*, and Michael Scheuer's *Through Our Enemies' Eyes* (published under the pseudonym Anonymous).[15] However, terrorist training camps have existed in a wide variety of locations throughout the world—indeed, the geography of former and current centers of terrorist learning includes failed states, dictatorships, and advanced industrial democracies.

In the Middle East, groups like the Palestinian Liberation Organization and Hizballah have established training camps in the Bekaa Valley of eastern Lebanon.[16] During the 1970s, Libya began providing a safe haven for a variety of terrorist training camps, and particularly for groups committed to the spread of Islam.[17] During the early 1990s, Islamic separatist groups in Algeria built and used training camps both within their country and across the border in Tunisia, where new recruits were taught combat tactics, explosives production, and weapons handling.

In Southeast Asia, Jemaah Islamiyah—a religious extremist organization which seeks to create a pan-Islamic state uniting Indonesia, Brunei, Malaysia, Singapore, and the Southern Philippines—developed and operated several training facilities, such as Camp Jabal Quba on Mount Kararao, where courses in weapons and explosives have been provided.[18] One of the most notorious Southeast Asian terrorist training facilities was known as the Camp Abu Bakar complex in Mindanao, the Philippines, built by the Moro Islamic Liberation Front (MILF).[19] Jemaah Islamiyah built three of its own terrorist training camps in this same location: Camp Vietnam, Camp Palestine, and Camp Hudaybiyya. In Sri Lanka, the guerrilla/terrorist group Liberation Tigers of Tamil Eelam (LTTE) operates a number of training facilities in Jaffna and remote areas in the northern part of the country.

Training for the Irish Republican Army (IRA) took place, according to one account, "in most parts of the [Irish] republic, even as far south as Cork. . . . Training camps [were] of various types: a deserted farmhouse, a beach or remote wood, dependent mainly on the security of the area."[20] In February 2003, French police discovered a training area in the secluded Landes forest in southwestern France, which had been used to teach members of the Spanish separatist group *Euzkadi Ta Askatasuna* (ETA) how to use homemade grenade-launchers capable of piercing armored cars.[21] Insurgent groups like Sendero Luminoso (the Shining Path) and Tupac Amaru in Peru have operated training facilities in various remote regions of the country, where new recruits are taught guerilla strategy and the use of firearms and explosives.[22]

Even the United States has played host to terrorist training camps in recent decades. In Northern Idaho, the Aryan Nations Church's 20-acre, gated fortress with guard towers provided a sanctuary in which Christian Identity adherents received weapons training, combat tactics, and indoctrination. The closely-related Covenant, Sword and the Arm of the Lord, headquartered on the Missouri-Arkansas border, amassed one of the largest private arms caches ever uncovered in American history on its 224-acre base, Zarepath-Horeb, consisting of a 30-gallon oil drum of arsenic, at least one improvised armored vehicle, facilities for retooling machineguns out of semi-automatic weapons, grenades, RPGs, silencers, and thousands of rounds of ammunition.[23]

Prisons have also been places of increasing concern when studying terrorist training. As researcher Ian Cuthbertson recently observed, prisons can serve as "universities for terrorists," where inmates learn ideology, strategy, and tactics of terrorist organizations. Recent studies of the Irish Republican Army, for example, have highlighted how prisons aided in training new recruits for terrorism.[24] According to one account, when members of the IRA were captured and sent to British or Irish prisons, they were immediately debriefed by other inmates, who then smuggled the information (and lessons learned) to IRA members outside the prison walls. Particularly useful information passed on by the imprisoned terrorists could include how they were caught, what information the captors were looking for, what (if anything) might have gone awry with a planned attack being carried out, and who (if anyone) might have played a role in their capture.[25]

Finally, another important "place" where terrorist training occurs is the Internet. Madeleine Gruen, an intelligence analyst at the New York City Police Department's Counter Terrorism Division, notes that both Islamic extremist groups and American extremist groups use the Internet as a means for both recruitment and training. For example, the Lebanese terrorist group Hizballah has recently developed a video game called "Special Force,"[26] which gives players a simulated experience of military operations against Israeli soldiers in battles recreated from actual encounters in the south of Lebanon. This approach, Gruen explains, was learned directly from the "first-person shooter" games developed by white supremacist groups in the United States. For example, the racist organization National Alliance offers video games on its website with titles like "Nigger Hunt" and "Rattenjagt"—games with violent graphics, depicting real-life scenarios in which the player is the central character, killing Jews and other racial minorities.[27]

In addition to indoctrination, tactical and strategic training, and a location in which these activities can take place, researchers point to another, more personal level of the transformation that takes place in becoming a true terrorist. It is one thing to learn how to pull a trigger or detonate a bomb, or to simulate the killing of others through video games and role playing, but in real life, killing is not as easy as it might seem. As several psychologists have observed, most human beings develop a certain set of moral guidelines that generally work to restrict their willingness to murder a particular person or blow up a café full of innocent bystanders.[28] The terrorist organization therefore faces the challenge of ensuring that a new recruit will be able to follow a lethal mission through to its completion.

Developing the will and ability to kill involves a range of psychological conditioning activities. Few—if any—individuals are born to be terrorists or become lethal terrorists overnight. Indeed, recent studies have revealed that the isolation of attributes or traits shared by terrorists is fraught with difficulty, and efforts to create a profile or "typical" terrorist have yielded mixed results.[29] Instead, terrorist experts like Ehud Sprinzak and Ariel Merari have shown that new recruits evolve gradually into terrorists through a process of radicalization that involves a disengagement of moral self-sanctions from violent conduct.[30] In exploring this "moral disengagement," renowned psychologist Albert Bandura identified several developmental processes that can disengage morality from an individual's conduct, such as reconstruing conduct as serving moral purposes; obscuring personal agency in bad activities; disregarding consequences of actions; and blaming or dehumanizing victims.[31]

According to this body of research, in order for individuals to become lethal terrorists, they must acquire an ability to sanctify harmful conduct as honorable and righteous, which explains why terrorists often see themselves as patriots doing the bidding of the group's leaders (in religious groups, the bidding of God; or, in state terrorism, the state), thus absolving them of responsibility for their actions.[32] For example, Masami Tsuchiya, a brilliant chemist, used his skills to help Aum Shinrikyō develop poison gas and the hallucinogen PCP. Throughout his trial—at which he was sentenced to death for his role in the production of sarin that was used in two deadly nerve gas attacks—Tsuchiya consistently described himself as a "direct disciple of the guru" (in reference to Aum's leader, Shoko Asahara) and refused to accept responsibility for doing anything wrong in serving his "sonshi" (or honorable master).[33]

Moral disengagement also involves the ability of individuals to minimize the consequences of murderous acts for which they are responsible. This disregard for consequences makes it easier for a new terrorist recruit to hurt or kill others, particularly when decisions are made by superiors who are removed from those in the group who follow orders. And finally, Bandura notes, people find violence easier if they do not consider their victims as human beings.[34]

Psychologist Jerrold Post agrees with Sprinzak, Bandura, and other scholars that powerful psychological forces are involved in transforming an individual into a terrorist.[35] His research led him to coin the term "psycho-logic" to describe how the terrorist constructs a personal rationalization for acts they are psychologically compelled to commit. In essence, a polarizing and absolutist "us versus them" rhetoric of terrorists reflects their underlying views of "the establishment" as the source of all evil, and provides a psychologically satisfying explanation for what has gone wrong in their lives. According to Post, the fixed logical conclusion of the terrorist—that the establishment must be destroyed—is driven by the terrorist's search for identity, and as he strikes out against the establishment, he is attempting to destroy the enemy within.[36]

Several studies of terrorism have indicated that of all terrorist organizations, religiously motivated ones offer the highest potential for mass casualties, in part because for them, violence is perceived to be part of an all-encompassing struggle between good and evil.[37] Characterizing the victims of a terrorist attack as a dehumanized form of evil enables perhaps the most potent type of "moral disengagement" suggested by Sprinzak, Bandura, and others. Some groups, however—even religiously oriented ones—may incorporate additional methods to ensure the lethality of their members. For example, Aum Shinrikyō—the terrorist cult responsible for the lethal attack on the Tokyo subway in 1995—is known to have used hypnosis, drugs, and a strenuous physical regimen to increase the "suggestibility" of new recruits to the messages of its leader, Shoko Asahara.[38]

Often, terrorist training also involves certain forms of coercive psychological persuasion. According to the late Margaret Singer, a professor emerita at UC Berkeley and a leading authority on mind control and cults, "Coercive psychological systems are behavioral change programs which use psychological force in a coercive way to cause the learning and adoption of an ideology or designated set of beliefs, ideas, attitudes or behaviors."[39] Similar to cults, terrorist organizations need to establish control over the new recruit's personal social environment, time, and sources of social support. Cults will often use a system of rewards and punishments, social isolation is promoted, and in many cases new recruits are brought to a geographically remote location to ensure they have contact only with other members of the group during this formative period.[40]

In both cults and terrorist organizations, communication among members may also be closely monitored and controlled. Certain topics may be forbidden, and expression of dissent—particularly against group values, objectives, or leaders—could lead to punishment, expulsion from the group, or possibly even execution.[41] For many terrorist organizations, group cohesion becomes an important component of the motivational training experience, as is highlighted in several chapters of this volume.

Conclusion

In sum, much has been learned about various dimensions of training for terrorism. Given the aim of most terrorists—to inflict pain and damage in order to create fear among a target audience and compel some form of policy or behavioral change desired by the terrorists—it is clear why training is such an important topic within the study of terrorism. With this in mind, the chapters of this volume seek to advance our understanding of developmental processes, teaching tools and centers of learning which help transform an ordinary individual into a lethal terrorist.

Acknowledgments

The views expressed herein are those of the author and do not purport to reflect the position of the United States Military Academy, the Department of the Army, or the Department of Defense.

PART I

TEACHING TOOLS AND DEVELOPMENTAL EXPERIENCES

CHAPTER 2

"When Hatred Is Bred in the Bone": The Sociocultural Underpinnings of Terrorist Psychology

JERROLD M. POST

Terrorist psychology and motivation is poorly understood. While the lay public often considers terrorists to be crazed fanatics, in fact terrorist groups regularly exclude emotionally disturbed individuals from their ranks—after all, they represent a security risk. Indeed, terrorism scholars have regularly emphasized that the outstanding feature of terrorists is their normality.[1] While many opinions have been offered on terrorist psychology and motivations, the commentators' analyses are more often than not spared the inconvenience of material deriving from interviews. Members of terrorist groups, after all, usually lead an underground life, may be on "Most Wanted" lists, and are not readily available for interviews. More-over, when they are in custody and are interrogated, the interrogations are characteristically geared at obtaining operational intelligence, rather than questions designed to understand "what makes the terrorist tick." Jour-nalists have sometimes been able to interview terrorists, and while these in-terviews have sometimes provided rich information, they often lack a psychological framework, and it has been difficult to generalize from these interviews.

This chapter is based on several decades of experience studying the psy-chology of terrorism—including interviews with a number of terrorists while the author was serving as expert witness in terrorist trials, a review of thousands of pages of documents in connection with these trials, and a major research project interviewing Middle Eastern terrorists incarcerated in Israeli and Palestinian prisons.[2] This research, supported by a generous grant from the Smith-Richardson foundation, sheds new light on the psy-chological dimensions of terrorist recruitment and training. As a whole, these interviews illuminated how the lives of individuals were shaped by powerful sociopsychological forces that led them onto the path of terrorism. As highlighted by the direct quotes presented in this chapter, an understanding of these forces reveals how "hatred is bred in the bone."

Interviews with Incarcerated Middle East Terrorists

The research discussed in this chapter took place over an eighteen-month period prior to the outbreak of violence that erupted after the failure of the Camp David talks during the fall of 2000. Interviews were conducted with thirty-one Palestinian terrorists and three members of the Lebanese terrorist group Hizballah. The majority of those interviewed were in prison in Israel at the time of the interview, serving sentences ranging from several months to multiple life sentences. All subjects had served at least some time in prison for their activities in conjunction with the organization to which they belong. Included in the group were two individuals serving forty-six and twenty-six consecutive life terms, respectively, for their role in orchestrating suicide bombing campaigns resulting in the loss of over eighty lives.

Subjects represented both Islamic and secular groups. The radical Islamic groups included in the study are Hamas (and its armed wing Izz a-Din al-Qassam), Islamic Jihad, and Hizballah. The secular groups included are Fatah (and its armed wing the Black Panthers), the Popular Front for the Liberation of Palestine (PFLP), and the Democratic Front for the Liberation of Palestine (DFLP). The interviewers were trained in developing a comfortable interpersonal situation which was neither coercive nor threatening.

The interviews were specifically designed to understand the terrorists in their social context, to better understand what led them onto the path of terrorism, and to learn how that journey has affected them. Employing a semistructured interview template, subjects were asked to discuss their personal, family, and social background; early life experiences; recruitment into the group and socialization to terrorism; group dynamics and decision-making processes within the organization they joined; effects of the prison experience; and attitudes toward armed action, casualties, and the use of weapons of mass destruction. The interviews focused specifically on issues of socialization and personal experience, as opposed to operational and tactical procedures, and interviewers were trained to avoid questions that could be considered interrogation aiming at eliciting tactical intelligence.

This study explored the similarities and differences between secular and Islamist organizations operating in Israel in relation to the individual members of the organization, socialization within the group, the fusion of individual and group identity, group dynamics and decision-making, and the resulting impact on the propensity of these organizations to engage in mass casualty acts of terrorism. The findings are quite remarkable and the material elicited from the terrorists who were interviewed vastly exceeded the researchers' expectations, providing a level of rich contextual detail on their individual pathways into the world of terrorism, the power of the group, the commitment to armed struggle, and the spectrum of rationalizations and justifications for their acts of terror.

The Individual and Family Influence

The interviews revealed few differences between members of Islamist and secular groups concerning the influence of family and the surrounding community in the development of individual ideology and organizational affiliation among the interviewees. Regardless of group affiliation, almost all interview subjects reported that their families were well respected socially and that as individuals they were respected and popular among their peers. There were divergent economic and religious activity backgrounds among all the interviewees, but no specific linkage between these factors and group affiliation. While there was a higher correlation between members of Islamic groups and participation in Islamic activities—such as attendance at the mosque or involvement in other religiously based activities—prior to joining the group, there were religiously active and devoted Muslims in both the secular and Islamist based organizations. One interviewee's personal story reflects the important influence of Islam:

> I came from a religious family which used to observe all the Islamic traditions. My initial political awareness came during the prayers at the mosque. That's where I was also asked to join religious classes. In the context of these studies, the sheik used to inject some historical background in which he would tell us how we were effectively evicted from Palestine.

Another interviewee noted that "the sheik also used to explain to us the significance of the fact that there was an IDF military outpost in the heart of the camp. He compared it to a cancer in the human body, which was threatening its very existence."

Although introduction to "the cause" varies among the interview subjects, almost all subjects reported growing up in villages or refugee camps that were extremely active in the struggle. Over 80 percent of the secular group members reported growing up in communities that were radically involved, and slightly more than 75 percent of the Islamist members reported a similar experience.

The social status and prestige associated with group membership was evident among all interview subjects. Clearly, families who were politically active socialized their sons to the movement at an early age and were supportive of their involvement in terrorist groups; however, families who were not politically active did not appear to dissuade active involvement by their children.

Interestingly, religiously active families seemed more likely to have sons who joined religiously based groups such as Hamas or Islamic Jihad, but there was no correlation between politically active families and the organizational choice of their sons. Equal numbers of group members came from politically active and nonreligious families had joined Islamist groups and non-Islamist groups. There were similar corollaries in looking at the childhood heroes of the group members. Children with primarily religious childhood heroes—such as the Prophet Muhammed and other prophets—seemed more likely to join the Islamist groups, while both secular and non-secular members reported nonreligious heroes. However, Fatah members did report a higher number of nonreligious hero figures, such as Che Guevara and Fidel Castro, whom they viewed as classic revolutionaries leading a struggle for the liberation of their people, while the Islamist group members identified with heroic figures who were both perceived as fighting for the liberation of their people as well as being associated with Islam.

The relationship of group members to their families was relatively strong, with interviewees reporting a high degree of support from their families. There was a stronger connection to family among the secular group members, with slightly over 60 percent reporting a high degree of loyalty to the family and the family being very important to them. Less than 50 percent of the Islamist group reported a similar familial connection. The remainder of both groups reported that their relationship with their family was average or not that important in their lives. Families with a personal connection to "the cause"—such as refugees who had been forcibly moved or had politically active fathers and/or older siblings involved with an organization—provided increased incentive to the young men during their childhood years to affiliate with a group. These children were routinely exposed to family stories about persecution, forced deportation, and their active parent/siblings. This early exposure to the Palestinian/Israeli conflict made the struggle more personal—it became a source of honor to right the injustice done to their families. Their personal family stories allowed these young men to identify with the larger struggle and increased their dedication to the cause. Members of the more militant armed wings of a terrorist group reported more instances of family storytelling during their youth and a greater percentage of personal connections to the struggle, such as family history with Israeli security forces or forced relocation.

As with most of the other Palestinian terrorist organizations, there is a dichotomy between how families felt, in theory, about their sons joining organizations and how they felt in reality. Publicly, families supported the organization and were proud of their sons for joining. Privately, they feared for their sons and often for what the security forces might do to their families. Members were seen as heroes, but, according to one interviewee, "On

the other hand, families who had paid their dues to the war effort by allowing the recruitment of a son tried to prevent other sons from enlisting
too."

While most Fatah members reported their families had good social standing, their status and experience as refugees was paramount in their development of self-identity. As one interviewee put it:

> I belong to the generation of occupation. My family are refugees from the
> 1967 war. The war and my refugee status were the seminal events that formed
> my political consciousness, and provided the incentive for doing all I could
> to help regain our legitimate rights in our occupied country.

For the secular terrorists too, enlistment was a natural step. One interviewee explained, "Enlistment was for me the natural and done thing. . . . In
a way, it can be compared to a young Israeli from a nationalist Zionist family who wants to fulfill himself through army service." Another interviewed
terrorist noted that "my motivation in joining Fatah was both ideological
and personal. It was a question of self-fulfillment, of honor and a feeling
of independence . . . the goal of every young Palestinian was to be a fighter."

The views and objectives illustrated by these statements, gathered from
incarcerated terrorists in the Middle East, help us gain a better understanding of terrorist recruitment. However, this research revealed that the
social contexts within which an individual's views toward terrorism are developed play an even more important role.

Group Socialization

Among those interviewed for this research, the most dominant factor in de-
ciding which organization to join was clearly their social environment. For
the secular groups, their social environment centered on school and social
clubs, while for the Islamist group members, their social environment was
dominated by the mosque, religious organizations, and religious instruction. The mosque in particular was consistently cited as the place where
most members were initially introduced to the Palestinian/Israeli conflict,
including members of the secular groups. As one interviewee explained,

> At the age of 16, I developed an interest in religion. I was exposed to the
> Moslem brotherhood and I began to pray in a mosque and to study Islam.
> The Koran and my religious studies were the tools that shaped my political
> consciousness. The mosque and the religious clerics in my village provided
> the focal point of my social life.

Many of the secular members also reported that while activism within
the community was most influential in their decision to join, their first in-

troduction to the cause was at the mosque or in another religious setting. Authority figures from the mosque were prominent in all conversations with group members and most dramatically for members of the Islamist organizations. According to one of the interviewees, "Major actions become the subject of sermons in the mosque, glorifying the attack and the attackers."

The introduction to authority in these societies—and the development of unquestioning obedience to Allah and authority—is instilled at a young age, and continues to be evident in the individual member's subservience to the larger organization. This emphasis on unquestioning acceptance of authority was most evident among the members of the Islamist groups such as Hamas and Islamic Jihad.

The recruitment process is predominantly a casual or informal process among both secular and Islamist groups, with only 15 percent of secular group members reporting a formal recruitment process and 30 percent of Islamist members reporting a similar experience. For the vast majority of those citing a well-defined recruitment process, the process involved either a formal swearing of allegiance or probationary period. Over half the members of each group type knew their recruiter prior to recruitment. For some this was a family member and for others someone from the community they knew casually. A few members with active siblings or family members reported no recruitment process; their membership was assigned to them through the family, the community, and the organization.

Group membership provided members with a level of social status and acceptance that many did not have prior to recruitment. Regardless of group affiliation, interviewees report increased social standing as well as improved self-esteem and pride after joining the group. As one terrorist interviewee explained, "After recruitment, my social status was greatly enhanced. I got a lot of respect from my acquaintances, and from the young people in the village." Another interviewee observed that "recruits were treated with great respect. A youngster who belonged to Hamas or Fatah was regarded more highly than one who didn't belong to a group, and got better treatment than unaffiliated kids."

Community support was important to the families of the fighters as well. According to one of the interviewed terrorists, "Families of terrorists who were wounded, killed or captured enjoyed a great deal of economic aid and attention. And that strengthened popular support for the attacks." Another pointed out that "perpetrators of armed attacks were seen as heroes; their families got a great deal of material assistance, including the construction of new homes to replace those destroyed by the Israeli authorities as punishment for terrorist acts."

One group member did note, though, that occasionally there was competition to stage the largest or most dramatic event because it helped recruiting, but that it was not viewed as competition between the groups.

There was, however, a great deal of tension between the secular groups and the Islamist groups as a whole. The secular groups tended to be more accommodating of the Islamist groups, although many interviewees noted that they disagreed with the tactics of the Islamist groups. In contrast, the Islamist groups were very clear in their absolutist approach to the Palestinian/Israeli conflict, and regarded the secular groups as heretics and as "selling out" to the Israelis. Although they did not go so far as calling the secular groups an enemy, it was clear that there were strong feelings of distrust and dislike directed at the secular groups.

Fusion of the Individual and the Group

Once recruited, there is a clear fusing of individual identity and group identity, particularly among the more radical elements of each organization. Many of the interviewees reported growing up or living in a repressed or limited socioeconomic status. Their ability to work was regulated, their ability to travel freely was severely restricted, and there was a general impression that they were denied the opportunity to advance economically. There was a common theme of having been "unjustly evicted" from their land, of being relegated to refugee status or living in refugee camps in a land that was once considered theirs. Many of the interviewees expressed an almost fatalistic view of the Palestinian/Israeli relationship and a sense of despair or bleakness about the future under Israeli rule.

The socialized hatred towards the Israelis was remarkable, especially given that few reported having had any contact with an Israeli. As one interviewee stated,

> You Israelis are Nazis in your souls and in your conduct. In your occupation you never distinguish between men and women, or between old people and children. You adopted methods of collective punishment; you uprooted people from their homeland and from their homes and chased them into exile. You fired live ammunition at women and children. You smashed the skulls of defenseless civilians. You set up detention camps for thousands of people in sub-human conditions. You destroyed homes and turned children into orphans. You prevented people from making a living, you stole their property, you trampled on their honor. Given that kind of conduct, there is no choice but to strike at you without mercy in every possible way.

Overall, the language used by the interviewees is remarkably dehumanizing. In addition, it is striking to note that few of the interviewees were able to identify personal goals that were separate from those of the organization to which they belonged.

In a society where social and economic advancement and professional opportunities are limited, many interviewees had adopted the organization as a path to success. There was a heightened sense of the heroic associated with fallen group members and the community supported and rallied around families of the fallen or incarcerated. Most interviewees reported not only enhanced social status for the families of fallen or incarcerated members, but financial and material support from the organization and community for these families as well. According to this analysis, "success" within the community is defined as fighting for "the cause": Liberation and religious freedom are the values that define success, not necessarily academic or economic accomplishment. As the young men adopt this view of success, their own self-image then becomes more intimately intertwined with the success of the organization. With no other means to achieve status and "success," the organization's success becomes central to individual identity and provides their *raison d'être*.

This fusing of the individual to the group was found across all organizations regardless of ideological affiliation. As individual identity succumbs to the organization, there is no room for individuality—individual ideas, individual identity, and individual decision making—while at the same time, self-perceived success becomes increasingly linked to the organization. Individual self-worth is again intimately tied to the "value" or prominence of the group—therefore, each individual has a vested interest in ensuring not only the success of the organization, but to increase its prominence and exposure. The more prominent and more important (and often times the more violent) a group is, the greater the prestige that is then projected onto group members. This creates a cycle in which group members have a direct need to increase the power and prestige of the group through increasingly dramatic and violent operations.

As the individual and group fuse, the struggle becomes more personal for the group members. There is a symbiotic relationship created between the individual's need to belong to a group, their need to ensure success of the group, and an enhanced desire to be an increasingly more active part of the group. Regardless of group affiliation, interviewees painted a similar picture of this personalization of the struggle. Interviewees were unable to distinguish between personal goals and those of the organization; they were one and the same. In their discussion of armed action and other actions taken, the success or failure of the group's action was personal—if the group succeeded, then as an individual they succeeded; if the group failed, they failed. Pride and shame, as expressed by the individual, were reflections of group actions, not individual actions, feelings or experiences. There was an overarching sense of the collective that consumed the individual. This fusion with the group seems to provide the necessary justification for their actions and absolution, or loss of responsibility, to the individual—if the group says it is ok, then it is ok. If the authority figure orders an action, then the action is justified. Guilt or remorse by the individual is not tolerated because the organization does not express it. Again, this is intensified among Islamist groups, who feel they have a moral obligation to the cause and a religiously sanctioned justification for their actions.

Most illustrative of this concept of individual and group fusion are the perceptions and characterizations of "the enemy." While there are slight differences between the secular and Islamist groups in the exact definition of the enemy, the overall experience in defining the enemy is remarkably similar. The enemy is uniformly identified as Israel. While the secular groups tend to focus on the Israeli military, security forces, and settlers, the Islamist groups expand their definition of the enemy to include all Israeli citizens, including civilians. The Islamist groups are fighting for a pure Islamic state. Many interviewees cited Iran as an example of the type of state they would like to create. While the secular groups have constrained (to a degree) their view of the struggle, the Islamist groups have no such restraint. There is no concern about alienating any "earthly" population, as the only "audience" they are seeking to satisfy is Allah. With their direction coming in the form of *fatwas* (religious edicts) and sanctioned by religious clerics and other figures, the identification of the enemy is clear and simple for these Islamist groups—it is anyone who is opposed to the creation of an Islamic Palestine. Indeed, according to one interviewee, "anyone who didn't enlist during that period (*intifada*) would have been ostracized."

As a member of a radical group (secular or Islamist), individuals are able to establish their identity within a framework that is valued within the context of their social community; the group provides others of a like mind with whom the individual has a common bond of belief. The struggle for identity in a culture at odds with itself leads to a fusing of the individual and the group. The need of individuals to belong and to exercise control in their own lives is paramount for every individual, but is intensified in communities where segments of the population are ostracized or persecuted based on ethnic, religious, or social background. By belonging to a radical group, otherwise powerless individuals become powerful. Group identity provides a foundation of relative stability upon which disenfranchised or isolated members of a society build a base of commonality and join together. This common perspective toward the enemy and the group's righteousness was especially observed among the interviewees' attitudes toward armed action and suicide terrorism.

View of Armed Attacks

Armed attacks were viewed by the interviewees as essential to the operation of the group. There was no question about the necessity of these types of attacks in order to ensure the success of the cause. The focus on the use of violence as part of a strategy was exemplified by one interviewee's statement:

> You have to understand that armed attacks are an integral part of the orga-
> nization's struggle against the Zionist occupier. There is no other way to re-
> deem the land of Palestine and expel the occupier. Our goals can only be
> achieved through force, but force is the means, not the end. History shows
> that without force it will be impossible to achieve independence. Those who
> carry out the attacks are doing Allah's work.

Another interviewee emphasized the strategic need to cause innocent casualties:

> The more an attack hurts the enemy, the more important it is. That is the
> measure. The mass killings, especially the martyrdom operations, were the
> biggest threat to the Israeli public and so most effort was devoted to these.
> The extent of the damage and the number of casualties are of primary im-
> portance.

Another interviewee took umbrage at the perceived accusation that he was
a murderer and provided his justification for suicide terrorism:

> I am not a murderer. A murderer is someone with a psychological problem;
> armed actions have a goal. Even if civilians are killed, it is not because we
> like it or are blood thirsty. It is a fact of life in a people's struggle—the group
> doesn't do it because it wants to kill civilians, but because the jihad must go
> on.

For secular groups in particular, armed action provided a sense of control or power for Palestinians in a society that had stripped them of it. Inflicting pain on the enemy was paramount during the early days of the
Fatah movement. As one interviewee explained:

> I regarded armed actions to be essential, it is the very basis of my organiza-
> tion and I am sure that was the case in the other Palestinian organizations.
> An armed action proclaims that I am here, I exist, I am strong, I am in con-
> trol, I am in the field, I am on the map. An armed action against soldiers was
> the most admired. . . . The armed actions and their results were a major tool
> for penetrating the public consciousness.

Overall, interviewees viewed armed attacks as a vital part of their struggle
against the Israelis. This view was particularly intense among those who
supported the use of suicide bombings.

The Justification for Suicide Bombings

In a recent publication, terrorism researcher Mohammad Hafez emphasized
that three conditions are necessary to support suicide terrorism: a culture

that values martyrdom, an organization that chooses this strategy as forwarding their goals, and individuals in a recruitment pool who are alienated and despairing and psychologically available to pursue this course.[3] The Islamist terrorists interviewed in this study offered an additional dimension to this analysis—a religious basis for suicide terrorism as the most valued technique of jihad, distinguishing it from suicide (which is prohibited by the Koran). In fact, one terrorist became quite upset when the term suicide was used in his interview, angrily exclaiming, "This is not suicide. Suicide is selfish, it is weak, it is mentally disturbed. This is *istishad* [martyrdom or self sacrifice in the service of Allah]."

Several of the Islamist terrorist commanders interviewed called the suicide bombers holy warriors who were carrying out the highest level of jihad. A major example is provided by Hassan Salame, the most notorious Palestinian suicide bomb commander, who bears primary responsibility for the wave of suicide bombings in Israel in the run-up to the 1996 general election. Convicted of being personally responsible for forty-six deaths, he is now serving forty-six consecutive life sentences. In his interview, Hassan explained that "a martyrdom operation is the highest level of jihad, and highlights the depth of our faith. The bombers are holy fighters who carry out one of the more important articles of faith."

Another terrorist, who was sentenced to twenty-six life terms for his role in several suicide-bombing campaigns, noted that "it is the attack when the member gives his life that earns the most respect and elevate the bombers to the highest possible level of martyrdom." He also provided a personal story which further illuminates how an Islamic terrorist group views the act of suicide bombing. The normality of the act is striking:

I asked Halil what is was all about and he told me that he had been on the wanted list for a long time and did not want to get caught without realizing his dream of being a martyrdom operation bomber. He was completely calm and explained to the other two bombers, Yusuf and Beshar, how to detonate the bombs, exactly the way he had explained things to the bombers in the Mahane Yehuda attack. I remember that besides the tremendous respect I had for Halil, and the fact that I was jealous of him, I also felt slighted that he had not asked me to be the third martyrdom operation bomber. But I understood that my role in the movement had not come to an end and the fact that I was not on the wanted list and could operate relatively freely could be very advantageous to the movement in the future.

The normality of this language is striking and chilling. He could as well have been talking of not having been chosen for a pick-up soccer team. His feelings were hurt that he was not chosen for this pick-up suicide bomb team. This was reminiscent of the normality of this pursuit as ironically described by Ariel Merari, an Israeli expert on terrorism who teaches at Harvard each fall. He observed that "teenagers are the same the world around."[4] He observed teenagers in Harvard Square, talking over pizza about their team (the Super Bowl–bound New England Patriots), the stars they worshipped on the team, and their dreams of becoming a National Football League star when they grew up. It was just the same, Merari remarked ironically, for Palestinian teenagers in the refugee camps, only their favorite team was Hamas, the stars they worshipped were the latest *shaheeds* (martyrs), and they hoped to become a *shaheed* when they grew up. In his own research, Merari has described the shaping of Palestinian suicide bombers as a "suicide terrorist assembly line." First they are recruited or volunteer, agreeing to be trained to become a suicide bomber. Then they are identified as "living martyrs," gaining prestige in the community, and finally they make a video, talking about their motivation for their mission. These tapes, which are used for recruitment, are a crucial last step, a public declaration. After this sequence, Merari notes, it is almost impossible for the suicide bomber to back down, for the shame would be unbearable. Thus, it is much more a phenomenon of social psychology than individual psychopathology.

Through these interviews, the issue of social psychology, of social group membership as the primary determinant emerges clearly. The suicide bomber (or in their terms, martyrdom operation bomber) has subordinated his individuality to the larger group, and if the individual's death serves the larger group, then the individual carrier out this act. The group's frame of reference also appears to have an important role in framing questions of ethics and morality with regard to killing others.

Sense of Remorse/Moral Red Lines

Interviewees were asked a number of questions about their views toward the morality of armed action, casualties, and the use of weapons of mass destruction. Their responses were strikingly similar in tone, indicating that a belief in the greater good outweighed the need of the individual. For example, one incarcerated terrorist observed that "when it came to moral considerations, we believed in the justice of our cause and in our leaders. . . . I don't recall every being troubled by moral questions." Another interviewee noted that "the organization had no red lines or moral constraints in actions against Jews. Any killing of a Jew was considered a success, and the more the better."

The lack of remorse or moral considerations observed in these interviews was particularly striking in the military wing of Hamas, Izz a-Din al-Qassam. There was a deep sense of righteousness in their discussion of their actions and the legitimacy of action undertaken in the fight for their cause. There was also a sense that the actions of the Israeli Security Forces provide justification for any action they might take. The language became more forceful during this portion of the interviews, as the Israelis were referred to as "the enemy" and "foreign occupiers"—in essence, the Israelis were depicted as "them," not as people living within the same community. For example, one interviewee echoed these sentiments: "The organization has no moral red lines. We must do everything to force the enemy to retreat from out lands. Nothing is illegitimate in achieving this." Another interviewee noted that "as for the organization's moral red lines, there were none. We considered every attack on the occupier legitimate. The more you hurt the enemy, the more he understands."

Yet another terrorist explained that "In a jihad, there are no red lines." In a world of such absolutist perceptions, the group's perspective and reinforced code comes to determines the terrorist recruit's moral code, This holds true not only for members of Palestinian Islamic groups, but can also be seen among members of the global jihad network led by al Qaeda.

Palestinian Islamic Groups in Comparison to al Qaeda: Similarities and Differences

Becoming a member of al Qaeda and supporting its cause has been found to be attractive among alienated Muslim youth, many of whom were sensitized in the madrasas, focused in the mosques. For them, Osama bin Laden is a romantic hero. During the 2001 trial (in a federal court in New York) of the al Qaeda bombers who destroyed the U.S. embassies in Tanzania and Nairobi, seventeen hours of personal interviews with Kalfan Khamis Muhammed—one of the lower-level participants in the bombing in Dar-es-Salaam, as well as one of the senior members of the organization—revealed the compelling role of the madrasa and the mosque in recruitment and mobilization of Islamic terrorism.[5] In the madrasa in Zanzibar (where he grew up), Muhammed was taught to never question learned authorities, especially those with religious credentials. When he dropped out of school and moved to Dar-es-Salaam—at the request of his older brother, to become a clerk in his grocery store—he was miserable, alone, isolated, and friendless. The one place he felt acceptance was in the mosque in Dar-es-Salaam, where he felt welcomed as a member of the *umma*, the community of observant Muslims. He learned of the obligations of Muslims to help other Muslims, wherever they were. He was shown films of Muslim mass graves in Bosnia, created by Serbian soldiers, and the bodies of Muslim women and children in Chechnya, killed by Russian soldiers.

Alone and isolated except for the mosque, Muhammed vowed (in his words) to become "a soldier for Allah" and defend these innocent victims against the soldiers of Serbia and Russia. When he gave voice to these sentiments, he was informed by a man (who was likely a spotter for al Qaeda) that to be a soldier for Allah, he must get training. Thus, using his own money, Muhammed went to Pakistan, was screened, and then was sent to an al Qaeda training camp in Afghanistan. After seven months of training, when he was offered only participation in the Kashmir struggle instead of fighting the soldiers in either Bosnia or Chechnya, he returned to Dar-es-Salaam—again isolated, aimless, and friendless—to take up his previous menial job as a grocery clerk. But he remained involved in the mosque, the one place where he felt a sense of community and meaning.

Then, three years later, he received a call and was asked if he wanted to participate "in a jihad job." Without further question, he responded "yes" and entered the al Qaeda pathway of terrorism. His pious wish to defend Muslim victims was bent into participating in an act of mass casualty terrorism. As he was confronted with the consequences of the bombing in which he had participated, in contrast to other terrorists, Muhammed was overwhelmed emotionally with the death of innocents, recognizing that what he had done was inconsistent with his views of jihad. "Their jihad," he said, "is not my jihad."

Nor, however, is it the jihad of the majority of mainstream Muslims; and yet, they have been remarkably mute, giving free rein to bin Laden and his colleagues to steer alienated youth into this extremist path in the name of Islam. Bin Laden's justifications—as spelled out in his speeches, al Qaeda's terrorism manual, and other documents—are inconsistent with the Koran, and yet to the unquestioning alienated youth, they are taken as religious justification for killing in the name of God.[6]

It is useful to contrast the suicide bombers of Hamas and Islamic Jihad—whose commanders were interviewed in the study described in this chapter—with the suicidal hijackers of 9/11. Investigations of nearly a hundred Palestinian suicide bombers have been conducted by Israeli authorities. These young men, mostly between the ages of seventeen and twenty-two, were unemployed, uneducated, and unmarried. (More recently, the age range of suicide bombers has expanded to fifteen to forty-three, and women have also joined the ranks of suicide bombers.) These youth, when they were recruited (or volunteered) to become martyrdom operation bombers, were informed by the suicide bomb commanders, who were very skillful at manipulating them, that they had a wretched life to look forward to (the unemployment rate in the Palestinian camps was running 40 percent, more so for those with no education). However, the commanders told them that they could do something significant with their lives, that they would enter the hall of martyrs, and that their parents would be proud of them and would gain prestige and financial benefit. From the moment they entered the terrorist group's safe house, they were never left alone. On the night before the operation, someone would sleep in the same room, to ensure that they did not backslide. On the day of the action, they would be physically escorted to the targeted pizza parlor or disco.

In vivid contrast, the suicidal hijackers of 9/11 were older (between the ages of twenty-eight and thirty-three), had higher education, and came from comfortable middle-class homes in Saudi Arabia or Egypt. Mohammed Atta, the group's leader, was thirty-three, and he and two of his colleagues had enrolled in masters' degree programs at the technological university in Hamburg, Germany. These were fully formed adults who had subordinated their individuality to the group, and uncritically accepted the dictates of their destructive charismatic leader, Osama bin Laden. Their major identification was as members of the al Qaeda organization, and if the action required brought benefit to the organization, they would give their lives for the cause. Most interesting, they had been on their own in the West for upwards of seven years, blending in with society, while keeping like a laser beam within them their mission to give of their lives while claiming the lives of thousands of victims, all of this in the name of Allah.

Other major differences between the radical Palestinian terrorist groups and the transnational terrorist network al Qaeda relates to organizational structure and decision making. While both recruit informally from friends and relatives, Hamas and Islamic Jihad are much more hierarchical and authoritarian in their decision making. Decisions are passed down from organizational leadership as to what operations to mount. While a group's members could discuss tactical variation, whether or not to carry out the operation was not a matter for group debate or discussion. Al Qaeda, in contrast—perhaps reflecting Osama bin Laden's studies of organization behavior and managerial leadership at the University in Jeddah—had a much flatter organization, and the organizations and groups under the umbrella were semiautonomous. Indeed, Osama bin Laden is seen to be in effect the Chairman of the Board of Radical Islam, Inc., who has grown his corporation through mergers and acquisitions and has a flat organizational structure.

In other charismatically led terrorist organizations, the capture of the leader was a mortal wound to the organization, as exemplified by Abimael Guzman of the Sendero Luminoso and Abdullah Ocalan of the Kurdish Workers Party (PKK). In contrast, bin Laden has already designated his successor—Ayman al-Zawahiri, who co-founded al Qaeda with him and serves as the principal ideologue, is much more concerned with the day-to-day operations of the organization, and (before 9/11) was in effect serving as CEO. Al Qaeda is an adaptive organization which has swiftly replaced senior officials who were killed or captured. For example, after Mohammad Atef—al Qaeda's chief of operations and military commander—was killed in an air strike south of Kabul in November 2001, he was replaced by Abu Zubaydeh, who had earlier served as chief recruiter. When Zubaydeh was captured in April 2002, he was replaced by Khalid Sheikh Mohammad, who has also been captured. Should bin Laden be killed or captured, the reins would pass seamlessly to al-Zawahiri. Should al-Zawahiri be killed or captured, it would be a blow to bin Laden, who has strongly relied on his managerial leadership, but this would only be a temporary setback. Should the entire leadership echelon be eliminated, the component organizations would revert to their previous semiautonomous structure. The issue here is not so much bin Laden and al Qaeda, as the international jihadist network.

Similar adaptive mechanisms—whereby an individual gives up virtually all his independence in conforming to the needs of the group—can also be observed among secular terrorist organizations. While the religious dimension of Islamic fundamentalist groups plays a powerful role in ensuring individual conformity to the group's authority, secular terrorist groups in the Middle East emphasize the rationalization of violent actions against Israel as justified retaliation for injustices against the Palestinian people. An example of the power of the generational transmission of hatred is seen in the following case study of a member of the Abu Nidal terrorist organization.

A Case Study: Life Experiences of an Abu Nidal Terrorist

In 1997, the U.S. Department of Justice brought to trial (in a federal court in Washington, DC) a man named Omar Rezaq, an Abu Nidal terrorist who had played a leading role in the skyjacking of an Egypt Air passenger jet in which more than fifty men and women lost their lives during the skyjacking and the subsequent SWAT team attack on the hijacked plane in Malta.[7] Rezaq epitomized the life and psychology of the nationalist-separatist terrorist. He did not believe that what he had done was wrong, as from boyhood on Rezaq had been socialized to be a heroic revolutionary fighting for the Palestinian nation.

Rezaq's Social History

In 1948, Rezaq's mother (who was eight years old at the time) was forced to flee with her family from their home in Jaffa when the Arab-Israeli War erupted. The family fled to the West Bank, where they initially lived in refugee camps. The mother's displacement from her ancestral home by Israel was an event of crucial importance that became a key element in the family legend.

Rezaq, born in 1958, spent his childhood in the West Bank village where his grandfather was a farmer. During his interview, Rezaq described his boyhood in the village as pleasant; they lived in their own home, with no economic problems, no worries about food or money. His relatively pleasant existence changed abruptly in the aftermath of the 1967 Arab-Israeli war, and, when Rezaq was eight, his family was forced to flee to Jordan. As Rezaq explained, "From this time, everything changed."

At the time, Jordan was overflowing with refugees. Rezaq's family moved into crowded circumstances, initially with their cousin. Rezaq's mother discussed that this was the second time the Israelis had forced her from her home. After staying in Amman for one year, they moved to the refugee camp Talibiya, some 25–35 kilometers outside of Amman. The living circumstances there were very difficult; the whole family was crowded into two rooms, with no bathroom or kitchen and little privacy. The UN supplied food. There was little money.

Indoctrination in Palestinian Nationalism and Recruitment into the Movement

In 1968, Yassir Arafat led a group of Palestinian guerrillas in the battle of Karameh, a twelve-hour battle against a superior Israeli force, galvanizing the previously dispirited Palestinian population. The energy of the revolution was everywhere, especially in the camps, and the Palestine Liberation Organization (PLO) became a rallying point. In Rezaq's words, "The revolution was the only hope."

In the UN-supported school where Rezaq was an average student, he was rewarded for learning Palestinian songs. He had Palestinian teachers who would propagandize the students, focusing their resentment toward Israel for their difficult living circumstances and instilling a sense of Palestinian nationalism. As young teenagers, Rezaq (now twelve) and his friends went to a youth camp for two to three hours a day, where they received some political indoctrination and began military training, learning how to clean and handle guns, jump barriers, and so on. His Palestinian teacher, who was in the PLO and was a member of Fatah, served as a role model for him. He was taught that the only way to become a man was to join the revolution and regain the lands stolen from his parents and grandparents. He was taught that the only way to get back his country was if the PLO would fight against Israel, and he was increasingly determined to join that fight.

After finishing intermediate school, he went on to technical school under UN auspices. There were branches of the revolution in this school; each group tried to recruit the new students. Rezaq became more deeply involved in politics. Afterwards, two years of obligatory service in the Jordanian army were required, so in 1977, at age nineteen, he was sent to a camp near Iraq for military training in the Jordanian army. There the Palestinians were treated as second-class citizens. After only three months in the Jordanian army, Rezaq went AWOL and joined Fatah. He went to a military camp where he was given a military uniform and was trained in the use of machine guns, pistols, and hand grenades. He also received intense political indoctrination. This was the first time he heard of Zionism. Now he was energized, a fully committed member of a fighting revolutionary organization. There was only one way to restore Palestine, he believed, and that was to fight Israel in order "to regain all of Palestine, from the sea to the river."

Rezaq moved from group to group within the general network of Palestinian terrorists, initially enthused, then disillusioned, each group more militant than the preceding. At last, he joined the most violent secular terrorist group, the Abu Nidal Organization. When he ultimately was chosen to play a lead role in the skyjacking of the Egypt Air passenger jet, it was the fulfillment of his destiny. At last he was carrying out an action that would help the Palestinian people regain the lands that had been stolen from them.

Like many of his generation, the developmental experiences of Omar Rezaq shaped his attraction to the path of terrorism, defined in his mind as "joining the revolution." The psychological soil had already been prepared by his mother's stories of the expulsion from Jaffa in 1948 and again when his family was uprooted in 1967 and forced into the refugee camp.

Like many young men of his generation in the camps, Rezaq was psychologically lost, with no clear path before him. His teachers both focused his hatred against Israel as the cause of his people's problems, and charted a valued identity, fighting for the revolution. He knew exactly what he was doing when he shot two Israeli women and the Americans aboard the Egypt Air passenger jet. He was executing the operational plan according to instructions, a soldier carrying out orders, killing the enemy.

Like his fellow terrorists, he believed that his actions were justified and were righteous acts in the service of the Palestinian revolution. He had been socialized to blame all of his and his people's difficulties on the enemy, and believed that violent actions against the enemy were justified. He rationalized that the injustices against the Palestinian people justified his violent acts. When one has been nursed on the mother's milk of hatred and bitterness, the need for vengeance is "bred in the bone." In ethnic/nationalist conflicts, hatred has been transmitted generationally, and the psychopolitics of hatred are deeply rooted.

Demonstrating the generational transmission of hatred, Rezaq's case can be considered emblematic of many from the ranks of ethnic/nationalist terrorist groups, from Northern Ireland to Palestine, from Armenia to the Basque region of Spain. This is illustrated in the following generational matrix,[8] which indicates that the nationalist separatist terrorists are carrying on the mission of their parents. Their acts of terrorism are acts of retaliation for injuries and injustices done to their parents and grandparents by society. They are loyal to parents damaged by the corrupt regime.

This family-oriented dynamic stands in vivid contrast to the dynamics of Osama bin Laden,[9] which resembles that of the social revolutionary terrorists, rebelling against the generation of their parents who are loyal to

Figure 2.1
Generational Pathways to Terrorism

	Parents' Relationship to the Regime	
Youths' Relationship to Parents	Loyal	Disloyal Damaged Dissident
Loyal	✕	National Separatist Terrorism ✓
Disloyal	Social Revolutionary Terrorism ✓	

the corrupt regime. After all, it was the support of the Saudi royal family which enriched Mohammad bin Laden, a remarkable entrepreneur, who at his death (when young bin Laden was eleven) was estimated to be worth between two and three billion dollars. When bin Laden, after the first Afghanistan campaign (and living in Sudan at the time), actively criticized the Saudi leadership for permitting the U.S. military to have bases in "the land of the two cities," he was criticizing the regime that had enriched his family, a family whose members were intensely loyal to (and beholden to) the Saudi regime. This led the Saudis to cancel bin Laden's passport, and his family took steps to distance themselves from him, lest they lose their royal patrons.

This turn of events only added to the already God-like image of bin Laden in the Islamic fundamentalist community. Bin Laden was initially revered for his leadership role in the struggle in the first Afghanistan war to expel the Godless Soviets from the Islamic land of Afghanistan, He lived in the caves with the Afghan Arabs he had recruited, giving generously of his fortune to support their cause. And when they succeeded, this confirmed that Allah blessed their cause. Now he was giving up his wealthy family ties on principle, in the name of a greater cause—calling attention to the corruption and infidelity of the Saudi regime. Surely, this example serves as a motivation for members of al Qaeda (and other like-minded organizations) to also sacrifice for the good of the cause. As with the Palestinians interviewed for the study described earlier in this chapter, the fusion of individual and group identity subsequently plays a powerful role in terrorist group recruitment and cohesion.

Conclusion

This chapter illuminates how the social context and group forces dominate perceptions in the world of the terrorist. The individual comes to subordinate his individuality to the group, which becomes the central pillar of his identity. The need of individuals to belong and to exercise control in their own lives is paramount for every individual, but is intensified in communities where segments of the population are ostracized or persecuted based on ethnic, religious, or social background. By belonging to a radical group, otherwise powerless individuals become powerful. Group identity provides a foundation of relative stability upon which disenfranchised or isolated members of a society build a base of commonality and join together.

According to this study of incarcerated terrorists, joining a terrorist group increasingly was seen as the path of normality, with positive social value attached to joining a terrorist group, especially in the constituencies of particular concern to Israel. Once an individual is in the terrorist group, especially if it is an underground group, the power of group dynamics will enforce his psychological commitment to the group and its goals. Further, although studies of group dynamics in terrorist groups indicate that they are virtual hothouses of tension, when they are attacked, internal tensions and disunity disappear, and the group members become a united whole, dominated by a sense of "us against them."[10]

In sum, powerful psychological forces are involved in transforming an individual into a terrorist. Understanding these forces is critical in developing effective psychology-based counterterrorism efforts in the global war on terrorism.[11] Four components of a counterterrorism strategy based on psychological understandings of the power of group and organizational dynamics in determining terrorist identity and behavior are 1) inhibiting potential terrorists from joining the group in the first place; 2) creating dissension within the group; 3) facilitating exit from the group; and 4) reducing support for the group and its leader. For example, Osama bin Laden has for years been trying to marshal support for his malevolent Wahhabi view of Islam and the West, a pursuit in which he has been largely unchallenged. The virulent brand of Islam that he has championed, the violence and destruction that he has called for as a sacred obligation for which he has found justification in his extreme interpretation of the Koran—these views, which of course are quite consistent with those promoted by leaders of Hamas and Islamic Jihad, have not been countered. Bin Laden is considered a hero figure by alienated Islamic youth. He has no religious credentials, but has regularly cited verses from the Koran, which are taken out of context, to justify acts that are prohibited by the Koran. The United States cannot directly counter his destructive charismatic leadership. It is thus important to encourage moderate religious clerics to counter and undermine his religiously justified calls for violent action and reclaim their hijacked religion.

More broadly, this analysis suggests that terrorism thrives among communities of hate, reinforced by aggression and oppression (real or perceived), and a slim chance of a brighter future for its youth. Communities such as these are rarely found in the Western developed world, but they are all too common throughout Africa, Asia, and the Middle East. Thus, analyzing how communities breed hatred, as well as the other sociocultural dimensions of terrorist psychology covered in this chapter, is vital to our understanding of global terrorism, and can provide the knowledge foundation for developing long-range strategies for countering terrorism.

CHAPTER 3

Training for Terrorism through Selective Moral Disengagement

ALBERT BANDURA

Self-sanctions play a central role in the regulation of inhumane conduct.[1] In the course of socialization, people adopt moral standards that serve as guides and deterrents in the management of their everyday lives. Once personal control has developed, people regulate their actions by the sanctions they apply to themselves. They do things that give them self-satisfaction and a sense of self-worth. They refrain from behaving in ways that violate their moral standards because such behavior will bring self-condemnation. Self-sanctions thus keep conduct in line with internal standards.

Moral standards do not function as fixed internal regulators of conduct, however. Self-regulatory mechanisms do not operate unless they are activated, and there are many psychological processes by which moral self-sanctions can be disengaged from inhumane conduct.[2] Selective activation and disengagement of moral control permit different types of conduct with the same moral standards. Figure 3.1 shows the place in the control process where moral self-sanctions can be disengaged from reprehensible conduct. The disengagement may center on the behavior by sanctifying harmful conduct as honorable and righteous. This is achieved by moral justification, exonerating comparison with graver inhumanities, and sanitizing language. Disengagement may center on one's sense of personal accountability, where perpetrators minimize their role in causing harm by diffusion and displacement of responsibility. Disengagement may focus on the seriousness of the outcome, by minimizing or distorting the harm that flows from detrimental actions. And the disengagement may also occur through characterizations of the recipients, by dehumanizing the victims and blaming them for bringing the suffering upon themselves.

The way in which these moral disengagement practices operate in the perpetration of inhumanities is analyzed in detail in later sections of this chapter.

Figure 3.1

Mechanisms through which moral self-sanctions are selectively activated and disengaged from detrimental behavior at different points in the self-regulatory process

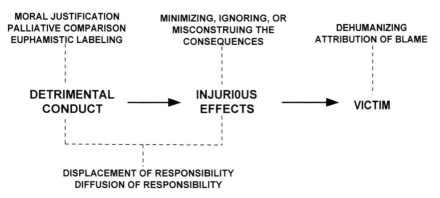

(Albert Bandura, *Social Foundations of Thought and Action* [Englewood Cliffs, NJ: Prentice-Hall, 1986]).

These psychosocial mechanisms of moral disengagement have been examined most extensively in political and military violence. This limited investigatory focus conveys the impression that selective disengagement of moral self-sanctions occurs only under extraordinary circumstances. Quite the contrary. Such mechanisms operate in everyday situations in which decent people routinely perform activities that further their interests but have injurious human effects. Self-exonerations are needed to eliminate self-prohibitions and self-censure. This chapter analyzes how the mechanisms of moral disengagement function in terrorist operations.

Terrorism is a strategy of violence designed to promote desired outcomes by instilling fear in the public at large.[3] Public intimidation is a key element that distinguishes terrorist violence from other forms of violence. Customary violence involves two-party violence in which detested victims are personally targeted. Terrorism involves third-party violence. What makes terrorism distinctive is its choice of targets. The victims are incidental to the terrorists' intended aims because the violence directed toward them is used mainly to provoke conditions and actions designed to topple rulers and force desired sociopolitical changes.

Several features of terrorist acts give power to a few incidents to incite widespread public fear that vastly exceeds the objective threat. The first terrorizing feature is the unpredictability of who will be targeted and when or where a terrorist act will occur. The second feature is the gravity of terrorist acts that maim and kill; with the magnified lethality of today's weapons technology, terrorists can now wreak destruction on a massive scale. A third feature of terrorist acts that render them so terrorizing is the sense of uncontrollability of the threat. The fourth feature that contributes to a sense of personal and societal vulnerability is the high centralization and interdependence of essential service systems in modern day life; a single destructive act that knocks out communications, transportation, and power systems and damages safe water and food supplies can instantly frighten and harm vast numbers of people. The combination of unpredictability, gravity, perceived protective inefficacy, and vulnerable interdependence is especially intimidating and socially constraining.[4]

In coping with problems of terrorism, societies are faced with a dual task. The first is how to reduce terrorist acts. The second is how to combat the fear of terrorism. Even though the number of terrorist acts is relatively small, the widespread public fear and the intrusive and costly security counter-measures pose serious problems. Utilitarian justifications can readily win the support of a frightened public for curtailment of civil liberties and violent counterterrorist measures. A frightened and angered citizenry does not spend much time agonizing over the morality of lethal modes of self-defense.

The term terrorism is often applied to violent acts that dissident groups direct surreptitiously at officials of regimes to force social or political changes. So defined, terrorism becomes indistinguishable from straightforward political violence. Particularized threats are certainly intimidating to prominent social and political figures who are personally targeted for assassination and may create some public apprehension over destabilizing societal effects. But such threats do not necessarily terrify the members of the general public as long as they are not targeted as the objects of victimization. Terrorist tactics, relying on public intimidation, can of course serve other purposes as well as a political weapon.

From a psychological standpoint, third-party violence directed at innocent people is a much more horrific personal undertaking than political violence in which detested figures are personally targeted. It is easier to get individuals who harbor strong grievances to kill hated political officials or to abduct advisors and consular staffs of foreign nations that support oppressive regimes. However, to cold-bloodedly slaughter innocent women and children in buses, department stores, and airports requires more powerful psychological machinations of moral disengagement. Intensive psychological training in moral disengagement is thus needed in order to create the capacity to kill innocent human beings as a way of toppling rulers or regimes, or achieving other political ends.

Moral Justification

One set of disengagement practices operates on the interpretation of the behavior itself. People do not ordinarily engage in reprehensible conduct until they have justified to themselves the morality of their actions. In this process, destructive conduct is made personally and socially acceptable by portraying it as serving socially worthy and moral purposes. Moral justification sanctifies violent means. People can then act on a moral imperative.

Radical shifts in destructive behavior through moral justification are most strikingly revealed in military conduct. People who have been socialized to deplore killing as morally condemnable can be rapidly transformed into skilled combatants, who may feel little compunction and even a sense of pride in taking human life. Moral reinterpretation of killing is dramatically illustrated in the case of Sergeant York, one of the phenomenal fighters in the history of modern warfare.[5] Because of his deep religious convictions, he registered as a conscientious objector, but his numerous appeals were denied. At training camp, his battalion commander quoted chapter and verse from the Bible to persuade him that under appropriate conditions it was Christian to fight and kill. A marathon of mountainside prayer finally convinced him that he could serve both God and country by becoming a dedicated fighter.

The transformation of socialized people into dedicated fighters is achieved not by altering their personality structures, aggressive drives, or moral standards. Rather, it is accomplished by cognitively redefining the morality of killing, so that it can be done free from self-censuring restraints. Through moral sanction of violent means, people see themselves as fighting ruthless oppressors, protecting cherished values and way of life, preserving world peace, saving humanity from subjugation to an evil ideology, and honoring one's country's international commitments.

Over the centuries, much destructive conduct has been perpetrated by ordinary, decent people in the name of legitimizing and sanctifying ideologies; including religious principles, righteous ideologies, and nationalistic imperatives.[6] Throughout history countless people have suffered at the hands of self-righteous crusaders bent on stamping out what they considered evil. Voltaire put it well when he said, "Those who can make you believe absurdities, can make you commit atrocities."[7] Members of one group sanctify their militant actions, but condemn those of their adversaries as barbarity masquerading under a mask of outrageous moral reasoning. Each side feels morally superior to the other. Acting on moral or ideological imperatives reflects a conscious offensive mechanism, not an unconscious defensive mechanism.

The politicization of religion has a long-blooded history. In holy terror, perpetrators twist theology and see themselves as courageously doing God's will. Pope Urban launched the Crusades with the following impassioned holy imperative: "I address those present, I proclaim it, to those absent, Christ commands it. For all those going thither, there will be remission of sins if they come to the end of this fettered life."[8] He then dehumanizes and beastializes the Muslim enemies: "What a disgrace if a race so despicable, degenerate, and enslaved by demons, should overcome a people endowed with faith in Almighty God and resplendent in the name of Christ! Let those who once fought against brothers and relatives now rightfully fight against the barbarians under the guidance of the Lord."[9]

In modern times, Islamic extremists mount their jihad, construed as self-defense against tyrannical, decadent infidels who seek to enslave the Muslim world and destroy its way of life. In his Islamic radicalism, bin Laden enobled his global terrorism as serving a holy imperative.[10] "We will continue this course because it is part of our religion and because Allah, praise and glory be to him, ordered us to carry out jihad so that the word of Allah may remain exalted to the heights."[11] In the jihad they are carrying out Allah's will as a "religious duty." The prime agency for the holy terror is thus displaced to Allah. By attribution of blame, terrorist strikes are construed as morally justifiable defensive reactions to humiliation and atrocities perpetrated by atheistic forces. "We are only defending ourselves. This is defensive jihad." By advantageous comparison with the nuclear bombing of Japan and the toll of the Iraqi sanctions on children, the jihad takes on an altruistic appearance: "When people at the ends of the earth, Japan, were killed by their hundreds of thousands, young and old, it was not considered a war crime, it is something that has justification. Millions of children in Iraq is something that has justification."[12] Bin Laden bestializes the American enemy as "lowly people" perpetrating acts that "the most ravenous of animals would not descend to." Terrorism is sanitized as "the winds of faith have come" to eradicate the "debauched" oppressors.[13] His followers see themselves as holy warriors who gain a blessed eternal life through their martyrdom.

Israeli Prime Minister Yitzhak Rabin's assassin was similarly acting on a divine mandate using the rabbinical pursuer's decree as moral justification. Those who give over their people and land to the enemy must be killed. As he explained the killing to prevent transfer of land to Palestinian control: "Maybe physically, I acted alone but what pulled the trigger was not only my finger but the finger of this whole nation which, for 2,000 years, yearned for this land and dreamed of it."[14] Paul Hill, the Presbyterian minister, also justified the killing of a doctor and his elderly assistant outside the abortion clinic as carrying out God's will: "God's law positively requires us to defend helpless people. God has used people, who are willing to die for their cause to save human life. I'm willing to do that."[15]

Although moral cognitive restructuring can be easily used to support self-serving and destructive purposes, it can also serve militant action aimed at changing inhumane social conditions. By appealing to morality, social reformers are able to use coercive—and even violent—tactics to force social change. Vigorous disputes arise over the morality of aggressive action directed against institutional practices. Powerholders often resist, by forcible means if necessary, pressures to make needed social changes that jeopardize their own self-interests. Such tactics provoke social activism. Challengers consider their militant actions to be morally justifiable because they serve to eradicate harmful social practices. Powerholders condemn violent means as unjustified and unnecessary because nonviolent means exist to effect social change. They tend to view resorts to violence as efforts to coerce changes that lack popular support. Finally, they may argue that terrorist acts are condemnable because they violate civilized standards of conduct. Clearly, anarchy would flourish in a climate in which individuals considered violent tactics acceptable whenever they disliked particular social practices or policies.

Challengers refute such moral arguments by appealing to what they regard as a higher level of morality derived from communal concerns. They see their constituencies as comprising all people, both at home and abroad, who are victimized either directly or indirectly by injurious institutional practices. Challengers argue that, when many people benefit from a system that is deleterious to disfavored segments of the society, the harmful social practices secure widespread public support. From the challengers' perspective, they are acting under a moral imperative to stop the maltreatment of people who have no way of modifying injurious social policies because they are either outside the system that victimizes them or they lack the social power to effect changes from within by peaceable means. Their defendants regard militant action as the only recourse available to them.

Clearly, adversaries can easily marshal moral reasons for the use of aggressive actions for social control or for social change. When viewed from divergent perspectives, violent acts are different things to different people. In conflicts of power, one person's violence is another person's selfless benevolence. It is often proclaimed that one group's terrorist activity is another group's liberation movement fought by heroic freedom fighters. This is why moral appeals against violence usually fall on deaf ears.

Moral Justifications and the Mass Media

The mass media, especially television and the Internet, provide the best access to the public because of their strong drawing power. For this reason, television is increasingly used as the principal vehicle for communicating social and moral justifications of goals and violent means. Struggles to legitimize and gain support for one's causes, and to discredit those of one's foes, are now waged more and more through the electronic media.[16]

Terrorists try to exercise influence over targeted officials and nations through intimidation of the public and arousal of sympathy for the social and political causes they espouse. Without widespread publicity, terrorist acts can achieve neither of these effects. Terrorists, therefore, require access to the media in order to publicize their grievances to the international community. They use television (and increasingly, Internet websites and chat rooms) as the main instrument for gaining sympathy and support for their cause by presenting themselves as risking their lives for the welfare of a victimized constituency subjected to inhumane forms of oppression. The media, in turn, come under heavy fire from governmental officials and the targeted populace, who regard granting terrorists a worldwide forum as aiding terrorist causes. Security forces do not like media personnel tracking their conduct and broadcasting tactical information that terrorists can put to good use and interposing themselves as intermediaries in risky negotiation situations. Social pressures mount to curtail media coverage of terrorist events and to present the societal efforts at countercontrol in patriotic terms.

With the advent of satellite transmission, battles are now fought in the airways over terrorist carnage and "collateral" damage inflicted by counterattacks. In the escalating cycle of terrorism and military retaliation in the Middle East, the Arab news network al-Jazeera airs graphic real-time images of death and destruction around the clock, while the Western media try to highlight the humanitarian benefits of military force.[17] Satellite television has thus become a strategic tool in the social management of moral disengagement at the critical juncture of the human consequences of lethal means.

The Internet is providing a particularly useful vehicle for sanctifying violent means, mobilizing supporters to one's cause, and implementing terrorist activities. The Internet is swift, wide-reaching, and free of institutional controls. There are several unique features of electronic information technologies that make them perilous if used for destructive purposes. They are readily accessible, portable, easily implementable remotely by pushbutton, connected worldwide for far-reaching consequences, and exceedingly difficult to control. Societal vulnerabilities are enormously magnified because virtually all of the systems on which people depend in their everyday life are interdependently run by computer network systems. These can be easily knocked out, as shown by the computer student in the Philippines who wreaked havoc worldwide by crippling e-mail systems costing billions of dollars. Smart hackers can do much more serious damage. Cyberterrorism, enacted through the Internet, is a dark side of the cyberworld that will increasingly command societal attention.[18]

Advantageous Comparison

Interpretations of behavior are colored by what they are compared against. By exploiting comparisons and contrasts, reprehensible acts can be made righteous. The more flagrant the contrasting inhumanities, the more likely it is that one's own destructive conduct will appear trifling or even benevolent. Thus, terrorists minimize their killings as the only defensive weapon they have to curb the widespread cruelties inflicted on their people by tyrannical regimes. In the eyes of their supporters, risky attacks directed at the apparatus of oppression are acts of selflessness and martyrdom. Those who are the objects of terrorist attacks, in turn, characterize their own retaliatory violence as trifling, or even laudable, by comparing it with the carnage and terror perpetrated by terrorists. Such social conflicts breed increasing levels of violence, with each side lauding its own behavior but condemning that of its adversaries as heinous.

Advantageous comparisons also draw heavily on history to justify violence. Terrorists are quick to note that the French and Americans earned their democracies through violent overthrow of oppressive rule, and the Jewish people got their homeland by paramilitary violence. Terrorists claim entitlement to the same tactics to rout those they regard as their oppressors. A former director of the CIA effectively deflected, by expedient comparison, embarrassing questions about the morality and legality of CIA-directed covert operations designed to overthrow an authoritarian regime. He explained that French covert operations and military supplies greatly aided the overthrow of oppressive British rule during the War of Independence, thereby creating the modern model of democracy for other subjugated people to emulate.

Social comparisons are similarly used to show that the social labeling of acts as terrorism depends more on the ideological allegiances of the labelers than on the acts themselves. Airline hijackings were applauded as heroic deeds when East Europeans and Cubans initiated this practice, but condemned as terrorist acts when the airlines of Western nations and friendly countries were commandeered. The degree of psychopathology ascribed to hijackers varied depending on the direction of the rerouted flights. Moral condemnations of politically motivated terrorism are easily blunted by social comparison because, in international contests of power, it is hard to find nations that categorically condemn terrorism. Rather, they often back the perpetrators they like but condemn those they repudiate.

Euphemistic Language

Language shapes people's thought patterns upon which they base many of their actions. Activities, therefore, can take on a markedly different character depending on what they are called. Euphemistic language is used widely to make harmful conduct respectable and to reduce personal responsibility for it.[19] Euphemizing is an injurious weapon. People behave much more cruelly when assaultive actions are given a sanitized label than when they are called aggression.[20]

In an insightful analysis of the language of nonresponsibility, Richard Gambino identified the different varieties of euphemisms.[21] One form relies on sanitizing language. Through the power of sanitized language, even killing a human being loses much of its repugnancy. Soldiers "waste" people rather than kill them. The military calls them "vertically deployed anti-personal devices"; we call them bombs. Bombing missions are described as "servicing the target," in the likeness of a public utility. The attacks become "clean, surgical strikes," arousing imagery of helpful medical procedures. The civilians killed by the bombs are linguistically converted to "collateral damage." Many are victims of bombs that were "outside current accuracy requirements." Soldiers killed by misdirected missiles fired by their own forces are the tragic recipients of "friendly fire."

The agentless passive form serves as a linguistic device for creating the appearance that culpable acts are the work of nameless forces, rather than people.[22] It is as though people are moved mechanically but are not really the agents of their own acts. Gambino further documented how the specialized jargon of a legitimate enterprise can be misused to lend an aura of respectability to an illegitimate one. Deadly activities are framed as "game plans," and the perpetrators become "team players," a status calling for the qualities and behavior befitting the best sportsmen.[23] For the religious suicide bomber, euphemistic language helps redefine the terrorist act as using one's body as a tool of God. The liberating power of language can be boosted further by colorful metaphors that change the nature of culpable activities.

Cognitive restructuring of harmful conduct by moral justifications, sanitizing language, and expedient comparisons is the most effective set of psychological mechanisms for disengaging moral control. Investing harmful conduct with high moral purpose not only eliminates self-censure so destructive acts can be performed without personal distress and moral qualms. Sanctification engages self-approval in the service of destructive exploits. What was once morally condemnable becomes a source of self-valuation. Functionaries work hard to become proficient at them and take pride in their destructive accomplishments.

Displacement of Responsibility

Moral control operates most strongly when people acknowledge that they are contributors to harmful outcomes. The second set of disengagement practices operates by obscuring or minimizing the agentive role in the harm one causes. People will behave in ways they normally repudiate if a legitimate authority accepts responsibility for the effects of their conduct.[24] Under displaced responsibility, they view their actions as stemming from the dictates of authorities rather than from their own personal responsibility. Because they feel they are not the actual agent of their actions, they are spared self-condemning reactions.

In terrorism sponsored by states or governments in exile, functionaries view themselves as patriots fulfilling nationalistic duties rather than as free-lancing criminals. Displacement of responsibility not only weakens moral restraints over one's own detrimental actions but diminishes social concern over the well-being of those mistreated by others.[25]

Self-exemption from gross inhumanities by displacement of responsibility is most gruesomely revealed in socially sanctioned mass executions. Nazi prison commandants and their staffs divested themselves of personal responsibility for their unprecedented inhumanities;[26] they claimed they were simply carrying out orders. Self-exonerating obedience to horrific orders is similarly evident in military atrocities, such as the My Lai massacre.[27]

In an effort to deter institutionally sanctioned atrocities, the Nuremberg Accords declared that obedience to inhumane orders, even from the highest authorities, does not relieve subordinates of the responsibility for their actions. However, because victors are disinclined to try themselves as criminals, such decrees have limited deterrence effect without an international judiciary system empowered to impose penalties on victors and losers alike.

In psychological studies of disengagement of moral control by displacement of responsibility, authorities explicitly authorize injurious actions and hold themselves responsible for the harm caused by their followers.[28] However, the sanctioning of pernicious conduct in everyday life differs from this in two important ways. Responsibility is rarely assumed that openly. Only obtuse authorities would leave themselves accusable of authorizing destructive acts. They usually invite and support harmful conduct in insidious ways by surreptitious sanctioning systems for personal and social reasons. Sanctioning by indirection shields them from social condemnation in case things go awry. It also enables them to protect against loss of self-respect for authorizing human cruelty that leaves blood on their hands. Implicit agreements and insulating social arrangements are created that leave the higher echelons unblamable.

In his psychological study of Hizballah, Martin Kramer describes the great lengths to which Shiite clerics go to produce moral justifications for violent acts that breach Islamic law, such as suicidal bombings and hostage taking.[29] These efforts are designed not only to persuade themselves of the morality of their actions but to preserve their integrity in the eyes of rival clerics and other nations. The Islamic religious code permits neither suicide nor the terrorizing of innocent people. On the one hand, the clerics justify such acts by invoking situational imperatives and utilitarian reasons, namely that tyrannical regimes drive oppressed people to resort to desperate means to rout aggressors who wield massive destructive power. On the other hand, they reinterpret terrorist acts as conventional means in which dying in a suicidal bombing for a moral cause is no different than dying at the hands of an enemy soldier. Hostages are typically relabeled as enemy spies or assisters. When the linguistic solution defies credibility, personal moral responsibility is disengaged by interpreting terrorist acts as dictated by their foe's tyranny. Because of the shaky moral logic and disputable rein-terpretations involved, clerics sanction terrorism by indirection, they vin-dicate successful ventures retrospectively, and they disclaim endorsements of terrorist operations beforehand.

Nation-states sponsor terrorist operations through disguised, round-about routes that make it difficult to pin the blame on them. Moreover, the intended purpose of sanctioned destructiveness is usually linguistically disguised so that neither issuers nor perpetrators regard the activity as cen-surable. When culpable practices gain public attention, they are officially dismissed as only isolated incidents arising through misunderstanding of what, in fact, had been authorized. Efforts are made to limit the blame to subordinates, who are portrayed as misguided or overzealous.

A number of social factors affect the ease with which responsibility for one's actions can be surrendered to others. High justification and social consensus about the morality of an enterprise aid in the relinquishment of personal control. The legitimacy of the authorizers is another important determinant. The higher the authorities, the more legitimacy, respect, and coercive power they command, the more willing are people to defer to them. Modeled disobedience, which challenges the legitimacy of the activ-ities—if not the authorizers themselves—reduces the willingness of ob-servers to carry out the actions called for by the orders of a superior.[30] It is difficult to continue to disown personal agency in the face of evident harm that results directly from one's actions. People are, therefore, less will-ing to obey authoritarian orders to carry out injurious behavior when they see firsthand how they are hurting others.[31]

Perpetration of inhumanities requires obedient functionaries. They do not cast off all responsibility for their behavior as if they were mindless ex-tensions of others. If they disowned all responsibility, they would be quite unreliable, performing their duties only when commanded to do so. In sit-uations involving obedience to authority, people carry out orders partly to honor the obligations they have undertaken.[32] In fact, they tend to be con-scientious and self-directed in the performance of their duties. It requires a strong sense of responsibility to be a good functionary. One must, there-fore, distinguish between two levels of responsibility: a strong sense of duty to one's superiors and overall organizational mission, and accountability for the effects of one's actions. The best functionaries are those who honor their obligations to authorities but feel no personal responsibility for the harm they cause.

Displacement of responsibility also operates in situations in which hostages are taken. Terrorists warn officials of targeted nations that if they take retaliatory action they will be held accountable for the lives of the hostages. At different steps in negotiations for the hostages' release, ter-rorists continue to displace responsibility for the safety of hostages on the reactions of the national officials they are fighting. If the captivity drags on, terrorists blame government officials for the suffering and injuries they inflict on their hostages because these officials are failing to make what they regard as warranted concessions to remedy social grievances. This practice has escalated to a new level, using emotionally wrenching videos of anguished captives questioning their nation's policy, or pleading with their government to spare their lives by meeting the terrorists' demands.[33]

Diffusion of Responsibility

The deterrent power of self-sanctions is weakened when the link between detrimental conduct and its effects is obscured by diffusing responsibility. This is achieved in several ways. Responsibility can be diffused by division of labor. Most organizations require the services of many people, each performing individual tasks that seem harmless in themselves. The partial contribution of each task can be easily isolated from the overall organizational mission, especially when participants exercise little personal judgment in carrying out a task that is related by remote, complex links to the end result. Once activities become standard routines and operating procedures, people shift their attention from the meaning of what they are doing to the details of their job.[34]

Group decision making is another common bureaucratic practice that enables otherwise considerate people to behave inhumanely, because no single individual feels responsible for policies arrived at collectively. Where everyone is responsible, no one really feels responsible. Social organizations go to great lengths to devise sophisticated mechanisms for obscuring responsibility for decisions that will affect others adversely. Collective action, which provides anonymity, is yet another diffusion expedient for weakening self-restraints. Any harm done by a group can always be attributed in large part to the behavior of other members. People act more cruelly under group responsibility than when they hold themselves personally accountable for their actions.[35]

Disregard or Distortion of Harmful Consequences

To be able to perpetrate inhumanities requires more than absolving personal responsibility. Other ways of weakening moral self-sanctions operate by minimizing, disregarding, or distorting the effects of one's action. When people pursue activities that harm others, they avoid facing the harm they cause or minimize it. If minimization does not work, the evidence of harm can be discredited. As long as the harmful results of one's conduct are ignored, minimized, distorted, or disbelieved there is little reason for self-censure to be activated.

It is easier to harm others when their suffering is not visible and when destructive actions are physically and temporally remote from their injurious effects. Our technologies for causing death have become highly lethal and depersonalized. We are now in the era of faceless electronic warfare, in which mass destruction can be delivered remotely with deadly accuracy by computer and laser controlled systems.

When people can see and hear the suffering they cause, vicariously aroused distress and self-censure typically serve as self-restrainers.[36] In studies of obedient aggression, people are less compliant to the injurious commands of authorities when the victims' pain becomes more evident and personalized.[37] Even a high sense of personal responsibility for the effects of one's actions is a weak restrainer of injurious conduct when aggressors do not see the harm they inflict on their victims.[38]

Most organizations involve hierarchical chains of command, in which superiors formulate plans and intermediaries transmit them to functionaries who then carry them out. The further removed individuals are from the destructive end results, the weaker is the restraining power of injurious effects. Disengagement of moral control is easiest for the intermediaries in a hierarchical system—they neither bear responsibility for the decisions nor do they carry them out and face the harm being inflicted.[39] In performing the transmitter role, they model dutiful behavior and further legitimize their superiors and their social policies and practices.

Attribution of Blame

Blaming one's adversaries or compelling circumstances is still another expedient that can serve the purpose of exonerating one's actions. In this process, people view themselves as faultless victims driven to extreme means by forcible provocation, rather than acting on a deliberative decision. A series of reciprocal actions in any given conflict tend to increase in intensity and potential damage. One can select from the chain of events a defensive act by the adversary and portray it as the initiating provocation. Victims then get blamed for bringing suffering upon themselves. Those who are victimized are not entirely faultless because, by their behavior, they contributed partly to their own plight. Victims can, therefore, be blamed for their own suffering. By fixing the blame on others or on circumstances, not only are one's own injurious actions made excusable, but one can even feel self-righteous in the process.

Victim blaming by ascription of responsibility figures prominently in attrition theory.[40] However, the mechanism by which blaming spawns inhumane conduct has received less attention. In social cognitive theory,[41] victim blaming functions as a means of disengaging moral self-sanctions that operates in concert with other means serving the same purpose.

Terrorist acts that take a heavy toll on civilian lives create special personal pressures to lay blame elsewhere. IRA guerrillas planted a large bomb that killed eleven and injured sixty people attending a war memorial ceremony in a town square in Enniskillen, County Fermanagh.[42] The guerrillas promptly ascribed the blame for the civilian massacre to the British army for having detonated the bomb prematurely with an electronic scanning device. The government denounced the "pathetic attempt to transfer blame" because no scanning equipment was in use at the time.

Observers of victimization can be disinhibited in much the same way as perpetrators are by the tendency to infer culpability from misfortune. Seeing victims suffer maltreatment for which they are held partially responsible leads observers to view them less sympathetically.[43] The devaluation and indignation aroused by ascribed culpability, in turn, provides moral justification for even greater maltreatment. The fact that attribution of blame can give rise to devaluation and moral justification illustrates how the various disengagement mechanisms are often interrelated and work together in weakening moral control.

Self-vindication is easily achievable by terrorists when legitimate grievances of maltreatment are willfully disregarded by power holders, so that terrorist activities are construed as acts of self-protection or desperation. Oppressive and inhumane social conditions and thwarted political efforts breed terrorists. Those who become radicalized carry out terrorist acts against the regime as well as nations seen as supporting its oppressive actions. Violent countermeasures are readily resorted to in efforts to control terrorist activities when the social conditions breeding discontent and violent protest are firmly entrenched in political systems that obstruct legitimate efforts at change. It is much easier to attack violent protests than to change the sociopolitical conditions that fuel them. In such skirmishes, one person's victim is another person's victimizer.

Dehumanization

The final set of disengagement practices operates on the targets of violent acts. The strength of moral self-sanctions partly depends on how perpetrators view the people toward whom the violence is directed. To perceive another as human enhances empathetic reactions through a sense of common humanity.[44] The joys and suffering of familiar persons are more vicariously arousing than are those of strangers or of those divested of human qualities. Personalizing the injurious effects experienced by others also makes their suffering much more salient. As a result, it is difficult to mistreat humanized persons without risking self-condemnation.

Self-censure against cruel conduct can be disengaged or blunted by stripping people of human qualities. After they are dehumanized, they are no longer viewed as persons with feelings, hopes, and concerns but as subhuman forms. They are portrayed as mindless "savages," "gooks," "satanic fiends," and the like. Subhumans are regarded as insensitive to maltreatment and influenceable only by harsh methods. If dispossessing one's foes of humanness does not weaken self-censure, it can be eliminated by attributing demonic or bestial qualities to them. They become "beasts," "vermin," or other undesirable creatures. It is easier to brutalize victims, for example, when they are referred to as "worms."[45]

"Evil" has become very much in vogue as the current form of demonization. It conjures up the image of an unfathomable pernicious force that drives "evildoers" ruthlessly. As previously noted, inhumanities are typically perpetrated by people who can be quite considerate and compassionate in other areas of their lives. They can even be ruthless and humane simultaneously toward different individuals. This selectivity of moral engagement is strikingly illustrated by a scene in the movie *Schindler's List* involving Amon Goeth, the Commandant of the Nazi labor camp in Plaszow, Poland. While dictating a letter replete with empathy and compassion for his ailing father, he sees a captive on the grounds who he thinks is not working hard enough. He whips out his revolver and callously shoots the captive. The commandant is both overcome with compassion and is savagely cruel at the same time. By using a description in the guise of an explanation, ready attribution of violence to evil stifles analysis of the determinants governing inhumane conduct.

Studies of interpersonal aggression give vivid testimony to the liberating power of dehumanization.[46] Dehumanized individuals are treated much more punitively than those who have been invested with human qualities. When punitiveness fails to achieve results, this is taken as further evidence of the unworthiness of dehumanized persons, thus justifying their even greater maltreatment. Dehumanization fosters different self-exonerative patterns of thought. People seldom condemn punitive conduct, and they create justifications for it when they are directing their aggression at persons who have been deprived of their humanness. By contrast, people strongly disapprove of punitive actions, and rarely excuse them when they are directed at persons depicted in humanized terms.

The overall findings from research on the different mechanisms of moral disengagement corroborate the historical chronicle of human atrocities: it requires conducive social conditions rather than monstrous people to produce heinous deeds. Given appropriate social conditions, decent, ordinary people can be led to do extraordinarily cruel things.[47]

As alluded to in previous analyses, moral disengagement involves social machinations not just personal intrapsychic ones. In moral justification, for example, people may be misled by those they trust into believing that violent means will prevent more harm than they cause. The benefits that are socially declared may be exaggerated or simply pious rhetoric masking less honorable purposes. Cultural prejudices shape which human beings get grouped and dehumanized, and the types of depraved attributes ascribed to them. Social systems are structured in ways that make it easy for its members to absolve themselves of responsibility for the effects of their actions. Communication systems can be manipulated and institutionally managed in ways that keep people uninformed or misinformed about the harm caused. In short, moral disengagement is a product of the interplay of both self-persuasion and social machinations.

Gradualistic Moral Disengagement

These dimensions of moral disengagement will not instantly transform considerate persons into cruel ones who purposely set out to kill human beings. Rather, the change is achieved by gradual disengagement of self-censure. Terrorist behavior evolves through extensive training in moral disengagement and terrorist prowess rather than emerging full blown. The path to terrorism can be shaped by fortuitous factors as well as by the shared influence of personal preferences and sociopolitical incentives.[48] Development of the willingness to kill is usually achieved through an evolvement process, in which recruits may not recognize the transformation they are undergoing.[49] The training for moral disengagement is usually conducted within a communal setting of intense interpersonal influences insulated from mainstream social life. The recruits become deeply immersed in the ideology and functional roles of the group. Initially, they are prompted to perform unpleasant acts that they can tolerate without much self-censure. Gradually, their discomfort and self-criticism are weakened to ever higher levels of ruthlessness through extensive performance and exposure to aggressive modeling by more experienced associates. The various disengagement practices form an integral part of the training for terrorism. Eventually, acts originally regarded as abhorrent can be performed callously. Inhumane practices become thoughtlessly routinized.

The removal of one's inhibitions is accelerated if violent courses of action are presented as serving a moral imperative, and the targeted people are divested of human qualities.[50] The training not only instills the moral rightness and importance of the cause for militant action. It also creates a sense of eliteness and provides the social rewards of solidarity and group esteem for excelling in terrorist exploits.

Terrorism expert Ehud Sprinzak has shown that terrorists, whether on the political left or political right, evolve gradually rather than set out to become militants.[51] The process of radicalization involves a gradual disengagement of moral self-sanctions from violent conduct. It begins with nonviolent efforts to change particular policies, and voicing opposition to officials who are intent on keeping things as they are. Failure to accomplish social change, combined with hostile confrontations with authorities and police, lead to growing disillusionment and alienation from the whole system. Intensifying battles then culminate in terrorists' efforts to destroy the system and its dehumanized rulers.

There are many determinants and evolving paths to militant activism. However, it is often the more effective members who have become alienated and radicalized, that spearhead militant activism.[52] For example, the Islamic radicalists bent on establishing Muslim theocracies through guerrilla combat and suicidal terrorism did not necessarily come from the ranks of the impoverished and uneducated. However, widespread discontent provides a fertile ground for ideological indoctrination recruitment and collusive support of terrorist activities. In cultural settings where suicidal bombing is hailed as gaining blessed martyrdom, this mode of terrorism is institutionally embraced and socially applauded as divine retribution for the humiliation and suffering inflicted on their people by the enemy.[53] This invests suicide with noble, humanitarian meaning.

Middle East militants modeled suicidal terrorism after the Tamil Tigers of Sri Lanka, who professionalized and institutionalized it as a powerful offensive weapon used for political ends. They regard a suicide as a humanitarian self-gift rather than as self-destruction. There is little defense against individuals who are willing to detonate themselves. For self-protection, terrorists avoid candidates with emotional instabilities who can be readily dissuaded or turned into informants under aversive coercion. They are weeded out in favor of trustworthy ones with unshakeable commitment to what they regard as a humanitarian cause.[54] Within the terrorist subculture, suicidal bombers are celebrated as heroic figures.

Concluding Remarks

The various complementary analyses provided in this chapter shed light on the various psychosocial processes by which individuals can remove humanity from their destructive conduct and spare themselves self-condemning reactions that serve as restraints on cruelty. In so doing, otherwise considerate individuals can commit atrocities of appalling proportions. Terrorism can thus be seen as the product of a complex network of influences that enable and motivate people to perpetrate terrorist acts rather than stemming mainly from a pernicious nature.

CHAPTER 4

Cults, Charismatic Groups, and Social Systems: Understanding the Transformation of Terrorist Recruits

MARC GALANTER AND JAMES J. F. FOREST

Given the rise in terrorist activity throughout the world in recent decades, there is much we can learn from examining how cults engage the minds of their recruits, how they generate their unique psychological and social forces, and how they acquire structure as a social system.[1] Of particular salience, a fairly substantial body of research on religious cults has been developed over the past several years, illustrating (among other topics) the importance of social identity processes for individuals who become cult members. Religious cults—typically driven by a charismatic leader—are highly cohesive, collectivist, and authoritarian. Within the group there is a great deal of harmony and positive regard for group members combined with negative perceptions of outsiders. Studies have revealed how individuals experience a profound increase in psychological well-being when they join these groups. Further, individuals who are particularly distressed prior to joining—such as those experiencing economic, social, and/or psychological stresses—are particularly more likely to experience a significant sense of relief upon joining a cult. Meanwhile, growth in cult membership helps to reinforce the merit of the group's ideology and validate the group's existence.

It is not uncommon to think of cults as anomalies. When described in the news, a cult is often portrayed as a sort of oddity, with little attention paid to the psychology and social structure that most cults have in common. However, the beliefs and behaviors of cult members become more understandable when the patterns underlying these organizations are viewed within the context of social systems. This chapter will expand the research of such patterns by exploring the role of cults and other charismatic groups in the terrorist world. In doing so, this discussion contributes to our understanding of how an average individual is transformed into a terrorist. But first, a definition of what is meant by the term "charismatic group" is necessary.

The Charismatic Group

A cult is one of several types of charismatic groups. A charismatic group consists of a dozen or more members, even hundreds of thousands. It is characterized by the following psychological elements: members (1) have a *shared belief system*, (2) sustain a high level of *social cohesiveness*, (3) are strongly influenced by the group's *behavioral norms*, and (4) impute *charismatic* (or sometimes *divine*) *power* to the group or its leadership. In a charismatic group, commitments can be elicited by relative strangers in a way rarely seen in other groups. Even Freud, who championed the compelling nature of individual motives, addressed this impressive capacity at length in his book *Group Psychology and the Analysis of the Ego*.[2] He discussed these forces in terms of the "primitive sympathetic response of the group," and said that "something is unmistakably at work in the nature of a compulsion to do the same as others, to remain in harmony with the many."

The cognitive basis for this conformity is a *shared belief system*. The beliefs held in common by members of charismatic groups are a vital force in the group's operation. They bind members together, shape their attitudes, and motivate them to act in self-sacrifice. When these groups are religious in nature, their beliefs are often codified, but some groups have no more than an ill-defined ideological orientation. In some religious cults, converts are introduced to the group's ideology only after they have affiliated.[3] Once they have identified with the group's general orientation, though, they tend to accept their beliefs quite readily when these are spelled out. Members of these groups tend to be intensely concerned about each other's well-being and are deeply committed to joint activities. Their social cohesiveness, essential to the group's integrity, is reflected in the close intertwining of the individual's life circumstances with those of all group members. Meetings are frequent; they serve as a focus for group functions and articulate their cohesiveness. Members often express their need to associate regularly with each other by developing joint activities such as minor group tasks and rituals, which in turn justify such meetings. Both cult and self-help group members are always aware of when their next group meeting will be held, and look to them as a means of instilling commitment and a sense of purpose. A member's emotional state may be highly vulnerable to disruptions of this routine, and a group gathering missed can become a source of distress.

All charismatic groups engage the emotional needs of their members in an intensely *cohesive social system*. Group cohesiveness may be defined as the result of all the forces acting on members to keep them engaged in the group.[4] When cohesiveness is strong, participants work to retain the commitment of their fellow members, protect them from threat, and ensure the safety of shared resources. With weak cohesiveness, there is less concern over the group's potential dissolution or the loss of its distinctive identity, and joint action is less likely.

Group cohesiveness[5] is seen in informally structured groups, such as a clique of teenagers who make every effort to get together, even when forcibly separated by their elders. It also exists in formally structured groups, such as professional sports teams or military platoons, whose members undergo great sacrifice to assist each other in their common mission, particularly when confronted by adversaries. In most organized groups, however, cohesiveness is characterized by neither adversity nor great drama; in a fraternal organization, for example, members meet regularly to share experiences and give each other practical assistance.

Our understanding of group cohesiveness—particularly as applied to charismatic groups—is informed by studies of family relationships. The concept of "differentiation of self," developed by family theorists such as Murray Bowen and Lyman Wynne,[6] helps explain the interaction between the individual and his or her family, and can be assessed independently of a person's diagnosis, social class, and cultural background. At one end of this scale lies the highly differentiated individual, characterized by autonomy and even rugged individualism. At the other end, family relationships exhibit emotional fusion and an inability to make critical judgments because of a need to assure harmony with others.

Emotional fusion in families is akin to group cohesiveness in its merging of identity and decision-making functions. It occurs in large charismatic groups as well as in families, because members of both may be highly dependent on each other and rely excessively on their compatriots for emotional support and decision making.[7] This is also seen among certain families who are unable to tolerate disruptions in the balance of their members' relationships. For example, if a psychiatrist attempts to change an apparently harmful pattern of interaction within a family, one way or another that pattern will soon reestablish itself; this takes place without any formal understanding among family members, as if a governing structure existed outside their awareness.

Preserving intense interrelatedness is also essential to a religious cult.[8] Because of the need to preserve cohesiveness and interdependency, close-knit families and religious cults employ adaptive strategies to maintain stability in the face of internal or external threat. A distorted consensus emerges, a mutually-held point of view that allows the perception of equilibrium to be maintained. This consensus is often achieved by denying reality and rationalizing a shared perspective. In essence, reality becomes less important to certain groups than the preservation of their ties. Freud's observation about group psychology and the pressures that draw individuals into consensual and irrational response is particularly apt here. The evolution of a crowd, he noted, is based on a compulsion in people to do the same as others, "to remain in harmony with the many."[9]

The *norms for behavior* in a charismatic group also play an important role in determining how its members conduct themselves. Members typically look to group norms for learning ways to behave in new situations. They may respond in a similar fashion to strangers perceived as threatening—in some groups, with a blunted and distant stare. Often they are implicitly aware of their style of behavior in an unexpected situation, while at other times it emerges without conscious appreciation of how they act. Behavioral change may also extend to mimicking the symptoms of mental illness. In these groups, transcendental experiences—often hallucinatory—are quite common. A deceased comrade "literally" stands by a member or a historical figure, bringing divinely inspired advice. Intense emotional experiences are reported, such as profound euphoria or malaise. Such phenomena, which are often seen among the mentally ill, occur among individuals who give no evidence of psychiatric disorder.

Finally, *charismatic powers* are typically imputed to leaders of these groups, but can also be ascribed to the group or its mission. Some contemporary terrorist groups, for example, are viewed by their members as heralding an inevitable new world order. The leaders of some religious-oriented groups are believed by their followers to have a uniquely close relationship with God, giving a virtually uncontestable authority for that leader's decisions. These four psychological elements—shared belief system, social cohesiveness, behavioral norms, and charismatic power—are common to most charismatic groups. Further, they reinforce each other through a series of interactions that are similar in virtually any social system.

The Charismatic Group as a Social System

At the interface between charismatic group and society at large, strange things happen. Many people have noted the glazed look of members of such cults as the Unification Church when they venture outside the fold and mix with nonmembers. It has been suggested that such behavior is symptomatic of psychopathology, specifically a detached state. Others who have studied cults and other charismatic groups, however, have not made such observations. This discrepancy represents different aspects of behavior at the boundary of a social system.

Another common observation is the animosity such groups elicit from outsiders. In a pluralistic society such as the United States, one may wonder why such hostility exists. Again, this reaction represents a characteristic process that occurs at a cult's boundaries and will explain some troublesome interactions between members and nonmembers.

All social systems have certain functions that act to protect their integrity and implement their goals. To view cults more clearly in the broad social context, and to understand their interactions with society better, it is useful to draw upon systems theory. Four functions characteristic of systems are transformation, monitoring, feedback, and boundary control.

Transformation

Systems have been likened to factories; they take input from the outside, which can be raw material, energy, or information, and process it into output, a product. This function, called transformation, allows the system to carry out operations essential to its own continuity or to the needs of a larger suprasystem to which it belongs. In a given system, the most important transformation—the one that typically defines its identity—is its *primary task*; most components of the system are geared toward either carrying out this primary task or preventing its disruption. The primary task of many religious cults is to prepare for the messianic end they envision, while the equivalent task of terrorist groups is to compel—through the use of terror—some sort of political, social, religious, or other type of change by a government or target population.

An unstable system, such as a cult in its earlier stages, is particularly susceptible to dissolution. Members may disaffiliate at any time, since the ties that bind them together have yet to be woven into the stable network of a social structure. In this regard, the concept of transformation can be used as a model for the persistent attempts of certain charismatic groups to stabilize themselves by acquiring new members. This may be why members can become so deeply involved in conversion activities; they themselves are motivated only by an inherent need to become engaged in the charismatic group, but they begin conforming to the group's needs as a system. Members would not on their own be inclined to go out and recruit for the group, but as parts of its system they come to act in accordance with its goals.

At some point in their evolution, most charismatic groups focus on recruitment as a primary task. The process may ensure a larger and stronger group and, when successful, can also help confer legitimacy to the group's own ideology, thereby consolidating the commitment of its long-standing members.

Another important aspect of that transformation function is how it disrupts the psychological stability of potential recruits, the "input" to this process. Since an intensive mobilization of a charismatic group's psychological and material resources may be directed at the conversion of new members, they can create deep turmoil in the individual convert. On the one hand, the group is intensely seductive in its attempt to attract new members; on the other, it demands a disruption of antecedent social ties and a metamorphosis in the new member's worldview. Thus, when the full resources of the group are focused on a recruit, the potential for tearing the fabric of that individual's psychological stability is considerable. The result may be psychiatric symptoms in people with no history of mental disorder or psychological instability. The genesis of these symptoms may lie more in the conflict between the recruit's needs and the group's demands than in an underlying psychological impairment of the individual. In essence, an effective cult is able to engage and transform individuals in ways that disrupt an otherwise stable psychological condition, in many cases causing significant guilt and resulting in a severe psychiatric reaction.

A variety of devices are employed in this group to intensify the forces operating on potential recruits. The "training" is carried out in protracted sessions where disagreement with the trainer is actively discouraged, often by harsh verbal abuse. Little respite is afforded from the intensity of the group experience, and the training setting includes as many as two hundred potential recruits herded together, with their behavior tightly controlled. The dynamism of the experience further heightens the potential for energetic group influence and emotional contagion, and altered consciousness is promoted by a variety of contextual cues and behavioral controls.

Conversion is in fact a primary task of terrorist training. Casualties incurred during the difficult training regimen may have to be ignored, and the problematic issues they raise, repressed. This reinforces the "shared beliefs" of other followers, those who see "getting it" as more important than attention to specific personal conflicts or day-to-day relationships. Suppression of concerns that might detract from the primary task of an intensely committed social system is actually quite common. In the time of battle, for example, an army may be mobilized to achieve its immediate military objectives, and its primary task is therefore the transformation of all personnel and material into a fighting force. The psychology of the troops is bent to this mission to the exclusion of all else, since victory in battle is paramount. Concern for the needs of the wounded may be secondary, since this could detract from the thrust into battle. In a similar way, mobilization for the transformation process in the terrorist group cannot be deflected by the difficulties experienced by individual recruits because the usual constraints on exerting social pressure are suppressed.

Monitoring and Identification

To operate effectively, a system must transform input from the environment into a form that meets its needs, but must also observe and regulate the actions of its component parts, thereby assuring that their respective activities are properly carried out and coordinated. This constitutes its monitoring function. Such monitoring is essential to any system, in order to ensure the effective implementation of its primary task, whether that system is a living organism, a social organization, or a factory. The system must have an apparatus for monitoring its components. In the living organism, its nervous system serves this function, and in social organizations and factories, it is some form of management structure.

In the terrorist organization, monitoring is necessarily conducted by the trainers (in training camps) and by cell leaders. These monitors must know how to observe and govern the group's members in order to ensure the stability of the social system. In an effective system, the monitoring function will operate without undue need for communication or conflict resolution. The system's components—the group members—will respond automatically to the suggestions of the leadership. Whether consciously controlled or not, compliance with the group's announced perspective is expected.

To understand the means by which the charismatic group rapidly and effectively monitors the thinking and behavioral norms of its members, one must consider the psychological defense mechanisms employed by the group as a whole, which are unlike those operating in individuals. These defenses are employed for the unconscious management of conflicting motives so that the group can function smoothly in the face of conflict. Although similar defenses may be observed in other social systems, the charismatic group responds in particular ways that distinguish it from less tightly knit groups, since the forces of group cohesiveness and shared beliefs in the charismatic group facilitate its operation as a functional whole. These psychological defenses protect the group culture from unacceptable ideas, often "realities" produced by outdated initiatives or outside influences. Such realities may be ignored outright, by means of denial; forgotten through repression; or distorted through rationalization.

In a social system, monitoring is most easily implemented when a voluntary collaboration exists between those in control and those being managed, since outright coercion necessitates undue expenditure of resources and detracts from cooperative efforts to carry out the system's primary task. It is best, in fact, if those monitored accept the leadership without conscious deliberation and, since the defense mechanism of identification operates in an unconscious fashion, those who adopt the attitudes of their leaders do so without deliberating over the wisdom of their actions.

Perhaps the most unusual type of identification takes place when the members' own safety and well-being are jeopardized by their leadership. In terrorist training camps, recruits typically develop a positive bond with their trainers, not only complying with their expectations but even defending them against outside forces. Thus, despite the physical pain and rigor of terrorist training, the agent inflicting distress on the dependent person (the recruit) is also perceived as the party who can provide relief. Training for terrorism necessitates enduring unpleasant activities, while in some of the more nefarious cults (religious or otherwise) members may be subject to various forms of abuse. Members nonetheless have their own psychological need for maintaining affiliation with the leader and the group, since they are captives by virtue of a pincer effect, which makes their emotional well-being dependent upon involvement in the group that inflicts distress. In a sense, they have no choice but to unconsciously make peace with the potentially threatening agenda of the leadership and comply with its expectations in order to achieve emotional relief.

A subcomponent of identification in certain cults and terrorist groups involves the suppression of autonomy. For a social system to regulate its functioning effectively, it must have the capacity to suppress members' deviation from its implicit or explicit goals. In charismatic groups, the penalty for those who deviate from norms is psychological distress; overt coercion usually is not necessary to induce compliance. From this, it can be inferred that attempts at achieving independence from such groups become rare, and would tend to be easily extinguished by the groups' leaders. In extreme cases, attempts to leave a group's membership may even result in execution.[10]

Feedback

Feedback is one way for a system to obtain information about how well it is carrying out its primary task. Analysis of results is fed back into the system, and this provides information for planning future operations. For example, if a cult is trying to recruit, information on the relative response of potential members can be fed back to the cult leaders and guide them in improving the group's recruitment techniques.

Feedback may be either positive or negative. Positive feedback gives the system information that will increase the effectiveness in achieving desired results. When negative feedback ceases to be available, the organization loses an important aspect of its ability to self-correct for actions which may be detrimental to the group's members. Transformation activities may go unmoderated, and the system's boundaries can be disrupted.[11] Consequently, the system must have unrestrained access to negative feedback to exercise a proper degree of self-regulation and not dissipate its energies.

This latter function is important in charismatic groups because they are prone to suppress negative feedback when it runs contrary to the group's internal stability. It is a special risk because of the highly effective monitoring function that allows the cult system to control the information made available to its members. Means of avoiding undue negative feedback are essential to charismatic groups because their ideology and practices often elicit hostility from the general society. If allowed to enter the system unobstructed, such negative feedback leads to suppression of the group's transcendent vision and a decline in members' morale.

Certain charismatic groups try hard to isolate their members from all negative feedback, but this can be dangerous, as the group may lose information valuable to its own self-regulation. These groups usually are no longer actively recruiting and have little need for protracted contact with outsiders. Other groups, however, rely on the successful recruitment of new members to provide them with positive feedback. Such successes are used to reinforce the merit of the group's own ideology and promote new initiatives that validate the group's chosen course. New recruits give legitimacy to a group in the face of a hostile world, and encourage members to carry the group's mission forward. Such feedback can be a useful tool for social regulation.

Boundary Control

In sum, an open system must carry out its transformation functions while maintaining internal stability by monitoring its own components and responding to feedback. These functions, however, can be disrupted by intrusions from outside. For this reason, boundary control is a vital function of any social system.

Boundary control protects social systems against dangerous outsiders. It includes not only the screening of people but also of information, since information is a potent determinant of behavior. If a charismatic group is to maintain a system of shared beliefs markedly at variance with that of the surrounding culture, members must sometimes be rigidly isolated from consensual information from the general society that would unsettle this belief system. During the initial phases of conversion to charismatic groups, novices may be regarded as vulnerable, and discouraged from establishing contact with their families. Similar processes of individual isolation from family, friends, and society often takes place in the setting of terrorist training camps. After their integration into the group, when their beliefs have been consolidated, these new members may be encouraged to reestablish ties with their families so as to promote a benign public image and perhaps help recruit other new members.

Any group that coalesces around a cause or function must soon establish a boundary to differentiate those who are participating from those who are not. Two important facets of activity form the boundary of charismatic groups, each mirroring the other. The first is a set of behaviors and attitudes of members, often deviant, that is directed at outsiders. It reflects how the system focuses its social forces to protect its boundaries. The second is a reciprocal set of behaviors and attitudes of the surrounding society, often an aggressive response of outsiders to the group's members.

The boundary of behavior of cult members that has made the deepest impression on outsiders involves the glazed, withdrawn look and trance-like state that some find most unsettling. Although this may appear pathologic, it can help group membership by reducing the possibility of direct exchanges with outsiders—it has an insulating effect. Thus, the trancelike appearance protects the group's boundary. It would be more likely to develop in settings that threaten the group's integrity, so that an observer who is perceived as an antagonist is more likely to see the behavior than one who is not.

Fearfulness of outsiders, or xenophobia—a common characteristic of cults—is another important manifestation of boundary control. It holds groups together, but it can reach the dimensions of outright paranoia. It represents a boundary control function carried to the extreme and is seen among those group members pressed by family or strangers to give up their ties to the group. It is also evident in the way outsiders are often treated with a different standard of openness or honesty.

Defensiveness and paranoia associated with the boundary function of a charismatic group elicit a complementary reaction from the surrounding community. This is seen in the animosity between family members of converts and the sects, in the breakdown in communication between sects and some religious groups, and in the hostility toward sects voiced by some former members.

Attempts at communication between parents and their children who have joined contemporary groups are often rife with misunderstanding and hostility. The new recruit often becomes an agent of the group's boundary control function and regards the relatives who make contact as attempting to disengage the person from the movement, whereas the parents, operating at the boundary of a highly cohesive group, frequently become preoccupied with the effort to dislodge the new member. Communications are often frozen at this level.

Overall, members of a cult may be driven to behave as they do by forces that act within the social system to assure its stability and implement its primary task. On the other hand, the openness of each member to such influence can only be understood by recourse to one's biologically grounded responsiveness to group influence. In the world of the terrorist organization, then, an individual is transformed by group forces as well as by their personal willingness to be transformed by these forces.

The Charismatic Group in the Terrorist World

For the Islamic fundamentalist, becoming a member of the global jihad can be viewed as a complex process, and the social bonds and psychological forces involved in this act are similar to those of religious cult membership. For example, the membership of terrorist groups develop and maintain their own organizational saga and negative perceptions of outsiders. Similar examples of shared beliefs, altered consciousness, and behavioral con-

formity that contribute to cult membership are seen among terrorist organizations—particularly those driven by charismatic leaders. Thus, a discussion of the social and psychological forces that reinforce an individual's
commitment within cults has clear implications for our understanding of
how groups like Hamas or al Qaeda maintain their membership despite
rather grueling living conditions. Much the same as cults, terrorist groups
merge identity and decision-making functions into a common membership
framework and work to replace an individual's psychological distress with
an enhanced sense of self-being and belonging.

Studies of terrorist groups—ranging from the Red Army Faction of Germany to the myriad Islamic militant groups in Egypt—have all emphasized
the important relationship between individual well-being and complete loyalty to the group. While there are clear distinctions between social networks
and formal cults, our understanding of cult mentality allows us to shed
light on terrorist behavior.

To begin with, like other charismatic groups, the traits of terrorist-
oriented cult organizations are often best illustrated by the way they bring
about changes in the thinking and behavior of individual members. Much
has been written—in this three-volume publication and elsewhere—about
the role of ideology and indoctrination by terrorist organizations. Clearly,
the doctrine and pronouncements of al Qaeda leaders, for example, is
meant to solidify group goals and ensure that new recruits embrace the
concepts of global jihad. The expansive network of alumni from al Qaeda's
training camps in Afghanistan serves to maintain interpersonal connections,
relationships which lead to what Freud would call remaining "in harmony
with the many"[12] even at the expense of human security.[13]

Other parallels between religious cults and terrorist organizations include
the role of a charismatic leader in providing direction to the collective energies of group members. Cult leaders are often seen as powerful personalities who inspire, even hypnotize their audiences, and who may punish
dissent or deviation from the group's values or objectives.[14] At a basic level,
an individual like David Koresh—of the infamous Branch Davidians compound in Waco, Texas—can use his charismatic power to force a group of
people to do things they would not ordinarily do. More extreme cases include Jim Jones, who led his followers to commit mass suicide in Guyana.
But wherever cults have been organized by a charismatic leader, the changes
in thinking and behavior that are brought about within individual group
members have not been achieved solely by the leader's power; rather, the
four psychological elements discussed earlier in this chapter—shared belief
system, social cohesiveness, behavioral norms, and charismatic power—
play a critical role in the evolutionary process of virtually all charismatic
groups. A case in point, which clearly lies within the realm of the terrorist
world, can be seen in the Aum Shinrikyō cult and its leader, Shoko Asahara.

A Case Study: Aum Shinrikyō

During a morning rush hour, in March 1995, two five-man teams converged on the Kasumigaseki station, the hub of Tokyo's underground transit system and a short walk from the Japanese Parliament. They carried plastic bags of sarin, a liquefied poison gas, along with their umbrellas. Already protected by antidotes to the poison, they punctured the bags with the umbrellas, releasing vapors from the liquefied gas, and fled quickly. Sarin, which was developed in Nazi Germany, attacks the central nervous system and is deadly in the smallest quantities. In this case, the attack killed twelve subway riders, and many others were temporarily blinded and collapsed on sidewalks as they tried to run for safety.

Aum Shinrikyō was a religious sect that claimed to have 10,000 members in Japan and 20,000 abroad, mostly in Russia. It had been previously suspected of wrongdoing by the Japanese police, and was now presumed to be responsible for the subway poisonings. After the subway attack, more than 2,500 officers raided Aum's various offices, while hundreds of Aum priests continued to meditate and pray at its headquarters. The public's anxiety was only heightened when statements of the group's leader, Shoko Asahara, were beamed to Japan by radio from Vladivostok and Sakhalin in Russia—statements such as "Let us face death without regret."

At the cult's main compound in Kamikuishiki, a small farming village in the shadow of Mount Fuji, riot policemen entered warehouses carrying caged canaries, a means of alerting them to the presence of toxic fumes. They found some 500 metal drums containing deadly poisons like sodium cyanide. The discovery of huge stocks of the chemicals used to make sarin was particularly startling, because even minute quantities of the poison are extremely lethal.

An investigation by Japanese authorities revealed that Aum's leadership had managed to acquire or build a vast, diversified arsenal, including computer-controlled laboratories and remote-controlled machinery for sealing plastic pouches. They had recruited large numbers of university science graduates, who were conducting research into botulism and other biological weapons. The police seized raw materials that could have been used to cultivate viruses. Aum operated three companies of its own to buy chemicals, and in Moscow—where the group claimed a considerable following—there were reports of members having met with Russian nuclear specialists, indicating Aum's interest in acquiring nuclear weapons. There was also evidence that the group had purchased a large Russian military helicopter and had priced Russian tanks, submarines, and military aircraft.

The 1995 attack was not the first violent act committed by this organization. In 1989, agents of Aum had murdered lawyer Tsutsumi Sakamoto, along with his wife and infant son. Sakamoto had represented families of cult members who were trying to get their relatives back from

Aum Shinrikyō, and had appeared on television to present his case shortly before being murdered. Police found the bodies only when they undertook a search after the Tokyo attack six years later. Cult members later testified that the victims had been injected with a drug, struck with a hammer, and then strangled.[15]

Aum leaders had even considered releasing nerve gas in the United States, a country thought by Asahara to be hostile to his group.[16] Dr. Ikuo Hayashi, who had served as medical director of Aum, said that the U.S. attacks were planned for June 1994 but were suspended. The intelligence director of the group had even instructed him to go to the United States to pick up a package of sarin that was to arrive in a shipment of ornaments. Hayashi, by the way, a respected cardiologist who had worked in an American hospital before joining the cult, is illustrative of the talent that was inducted into the group.

Asahara as a Cult Leader

In his pamphlets, Shoko Asahara urged people to join his program of "Death and Rebirth," pointing out that "as we move toward the year 2000 there will be a series of events of inexpressible ferocity and terror"; that "Japan has been unjustly deprived of the concept of death and life after death"; and that he would teach people about both.[17] Japanese newspapers estimate that Asahara's chemical stockpile could have created enough nerve gas to kill between 4.2 million and 10 million people.

Asahara was described by followers as an intelligent, soft-spoken married man with six children. He had a long beard, a beatific smile, and wore oriental robes. He was the sixth of seven children born to a maker of tatami mats in a small Japanese village. One of his older brothers was almost completely blind and had to attend a school for children with limited vision. Shoko's parents decided to enroll him there as well, since his vision was also limited, but because his sight was better than that of the other students he became a leader among them. He later experienced a string of failures during his school years, including unsuccessful runs for student body president in elementary, junior high, and senior high schools. After failing his college entrance exams, he moved to a Tokyo suburb to work as an acupuncturist.

In the early 1980s, Asahara opened a shop selling concocted Chinese medicines, and was arrested and fined for marketing drugs of unproven effectiveness. He later launched a company called "Aum," which ran a yoga school and operated health-related activities. He traveled to Nepal and India and came back with photographs of himself with senior Tibetan lamas, even the Dalai Lama. He promoted his school with some success, using these pictures to present himself as an internationally respected religious leader.

By 1987, Asahara had acquired a small following and had founded Aum Shinrikyō as a religious sect. It was a time when a number of similar Buddhist- or Shinto-oriented sects were emerging in Japan and attracting young people who were disenchanted with the country's materialist orientation. Aum appeared to offer a clear alternative. As though to prove its special power, it promised its members the ability to levitate and would present recruits with photographs of Asahara poised inches above the ground in a yogic position. It also provided recruits with headgear containing batteries and electrodes designed to align their brain waves with those of their leader. Asahara had a knack for recruitment, and Aum began to attract many bright, discontented university students, particularly those trained in the sciences. As his sect grew richer, he developed a paunch and began to drive around in a Rolls Royce.

The group's tactics for securing members reflected many of the worst aspects of other cultic groups. These included alterations in consciousness and sensation, as the recruits were sometimes starved and given psychotomimetic drugs. In one account given after the sarin attack, a woman described how she and her daughter were locked inside a dark, windowless room shortly after joining the sect and were forced to watch a continuously running tape of Asahara. Furthermore, when police raided the cult's training compound in Kamikuishiki shortly after the subway attack, they found fifty people in an advanced state of malnutrition and dehydration, some barely conscious; remarkably, they eschewed the medical attention offered them.

Intense cohesiveness, bolstered by physical isolation, was also a vehicle for sustaining members' involvement. Asahara demanded that many of his followers live in communes, cut off from relatives and family. There was a striking inconsistency between the activities of Aum's leadership and the Buddhist-derived philosophy maintained by the large majority of its members. Most members knew nothing about the criminal activities of the group's leaders, a fact that reflects the profound discrepancy between the means employed by the core leadership and the pacific attitudes shown by members.

As is typical of many charismatic sects, recruits were often told to sign over their property to the group, and Aum went so far as to murder one person who opposed the expropriation. The relative of a recruit was kidnapped in the street after protesting that his sister had been required to give away all her assets, and later police unearthed evidence that the man had been murdered by Aum members.

Surprisingly, the Tokyo disaster made only a modest impression on most members of the cult. A few weeks after the event, one graduate student reported that he was urged by his family and friends to leave the group. He insisted on staying, and said, "I've got to do this, and that's all I can say. I'm sorry, Mom. Sorry Dad . . . if I were head of the public security commission in Japan, and if I were thinking of what group is the most dangerous for the present social system in Japan, it would be Aum . . . because Aum has such potential for the future."[18] A disaffiliated member, questioned about his experience in the group, had eaten only root vegetables that were often rotten and caused diarrhea. Nonetheless, he said that even after leaving Aum, he often found himself singing Aum songs and recalling his experience with the group fondly.

Fumihiro Joyu, a thirty-two-year-old spokesman for Aum, was something of a media star in Japan and an idol of many teenage girls and young women. As a monk in the movement, Joyu said that he shunned wine, woman, and sex. Even after the Tokyo attack, he attracted a bevy of young girls in front of the sect's headquarters waiting to see him emerge. Some of them indicated belonging to a Joyu fan club. He continued to deny the cult's responsibility for the gas attack months after the event.

The sustained commitment of members, as exemplified by the graduate student and the group's spokesman, flew in the face of reality and reflected a need to retain fidelity to a failed movement even when it was proven unworthy. This is very much aligned with what other research has discovered about doomsday cults. Members of such groups remain committed even after their leaders' predictions of the world's end came to naught; many simply rationalized this failure and retained their fidelity to the movement.[19]

Discussion

The case of Aum Shinrikyō offers a useful example of how cults and terrorist organizations engage the minds of their recruits, how they generate their unique psychological and social forces, and how they acquire structure as a social system. There are four elements in particular by which Aum exemplifies the transformative process of other charismatic groups: isolation, paranoia, grandiosity, and absolute dominion. Regarding *isolation*, a group can remove or distance itself from the values of our common culture, even the importance of preserving life. This can take the form of geographic isolation, such as Aum's training facilities. For example, Shoko Asahara established an isolated compound in rural Japan; he also maintained a gulf in communication between his inner circle and his widely dispersed adherents, thus isolating the decision makers from the flock of followers.

An isolated cultic group provides fertile soil for the emergence of *paranoia* and *grandiosity* in its leader, and will aggravate these traits in the leader who already sees himself as espousing a philosophy of absolute truth. Paranoia and grandiosity are interdependent—a person who needs to sustain full control over his flock, in order to maintain the appearance of divinity that most charismatic group leaders enjoy, will inevitably begin to suspect others of trying to take it away. He fears that the government or even parties inside his own sect will envy his powers and try to obstruct his mission. This sets up a siege mentality and leaves the leader awaiting the moment of assault. The interweaving of grandiosity and paranoia sets the stage for thinking that a fight to the death—or in some cases, mass suicide or martyrdom—following a confrontation with the government is legitimate. Isolation, grandiosity, and paranoia all set the stage for a leader to establish *absolute domain* over his followers. This can be achieved through the intensification of the system's monitoring of members' behavior—that is, observation and regulation of members to ensure that the group's tasks are carried out as the leader's control continues.

Controlling perception and behavior. As discussed earlier, the traits of charismatic groups are often best illustrated by the way they bring about changes in the thinking and behavior of individual members. Indeed, virtually all types of charismatic groups seek control over their members' behavior, thoughts, information and emotion. People are more vulnerable to social influence when they are made to think, sense, and feel differently than usual, when someone or something disrupts their emotional balance. Such changes in subjective experience (or alterations in consciousness) can undermine the psychological matrix in which our views are rooted, so that we lose track of customary internal signposts. They may also introduce a feeling of mystery, or a sense that forces beyond our control are operating. Thus, they can prime us to accept unaccustomed explanations for our experiences and adopt new attitudes implied in these explanations. In this regard, it is perhaps no surprise to learn of Aum's use of drugs, meditation, and other psychologically-related activities in transforming their new recruits into full members, given that altered consciousness can help shape members' attitudes in a charismatic group.

Social cohesion. Preserving intense interrelatedness is also essential to both a religious cult and terrorist group.[20] Because of the need to preserve cohesiveness and interdependency, close-knit families and religious cults employ adaptive strategies to maintain stability in the face of internal or external threat. As illustrated by the case of Aum Shinrikyō, a distorted consensus emerges, a mutually-held point of view that allows the perception of equilibrium to be maintained. This consensus is often achieved by denying reality and rationalizing a shared perspective. In essence, reality becomes less important to certain groups than the preservation of their ties. Freud's observation about group psychology and the pressures that draw individuals into consensual and irrational response is particularly apt here. As he noted, people are sometimes compelled to do the same as others, "to remain in harmony with the many."[21]

Shared belief systems. Members of Aum had a shared belief in a vision for the future, which served as a vital force in the group's operation. These beliefs bind Aum's members together, shape their attitudes, and motivate them to act in self-sacrifice. Members of Aum tend to be intensely concerned about each other's well-being, as well as that of their leader Asahara. These shared belief systems are particularly powerful when they include religious dimensions. From Islamic fundamentalist groups in Saudi Arabia or Indonesia to Christian militia groups in the United States, the belief that God endorses the values and objectives of the group is a particularly powerful motivator for group cohesion.

Belonging and psychological well-being. Members of Aum displayed the attributes of other cults—namely, the need to belong to the group, from which psychological well-being is drawn. Decades of psychological research have observed how group membership can replace an individual's psychological distress (which can be the product of any number of personal or social traumas) with an enhanced sense of self-being. This, in turn, helps explain the lengths to which group members will go to protect the group from outside forces, even when presented with evidence that the group is engaged in activities which society deems unacceptable.

Communication patterns among group members. As noted earlier, boundary setting plays a critical role in determining patterns of communication between group members and those deemed as "outsiders." In the case of Aum Shinrikyō, members were cordoned off from contact with the outside world, and Asahara maintained a gulf in communication between his inner circle and his widely dispersed adherents, thus isolating the decision makers from the flock of followers. Monitoring and controlling communication patterns, and restricting any form of dissent, enabled Aum Shinrikyō's leaders to ensure that new members of the group accept the beliefs and values of the group.

Together, these elements of isolation, paranoia, grandiosity, and absolute dominion exemplify how Aum Shinrikyō—as well as other cults and terrorist organizations—generate unique psychological and social forces that transform a fairly ordinary individual into a potentially lethal terrorist.

Conclusion

This chapter illustrates the usefulness of describing terrorist group membership more in terms of social adaptation rather than personal pathology. Instead of the typical Hollywood portrayal of terrorists as wild-eyed, mindless fanatics, this discussion suggests that psychological and social forces can be brought to bear in reducing the attractiveness of terrorist group membership. The social system forces found in cults and other types of charismatic groups—including those committed to terror—play a critical role in transforming an individual's values and belief systems, creating group members whose commitment to membership in (and objectives of) the group takes precedence over individual needs or desires. In extreme cases—including members of Aum Shinrikyō or the hijackers responsible for the 9/11 attacks in New York and Washington, DC—a dedication to committing terrible acts of homicide and suicide, and protecting the group (or the al Qaeda cell) from discovery beforehand, is more important than an individual's fundamental desire to remain alive. This dedication, in turn, can be seen as the product of forces common to most any charismatic group.

To summarize this chapter, the charismatic group can be viewed as a close-knit community defined by the following primary characteristics: It has a strongly-held belief system and a high level of social cohesiveness; its members are deeply influenced by the group's behavioral norms and impute a transcendent (or divine) role to their leader. These groups may differ among themselves in the particulars of their ideology and ritual behavior, but they do have several traits in common, including 1) an attraction to joining the group; 2) the transformative experience of membership; and 3) the social system forces that surround members, giving meaning and structure.

The attraction of entry into the group. Charismatic groups are likely to emerge at a time when the values of a society are felt to be inadequate for addressing major social issues. Individuals are more prone to join if they are unhappy because of situational problems or chronic distress and if they have limited affiliate ties to family and friends. Groups generally engage new members by creating an atmosphere of unconditional acceptance and support, and offering a worldview that promises a solution for all existential problems. Engagement (or conversion) entails experiences of intensely felt emotion or perceptual change. It also provides a relief of neurotic distress and a feeling of well-being. For newly recruited members of the group, these experiences serve to validate the group's mission.

The transformative experience of group membership. The group's leader is reputed to have the potential of bringing a resolution to the problems of humanity. In interacting with followers, the leader is also drawn into believing the grandiose role accorded him and then justifies his behavior by referring to the transcendent mission suggested by the group's philosophy. This can cause him to make demands on his followers that outsiders would see as petulant and abusive. The group attributes special meaning, colored by its philosophy, to everyday language and events; this meaning is usually related to dogma or written code attributed to the group's leader or progenitor. Recruits experience a *relief effect* with membership. That is, the closer they feel to their fellow members and the group's values, the greater the relief in their emotional distress; the more they become emotionally distanced from the group, the greater their experience of distress. This relief effect serves as the basis for reinforcing compliance with the group's norms, as it implicitly rewards conformity with enhanced well-being and punishes alienation with feelings of distress. It also keeps members from leaving the group, because they are conditioned to avoid the distress that results from relinquishing the benefits of the relief effect.

Group behavioral norms generally structure all areas of members' lives, their work, sexuality, socialization, and intellectual pursuits. Activities in these areas are preferentially carried out with other members, so that friends and colleagues are generally shunned as outsiders. Membership is characterized by levels of "sanctity," so that a member is continually striving to achieve a higher level of acceptance by conforming all the more with the group's expectations. Such conformity generally results in members' experiencing considerable hardship.

The charismatic group as a social system. The group operates as a close-knit social system to ensure its stability. It does this by manipulating the activities and views of its members. Members' activities are monitored closely, either by formally designated observers or other general members. Compliance with the group's norms is assured by the members' need to avoid estrangement and resulting distress if they appear to question those values. Scapegoating or vilifying members who go astray helps to maintain a sense of goodness and trust among members. Information is managed, in order to minimize dissonance between the views of the group and the contrasting attitudes of the general society. The group may therefore engender attitudes and views that fly in the face of reality to prevent destabilization in members' commitment. Implicit "evidence" of the credibility of the group's ethos is also provided by new members, and aggressive recruitment therefore helps stabilize the entire system.

Boundary control is exercised by the group to protect it from threatening incursions from without. The group will therefore engender a suspicious attitude toward the general society in order to protect its members from assimilation. A clear difference is drawn between members and nonmembers, in terms of their innate value as people. Nonmembers are accorded less moral weight and may be deceived or snubbed to assure the stability of the group as a social system. Charismatic groups come into conflict with the surrounding society in a number of ways. They disregard the concern of the families of new members. They behave in a defensive and paranoid way toward outsiders suspected of being hostile to the group. They aggressively maintain ideological positions at variance with those of the general public. And to maintain group cohesiveness, many find it necessary to migrate to an isolated setting.

These traits of charismatic groups help explain the behavioral transformations described in many of the chapters of this volume. Through a mix of psychological and social dimensions observed in this discussion, the charismatic group and the individual form a symbiotic relationship, serving each other's needs. When joining a charismatic group, an individual is transformed by powerful forces into a personal extension of the group's identity, which compels him or her to carry out activities that were unthinkable prior to group membership. Even when a suicide terrorists attack is the goal, this act can be justified as serving the needs of the group, needs which take primacy over the individual's basic desire for a longer life. Overall, this analysis of cults and charismatic groups enables one to better understand the behavioral transformation that takes place among new recruits to certain terrorist organizations.

Acknowledgments

The views expressed herein are those of the author and do not purport to reflect the position of the United States Military Academy, the Department of the Army, or the Department of Defense.

CHAPTER 5

The Psychological Power of Charismatic Leaders in Cults and Terrorist Organizations[1]

ARTHUR J. DEIKMAN

The role of the charismatic leader in terrorist groups is clearly one of importance. This chapter explores the psychological dimension of power held by charismatic leaders of all types—whether in cults or normal-appearing businesses—and focuses on what this can tell us about the dynamics of terrorist groups.

The Charismatic Leader

All groups have leaders. Whether the leader is formally recognized or not, someone makes the decisions, someone leads while the rest follow. The first leader we encounter is most likely to be a parent, usually our mother, the one who gives or withholds food, affection, praise, and security. Later, the father and/or other family members may take similar dominant positions in our life. Biological survival requires that we become adept at pleasing these powerful people, so as children we try to win their love and care, avoid their wrath, and control their comings and goings as best we can. As adults, we bring to other groups the attitudes and behaviors we learned so early, directing them toward new leaders who, in the psychological sense at least, stand above us. Leaders of cults and terrorist organizations exploit this tendency.

It is customary to think of cult leaders as powerful personalities who inspire, even hypnotize their audiences. Jim Jones, David Koresh, and Adolph Hitler have been described as having this hypnotic power. But a cult leader need not be all that impressive. He or she can develop power by distorting their followers' idealism, dividing their loyalties, using flattery, threats, and spurious logic to defeat objections and rationalize their demands. However, one particular characteristic links all cult leaders: They are authoritarian.

Authoritarians emphasize obedience, loyalty, and the suppression of criticism. In the groups they lead, hierarchies of rank are emphasized and autonomy discouraged. (Sometimes such a leader takes a benign, "loving," tolerant position, but allows his or her lieutenants to enforce an authoritarian regime.) Authoritarian leaders draw their power from the dependency fantasy, the wish for an idealized parent, the longing to ride in the back seat of the car—a desire conveyed so poignantly by the *Peanuts* cartoon below.

If we are sophisticated, we may reject, criticize, or look down on any public leader, but the dependency wish remains, engendering seldom-noticed fantasies of someone (or something) who observes our behavior and rewards or punishes. It is not surprising that under certain conditions skepticism about a cult and its leader may be overthrown and conversion occur—as in the case of a prominent 1960s radical who one day called a meeting and dismayed his admirers by announcing that he had become a follower of an Indian guru.

Figure 5.1

Source: Peanuts © United Feature Syndicate, Inc.

In our society, the tendency to look up to others while feeling small oneself is expressed in the enormous number of celebrities that clutter our minds. Statesmen, movie stars, sports figures, socialites, and the super-rich are given larger-than-life status by television and movies, by newspapers and magazines, all of which cater to this fantasy.

Thus, we can trace our susceptibility to authoritarian leaders to the family structure, but in doing so we should not forget that the authoritarian character of the family is both functional and appropriate. Within the family, parents and other elders are in fact superior in knowledge, experience, and strength to the children who depend on them for protection and satisfaction of needs. That parents command and children obey is realistic because of the large discrepancy in their respective capacities.

In a healthy family, as children mature and become more responsible and capable, the hierarchical, authoritarian structure moderates and becomes more democratic. Children are given appropriate responsibility and choice, which acts to reward competence and stimulate further growth. Eventually, the child's relationship to the parent reaches eye level psychologically as well as physically. This eye-level perspective is the hallmark of the mature adult. Such a perspective does not imply a denial of another's superior ability and knowledge; rather, feelings of appreciation and respect replace fear, awe, and dependency. The encounter with the leader is at eye-level.

Just as the good parent welcomes the child's ascent to equality and supports his or her maturation, the good leader can and should exercise a similar function, according subordinates increasing responsibility, choice, and authority as they become capable. If this does not take place, subordinates remain in the position of children while the leader plays out the role of omnipotent parent. Thus, the key issue is not the strength of the leader, but the development or suppression of autonomy.

From this point of view, a hierarchical structure is not inherently bad; it can contribute to learning and is necessary when real differences in capacity exist. Furthermore, groups usually require a hierarchy for efficient performance of tasks. But a truly authoritarian leader is repressive and regressive.

Mainstream politics provides many examples of the power of a charismatic leader. Often, the key to a politician's popularity stems from the capacity to present the image of a strong, good parent; to convey an optimistic, sincere self-confidence; and to communicate belief in a golden future. Apparent self-confidence and freedom from doubt are characteristics of all successful cult leaders, because these postures resonate so strongly with the universal fantasy of a powerful, benign father or mother who will remove all difficulties and reassure the frightened child.

As powerful as he or she might seem, a leader is also the captive of the group and may not fail the group's expectation or waver on the pedestal. If a leader does, the group may annihilate him. And so, the eminence initially sought by the leader can become a prison; the tyrant is tyrannized. Leader and follower alike to some degree enact a dependency fantasy that requires an all-powerful parent who protects and rewards and a group of children who have no responsibilities other than obedience. The leader, as much as the group members, wishes to believe that an omnipotent, perfect parent is possible. And when a person assumes the mantle, he or she participates in the concept as faithfully as does the follower. The psychologist Margaret Rioch commented,

> We do indeed long for a shepherd who will guide us into green and safe pastures. The trouble with this simile, when applied to human beings, is that the shepherd is another sheep. He may be dressed up in a long cloak and accompanied by a tall staff with a crook on the end of it or by other formidable symbols of high office. But underneath the cloak is one of the sheep, and not, alas, a member of a more intelligent and more far-seeing species. But the wish—and sometimes, the need—for a leader is so strong that it is almost always possible for one of the sheep to play the role of shepherd of the flock.[2]

It is hard for leaders to remember that they are fallible when their followers attribute to them the qualities of a superparent. Furthermore, the leader's sense of personal power is reinforced when he or she finds they can wield enormous influence over group members through the gratification he or she can provide or withhold. That gratification is seen in its most intense form as "bliss," which in this context can be interpreted as the joy that springs up when an adult becomes a child once again. How wonderful to relinquish all choice and decision, to be secure in the belief that the superparent will take care of everything! When, at the same time, this regression is said to be for the good of the human race, to help bring about the salvation of the world, then the bliss is complete because it seems noble as well.

On occasions when a leader's actions conflict with the group's avowed principles or values, followers may twist words and meanings to reduce cognitive dissonance and maintain the fantasy of the leader's superior wisdom and morality. According to published accounts, one well-known Eastern guru with a propensity for drunkenness became angered at a visiting couple who had withdrawn from a wild party (held during a retreat) and secluded themselves in their room, refusing his commands to appear. He ordered his guards to bring them by force—which they did, breaking down the door and engaging the man in a fight during which he wielded broken glass as a weapon, wounding one of the guards. The couple was finally brought to stand before the guru, who then ordered that they be stripped naked. The woman and man were thrown to the floor and their clothes torn off. The woman called for help but only one onlooker came to their defense (and he was struck). The nude couple were then brought to stand before the guru. Shortly thereafter, everyone at the party stripped. The guru's actions were later justified by a follower: "Vajrayana teachings are ruthless; compassion takes many forms."[3]

Calling the drunken guru's behavior compassion is an example of what George Orwell, in his novel, *1984*, called "double-speak"—manipulating the abstractions of language to suggest a meaning and value opposite to the real situation. This is one way discrepancies between group fantasies and the actual behavior of the leader can be painted over.

The power of the dependency fantasy is underscored in the case cited above by the fact that the abused couple chose to stay on for the conclusion of the retreat. The man explained, "We'd come to study the whole course; we'd taken it (as he [the guru] knew) seriously; we wanted to finish what we'd begun, and not be scared off. The last lap, about to begin, was the famous Tantric teachings."

In such extreme cases, the individual's perception has to be narrowed and critical thinking suppressed. Groups have effective means of doing this. If a group member voices objections or criticism, he or she may be attacked as ignorant, unworthy, selfish, elitist—whatever term is used to define badness. Groups, as well as leaders, may punish dissent or deviation when maintenance of the superparent fantasy requires that no imperfections be revealed lest the whole structure be put in jeopardy.

When facts become impossible to ignore, the leader may be dethroned; but all too often the dependency fantasy continues and a new parent/leader is found and followed. The idealism of the group members can be exploited and become a source of a leader's power; he or she need only inspire and mobilize the readiness for self-sacrifice which exists within many people.

This can be seen in the business world, where the importance of generating emotional commitment was noted by Thomas Peters and Robert Waterman Jr. In their studies of "excellent" companies they found that charismatic leaders stirred the emotions of their employees so as to instill a sense of elevated purpose, fulfilling their need for meaning and purpose. Sometimes the meaning may not seem very profound to an outside observer. Charles Edward Wilson, president of General Electric from 1940 to 1950, created a strong impression on Reginald Jones (who himself later became president of the company):

> I still remember Charlie Wilson, the very epitome of the inspirational leader. He told us, in the Town Hall, how Westinghouse planned to surpass us in sales and earnings. "They should live so long!" he roared. "Their grandchildren should live so long." And then he got us out behind the marching band, and they led us out to the flagpole playing "Onward Christian Soldiers." At that moment, I would have followed him anywhere on earth—and beyond if necessary.[4]

So, whether the emotions mobilized are for religious, economic, or political goals, the energies mobilized can be quite similar—the final result is declared to be for the greater good, creating paradise on earth, saving the world. What matters is that people's deepest desires for the Good be mobilized. That is why the most effective leaders inspire rather than overpower. This was the conclusion of a study of audience reactions to a charismatic leader:

> They were apparently strengthened and uplifted by the experience; they felt more powerful, rather than less powerful or submissive. This suggests that the traditional way of explaining the influence of a leader on his followers has not been entirely correct. He does not force them to submit and follow him by the sheer overwhelming magic of his personality and persuasive powers ... he is influential by strengthening and inspiriting his audience.[5]

Most of us need to feel that our lives have meaning and purpose, that we are special and are living in a way that is consistent with our ideals. And it is not only the young that long to live idealistically; older people who have led practical lives and have accepted the necessity of compromising their ideals may respond with great commitment if offered the opportunity to sacrifice for a good cause. This appeal to the perception of a larger reality, to unsatisfied idealism and the wish for meaning, can be very powerful, and it can be put to good or bad use. Terrorist groups like al Qaeda make primary use of this appeal to recruit and train their members—even to the point of their becoming suicide bombers, for which they are declared to be martyrs for the Islamic cause.

Dependence on a charismatic leader is further supported and enhanced by three cult behaviors: compliance with the group, avoiding dissent, and devaluing the outsider. The group enforces compliance in order to protect the group's fantasy of having a wise parent driving the car. Avoiding dissent is required for the same reason. But the most telling aspect of cult behavior is devaluing the outsider. This is psychologically necessary because if those outside the group are just as good as those in the group, why belong? Why contribute money, sexual favors, and labor for the leader? Thus, the outsider is feared as a threat to those in the group who sacrifice so much for security.[6]

All these behaviors exist in many forms in normal society where their cult characteristics are seldom noticed. For example, authoritarian leadership tends to become established in large corporations where power has become overly centralized. Harold Geneen, who ran ITT like a potentate, knows whereof he speaks: "The authority vested in the chief executive of a large company is so great, so complete, and the demands made upon his time are so consuming, that most chief executives slip into authoritarian roles without realizing that the process is going on."[7]

The authoritarian attitude of such a leader results in an emphasis on punishment and the manifestation of power by saying no. The veto is safer and more impressive than granting permission. Although innovation and creativity may be given lip service, even insignificant mistakes are usually punished despite their being the inevitable price of developing a new approach or a new product.

Researchers Thomas Peters and Robert Waterman, in reviewing the problem, came to the conclusion that this behavior reflects the same superior/inferior perspective that psychologist Erich Fromm emphasized in his study of authoritarian political behavior. "Central to the whole notion . . . is the superior/subordinate relationship, the idea of manager as 'boss,' and the corollary that orders will be issued and followed. The threat of punishment is the principle implied power that underlies it all."[8]

The hierarchical emphasis is underlined by corporate class distinctions. The executive washroom, the special dining room for upper management, superior furnishings, and more space are all indicators of a higher position. Indeed, the top executives usually will be found on the highest floor. This institutionalization of the upward gaze is accepted almost everywhere and seldom questioned any more than is the assumption of parents having the largest bedroom in the home, a separate bathroom, and other special prerogatives.

Even when the chief executive officer wishes to make the organization less authoritarian, the task is not easy. Cornelle Meier, former CEO for Kaiser Aluminum, recalls a lesson he learned when his corporation began to decentralize decision making:

> As we started giving more authority to our operating divisions an interesting thing happened . . . all of the managers working for me felt that they should have a lot more authority in their decision-making: capital spending, personnel moves—what have you. That wasn't a surprise. What was a surprise was that nearly all of them felt that the people working for them shouldn't have more authority! . . . They wanted a lot more authority but they didn't want to give that authority away.[9]

Nor did they wish to give up the symbols of elevated status they had acquired as part of the superior/inferior authoritarian world.

The chief executive officer of a large corporation does not usually claim divine attributes. However, the CEO's power to hire, fire, reward, and punish is very great, and in the hands of an authoritarian personality this power can result in a suppression of critical thinking within the corporation and a mindless conformity and fawning support for whatever the CEO believes and decides to do. Whenever cult thinking occurs, a loss of realism is the result because the dependency fantasy corrupts critical judgment. Like similar leaders everywhere, authoritarian executives can easily end up valuing the conformity, loyalty, obedience, and subservience of subordinates more than actual performance. The charisma of the CEO may overcome the facts.

In more recent years, the CEO has gained almost mythical status as the magical leader who will take a company to new heights, or save it from its declining fortunes. This wish/belief has been accompanied by a grotesque salary structure. The compensation awarded celebrity CEOs is said to reflect their great effect on a company's success. However, research by Rakesh Khurana, an assistant professor at the Harvard Business School, found no such stable effect; instead, rewards seem independent of actual performance. Kharuna recounts an example where, at an AT&T board meeting in December 2000, CEO Mike Armstrong was asked to wait outside while the board reviewed his performance. In that year AT&T had cut its dividend for the first time in its history and its stock price had fallen from $60 a share to $18. When Mike Armstrong returned an hour later, "the board exploded with a standing ovation."[10] Kharuna attributes this situation to the quest for charismatic leadership. As summarized by *Harvard Magazine* editor Craig Lambert:

> Charismatic leadership, which grows from a personal magnetism that inspires devotion, reaches its apotheosis in religious cults. Its ascendance in corporate life is "a throwback to an earlier form of authority that proved to be very unstable". . . . The atavistic corporate quest for charismatic CEOs, with its deference to the personality and vision of a particular individual comes bundled with risks of abuse, misconduct, and incompetence. The results are now spread before us, and their name is not Legion, but Enron.[11]

Dimensions of Religion

These issues are particularly rampant in the field of religion, for what is God if not a supreme authority? In religions the world over, the devout acknowledge their god's divine wisdom, mercy, and awesome power; they pray for protection, forgiveness, and benefits. Even in Buddhism, whose founder declared that notions of gods and heavens were illusions, most believers bow to a Buddha idol with all the expectations found in theistic religions.

Formal religions tend to use the familiar relationship of parent and child as the model for a human being's relationship to the divine. This model inevitably creates cult dynamics in religious organizations. In part, the problem arises because the founding mystics of the theistic religions, in their attempts to communicate the ineffable, made use of the concept of God the Father, the supreme parent, although only as a metaphor. However, their listeners took the meaning literally. Thus, religions end up teaching, "Be good (obey God's wishes) and you will be rewarded (enter heaven or nirvana); if you are bad (disobey God) you will be punished (with hell or reincarnation)."

The dependency wish usually requires tangible authority figures and they are seldom in short supply. Muhammed abolished the priesthood, but equivalent ecclesiastical officials—the mullahs—arose after his death and in some areas, such as Iran (now a theocracy), the chief mullah rules with more authority than the present-day Pope. Another example is provided by Hinduism. Although the Upanishads preach the oneness of all being, the Brahmin priests—whose function it is to transmit Hindu teaching—maintained the caste system and their superior status within it. It took all the charismatic power of Gandhi to begin to crack the caste barriers enclosing the untouchables of India.

Theistic religions—such as Christianity, Judaism, or Islam—are intrinsically authoritarian, expressing the belief in God as a Supreme Being who transcends the material world, is infinitely superior to human beings, and to whom we owe obedience. God's absolute superiority in power, goodness, and knowledge may be used by religious leaders to justify their own authority and to legitimize their demands for submission. For the most part, theistic religions teach that compliance with God's will, coupled with an appropriately humble attitude, will be rewarded by protection and help for the supplicant. Pride (putting oneself at eye level with God) is a sin; submission a virtue. The greater the emphasis on the supreme god (the superparent) versus the inferior follower (the child), the more the stage is set for cult behavior in any religion, orthodox or not.

Although a person may be drawn to a religion through the admirable wish to find meaning and purpose, and often to serve God and humanity, religious organizations all too often fail to avoid provoking cult responses by stimulating fear (of Hell), greed (for Heaven), or vanity (being one of the chosen). Consequently, the obedience commanded tends to evoke the attitude of the child toward its parent. Obedience is certainly necessary for certain kinds of learning and development, and has a definite function in religious instruction, but great religious teachers agree that the highest obedience is to the religion's essence. Obedience to the literal scriptures—to the form rather than the essence—opens the door to cult processes. This problem of form taking precedence over content is one that plagues all religions and is defined as idolatry. We see this in Islamic terrorist organizations, where the teachings of the Koran are twisted and distorted to justify the killing of women and children, something explicitly forbidden by Muhammed.

When a religion's texts are regarded as literally true and infallible, a likely next step is that the leader's interpretation becomes what is true and sacred. Then a member's obedience is transferred to the priest, rabbi, mullah, or minister; this is the lowest level of obedience, and most likely to lead to overt cult behavior. Reverend R. G. Puckett, the Baptist evangelist who heads Americans United, warned of this development taking place in American Christian fundamentalist churches:

> The church is centered in the pastor. He is the authority, the ruling force. Fal- well, Robinson, Robertson, all the rest—these are personality cults. People follow the person, the pastor, not Jesus Christ. He may say he is not telling anyone how to vote or how to live, but the very climate and mentality of the whole church says: what the pastor wants is what we do.[12]

Such preachers do not claim divinity, only that God speaks to them, in- spires them, guides them. That claim may be quite enough to demand com- plete obedience and to brand disagreement with their views and wishes as a sign that the defiant member is lost to salvation.

Religious leaders may be as attracted to the security of certainty and sur- render as are their followers. Many really believe they are commanded by God, that they have become instruments of his will, and that their pro- nouncements are beyond error. Others with less exalted views of themselves nevertheless succumb to the lure of certainty and rightness. From a priest who has faced the shortcomings of his church, we have an eloquent testi- mony to that attraction:

> I do not [now] live without worry or responsible concern. In fact, I have never felt so responsible since I discovered that the Church cannot absorb my con- science, nor replace my mind. Life was easier when I knew where everything fit, when I could lose myself in the structure of a massive organization. There heaven and hell were governed by careful laws. There God's friendship was certain and manageable, and I was satisfied when I kept the Church's rules.[13]

Since most of the examples cited in this discussion are from the funda- mentalist and conservative wings of established religions, some readers may feel the conclusions offered here do not apply to them because they are in- volved in less doctrinaire, more moderate, more acceptable beliefs and prac- tices. A reasonable response is that it is a matter of degree, and that each person needs to assess the extent to which cult behavior and the depen- dency fantasy are operative in his or her religious life. Certainly, if a reli- gious group (or any other group) provides us with security and identity, we will not see its cult features very readily. One's own group is thought to be above such behavior; a cult is seen as something that you yourself do not belong to. But perhaps in some ways you do. It just is not obvious when measured against Jonestown or the Branch Davidians.

Like most cults and formal religions, governments cite a higher principle or authority to justify their actions. This is probably what Samuel Johnson mocked when he said, "Patriotism is the last refuge of the scoundrel."[14] Cult leaders, tyrants, and terrorists invariably defend immoral and violent actions as serving God, truth, or country.

Once you become aware of the types of cult thinking, you begin to notice them in differing degrees in a wide variety of situations. Nevertheless, the quickest tip-off that cult thinking is operating is when you see members of a group devalue outsiders while ignoring the faults of the leader and fellow believers. Outsiders—Them—are declared to be inferior, bad, or damned. Those in the cult group view themselves as superior, good, or saved. We see this in its most extreme form in the mind of the terrorist.

Distinguished from the conventional violence of warfare, terrorism features the deliberate killing of civilians in order to coerce or intimidate a target group that goes beyond the victims of the attack. It is a sad fact that such terrorist acts have been perpetrated throughout history and in many parts of the world. Today, everyone is aware that the United States is a target of a terrorist organization of worldwide scope called al Qaeda that is devoted to a holy war, a jihad, against Western powers, particularly the United States and Jews.

Most Westerners find themselves asking the question, "How could anyone devote themselves to the wholesale murder of innocent men, women and children, and see this as a religious duty?" Although we have modern examples of slaughter for political and racist motives in the West—as in the case of Hitler and Stalin—we have to go back to the Crusades to find explicitly "holy" carnage. Nevertheless, the same fundamental cult behavior underlies the brutality and destruction evident in many political and religious movements; namely, devaluing the outsider. In the case of al Qaeda, its leader, Osama bin Laden, has defined the outsider as the non-Islamic West, the "infidel." Members of this rather large category are not only outsiders and different but have been declared by bin Laden to be of the party of Satan, abhorred by Allah, damned. It is from this perspective that militant extremists and clerics throughout the Islamic world—including bin Laden—preach it is a religious duty on the part of Muslims to kill the infidel. With such an outlook, the September 11th suicide attack on the World Trade Center and the Pentagon is labeled a holy action of martyrdom. Not only is such martyrdom to be revered and honored, a sumptuous payoff is promised:

> A martyr's privileges are guaranteed by Allah; forgiveness with the first gush of his blood, he will be shown his seat in paradise, he will be decorated with the jewels of Imam [belief], married off to the beautiful ones, protected from the test in the grave, assured security in the day of judgment . . . wedded to seventy two of the pure Houris [beautiful ones of paradise], and his intercession on behalf of seventy of his relatives will be accepted.[15]

This passage offers an excellent example of the religious form of the dependency fantasy—the individual's innate search for reward and security—discussed earlier in this chapter. Furthermore, the call to jihad—a religious war—advocated by Islamic militants offers many psychological benefits.

Mark Juergensmeyer, professor of sociology at the University of California, Santa Barbara, astutely observes,

> To live in a state of war is to live in a world in which individuals know who they are, why they have suffered, by whose hand they have been humiliated. . . . Perhaps most important, it holds out hope of victory and the means to achieve it. In the images of cosmic war this victorious triumph is a grand moment of social and personal transformation, transcending all worldly limitations. One does not easily abandon such expectations. To be without such images of war is almost to be without hope itself.[16]

Juergensmeyer goes on to point out that a process of devaluation—or "satanization," in the language of al Qaeda—sets the stage for an end to humiliation:

> In that sense, the conflict is not just an effort at delegitimization but at de-humiliation: it provides escape from humiliating and impossible predicaments for those who otherwise would feel immobilized by them. They become involved in terrorism not only to belittle their enemies but also to provide themselves with a sense of power . . . the scenario of cosmic war is a story; it carries a momentum toward its completion and contains the seeds of hope for its outcome. I use the term *hope* rather than *fear*, for no one wants to believe in a story that cannot produce a happy ending. Those who accept that their life struggles are part of a great struggle, a cosmic war, know that they are part of a grand tale that will ultimately end triumphantly, though not necessarily easily or quickly. The epic character of the story implies that the happy ending may indeed be long delayed—perhaps until after one's lifetime or after the lifetimes of one's descendents.[17]

Conclusion and Implications

The motivations of the terrorists are diverse, as are their educational and social backgrounds. However, a certain picture does emerge. In a recent book, researcher Malise Ruthven describes the majority of terrorists as "worldly-wise young adult males, unemployed or underemployed (except by terrorist groups), with weak social and familial family support and with poor prospects for economic improvement and advancement through legitimate work."[18]

In contrast, Daniel Pipes, director of The Middle East Forum, suggests that "like fascism and Marxism-Leninism in their heydays, militant Islam attracts highly competent, motivated, and ambitious individuals. Far from being the laggards of society, they are its leaders."[19] He cites other researchers who found that economic factors did not seem to be an important motivator, and quotes Princeton historian Sean Wilentze's ironic observation that "terrorism is caused by 'money, education and privilege.' "[20] Similarly, Palestinian journalist Khalid M. Amayreh observed that "a substantial majority of Islamists and their supporters come from the middle and upper socio-economic strata."[21]

The analysis provided in this chapter suggests that it is often not deprivation or injustice that is the decisive motivation for terror, but the need to see oneself as good and heroic, esteemed by the community and blessed by God—and in the case of al Qaeda, restoring honor to Islam. It has been remarked that the basic human instinct is not self-preservation but preservation of the self-image. The jihad solves that problem. We must not forget it in dealing with other countries, especially in the Middle East. Surely, that need for self respect—despite the horrific means chosen to achieve it—is not dissimilar to our own.

The suicide bomber is presented as heroic by bin Laden and his sympathizers, and we need to recognize that for many their sacrifice is heroic, if misguided. Human beings have a limitless capacity to rationalize their behavior. When such rationalizations are supported by their community, they are even harder to counter. Killing innocent civilians becomes a noble act to the suicide bomber who has been told it is a religious duty.

Devaluation is a basic cult dynamic that supports violence against the innocent and legitimizes terror. In turn, devaluation requires misinformation and distortion, so that the Other can be perceived as malignant, deserving extermination. Dependence on a leader and compliance with the group are the psychological forces by which misinformation is initiated; avoiding dissent enables misinformation to be maintained.

The cult thinking described in this chapter is basic to all human beings because of our childhood dependence on parents. Although later as adults we have at our disposal much more sophisticated mental capacities, we carry with us a heritage of dependency: the vision and hope for a super family, providing the security of the back seat of the car. This longing for the wise parent/leader, portrayed with so much charm in the *Peanuts* cartoon, can lead to terribly destructive results—beginning when the leader defines other humans as Them. The leader points to Them as the enemy so they cannot be good, as we are. We blame Them, hate Them, exploit Them, and kill Them. The irony is that we are all Them to someone else. Currently, we are Them to al Qaeda, and they try to kill Us. Can our own leaders be more realistic in response to this threat? Can we avoid selecting facts to support our own fantasy of being good, unlike Them? A more realistic view of the terrorist problem may seem to offer less security than does fantasy, but actually it offers more. If we allow ourselves to see our own fantasies as well as theirs, we can better understand cult thinking and respond to terrorism more effectively.

CHAPTER 6

Teaching Terrorism: Dimensions of Information and Technology

JAMES J. F. FOREST

In April 1999, after visiting an Internet cafe in the Victoria district of London, a young man downloaded two books—*The Terrorists' Handbook* and *How to Make Bombs, Book Two*—from a seemingly ordinary website.[1] Following the instructions provided in these texts, he packed a plastic pipe with flash powder he had removed from various fireworks and sealed the pipe with glue. This was put into a box surrounded by around 1,500 nails of differing sizes, which would act as shrapnel when the pipe was detonated. He added a modified timer and two battery-powered electrical igniters (which would serve as detonators), placed the device inside a sports bag, took a taxi to Brixton, South London, and left the bag on the corner of busy Electric Avenue. The explosion occurred at 5:25 P.M., injuring fifty people. The following Saturday, a second explosion took place, this time in Brick Lane, an East London neighborhood. The same type of device was used, this time injuring thirteen. Less than a week later, an explosion ripped apart the Admiral Duncan pub in Soho, London, at approximately 6:10 P.M. The pub had been full of Friday evening patrons; three were killed, four needed amputations, twenty-six suffered serious burns, and another fifty-three were injured in other ways.

Thanks to a series of tips to Scotland Yard, David Copeland's terrifying nail bombing campaign ended while the dead and maimed were still being counted from the wreckage of the Admiral Duncan pub. At his trial, Copeland told police that he was a Nazi, and that he hoped the explosions would "set fire to the country and stir up a racial war." The media focus on the trial of this young engineer from Farnborough, Hampshire, brought considerable public attention to the widespread availability of online resources like *The Terrorists' Handbook* and *How to Make Bombs, Book*

Two. Both titles are still easily accessible; a search for the keyword phrase "terrorist handbook" on the popular Google search engine found over 423,000 matches. One site gives instructions on how to acquire ammonium nitrate, Copeland's "first choice" of explosive material.

Most of the chapters in this volume address physical aspects of terrorist training, from the training camps in places like Afghanistan, Indonesia, and Syria to the various psychological and sociological forces involved in transforming a new recruit into a capable terrorist. This chapter explores a more virtual realm of terrorist learning, exploring the print and online materials that exist through which an individual can learn the skills and operational knowledge required for conducting successful terrorist attacks without necessarily affiliating with a particular terrorist-oriented group.

This discussion is placed within the context of the primacy of information—without appropriate operational knowledge, a would-be terrorist is limited in his or her capabilities to conduct a successful attack. Before the advent of the Internet, access to such forms of operational knowledge was fairly limited. In contrast, today it is accessible worldwide; at the touch of a keyboard, the click of the mouse, anyone—regardless of age, ethnicity, or intelligence level—can learn how to conduct a terrorist attack. Our understanding of the terrorist world must therefore include the dimensions of information and technology.

Two Types of Useful Information for Terrorism

Like terrorism, information can be seen as a primary tool to change behavior or bring about some action on either an individual or group level. There are basically two types of information useful to developing the would-be terrorist: *motivational* (most often of an ideological nature), and *operational* (that which provides strategic and tactical capabilities). Put another way, motivational/ideological information usually addresses the central question of *why* an individual or group seeks to use violent means to achieve political, social, and/or religious goals, while operational information addresses the question of *how* to most effectively use violent means for achieving these goals.

Motivational knowledge is typically disseminated in oral, print, and online formats, and largely deals in the realms of psychological, social, cultural, intellectual, and emotional development. Acquiring this knowledge (or indoctrination) is seen as vital to developing an individual's will to kill, and is addressed at length in Volume I of this publication.[2] However, it can be argued that operational information—a much more action-oriented realm of learning—arguably presents the greatest present danger to the civilized world. Motivational knowledge without operational capability is far less harmful than operational knowledge (with or without motivation). In contrast, operational knowledge—the skill to kill—is the primary key to any terrorist's capability to achieve his or her objectives.

The globalization of access to information technology has had a dramatic impact on the dissemination of this type of knowledge. As Bruce Hoffman aptly observed, "Using commercially published or otherwise readily accessible bomb-making manuals and operational guides to poisons, assassinations and chemical and biological weapons fabrication . . . the 'amateur' terrorist can be just as deadly and destructive as his more 'professional' counterpart."[3] In essence, operational knowledge can be seen as the most vital tool in the terrorist's toolkit, which accounts for why the would-be terrorist most often tends to seek out these sorts of information resources.

One can generate quite an extensive list of the types of strategic or tactical information terrorists need to acquire before conducting a successful attack. At the terrorist group level, required information includes how to organize cells, how to communicate between and among the organization's members, and how to get and exchange funds. In addition, a group—as well as a nonaffiliated individual seeking the ability to conduct a terrorist attack—may need to acquire information on document falsification, sabotage, target vulnerability assessment, and artillery training. Some terrorists need to learn how to move from one location to another without detection; how to mount rocket launchers in the beds of pickup trucks; how and where to launder money; how to successfully conduct a kidnapping; how to conduct target identification, surveillance and reconnaissance; how and where to build camouflage-covered trenches; and how to covertly communicate with other members of a group or network—for example, the use of personal messengers (particularly on horseback, motorcycle, or bicycle) rather than electronic communications, or changing frequencies when using electronic communications in battle.

A terrorist may also need certain kinds of information to help him or her decide what types of weapons will be most effective for a particular attack (and how they must be assembled, transported and used). Specialized information is needed to learn how to effectively fire handguns, machineguns, and rocket-propelled grenade launchers, or how to assemble bombs and TNT from the plastic explosive C4.[4] In many cases, surveillance and planning is needed for securing escape routes once the attack has been carried out. Terrorists must learn the nuances of securing organizational assets, planning the roles and responsibilities of members involved in the attack, identifying risks to the operation, and examining the advantages of using certain kinds of vehicles over others—for example, al Qaeda's use of Toyota Corollas for transporting militants and weapons on windy mountainous roads. Information for conducting urban warfare is also useful to the would-be terrorists, through which they can learn how to block roads, storm buildings, and attack the infrastructure of a country—including electrical power plants, airports, railroads, large corporations, and military installations.[5]

A terrorist's search for operational information is not limited to attacks of a physical nature. Indeed, as described later in this chapter, cyberterrorist attacks require a specialized mix of knowledge. While highly technical knowledge is required to successfully use the Internet to shut down power plants, banking systems, or other cyberterrorist targets, a successful terrorist must also have a solid understanding of human behavior, public policies, emergency awareness procedures, and so forth.

In sum, the skills and abilities of the would-be terrorist are developed through the acquisition of an array of operational information. As described in many of the chapters of this volume, this individual can acquire this information through formal training camps by joining any number of terrorist organizations, including al Qaeda, the FARC, Hizballah, or Jemaah Islamiyah. However, training for terrorism can also take place through many forms of distance education—defined as instruction (typically asynchronous) provided through print or electronic means to individuals in a geographic location separate from the instructor(s).[6]

Print and Electronic Sources of Information for Learning Terrorism

Throughout most of the nineteenth and twentieth centuries, the distribution of literature complemented face-to-face contact as primary vehicles for both recruitment and training of new supporters of terrorist organizations. Books and magazines have always played a particularly important role in disseminating both motivational/ideological knowledge and operational knowledge to new and potential terrorists worldwide. One of the earliest prominent examples was Carlos Marighella's book *The Liberation of Brazil*, portions of which were widely translated and employed by Latin American and European terrorists.[7] In one chapter of his book, entitled "Handbook of Urban Guerilla Warfare," Marighella encouraged physical training and manual skills, as well as the mastery of small arms and explosives, and stated that only a guerrilla who had passed initial tests should be selected for additional training or tasking.[8] In Northern Ireland, the Provisional Irish Republican Army produced a manual called *The Green Book*, covering ideology as well as basic military training for new recruits, weaponry, explosives, and battle tactics.[9]

In the world of the jihadists, prominent books include Sayyid Qutb's *Under the Umbrella of the Koran*, which underscored the importance of monotheism in Islam,[10] and his *Signposts along the Road*, in which he damned Western and Christian civilization and urged jihad against the enemies of Islam.[11] Qutb's teachings have had considerable influence over

Osama bin Laden and informed the writings of his deputy, Ayman al-Zawahiri, as reflected in his book *Knights Under the Banner of the Prophet*.[12] Another influential Islamic scholar was Sheik Abdullah Azzam, whose books on jihad include *Join the Caravan*, *Signs of Ar-Rahman in the Jihad of the Afghan*, *Defense of the Muslim Lands*, and *Lovers of the Paradise Maidens*. Azzam's combat experiences in the Palestinian territories and Afghanistan contributed to the unique reverence given to his writings by Islamist radicals.

In terms of U.S.-based domestic terrorist groups, one of the most oft-cited sources of motivational/ideological knowledge is *The Turner Diaries*. Written by William Pierce—a former physics professor and, at the time, the founding leader of the white supremacist group The National Alliance—and published under the pseudonym Andrew MacDonald, the book describes a fictional civil war in the United States in which white Aryans fight what the author and other right-wing extremists call the Zionist Occupation Government (ZOG), killing blacks and Jews indiscriminately. The dramatic highlights are the ruthless destruction of American cities to pave the way for the dream of a white America and a white world come true.[13] Since its publication in 1980, the book has influenced a whole generation of right-wing extremists, from Christian Identity adherents to Neo-Nazis, Klansmen, militia, and survivalist activists. *The Turner Diaries* was a favorite book of Oklahoma City bomber Timothy McVeigh, who used the description of the FBI headquarters' destruction as a blueprint for his real-life terror attack.[14]

While a significant majority of the publications in the terrorist world deal with the motivational/ideological realm of knowledge (most often of a religious and/or political flavor), the increasing proliferation of operationally-focused magazines and training manuals is cause for some concern. Al Qaeda's occasionally-published magazine *Mu'askar al-Battar* (The al-Battar Training Camp), features essays on military training amid a plethora of appeals for Muslims to join the fight. Issue 19, released October 2004, includes advice on survival techniques in the wild, the care and use of a revolver, and instruction in map reading and orientation.

Other jihadi periodicals, many linked to al Qaeda, include *Voice of Jihad* (in print and online circulation since 2000) and *Tora Bora*, the May 2004 issue of which included an analysis of Pakistan's campaign in the Waziristan province and an extended article on "The Secret of Success in Battle." In Algeria, a new magazine appeared in May 2004 (*Al-Jama'a*, or "The Group") which noticeably imitates al Qaeda publications. Posted on the website of the *Groupe Salafiste pour la Predication et le Combat* (GSPC), the first issue of this publication was large on motivational/ideological knowledge, but short on operational knowledge.[15] Another periodic jihadist publication, the "In the Shadow of the Lances" series, first appeared after 9/11. As of mid-2003, there have been nine installments, the majority of which were written by al Qaeda spokesman Sulaiman Abu Gaith and were largely focused on motivational/ideological knowledge transfer, while the fifth and sixth installments were written by Saif al-Adel (believed to be a high-ranking member of al Qaeda's military operations) and provided tactical lessons learned from the battle against U.S. forces in Afghanistan.[16]

Other prominent sources of operational knowledge include *The Anarchist Cookbook* and *The Mujahideen Poisons Handbook*. The latter was written by Abdel Aziz in 1996 and "published" on the official Hamas website, detailing in twenty-three pages how to prepare various homemade poisons, poisonous gases, and other deadly materials for use in terrorist attacks.[17] The *Terrorist's Handbook*, published by "Chaos Industries and Gunzenbombz Pyro Technologies," offers ninety-eight pages of step-by-step operational knowledge.[18] But the multivolume *Encyclopedia of the Afghan Jihad*, written in Arabic and distributed on paper and on CD-ROM, is perhaps one of the most oft-cited terrorist training manuals in existence today. It contains a wealth of operational knowledge for new terrorists, covering topics such as recruitment of new members, discharging weapons, constructing bombs, and conducting attacks. Specific examples are included, such as how to put small explosive charges in a cigarette, a pipe, or a lighter in order to maim a person; drawings of simple land mines that could be used to blow up a car (not unlike the improvised explosive devices seen most recently in Iraq); and radio-controlled devices that could be used to set off a whole truckload of explosives, like those used to destroy the U.S. embassies in Kenya and Tanzania in August 1998.

In the United States, Tom Metzger, the guru of the "lone wolf" or "leaderless resistance" model of activism, has provided right-wing extremist groups with strategic guidance for several decades. Through his *White Aryan Resistance* (WAR) monthly newspaper, books, a telephone hotline, a website, and a weekly e-mail newsletter (*Aryan Update*), Metzger's work can be seen as the operational-knowledge counterpart to the motivational/ideological knowledge contribution of the *Turner Diaries*. His primary contribution to the field of terrorist knowledge has been in advocating individual or small-cell underground activity, as opposed to above-ground membership organizations. He argues that individual and cellular resistance leaves behind the fewest clues for law enforcement authorities, decreasing the chances that activists will end up getting caught. Specific guidelines for this strategy include act alone and leave no evidence, do not commit robbery to obtain operating funds, act silently and anonymously, do not deface your body with identifiable tattoos, understand that you are expendable, and whatever happens, do not grovel.[19] While Metzger intended his operational knowledge to improve the capabilities of like-minded racists, some observers have noted its salience for (and adoption by) other terrorist-minded groups as well.

Another U.S.-focused terrorism resource is the *Field Manual for Free Militia*, which is available on the web.[20] This manual contains sections such as "Principles Justifying the Arming and Organizing of a Militia," which lays out a theological justification for the ideals and goals of the Christian Militia movement. Another section of the manual provides advice for buying and using weapons and other equipment considered necessary for violent confrontation with enemies of the movement. Christian militiamen are encouraged to acquire a medium- to high-power semiautomatic rifle with a magazine that is detachable, camouflaged clothing, protective gear needed in direct combat (like helmets and flak jackets), and basic radio equipment that would be necessary to keep a small force of men in contact during a battle.[21] Thus, like the al Qaeda manual and other jihadist resources described earlier, this popular Christian Militia publication contains both motivational/operational learning and operational training.

Beyond the printed word, terrorists are discovering what many Western institutions of higher learning have already recognized: CD-ROMS, video recordings, and other forms of multimedia offer powerful vehicles for motivational and operational knowledge transfer. Even audio recordings are useful; Osama bin Laden is said to have been considerably influenced by the tape recordings of fiery sermons by Abdullah Azzam, a Palestinian and a disciple of Qutb.[22]

However, perhaps no source of operational information is more important today than the Internet. Indeed, the global spread of Internet connectivity provides such a powerful medium for terrorists to engage in distance learning activities that some websites can truly be called—as in the words of Israeli terrorism researcher Gabriel Weimann—"virtual training camps."[23] For example, two "Jihad in Chechnya" websites (azzam.com and kavkaz.org) offer an array of motivational and tactical support to terrorist organizations, particularly through photo and video libraries. Much of the information found in the *Encyclopedia of the Afghan Jihad* volumes is now available on many websites and in multiple languages. The website of the French Anonymous Society (*Société Anonyme*) offers a two-volume *Sabotage Handbook* online, with sections on topics such as planning an assassination and antisurveillance methods.[24]

The invention and increasing availability of online language translation tools also offers a unique and important dimension to the transfer of knowledge in the terrorism world. With these tools, the U.S. Army website—which offers scores of publicly available field manuals on everything from conducting psychological operations to sniper training and how to install Claymore antipersonnel mines—can be translated online and used to educate non-English speaking terrorist-minded individuals. Further, the ability to rapidly transfer new information in electronic form to a global audience, simultaneously and in multiple languages, presents additional challenges to those seeking to curb the ability of terrorist organizations to train new members.

Online computer games are another form of Internet-based training for terrorism. Today, a whole variety of "first-person shooter" games—with violent graphics, depicting real-life scenarios in which the player is the central character, killing Jews and other racial minorities—can be obtained for free on the Internet.[25] As Madeleine Gruen notes, "a website associated with the racist organization National Alliance offers game titles and descriptions such as 'Shoot the Blacks' (Blast away the darkies as they appear), 'Nigger Hunt' (Safari in Africa: Kill all the Niggers you can) and 'Rattenjagt' (Kill the Jewish rats). Their strategy [in offering these games] is . . . to make them widely available on the web for free so that there can be no limit to the number of people exposed to the 'white power' message."[26]

The first computer game developed by a political Islamist group is called *Special Force*, and was launched in February 2003 by the Lebanese terrorist group Hizballah.[27] Another "first-person shooter" game, *Special Force* gives players a simulated experience of conducting Hizballah operations against Israeli soldiers in battles re-created from actual encounters in the south of Lebanon, and features a training mode where players can practice their shooting skills on targets such as Israeli Prime Minister Sharon and other Israeli political and military figures. The game can be played in Arabic, English, French, and Farsi, and is available on one of the Hizballah websites.[28] Mahmoud Rayya, a member of Hizballah, noted in an interview for the *Daily Star* that the decision to produce the game was made by leaders of Hizballah, and that "in a way, *Special Force* offers a mental and personal training for those who play it, allowing them to feel that they are in the shoes of the resistance fighters."[29]

According to terrorism analyst Madeleine Gruen, Hizballah's Central Internet Bureau developed the game in order to train children physically and mentally for military confrontation with their Israeli enemies.[30] By the end of May 2003, more than 10,000 copies of *Special Force* been sold in the United States, Australia, Lebanon, Syria, Iran, Bahrain, and United Arab Emirates. Games such as these, as Gruen notes, "are intended to dehumanize the victim and to diminish the act of killing." In essence, through simulating acts of violence, these games develop the players' skill to kill, without the players having to leave the comfort of their own home.

Websites operated by the global news media also play a role in teaching terrorism, each time they offer details of how a successful attack was carried out.[31] By offering online video clips of attacks and their aftermath, messages from prominent terrorist leaders (like Osama bin Laden or Abu Masab al-Zarqawi), and other types of information, these media websites are in essence providing a form of showcase for the display of both motivational and operational information.[32] Indeed, in some cases training for terrorism may in fact be an ultimate goal of providing such information—like, for example, the website of al-Manar (the Arabic word for beacon), a television station owned and operated by Hizballah. In other cases—such as the satellite television networks al-Jazeera and al-Arabiya, whose web-sites are relatively less one-sided in their coverage of the Middle East cri-sis but are much more global in their appeal throughout the Islamic world[33]—the goals are more journalistic in nature. In either case, would-be terrorists can learn much from the television broadcasts and websites of such media outlets.

Overall, much of the terrorist-oriented uses of the web involve one-way dissemination of ideology. Most websites of concern play a similar role as pamphlets, doctrinal statements, or other literature that seeks to motivate terrorist-oriented sentiments. However, a limited (but growing) number of online information sources are providing operational capability-building knowledge, a means by which motivated terrorists can acquire the know-how to actually carry out a successful attack. This is particularly true when considering the threat of cyberterrorism.

Tools and Training for Conducting Cyberterrorist Attacks

Cyberterrorism refers to the convergence of cyberspace and terrorism.[34] The Naval Postgraduate School defines cyberterrorism as the unlawful destruc-tion or disruption of digital property to intimidate or coerce people.[35] Mark Pollitt, special agent for the FBI, offers a more comprehensive definition: Cyberterrorism is the premeditated, politically motivated attack against in-formation, computer systems, computer programs, and data which result in violence against noncombatant targets by subnational or clandestine agents.[36] In 1996, the President's Commission on Critical Infrastructure Protection noted how the threat of cyberterrorism was changing the land-scape of homeland security:

> In the past, we have been protected from hostile attacks on the infrastructures by broad oceans and friendly neighbors. Today, the evolution of cyberthreats have changed the situation dramatically. In cyberspace, national borders are no longer relevant. Electrons don't stop to show passports. Potentially serious cyber attacks can be conceived and planned without detectable logistic prepa-ration. They can be invisibly reconnoitered, clandestinely rehearsed, and then mounted in a matter of minutes or even seconds without revealing the identity and location of the attacker.[37]

Clearly, the threat of a cyber attack is an important consideration for any-one working to improve national security, and deserves far more attention in the study of terrorism than has been seen to date. Indeed, much of the research literature on cyber attacks has been limited to focusing on crimi-nal aspects, such as credit card theft, bank fraud, identity theft, or more generally, computer hacking.

Hacking is a general term used to describe a variety of creative techniques through which individuals seek to gain access to computer systems.[38] Some, like "denial of service attacks" or "e-mail bombs," are meant to break these systems, or at least keep them from doing what they ordinarily do. For example, a denial of service attack on a web server floods it with bogus requests for pages. The server spends so much time trying to process these requests that it cannot respond to legitimate requests and may crash. An e-mail bomb is similar, but targets a victim's mail server.[39] Both attacks serve as a form of virtual blockade, and can result in a loss of service, computer system degradation, and even general insecurity among computer users. In what some U.S. intelligence authorities characterized as the first known attack by terrorists against a country's computer systems, the Tamil Tigers (ethnic separatists considered one of the most lethal terrorist groups in the world) swamped the computers at Sri Lankan embassies with thousands of e-mail messages, clogging their network systems and "generating fear in the embassies."[40]

In addition to cyber attacks that flood and disable websites or e-mail servers with a barrage of data, computer users also face a daily threat from computer viruses, worms, Trojan horses and logic bombs—malicious computer programs designed by hackers and spread over the Internet to steal or destroy computer data. A virus is a program that can attach itself to a file, corrupt a computer's data files, replicate itself, and even try to use all of the computer's processing resources in an attempt to crash the machine. Worms invade a computer and steal its resources to replicate themselves and spread to other computers on the network. A Trojan horse appears to do one thing but does something else—the system may accept it as one thing, but upon execution it may release a virus, worm, or logic bomb. A logic bomb is an attack triggered by an event, like the computer clock reaching a certain date. It might release a virus or be a virus itself.[41] To complicate matters further, these types of attacks are often difficult to identify until after they have taken place, and identifying the culprit—figuring out who attacked you, and how—can take enormous amounts of time and energy. Developers of computer viruses, worms, and so forth are quite innovative and creative, causing no end of trouble for the virus protection industry.

While most cyber attacks of major significance have been relatively harmless forms of political protest—or at worst, an annoyance for computer network professionals to deal with—they have also occasionally caused significant economic and political trouble. For example, the CODE RED attack in 2001 infected 50,000 machines per hour, ultimately causing billions of dollars in damage.[42] During the Gulf War, Dutch hackers stole information about U.S. troop movements from U.S. Defense Department computers and tried to sell it to the Iraqis, who thought it was a hoax and turned them down.[43] In March 1997, a fifteen-year-old Croatian penetrated computers at a U.S. Air Force base in Guam.[44] Government computers reportedly were crashed by terrorist groups during elections in Indonesia, Sri Lanka, and Mexico.[45]

In March 1994, two hackers, identified by the aliases Kuji and Datastream Cowboy, broke into the U.S. Air Force's lab in Rome, New York. Subsequent investigations led officials to Britain, and with the help of Scotland Yard it was discovered that Datastream Cowboy—a sixteen-year-old British student—had used various hacking techniques to access data from NATO headquarters, Goddard Space Flight Center, the South Korean Atomic Research Institution, and over a hundred other victims. Telecommunications networks in Colombia, Chile, the United States, and at least a half-dozen more countries were used as conduits for these attacks.[46] In February 1998, a number of Department of Defense networks were attacked by hackers using a well-known vulnerability in the Solaris (UNIX-based) computer system. The hackers probed, found, and exploited the vulnerabilities in the DOD computer network, planted a program to gather data, and then returned later to collect the data. Two high school students from California were eventually arrested, along with an eighteen-year-old Israeli accomplice.

To test the nation's defenses against a massive Internet-based attack, the National Security Agency hired thirty-five hackers in 1997 to launch simulated attacks on the U.S. electronic infrastructure, an exercise dubbed "Eligible Receiver."[47] The hackers gained access to thirty-six Department of Defense networks, "turned off" sections of the U.S. power grid (affecting cities like Los Angeles, Colorado Springs, St. Louis, Chicago, Detroit, and Tampa), "shut down" parts of the 911 emergency network in Washington, DC, and gained access to computer systems aboard a Navy cruiser at sea.[48] From this and other exercises, the U.S. government has learned that a coordinated cyber attack has the potential to bring down parts of the Internet, silence communications and commerce, paralyze federal agencies and businesses, hang up air traffic control systems, deny emergency 911 services, shut down water supplies, and interrupt power supplies to millions of homes.[49]

The global spread of the Internet presents attractive opportunities to would-be terrorists. Terrorists have obvious incentives to look for and exploit the weakest links in any system—including social systems. In most societies, the weakest links regarding Internet security are the average home users browsing the Internet, sending an e-mail to Uncle Joe with a photo of the new baby, checking a bank balance, and shopping for that latest U2 release. Malicious attacks against the average Internet user have become increasingly common, resulting in widespread computer crashes and many instances of credit card number theft, identity theft, and bank fraud, through which terrorist groups can gain funds to support their operations. Attacks of various types occur through cyberspace every day, even in the United

States; the world's greatest economic and military superpower cannot protect its citizens against a fourteen-year-old computer whiz in Malaysia. However, these small-scale attacks can also be seen as training exercises, whereby computer hackers develop the technical skills for future, more elaborate and complicated attacks—like that envisioned in the NSA's "Eligible Receiver" exercise. It is this latter point which causes the most concern for public and private security professionals worldwide.

While private firms like CERT and Symantec scramble to keep up with the evolution and proliferation of Internet viruses and newly invented hacking techniques, the U.S. government recently issued its first national strategy for securing cyberspace.[50] To its credit, this document highlights the importance of multinational cooperation, particularly since many of the most active websites are hosted in countries beyond those that are committed to the global war on terrorism. The National Strategy to Secure Cyberspace (2002) also emphasizes the nation's vulnerability, noting that "of primary concern is the threat of organized cyber attacks capable of causing debilitating disruption to our Nation's critical infrastructures, economy, or national security." Indeed, the threat of cyberterrorism is quite real and is ignored at our peril. For this reason, government agencies and units have been established through North America and Europe to investigate cyber crimes and to work with the private sector to identify and fix critical vulnerabilities in cyberspace.

Unfortunately, as most technology-savvy observers will agree, a vast array of tools and information resources for learning terrorism are all around us. The Internet offers a rich source of information through which self-styled hackers or crackers can learn how to conduct a wide variety of cyber attacks against any private or public online entity. Each year, thousands of new websites with hacker tips and tools appear, along with dozens of publications and newsgroups.[51] An entire world of hacker support communities also exists online. The website chat forums of hacking groups—with names such as the Chaos Computer Club, the Cult of the Dead Cow, !Hispahak, L0pht Heavy Industries, Phrack, Pulhas, and Legion of the Underground—serve as places where members share ideas and experiences, sometimes even boasting of their exploits in a perverse form of one-upmanship. These online arenas for shared learning provide a useful source of information for the would-be cyberterrorist.

Today, thousands of websites provide detailed step-by-step instructions for conducting denial of service attacks, packet sniffing, password cracking, buffer overflow attacks, network vulnerability testing, and so forth. Visitors can download free software (like the SuperScan vulnerability scanning tool or the Ethereal packet sniffing program) for use in finding and exploiting vulnerabilities in virtually any type of computer or network system. Tools can also be found online for protecting an attacker's anonymity and for conducting encrypted communications, including the use of steganography—a method known to be used by members of al Qaeda, whereby computer graphics and digital photos are used to hide data (such as the plans for future attacks), and can then be transferred openly over the Internet.[52]

According to a 1998 statement to Congress by Clark Staten, the executive director of the Emergency Response and Research Institute in Chicago, "Members of some Islamic extremist organizations have been attempting to develop a 'hacker network' to support their computer activities and even engage in offensive information warfare attacks."[53] As Israeli researcher Gabriel Weimann (2005) has noted, Islamic radical terrorists have an interest in conducting various forms of cyber attacks. In fact, Sheikh Abdul Aziz al-Alshaikh—the Grand Mufti of Saudi Arabia and the highest official cleric in the country—issued a special *fatwa* in December 2002 which in essence encourages Muslims "to send viruses to disable and destroy websites" that are deemed hostile to Islam.[54] It is thus unsurprising to find that the website of the Muslim Hackers Club offers tutorials in viruses, hacking strategies, and instructions and encouragement for exploiting various network vulnerabilities.[55] According to military analyst Timothy Thomas, "The website 7hj.7hj.com aims to teach Internet users how to conduct computer attacks . . . [and offers] a kind of database or encyclopedia for the dissemination of computer viruses, purportedly in the service of Islam."[56]

The Internet is also used for conducting surveillance on potential targets. One captured al Qaeda computer contained engineering and structural architecture features of a dam, enabling al Qaeda engineers and planners to simulate catastrophic failures.[57] In fact, an al Qaeda training manual recovered in Afghanistan informed its readers that "using public sources openly and without resorting to illegal means, it is possible to gather at least 80 percent of all information required about the enemy."[58] Thus, in addition to the wide range of instructions and free software applications for hacking into websites, e-mail systems, banking transactions, etc., the Internet also provides the cyberterrorist with such open source documents as plans, building schematics, maintenance schedules, emergency preparedness plans, and others that can be useful in planning an attack.

Overall, cyber attacks require a specialized mix of knowledge, and much of it is easily available on the Internet. While highly technical knowledge is required to successfully use the Internet to shut down power plants, banking systems, or other cyberterrorist targets, a host of manuals, instructions, and tools are freely available to the would-be terrorist. With the increasingly interconnected infrastructure of the United States and other advanced economies, it is plain to see why terrorists would be attracted to the opportunities of cyber attacks, and for them, the capabilities made available by the Internet must surely bring a sinister smile to their face.

Conclusion

This chapter offers a fairly bleak prognosis for the global war on terrorism. Because of the vast—and growing—amounts of information available both in print and online, through which an individual can learn the tools of terror, we will likely never see the complete eradication of terrorism. Through a process of independent study and distance learning, an individual—with limited, if any, guidance from seasoned veterans of terrorist organizations—can acquire both the ideological and operational knowledge needed to become a somewhat effective terrorist. The situation is even more grim in the world of cyberspace, where the unique tools needed to conduct cyber attacks are freely available, and there is a large, supportive community of hackers ready and willing to teach the "newbie" how to use these tools.

Books and websites can thus be seen as valuable sources of terrorist learning—at least, a certain type of independent, self-directed type of learning. However, it is virtually impossible to do anything about their existence without resorting to the type of widespread government censorship that very few in the world would want to see. This produces a difficult dilemma for the governments of most nation-states in the global war on terrorism. Most countries recognize that it is counterproductive to allow the exchange of terrorist-related learning on their soil. Thus, training camps are found in only a small number of countries. However, many countries do not yet seem to recognize that training for terrorism may already be taking place in a virtual form under their very noses. By allowing terrorist-training websites to exist on Internet servers within their jurisdiction, these countries are in essence playing host to online centers of knowledge transfer in the terrorist world. How the United States (and the civilized world) should respond to the challenges raised in this chapter, without violating the democratic principles and civil liberties so crucial to our way of life, is one of the more important challenges of the twenty-first century.

Acknowledgments

The views expressed herein are those of the author and do not purport to reflect the position of the United States Military Academy, the Department of the Army, or the Department of Defense.

CHAPTER 7

Mediated Terror: Teaching Terrorism through Propaganda and Publicity

BRIGITTE L. NACOS

Following the devastating terrorist attacks of September 11, 2001, Osama bin Laden and his al Qaeda organization became household names. Whether he and his lieutenants threatened more political violence or urged supporters to join their jihad, the news media publicized all of these communications immediately and repeatedly. As a result, whenever bin Laden or one of his associates spoke, the world listened—and reacted.

For example, consider the videotape of a bin Laden speech that the Arab television network al-Jazeera aired on 29 October 2004—five days before the presidential election in the United States. The tape and its content dominated the news in America and elsewhere. After claiming that he and his circle "had no difficulty in dealing with [President George W.] Bush and his administration because they resemble the regimes in our countries. . . . They have a lot of pride, arrogance, greed and thievery," bin Laden told Americans; "Your security is not in the hands of John F. Kerry or Bush or al Qaeda. Your security is in your own hands"[1] At first the Bush and Kerry campaigns refused to comment on what could be seen as an attempt to influence the American electorate. But before long both sides knew that most Americans were aware of bin Laden's propaganda message and therefore tried to spin the videotape to their advantage. While nobody knows whether and how bin Laden's message affected the outcome of the election, exit polls revealed that the majority of voters considered this particular bin Laden videotape as very or somewhat important—presumably within the context of their voting decisions.[2] Once again, global, national, regional, and local news organizations had facilitated terrorists' fundamental need for communication, publicity, and propaganda. Without the news media paying a great deal of attention to bin Laden's cleverly timed speech, the al Qaeda leader's rhetoric would have resembled the proverbial tree that falls in the forest without the press present to report. It would have been as if the tree did not fall—or, to return to terrorism, as if bin Laden did not speak at all.

Publicity has been called terrorism's lifeblood or oxygen. Terrorists at all times understood this and acted accordingly long before the printing press was invented. Thus, nearly 2,000 years ago the *Sicarii*, a particularly extreme segment in the Jewish Zealots' struggle against the Roman occupiers of Palestine, attacked their enemies typically on high religious holidays and at the most crowded places in order to assure the greatest amount of word-of-mouth publicity by eyewitnesses. Subsequent terrorist groups learned from and followed this example. In the second half of the nineteenth century, anarchists characterized their political violence as "propaganda by the deed," thereby acknowledging that their violent actions were meant to communicate messages that otherwise would not be read or heard by their foes or by potential supporters and recruits.

Contemporary terrorists, too, commit violence in order to spread the news of their deeds, to spread their propaganda. The difference is, of course, that today's terrorists have far greater opportunities in this respect than their predecessors, thanks to the advances in communication technology, the proliferation of global television networks, and the accessibility and reach of the Internet.

For more than a hundred years, terrorists circumvented the traditional news media's gatekeepers to communicate their messages directly to their target audiences. They prepared posters, wrote pamphlets, and published newspapers. More recently, terrorist groups have utilized their own radio transmitters on land and off-shore, their own global television network (in the case of the Lebanese Hizballah), satellite cell phones, and, most of all, the Internet. But while these communications means have grown in importance, the traditional mass media—newspapers, newsmagazines, radio, and television—remain for the time being the most important vehicles for terrorist publicity and propaganda because they continue to be the predominant sources of information.

Bin Laden, and al Qaeda in particular, perfected their media operations over the years and adapted their modes of communication to changing circumstances and opportunities. Thus, during the 1990s bin Laden recognized that granting interviews to Western news organizations, such as CNN or NBC News, was the surest way to get the attention of his foes in America and elsewhere in the West. But an equally important reason for using the media for his "going public" scheme was bin Laden's recognition that this sort of news showcased his brand of terrorism for the benefit of followers and potential recruits. To this end, footage of bin Laden's TV interviews became an integral part of al Qaeda instructional materials that were used in training camps in Afghanistan to familiarize recruits with the fundamentals of the organization's ideology and usefulness of bin Laden's communications skills.

When al Jazeera emerged as a major global television network, the al Qaeda leadership sent faxes and tapes and granted interviews exclusively to this particular Arab news organization. What bin Laden's skillful media specialists produced was not simply aired and commented on by al Jazeera but by broadcasters and print media around the world. Similarly, whenever websites publicized statements by bin Laden or other al Qaeda leaders, the postings triggered an avalanche of reports in the mainstream media.

Actually, the most extreme examples of terrorist news management and propaganda were provided by terrorists in Saudi Arabia and Iraq that kidnapped and executed American and other foreigners. In literally all cases the killers filmed their deeds and publicized these most brutal videotapes on their own websites or delivered them to a television network. In July 2004, for example, when Saudi police raided a house in Riyadh in which Paul Johnson Jr. (an American civilian) had been beheaded, they found cameras, video editing equipment, and computers. A few months later, U.S. soldiers found a whole range of videotape production and computer equipment in a house in Fallujah, Iraq, in which Kenneth Bigley (a British hostage) had been decapitated by terrorists.

The fact that these terrorists had the capability of showing their unspeakable violence—either on the Internet or on television—and thereby initiate worldwide breaking news coverage served to magnify the perceived power of such terrorist cells and the threats they posed. As one observer remarked, "This is a breakthrough in communication that has transformed the whole ethos of terrorism. What has changed is that the Arab world, the Muslim world, the Third World, now has access to communication."[3] In other words, neither terrorists nor their audiences in these parts of the world had to rely on Western media organizations to send and receive propaganda messages.

Given this easy access to worldwide communications, obscure terrorists were able to elevate the prominence of their image and causes on a global stage, simply by exploiting the effects of horrific images on the Internet or global television networks. Abu Musab al-Zarqawi, a Jordanian national, was a perfect example. Clips on the Internet showed gruesome scenes in which he and his associates beheaded hostages while raging against the American occupation of Iraq. As the mainstream media reported on this most extreme "propaganda of the deed," al-Zarqawi became a celebrity terrorist like bin Laden. While the strength of his cell and his ability to recruit were far from clear before his extensive "propaganda of the deed," eventually officials in Washington declared al-Zarqawi one of the world's most dangerous terrorists. Moreover, the U.S. government placed a $25 million bounty on al-Zarqawi—the same as the bounty on Osama bin Laden! Ironically, as al-Zarqawi's brand of terrorism triggered breaking news frequently, the al Qaeda leadership recognized the usefulness of this perceived terrorist powerhouse in Iraq. At the end of 2004 bin Laden used an audio taped message to declare al-Zarqawi "the prince of al Qaeda in Iraq" and urged "all our organization brethren to listen to him and obey him in his good deeds."[4]

Without communication, publicity, and propaganda, neither Osama bin Laden nor Abu Musab al-Zarqawi could have risen to global prominence or attract as many sympathizers, supporters, and actual recruits as they did. Still, the media-centered objectives of terrorists are not their most important goals. Instead, all terrorists strive to realize their political agenda, with political objectives such as national independence, regime change, and removing foreign troops or influence from a country or a region. Yet, terrorists have always been aware that propaganda is an absolutely necessary means to further their ultimate political ends.

According to *Webster's New Collegiate Dictionary*, propaganda is best defined as "ideas, facts, or allegations spread deliberately to further one's cause or to damage an opposing cause."[5] Terrorism researchers Anthony Pratkanis and Elliot Aronson offer the following definition of propaganda that is particularly useful in the context of terrorism:

> Propaganda is the communication of a point of view with the ultimate goal of having the recipient of the appeal come to "voluntarily" accept this position as if it were his or her own.[6]

Terrorists direct their publicity or propaganda to both their declared enemies and their actual and potential followers. As for its impact on enemy audiences, the terrorist propaganda is most effective when "it scares the hell out of people."[7] As for its effects on friendly audiences, the terrorist propaganda is most effective when perceived as providing useful information and education. As students of persuasion have pointed out, "Whether a person regards a particular course of instruction as educational or propagandistic depends, to a large extent, on his or her values."[8]

While contemporary terrorists have ample access to communication means that bypass the mainstream media, for the time being they continue to depend more on the "old" rather than the "new" media. In particular, when terrorists strike or threaten to commit violence, they aim at furthering four particular goals via news coverage:

- First, terrorists want attention—the attention of various audiences inside and outside their target society;
- Second, terrorists want recognition—the recognition of their motives, of the reasons why they resorted to violence against civilians and noncombatants;

- Third, terrorists want respectability—the respect of at least a segment of the population in the society they terrorize, as well as the respect of friendly or potentially friendly audiences in countries and regions in whose interest they claim to act; and

- Four, terrorists want quasi-legitimate status—the same or a similar status that is generally associated with legitimate political actors.

All of these goals are pursued by terrorists for the sake of persuading various audiences. In view of these objectives, one wonders whether and to what extent news coverage furthers one, several, or all of these terrorist imperatives. Further, an important outcome of a terrorist group's effective use of the media in furthering these goals comes in the form of demonstrating to others the effectiveness of publicity and propaganda. Groups who are able to communicate to their various audiences through the global media are considered more powerful and effective, thus setting an example for other groups—as well as individual terrorists—to follow. Clearly, the skillful use of the media by al Qaeda and bin Laden provides an obvious starting point for this discussion.

The "Attention-Getting" Goal

New York Times columnist Thomas Friedman has suggested that Osama bin Laden "is not a mere terrorist" but a "super-empowered" man with geopolitical aspirations who does not seek news coverage but wants to kill as many Americans as possible.[9] Some (including this author) disagree with this assessment because of al Qaeda's media-savvy operations, which included a video production team. Moreover, a training manual that was used in al Qaeda's training camps in Afghanistan advised recruits to target "sentimental landmarks" such as the Statue of Liberty in New York, the Big Ben clock tower in London, and the Eiffel Tower in Paris, because their destruction would "generate intense publicity."[10]

The architects of 9/11 (other than the kamikaze terrorists themselves) sought the media attention they received; they were certainly pleased with the blanket 'round-the-clock coverage in the United States (for days without interruptions for commercials) and around the world that resulted from the events of that day. Literally all Americans and almost all people abroad were quickly aware of the devastating attacks by a group of terrorists. Not since the 1972 Olympic Games in Munich, Germany, when the Palestinian "Black September" group killed Israeli competitors and took other members of Israel's Olympic team hostage, was a brutal terrorist incident so quickly and continuously reported to a worldwide audience. In 1972, it was estimated that between 600 and 800 million people around the globe watched the deadly drama in Munich; nearly thirty years later, the audience was far greater, given the technological advances of the last decades.

Similarly, the Madrid train bombings on 11 March 2004 were covered very extensively in Spain, in Europe, and in the rest of the world as was the aftermath of Spain's "3/11" attacks. Here again, the terrorist plotters were naturally interested in obtaining an extraordinary amount of media coverage, and in the process getting the attention of the Spanish government, the Spanish people, and the international community.

Closely tied to the terrorist goal of dominating (and even dictating) the content of breaking news, simply by committing shocking acts of political violence, is the desire to intimidate the target population, spread fear, and undermine the declared values of the targeted political system. This propaganda of fear has proven to be tremendously successful. In the days and weeks after 9/11, public opinion polls revealed that many Americans were traumatized: They suffered from sleeplessness, felt depressed, and feared that they or their loved ones could become the victims of future terrorism. While these feelings subsided, many people—especially in New York and Washington, as well as other places considered likely targets—retained their anxieties. Heavy news consumers were more plagued by fear of terrorism than those who did not follow the news very closely.[11]

This is precisely the reaction that terrorists desire. Certainly bin Laden and his associates aimed for such effects. Speaking about the impact of 9/11 on the American people, bin Laden remarked with obvious satisfaction, "There is America, full of fear from north to south, from west to east. Thank God for that."[12]

Given the magnitude of 9/11, the mere threat of new terrorism intimidated the American public in the years following the attacks. It did not matter whether Osama bin Laden threatened Americans with new violence or whether administration officials in Washington raised the color-coded threat alert, the effects were the same in every instance: The news media reported extensively, even excessively, and the public was frightened and intimidated all over again. All of this proved once and for all that terrorism is not simply *actual* political violence against civilians but also the *threat* thereof.

Further, it does not require major acts of political violence to trigger massive news coverage that results in the attention that terrorists aim for. For example, consider the small group of self-proclaimed anarchists that dominated the news of a summit meeting of the 1999 World Trade Organization (WTO) in Seattle, Washington, after they used hammers, baseball bats, and spray paint to damage store fronts and clashed with police. While the media all but ignored some 50,000 peaceful antiglobalization demonstrators and the summit proceedings, relatively minor acts of political violence took center stage in television and print news. Indeed, so carefully had the media-savvy anarchists prepared this stage media event that they referred reporters' requests for interviews to their own "publicist." After everything was said and done, the anarchist gang was utterly happy with the results of the media event they staged. Although chiding the "corporate media" for biased reporting, the anarchists recognized the value of nonstop media attention. "The WTO protests are a watershed," they proclaimed on one website and predicted that "after [what the media dubbed as] the Battle of Seattle, the anarchists will no longer be ignored."[13] If this seemed an overly optimistic assessment, it was not. The anarchists' publicity success in Seattle ignited a chain reaction, in that subsequent international meetings of the International Monetary Fund, the World Bank, and other international organizations attracted more (and a greater variety) of extremist groups and individuals, set on political violence for the sake of "selling" their propaganda via the media.

New terror groups see the effective use of media—as demonstrated by al Qaeda, al-Zarqawi's band of terrorists in Iraq, and others—and they learn from it. Terrorist groups, much like any collection of human beings, are capable of learning new tactics to achieve their goals, and thus many of them come to recognize that if the skillful use of the media works to get attention and spread fear in one instance, it will surely be a useful tool for their own cause. For example, al-Zarqawi's use of videotaped beheadings was mimicked by other groups outside the conflict in Iraq, in an effort to gain media attention for their cause. On 12 June 2004 Paul M. Johnson Jr, a forty-nine-year-old American engineer working for a Lockheed Martin Corp. project in Riyadh, Saudi Arabia, was kidnapped by Abdul Aziz al-Muqrin, the self-proclaimed military leader of al Qaeda in Saudi Arabia. Al-Muqrin and his group demanded that the Saudi government release all detained militants, and when this demand was rejected, Johnson was decapitated—a gruesome murder which was filmed in full detail and subsequently shown on websites and television networks around the world. Prior to this event, it can be argued that few observers outside Saudi Arabia or the Middle East had ever heard of al-Muqrin or knew that the Saudi government was detaining scores of Islamic militants. Thus, by staging a media-oriented act of political violence, his group gained the attention that they—and so many others—seek.

The "Getting Recognition" Goal

For terrorists, winning the attention of the news media, the public, and government officials—while intimidating their declared enemies and pleasing their own ranks and potential supporters—is not enough. They typically want to publicize their political causes and grievances, and depend on the mass media to explain and discuss their rationale for resorting to violence. Again, this exercise in utilizing the news for their strategic communication or public diplomacy is designed to inform and educate both friends and foes.

On this count, too, bin Laden and his comrades in arms were quite successful. Before September 11, 2001 the American news media did not report
a great deal about the growing anti-American sentiments among Arabs and
Muslims in the Middle East and in other parts of the world. This changed
after 9/11 in that the news media expanded their reporting from these regions. Instead of sticking to their typical episodic coverage of foreign news
(for example, events within the Israeli-Palestinian conflict), there was suddenly far more contextual reporting that provided viewers, listeners, and
readers with a better understanding of the Middle East and its peoples.

Suddenly, there were many stories that pondered the question that President George W. Bush had posed shortly after the events of 9/11: Why do
they hate us? The focus of this sort of reporting was not simply on the motives of the terrorists themselves, but, more importantly, on the many nonviolent Arabs and Muslims who resented the United States as well. More
than ever before, the American and Western media carried stories on Islam,
a religion most members of their audiences were not at all familiar with.
One comprehensive content analysis of religious news in ten American daily
newspapers, nine newsmagazines, and one wire service (the Associated
Press) found that stories on Islam and Muslims dominated this coverage in
the weeks following the events of 9/11. Indeed, 70 percent of the stories
fully devoted to religion concerned Islam and Muslims, while the remaining 30 percent dealt with Christianity and Christians, multifaith, Judaism
and Jews, nondenominational, and Buddhism and Buddhists.[14]

As a result, people in the United States and the West became far more
interested in (and knowledgeable of) the history of the Middle East and the
tradition of Islam. Never before were so many people in North America
and Europe interested in pertinent books and courses. This reaction in the
West was not lost on bin Laden. In a videotaped conversation with associates, the al Qaeda founder said.

> I heard someone on Islamic radio who owns a school in America say, "We
> don't have time to keep up with the demands of those who are asking about
> Islamic books to learn more about Islam." This event [9/11] made people
> think, which benefited Islam greatly.[15]

To be sure, frequent and contextual news coverage of countries and regions abroad is highly desirable. The problem with the described post 9/11
changes and improvements in the U.S. media was, of course, that they were
the direct results of horrific acts of terrorism, and in an ironic way fur-
thered the recognition goal of bin Laden and like-minded terrorists in the
United States and other western countries. Moreover, Arabs and Muslims
abroad, too, had access to media that dwelt on justifications for the terror
attacks on the United States. They learned much more about bin Laden as
well as his grievances and justifications for striking the United States.

When it comes to the recognition goal, 9/11 was not an exception but the rule. Whenever terrorists strike, sooner or later the news media search for and discuss the perpetrators' motives. The Oklahoma City Bombing in 1995—while left 168 persons dead, more than 800 injured, and the Murrah Federal Building completely destroyed—was a case in point as well. Without Timothy McVeigh explaining his motives, the news media ran with the clue he offered: By committing his deadly deed the on the second anniversary of an FBI raid on the Branch Davidian sect's compound in Waco, Texas, (during which cult leader David Koresh and eighty of his followers died), McVeigh received the news he craved—the media reported extensively on his own and like-minded people's causes and grievances against the federal government. More important, as the news revisited the tragedy at Waco and explored the sentiments of right-wing extremists opposed to the federal government's and its alleged abuse of power, the public was day-in, day-out reminded of the Waco inferno, and some observers changed their minds about how to interpret the event. According to one account,

> Shortly after the Oklahoma City bombing in April 1995, nearly three in four Americans approved of the actions of the FBI in Waco, but three months later, after an intensive mass-mediated debate of Waco and Oklahoma City, two in four Americans disapproved of the way the FBI and other federal agencies handled the Waco situation. Similarly, while two in four Americans did not support a new round of congressional hearings on Waco shortly after the Oklahoma bombing, several weeks later three in five supported additional hearings.[16]

A lethal act of terrorism achieved what legitimate political actions, such as contacting and pressuring political leaders, had not accomplished. First, the public and then the political class responded precisely the way McVeigh wanted them to react—although the U.S. Congress had held hearings into the Waco incident in 1993 and had exonerated the FBI, new hearings were conducted as a direct result of the mass-mediated debate triggered by the Oklahoma City bombing and surrounding McVeigh's grievances. The procedures in Washington initiated changes in the rules of engagement for the FBI and other federal agencies when in confrontations like Waco. What a success for terrorist McVeigh and his cause! And what an educational demonstration for the extreme right-wing fringe on how to succeed by violent means!

The "Getting Respect" Goal

Osama bin Laden and like-minded terrorists did not win the respect of the American people by committing heinous acts of political violence on U.S. soil. On the contrary, for Americans the architects and actual perpetrators of the 9/11 homicide/suicide attacks represented the personification of evil, with bin Laden seen as the villain-in-chief. This reaction did not come as a surprise to bin Laden and his kind. After all, when international terrorists strike abroad, they do not strive to be loved by their target audience; they want to be feared. But at the same time, they hope for increased respectability in those countries and societies on whose behalf they claim to act. This is precisely what bin Laden, his closest aides, and the al Qaeda organization achieved in the aftermath of 9/11: They won respect among many Arabs and Muslims. One result of this sudden jump in al Qaeda's respectability was an up-tick in the number of individuals who were inspired by the architects of the 9/11 attacks against the world's most powerful country. Muslims in many parts of the world heeded al Qaeda's call to arms against America, Westerners, and infidels in Saudi Arabia, Iraq, Afghanistan, Pakistan, and elsewhere.

Unlike international terrorists, their domestic counterparts figure that the news about their political violence will also bolster their respect in some circles within the very societies they target. Again, the Oklahoma City bombing and its architect, Timothy McVeigh, provide a good example here. The heavily reported lethal attack on the Murrah Federal Building earned the respect of right-wing opponents of the federal government and inspired them to join militia or patriot groups and thus enter a milieu, in which McVeigh and his circle had moved and nurtured their violent ideas.[17] Moreover, as the imprisoned Oklahoma City bomber awaited his trial, he received stacks of mail. According to Lou Michel and Dan Herbeck,

> Much of it was hate mail, but more than a few letters came from people who said they agreed with McVeigh's disdain for government. . . . And a woman in Baltimore sent a one-hundred-dollar check, telling McVeigh, "Don't give up, fight back."[18]

Needless to say, much of whatever these letter writers knew about Timothy McVeigh and his causes was based on reports in the news media that showcased his "propaganda by the deed."

The Quasi-Legitimate Status Goal

In April 2004, about five weeks after the train bombings in Madrid sent a shock wave through Western Europe, Osama bin Laden offered to halt terrorism in European countries that withdrew their military from Muslim lands. In an audio-taped message that was first aired on the Arab television network al Arabiya, bin Laden said, "The door to a truce is open for three months. The truce will begin when the last soldier leaves our countries."[19] Like all of his and his lieutenants' previous communications, this particular bin Laden message was prominently reported and commented on by the news media in the West. Within hours, the highest-level officials in Great Britain, Italy, Germany, Spain, and the United States went public with responses from their respective governments. Although all of these governments rejected the truce offer categorically, the immediate and official mass-mediated reaction to the utterings of the world's most notorious terrorist leader was a testament to bin Laden's quasi-legitimate status. In other words, government officials of leading Western nations responded to bin Laden's much-publicized communication as if he were a premier and legitimate political leader. They were likely prompted to respond quickly by the degree of attention the media paid to bin Laden's tape, if only for the sake of assuring their respective publics that they were on top of important matters. As German TV commentator Elmar Thevessen noted,

> I think it would be better not to react to the tape in the way many governments did today. Of course, one [presumably the media] shouldn't keep quiet about it, but by talking about bin Laden's message all the time, we are upgrading him to a global player.[20]

If there were doubts that bin Laden himself longed for the status that is reserved for world-class leaders and statesmen, they were laid to rest when the al Qaeda leader released a previously mentioned videotape five days before the 2004 U.S. presidential elections. Instead of wearing his familiar military attire, holding a weapon, and using threatening language, bin Laden was dressed in a softly flowing robe and spoke in the measured tone and style of a legitimate political leader. This change in style was not lost on experts who concluded that this particular speech was "carefully staged and worded to present him as a polished statesman and the voice of a broad movement, instead of a terrorism-obsessed religious fanatic."[21] While his new style hardly changed from one day to the other how bin Laden was viewed by friends and foes, the media nevertheless offered extraordinary air time and column inches to a "news" event that was staged by the al Qaeda leader's media-savvy staff.

To be sure, bin Laden was not the first terrorist leader to use the news media to cultivate his status and the image of a quasi-legitimate political leader. For example, Yassir Arafat exploited the media's obsession with terrorism to become an internationally recognized leader and eventually make the transition from terrorist to legitimate political leader in the eyes of many (although not everyone).

Wittingly or not, the news media bestow a certain status upon terrorist leaders simply by interviewing them. The mere fact that the terrorist is interviewed by respected media representatives and treated like a news source that is worthy of being part of serious public discourse elevates the person to the level of a legitimate political actor. For example, during the build-up phase to the first Persian Gulf War, Ted Koppel of ABC-TV's "Nightline" program interviewed Dr. George Habash of the Popular Front for the Liberation of Palestine (PFLP). Habash repeated and expanded on his threats of violence against Americans in case of military actions against Iraq and its occupation of Kuwait and spoke about Arab grievances against the United States. Saudi Arabia's ambassador to the United States was a guest on the same program and topic. While not sitting in the same room, the leader of a terrorist organization and a legitimate diplomat appeared on one of the most prestigious American television programs—clearly, a boost to the status of Dr. Habash. To be sure, target societies will rarely perceive leading terrorists as legitimate players because of the way the media treats them, but friendly audiences are likely to appreciate such boosts to their idols' quasi-legitimate status.

While recognizable terrorist leaders vie for public status and a degree of legitimacy, unknown terrorists also pursue the same goal. During the Iran Hostage Crisis (1979–81) and the much shorter TWA Hijacking and Hostage Crisis of 1985, for example, spokespersons for the captors were interviewed frequently by reporters and TV news anchors. During the TWA ordeal, news organizations did not hesitate to attend a press conference held by the same terrorists who had brutally killed Robert Stethem, a young U.S. Navy diver aboard the hijacked airliner. Former U.S. Secretary of State Alexander Haig was appalled, and complained that "when TV reporters interview kidnappers, it . . . risks making international outlaws seem like responsible personalities. Television should avoid being used that way."[22]

In Iraq, one could argue that al-Zarqawi and his *Tawhid and Jihad* terrorist organization would have had much greater difficulty gaining legitimacy—as well as sympathizers and recruits—without the use of videotaped attacks (and their subsequent replay over global news network channels). Further, another group in Iraq—the Army of Ansar al-Sunna, which has kidnapped and killed a number of civilians, sometimes by beheading, and which some suspect of having ties with al Qaeda—gained considerable global prominence by videotaping their bombing of a U.S. Army camp, which killed twenty-two people.[23] This videotape, posted on the group's website and subsequently replayed on various television stations, showed the planning of the attack. A militant pointed with an army knife to various areas on a map of the base with the dining hall clearly marked, and a masked attacker was shown embracing other group members before leaving on his mission, with a speaker urging God to accept the bomber as an Islamic martyr.[24] The Army of Ansar al-Sunna videotape served many purposes—all of them related to the goals described above—as well as showcasing to other groups an example of effective mass-mediated terrorism.

Publicity and the Terrorist Scorecard

Whether as a result of "super-terrorism"—à la al Qaeda—or minor acts of political violence—à la antiglobalization anarchists—the perpetrators of terrorism achieve their publicity goals to one degree or another in literally all cases. More specifically, thanks to generous news reporting, the media's habit to overcover violence-as-crime and violence-as-terrorism, modern-day terrorists are able to advance some, several, or all of their media-dependent objectives (as described above): attention, recognition, respect, and status. Terrorists manage to do so because violence wins them entrance to what can be called "The Triangle of Political Communication" (see Figure 7.1). The corners of this triangle are marked by the news media, the general public, and governmental decision makers. In mass societies in which direct contact and communication between citizens and their representatives are no longer the rule, the media provide the links that allow communications to flow between citizens and governments. It is this realm of communication which terrorists seek to influence through their "propaganda of the deed."

Of course, not all groups and individuals get past the gatekeepers of the conventional mass media, when they follow the rules of the game. However, when these circles resort to political violence, the media open their floodgates in favor of incident-related reporting, which affects the other players in the communication triangle—the general public and governmental decision makers. Moreover, given the global nature of communication and media, today's terrorists also exploit the international communication triangle, often by circumventing strictly domestic media, for their propaganda purposes.

Teaching Terror through Media-Showcased Acts of Violence

One consequence of the opportunity to showcase their "propaganda of the deed" on a global scale is undoubtedly is that terrorists in different parts of the world learn about and embrace the most successful methods of mass-mediated terrorism. Thus, the 9/11 attacks by hijackers willing to die in order to kill innocent civilians highlighted the effectiveness (from the terrorist perspective) of suicide terrorism. In the fall of 2002, when Chechen separatists seized a Moscow theater and threatened to kill themselves and hundreds of Russians, Anne Nivat—a reporter and expert on Chechnya—suggested, "There is definitely a 9/11 element in this new way of acting. They [the Chechen hostage holders] saw that it was really possible to have a huge impact by being ready to lose their lives."[25] Moreover, after terrorists in the Middle East beheaded a number of their kidnap victims in 2004, there were several copycat killings (or threats thereof) outside the Middle East. In Haiti, for example, the bodies of three headless policemen were found; they were victims of terrorists who used the label "Operation Baghdad," a label that had no meaning in Haiti's civil strife, except for the cruel method of murder. And then there was the beheading of a Buddhist official in a village in Thailand which was described as an act of revenge for violence against Muslim rioters. Finally, after the killing of Dutch film-

Figure 7.1
Terrorism and the Triangle of Political Communication

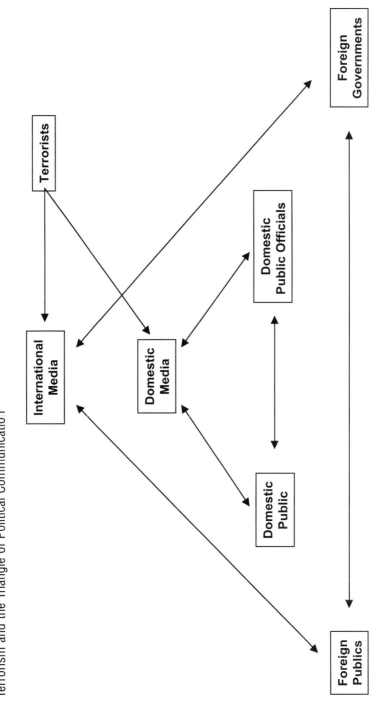

maker Theo van Gogh, self-proclaimed jihadists threatened to decapitate other critics of Muslim extremists. All of these perpetrators had recognized the shock value and media attractiveness of a news terrorist method.

Finding "significant evidence of a contagion effect wrought by [news] coverage," Gabriel Weimann and Conrad Winn observed,

> The suggestiveness of mediated terrorism operates on the minds not merely of the maladjusted but also on the minds of the relatively normal. Sane people may see the terrorist model as a plausible outlet for their sense of rational grievance. For suggestive normal people, mediated terrorism disseminates the precedence of violence and reinforces the sense of righteous anger.[26]

In essence, the uniquely public nature of mass-mediated terror allows individuals and groups worldwide to showcase (and learn from) effective terrorism tactics.

Terrorist Propaganda and the Media

While the press has always been interested in reporting violence, the proliferation of television and radio channels and the emergence of megamedia organizations has resulted in greater competition and insatiable appetite for shocking, sensational infotainment that is believed to keep audiences captivated and boost ratings, circulation, and, most importantly, increase profits. Few, perhaps no other events fulfill the requirements of gripping infotainment more than acts of terrorism and the plight of terrorist victims.

To be sure, the most fundamental function of the free press stems from its responsibility to fully inform the public. Thus, terrorism must be reported; the question is, how and how much to report on this sort of political violence. Is it in the public interest to replay the shocking images of deadly attacks over and over again? Is it responsible journalism to show the victims of terrorism regardless of the horror of such images? Should the news media display visual images of victims regardless of his or her condition? In the case of 9/11, the published images of people jumping to their death from highest floors of the World Trade Center's towers come to mind. Equally unsettling were the emotionally wrenching videotapes that depicted hostages begging for their lives in Iraq and Saudi Arabia. By displaying these sorts of images, the media provide terrorists with a platform for their propaganda of fear, addressed to the societies they terrorize. At the same time, these visuals also provide would-be terrorists with a set of "how-to" instructions.

Even without publishing the visuals of actual beheadings, detailed accounts of the victims' predicament can cross the line of what is ethical. For example, consider the following newspaper account of an American civilian's decapitation by his terrorist kidnappers:

> As the insurgent speaks, the gray-bearded man identified as Mr. Armstrong appears to be sobbing, a white blindfold wrapped around his eyes. He is wearing an orange jumpsuit. The masked man then pulls a knife, grabs his head and begins slicing through the neck. The killer places the head atop the body before the video cuts to a shot of him holding up the head and a third, more grainy shot showed the body from a different angle.[27]

There is absolutely no need to provide such graphic details without violating the press' responsibility to inform the public. Nor should there be room for critiquing the videotape of hostage ordeals and executions as if it were part of a Hollywood movie. For example, one such newspaper account first described a video released by a "militant group" in Iraq that showed "insurgents slicing off the head of a man identified as Kenneth Bigley, the British engineer who was kidnapped here last month."[28] Then, mentioning an earlier video by the same group that showed the same hostage in distress, the reporter wrote:

> The captors have shown a cold cinematic flair. At the end of the 11-minute video, they showed a series of title cards in Arabic and English on a black screen in which they asked whether a British civilian was worth anything to Blair. The last screen read, "Do leaders really care about their people?"[29]

More fitting terms for what this report called "militant groups," "insurgents," and "captors" would have been words like terrorists, killers, and murderers. Further, by referring to the "cold cinematic flair" of these terrorists as they produced real-life horror scenes, with a real-life victim, this reporter's description sounds almost like an instructional piece of propaganda.

Domestic versus International Media

Not so long ago, the news media operated mostly within national borders, despite foreign correspondents, international wire services, and broadcast networks that reached beyond the domestic spheres. But the international media and communication net of the past pales in comparison to today's global communication systems. Moreover, satellite television networks like al Jazeera, al Arabiya, or al-Manar challenge the international dominance of the American and Western media. Add to this the reach of the Internet! In short, today's global communication and media networks overshadow the domain of national media. This point was driven home in the fall of 2002, when Chechen terrorists seized a theater crowded with Russians. As soon as the Chechens controlled the hostage situation, their comrades outside delivered a preproduced videotape to the Moscow bureau of al Jazeera—not Russian TV—in which the terrorists articulated their demands and their willingness to die for their cause. Within hours, the clip was aired by television networks around the world. It did not matter that the Russian government censored their own television stations, because interested Russians were able to find ample information about the content of the videotaped propaganda in particular and about the hostage crisis in general thanks to the Internet, CNN, and other global news sources.

This particular case demonstrated first of all the limits of domestic media censorship by governments—which is, of course, incompatible with the values of liberal democracies. Secondly, the case illustrated the limitations of sensible self-restraint on the part of national media with respect to the terrorist propaganda scheme. If international terrorism remains a major threat, as experts in the field predict, the only antidote to news that showcases political violence would be a universal agreement on the part of domestic and global media to voluntarily restrict their coverage of terrorism. While highly unlikely, such a solution would still leave the Internet as an unrestricted carrier of terrorist propaganda that is designed to intimidate foes and to educate and embolden fellow terrorists and potential comrades and supporters.

Conclusion

To sum up, terrorism is often described as an act which is meant to compel change—a change of policy, behavior, and so forth on the part of a particular audience—in alignment with a terrorist's political agenda. The skillful use of the media plays an important role in advancing a terrorist's objectives and goals, including gaining attention, recognition, respect, and status. In addition, the effective uses of the media by terrorists demonstrate to others, particularly new or potential terrorist individuals and groups, how such publicity and propaganda aids in the achievement of political goals. Whether or not a terrorist group consciously uses media to teach their tactics to other groups is questionable, but the learning that takes place among the members of any particular audience is inevitable. Several terrorist groups have their own websites and, in the case of Hizballah, even their own television network, through which they can communicate with a variety of audiences in pursuit of these goals. Thus, in a way, terrorists' uses of the media can be seen as a teaching tool of sorts, training new cadres of violent individuals and groups how today's technologically advanced communication can further the goals and objectives of a terrorist's political agenda.

Terrorists' use of the media is a particularly public form of communicating goals and showcasing best practices for other terrorists to follow. Successful attacks are shown, learned from, and copied. Today's terrorists also learn from the successful use of videotapes to spread fear and panic and to compel government authorities to enact or change particular policies. Thus, the use of technologically-advanced studios to create audio and video tapes, which are then posted to websites and sent to satellite television networks, will undoubtedly increase in the foreseeable future.

PART II

CASE STUDIES OF TERRORIST LEARNING

CHAPTER 8

Training for Urban Resistance: The Case of the Provisional Irish Republican Army

BRIAN A. JACKSON

The difference between a well-trained and poorly-trained terrorist organization is the difference between tactically successful attacks and aborted operations, between groups that can persist under pressure and those which are penetrated and rolled up by intelligence and law enforcement. The well-trained terrorist sets a bomb that achieves his tactical and operational goals; the poorly trained terrorist sets a bomb that kills himself, rather than the intended victims of the attack.

Understanding the efficacy of terrorist training efforts is, therefore, a key element in assessing the threat posed by a terrorist group. Doing so requires more than simply process or content measures of group training: Information on the time a group spends training will be a poor indicator if little information is taught to members during that time, and listings of the topics of training will only be a partial picture if knowledge on those topics is poorly transmitted. Instead, assessing that efficacy requires insights into what training really accomplishes for the group, expressed by how the information passed to members meets the organization's needs and the impacts of training on group outcomes. As with many areas in the study of terrorism, there is seldom sufficient information readily accessible to characterize fully the value of group training efforts. Terrorists are less likely than educators to evaluate rigorously their training efforts and, if they do so, it is unlikely that the results will become public knowledge. Using the Provisional Irish Republican Army (PIRA) as an example case, this chapter will describe and, to the extent possible, evaluate a terrorist training effort based on the types of information available in the open literature.

Through the decades of conflict in Northern Ireland, the PIRA waged a persistent and high-intensity campaign of violence. Operating in areas ranging from urban Belfast to rural South Armagh, PIRA carried out thousands of separate operations in an attempt to advance their goal of Irish reunification and removal of British involvement in Northern Ireland. Applying tactics ranging from selective assassination to large-scale bombing operations, the group had to build expertise in a wide range of subject areas to maintain its desired level of military capability. Faced with the constant threat of penetration and compromise by technologically adept and sophisticated security forces, PIRA also had to build the capabilities required to persist under ongoing counterterrorist pressures.

Effective training processes to disseminate the knowledge required for both offensive and defensive operations among group members (or, as PIRA formally referred to them, Volunteers) were a major component of the group's activities throughout its operational history. Emphasizing the importance of training activities to the group's leadership, PIRA had a department within its general headquarters (GHQ) dedicated to Volunteer training. The training department was tasked with maintaining all the organizational and physical infrastructures needed to carry out required training of the group's membership.[1] The following sections will address PIRA training in three areas, focusing on how they

1. inducted new recruits to support its military activities;
2. taught Volunteers new skills to support and improve the group's operational capability; and
3. provided members with the intelligence and counterintelligence skills needed both to collect the information required for operations and to prevent security force penetration or disruption of group activities.

The discussion of each area will describe the relevance of training of this type, describe PIRA's efforts, and—to the extent possible—assess the effectiveness of those efforts based on available information.

Inducting the New Recruit: Socialization and "Political Training"

For any organization, new members must be educated about the group's history and taught what they need to know to become a part of the organization.[2] Terrorist and other clandestine organizations are no different. Such socialization brings new members into group culture and provides the ground rules for what it means to join and be an effective member of the organization.

Descriptions are available of the socialization processes PIRA had in place for training and inducting new members into the group and training them, written both by government and security force members opposing them and by PIRA Volunteers:

> In [his first] three months [the recruit] is asked to turn up once a week for a training session. During these sessions, which are taken by older men in the organization, the recruit is taught what Republicanism means, what it means to him, and is taught the policy of the movement.[3]

Other descriptions of initial recruit training from later in the conflict suggest that this element of Volunteer induction remained stable over time: "[In 1979, my contact] arranged for me to start receiving my official induction into the organization—a long series of lectures and talks . . . which [covered] the duties and responsibilities of volunteers, as well as explaining the history of the movement, the rules of military engagement, and anti-interrogation techniques."[4] J. Bowyer Bell, a scholar of insurgency and observer of PIRA for many years, emphasized the importance of such socialization—transmitting the philosophy of the movement—in PIRA's training programs, even taking precedence over the military goals of training: "An underground army inevitably has a training program, at least in theory . . . [but] they are far more concerned with maintaining the creed than in instilling the techniques of war."[5] While such a statement may overstate the ideological components of such training as compared to its more functional aspects, it does emphasize the importance of socialization of new recruits as part of a training effort. Although training may not directly build military capabilities on its own, its contribution to group cohesion and management means that it cannot be ignored.

Initial training also provides groups with the opportunity to assess new recruits and judge their fitness for membership. Such instances are important gatekeeping functions for groups, particularly clandestine ones. Moving beyond lectures to full participation in PIRA required a decision by the recruit,[6] and it required a similar decision by the trainer that the recruit was fit to join: "Throughout this initial training, the recruit is continually watched by the I.R.A. to make sure that he would not present a security risk to the organisation. 'If he drinks too much or talks too much we would not accept him,' the instructor said."[7]

Assessing the effectiveness of such initial training activities requires insight into what the group was trying to accomplish by doing it. Some group statements suggest that the goals of training in this area were relatively modest: "'The recruits are not taught to argue policy,' the instructor said in answer to a question, 'We leave that to Sinn Fein. In years gone by they would be, but our main priority at the moment is getting them fully trained and into active service.'"[8] Against this background, the stability of these elements in PIRA's training regimen through time suggests that the group valued their results and believed it was effective in accomplishing what was intended.

Although later descriptions of PIRA training suggest that political components were an enduring aspect of training, they also suggest that there were tradeoffs between socialization of new recruits and the need to transmit military knowledge. Statements suggest that military training increased in emphasis over political training for reasons of practicality:

> With all this talk of guns and ammunition, it'd be wrong to give the impression that an IRA training camp is purely a military experience. Practical limitations make it largely so—time is short, with a lot of weapons training that can't easily be done elsewhere, and there's not much point having formal political lectures surrounded by IRA guns.[9]

Military Training

The Provisional Irish Republican Army was formed as a result of a split in the Republican movement in 1969. Because many of its members had already acquired experience in earlier violent activities, PIRA did not begin from a standing start. Even with this advantage, however, the group's capabilities early in its operational career were quite limited: "It may be difficult nowadays to believe that inexperienced youths could pit small revolvers against rifles in the hands of trained soldiers, but this actually happened. I had never fired a revolver in training, nor had anyone I knew. We hoped to hit."[10] In the late 1960s and early 1970s, the primary activities of the organization were attacks that relied on very little training or expertise—throwing stones and gasoline bombs—and were, as a result, of limited impact.[11] This lack of expertise early on resulted in some significant costs to the organization.

One such cost of lack of experience is simple ineffectiveness. Published assessments of PIRA's capabilities cited several failed attacks and attributed the cause of failure to the poor training of its members: "Relatively few of the nightly shooting attacks on security force patrols, however, cause death or serious injury, since most appear to be carried out by relatively inexperienced volunteers and since individual soldiers and policemen and their vehicles are reasonably well protected."[12] Contemporary assessments by the security forces echo similar sentiments: "It is of interest that much of the IRA's shooting against the Security Forces, although greater in quantity, is becoming increasingly wild and is not pressed home."[13] The consequences of such expertise shortfalls can go beyond ineffectiveness, however. Reportedly, some early casualties to PIRA resulted from "friendly fire"—not because of difficulties in distinguishing friend from foe, but simply because a Volunteer lacked the expertise to control the submachine gun he was using during an attack.[14] In the use of explosives, shortfalls in training and expertise claimed even more group lives:

> Despite the number of bombing operations, the Provos' technique left much to be desired. Not only was the technical level of the various devices a generation out of date but also the volunteers' experience and training was limited. The inevitable result was a series of premature explosions that killed and maimed over a score of volunteers. Safety precautions were ignored in the name of expedience or out of ignorance—and the toll was worse than inflicted by the British Army during the height of bombing operations.[15]

Such failures and their associated costs provided a clear demonstration of the value of military training for the group—improved capabilities would pay off through reducing the toll on the group in casualties and ineffective operations.

General Military Training

One of PIRA's answers to these difficulties was to broaden training to arm its members not only with weapons but also with the expertise required to use them. Descriptions of the training curriculum from early in the conflict indicate that training covered a range of military skills, including the use of a variety of weapons. "The majority of recruits undergo a week's training at one of the camps in Eire, during which they are instructed in small arms handling, target practice, demolition techniques and field craft."[16] More experienced members would take the recruits through stripping down weapons, cleaning and loading them, and instruction in basic firearms safety.[17] Contemporary reports suggest that the full PIRA training program took at least six months,[18] though part of the duration was driven by the constraints imposed on covert training. Unlike a traditional military, individual training was often carried out in short blocks—such as the five-day figure cited above—or in weekend sessions[19] because of the risk of discovery. These early descriptions of training activities focus predominantly on use of arms, rather than broader military training in tactics and or unit operations.

Descriptions from later in the group's history are similar, but suggest the topics of training were gradually broadened to meet the group's evolving needs. Later training still included cleaning weapons, extensive "classroom" instruction in weapons and tactics, and some live-fire training, but also had a significant focus on sighting and aiming of weapons. These later training camps also reportedly covered operational planning and intelligence techniques (described below).[20] As the group built up more experience through its direct conflict with the security forces, the lessons learned were also incorporated into Volunteer training. For example, training was augmented to describe specific defensive measures taken by security force personnel and, as a result, "what parts of an armored vehicle to aim at, how to fire most effectively in teams, and where and how to fire constructively after the all-important first aimed shot."[21]

As part of the broader PIRA training effort, the group drew on published materials relevant to their military activities. Early on, the Provisionals drew on print sources for information on explosives and bombmaking: "I was surprised to find out how much information was available in the local library. I also studied the old IRA and British Army training manuals."[22] The group members were also encouraged to read other relevant sources such as the writings of "Che Guevara and the *International Revolutionary's Handbook* [section on] 'Urban Guerrilla Warfare,' "[23] although the methods for actually using the information in all such sources is not entirely clear.

To supplement what was available in published sources, the group also drew on the knowledge of former members of the military and other experts:

> I was also active in Sinn Fein and sold the IRA newspaper door-to-door. . . . One of my regular customers turned out to be a former British Army sapper. . . . I would go to his house during the day and over a cup of tea or two he would draw sketches of different booby traps, explaining the properties of different explosives. Updated IRA training manuals were now available; I would show these to him and he would scribble notes and make comments on any errors or deficiencies.[24]

Gaining access to such expert sources of information was particularly important because they can provide direct instruction critical to safely executing dangerous tasks such as working with explosives. First-person accounts of former PIRA members and other published reports cite the group drawing on other former members of the military, including the British Royal Marines Special Boat Squadron[25] and American veterans of the Vietnam conflict.[26] In a few cases, reports indicate the group developed its own experts through "sponsoring" individuals at educational institutions. In the early 1970s, PIRA reportedly persuaded a potential recruit to continue his education in Queen's University but to follow a nontraditional curriculum intended to provide him the skills needed to become a master bomb maker.[27]

In order to facilitate broader training among members of the group, PIRA devoted significant effort to preparing written resources to transmit training information. Training manuals were prepared covering weaponry, explosives, and battle tactics.[28] The best-known PIRA manual was *The Green Book* that, in addition to articulating the basis for the movement, also covered basic military information for new Volunteers.[29] The group also produced field manuals for particular weapons to instruct members in their use. Use of such manuals is cited in descriptions of PIRA training camps in the 1980s.[30]

A judgment about the effectiveness of group's military training would ideally be based on assessments of changes in its operational effectiveness before and after the training was carried out. Although comprehensive datasets to judge the efficacy of the training are not readily available, contemporary descriptions of the group's military activities suggest that PIRA's training efforts did pay off in increased effectiveness. Even early assessments of the group's activities cited improvement in PIRA operations in some areas: "In recent instances the gunmen [in Londonderry] have been hunting in packs, rather than individually. When in their packs, they are prepared to stand their ground and fight it out with the Security Forces. Gunmen are deploying to better fire positions and their aim seems to be more accurate."[31] In the mid- to late 1970s, after training measures had been in place for several years, another British military assessment noted improvement in firearms accuracy and in the use of relevant technologies to improve performance: "Until recently, PIRA's shooting attacks have been inaccurate. Zeroing of weapons has been poor. But simple telescopic sights have been fairly frequently used. Marksmanship has now improved probably due to better training."[32] The assessment of increased PIRA attention to sighting weapons echoes the description of shifts in training described above.[33]

An effort to gauge the impact of a training program on overall group capabilities must also consider the number of individuals the group can train. While PIRA's training programs did improve the group's capabilities in weapons use and tactics, their impact was bounded by the difficulties in training large numbers of Volunteers while maintaining group security. The limited time available to train individual recruits limited the amount of information that could be provided. However, given the operational requirements of the group, that amount of information could have been enough:

> The training carried out is . . . fairly basic. The standard of recruit is poor and with a maximum of ten days training, only the basic handling of one, or perhaps two, weapons can be covered. . . . General weapon training is [therefore] poor and achieves standards far inferior to those of a trained soldier. On the other hand, the standard required of a guerrilla . . . are not those required of a professional soldier. . . . The IRA standard is probably adequate for the operations they envisage.[34]

The benefits of training are also dependent on how well the content transmitted to group members matches the operational context and practicalities faced by the group. Some PIRA members raised criticisms, calling into question how well the group's training matched its circumstances, especially regarding the group's early efforts to train its membership. Those efforts were described as "very rudimentary [in] nature"[35] and were sometimes more appropriate to rural operations than the urban fight that made up a large part of PIRA's operations.[36]

Specialized Training

While the constraints of clandestine operations made it difficult to train large numbers of individuals to high degrees of expertise, PIRA carried out a number of specialized training programs that produced smaller numbers of operatives with much higher skill levels. This type of training makes it possible for a group to build up the necessary mix of skills at appropriate levels for its operations, without having to make the much larger investments required to develop all of its members into specialists. PIRA's route for selecting individuals with particular talents for tasks such as sniper operations or bomb making—candidate specialists—was to track their progress through the groups general training programs and, when they were identified, direct them into more advanced courses of training.[37]

This ability to specialize was made possible as the organization evolved and became more sophisticated; "as the IRA became more organized, volunteers began to specialize in areas such as sniping, explosives, logistics, or intelligence."[38] Such efforts were driven in part by effectiveness concerns, since it made it possible for some units to improve their capabilities in a specific area[39] and because certain weapons or tactics were more appropriate for operations in particular segments of the group's operational area. Specialization was supported by special "advanced courses" of training for particular areas[40] and ongoing "refresher" training for people with particular talents.[41] Such specialization allowed the group to develop very advanced expertise in areas like bomb making, significantly broadening the group's operational flexibility and increasing its lethality.

Different units of PIRA sought to enhance specialized knowledge in their particular members. At some points during PIRA's operational career, some units sought to build up specialized expertise by bringing together Volunteers engaged in similar activities. Such commingling would encourage cooperative learning and more general improvement of the group's capabilities:

> I tried to make fundamental changes to the way the [Derry] Brigade used explosives. . . . I sought to get all of the individual explosives officers, whether from the companies or battalions, into a pool over which I could exercise control, producing better training and improved safety standards. Pooling them would make higher quality operatives available to any unit or area, whereas before, each unit would have to rely on its own somewhat isolated explosives officer.[42]

Other units used rotation or "apprenticeship" processes to spread specific types of knowledge or expertise: "The next two weeks were spent in a bomb factory in Carrigart, learning how to make explosives from . . . nitrate fertilizer. Once trained, the idea was that we would use the expertise to establish similar bomb factories in the South."[43] The PIRA cell in South Armagh, a unit known for both its effectiveness and innovativeness, used a similar process of mixing experienced and new operatives so the veterans could provide mentoring and training within the unit:

> South Armagh developed a slow process of training the volunteer. They would have taken raw recruits and put them in with skilled people and took them on. They didn't push them too hard. And they got them used to what they were going to be faced with. This system meant that there were fewer mistakes and therefore fewer arrests in South Armagh than in any other IRA Brigade area.[44]

Training processes that bring together specialists within the organization for group training and knowledge exchange have obvious security risks, however. Such mechanisms also spread information about who is in the group broadly and increase the potential damage if the group is penetrated or a member persuaded to inform on group activities to the security forces or police. As a result of damage caused to the group by security force penetration, PIRA reorganized into a more compartmented cellular structure in the late 1970s. This made such broad rotation processes less viable. However, even then there was reportedly still exchange of some individuals among cells, providing the opportunity for mentoring of less experienced PIRA members by their more senior colleagues[45] or transfer of expertise from advanced units to other parts of the organization.[46]

Because of the heterogeneity they inherently create among different parts and members of a group, assessing the effectiveness of efforts at specialized training is more difficult. Unlike more general training, aggregate measures of group performance in areas such as marksmanship or concerns about the number of individuals that can be trained are not appropriate, because specialized training may focus on a very small number of group members. For individual units, performance at the unit level is relevant—such as the performance of the South Armagh unit described above. In some specialties, it is the outcomes of those specialists' performance that is important. Part of the reduction in PIRA fatalities from their own explosives (cited above with respect to individual training) was also likely a result of the success of the group's specialized training efforts as well, particularly in terms of the specialists who designed and constructed the devices used by other group members in their operations. However, because such assessments require much more specific data on a terrorist organization—down even to the individual level—the information required is frequently much more difficult to access.

Limitations in Clandestine Training

Although PIRA was quite successful in developing both general and specialized military training programs, the group's experience also demonstrates that the circumstances faced by clandestine groups can limit the scope and effectiveness of their training efforts. Three major areas impacting these kinds of group training programs are the need for secrecy, the resources required to carry out training, and the usefulness of obtaining training from sources outside the group.

Secrecy: Military Training and Risk to Group Security

In order to remain viable, terrorist organizations must maintain group security. Military training, however—particularly the "live fire" training that is required for individuals to build skills in the use of weapons—is difficult to conceal. At times, miscalculations associated with explosives training in particular were responsible for breaches in group security and significant risk to group members.[47] Although a considerable amount of information can be transferred to recruits about the use of weapons through lectures or other "dry training," such instruction cannot teach the intuitive or tacit knowledge required for individuals to use weapons well.[48] Lectures can teach how to fire a weapon, but marksmanship requires direct experience.

For much of its operational career, the Republic of Ireland provided PIRA with a comparatively safe haven for logistical and training activities. Because of a sympathetic population, limited security force enforcement activities, and large areas in which to hide their activities, the risk to activities in the Republic were much less than analogous actions in Northern Ireland. According to one account, "Training is carried out in most parts of the republic, even as far south as Cork. . . . Training camps are of various types: a deserted farmhouse, a beach, or remote wood, dependent mainly on the security of the area."[49] In addition to providing locations for broad organizational training in use of firearms and military tactics, the safe haven provided by the Republic was also important for training in louder, more destructive weapons like explosives and mortars:[50]

> Mortar firing using dummy shells usually took place at Inch Strand on the inner side of the Dingle peninsula—a six to seven-mile spit of firm white sand backed by dunes which was, in those days, out of the tourist season, a quiet and remote area. It was ideal for mortar training. You had a straight line of vision and could recover the dummy shells quite easily. The shells would also be undamaged from landing on the soft sand.[51]

The opportunity to test and experiment was significant in PIRA's ability to refine their explosives expertise, improve the operational functioning of

weapons systems they manufactured, and identify and correct design problems with their bombs and mortar systems.[52] Such training and experimentation could not be done without noise.

Security of training camps was always an issue, however, even in the relative safety of the Republic. To minimize noise, live firing focused on lighter
weapons

> as the likelihood of discovery . . . using the quieter .22 caliber ammunition
> was negligible, and this type of ammunition was cheap and easily available.
> Such freedom gave us a great opportunity to monitor development and to
> correct bad habits. Only those we felt had reached the required standard were
> allowed a short firing session with heavier weapons at a location deeper in
> the mountains.[53]

Camps were also located to minimize the impact of firearms noise, typically in areas where the noise would not carry far[54] or where the sound of
firing would not be out of place, such as close to rifle ranges used by the
Irish Army.[55] New recruits were also generally kept ignorant of the exact
locations of the camps where they were training.[56] Compromise of the
group's training facilities, which occurred at least once during the group's
operational career, could decimate their capability to teach new members
what they needed to know to become effective members of the organization. After one broad penetration and compromise of the training camps
in the Republic, "[i]t was almost a year before the training department was
able to resume normal business."[57]

Resources: Weapons Are Expended in Training

In order to use sophisticated weapons effectively in combat, users must be
sufficiently familiar with them to select appropriate targets for the
weapons, hit their desired targets, and do so effectively. One way to build
that familiarity is through live-fire training with the weapon. Beyond the
difficulties in maintaining secrecy during such training, the resources ex-
pended on training can be a major constraint for a group. For advanced
weapons in particular, which the terrorist may not have in large quantities,
groups may be hesitant to "waste" available stocks in training.

In PIRA's case, a particularly good example of this situation is the group's
use of rocket propelled grenade systems (specifically the RPG-7) early in its
operational career:

> Once the level of weapon sophistication is increased this problem of compe-
> tence becomes more serious. . . . To anyone with an exposure to the military,
> a bazooka or [antitank rocket] is quite a simple weapon used for obvious
> purposes. The IRA had never been trained to use a launcher. The GHQ was

not about to practice with the few rockets available. Instead the RPG-7 was used for IRA purposes rather than in the way the maker had intended. Fired into military and police posts the armor-piercing rocket zapped in one side and out the other. The entire exercise proved futile for the IRA.[58]

Contemporary assessments indicate that the weapon could have been effective, even for PIRA's desired applications against static targets "such as Security Force bases and prison walls," but that "[s]o far PIRA's inadequate training has resulted in the mishandling of the RPG-7."[59] The overall ineffectiveness of the weapons early in the group's career is likely a combination of shortcomings in target selection as well as the skills and practices of the individuals using the weapon. As cited by Bell, the limited availability of the weapons was important—most of the known arms shipments to the group included only a small number of the launchers (though they did include larger numbers of the grenades themselves).[60] The restricted supply increased the effective cost of certain types of training, specifically the live-fire training that could have improved end-user skills with the weapons,[61] and meant that the quantity the group required for the weapon to be "useful" was higher than might otherwise be assumed.[62]

Outside Training: Assistance from Sympathetic Groups Is Not Always Useful

One way individual groups can address the constraints placed on training in clandestine organizations, or the difficulties in finding and gaining access to the needed expertise and information, is to seek training from outside groups or sympathetic governments. In published sources on PIRA, there are a variety of reports that the group maintained links with—and obtained different types of training from—a range of international sources. One instance of "international interaction" may even predate the existence of the group itself. It has been reported that, "During the 1950s, those members of the IRA who were destined to form the core of the Provisional IRA in the 1970s were imprisoned in England with members of the Greek Cypriot terrorist group EOKA. By their own account they learned from them."[63]

One group that is frequently cited as interacting closely with PIRA for training and technology transfer is the Basque group, *Euskadi Ta Askatasuna* (Basque Homeland and Freedom, or ETA). A range of public acknowledgements of "good relations" between the groups reportedly go back as far as 1974.[64] Accounts of former PIRA members suggest that the relationship goes back even further, to soon after PIRA's founding: "The links between ETA and the IRA run deep; the two organizations have often cooperated and pooled ideas, technology and training. As far back as 1972, ETA supplied the IRA with weapons. The accounts of what was supplied differ but not the fact of it."[65] Over the course of both groups' careers, training was reportedly provided in both directions in a number of tactical and operational areas.[66]

PIRA also reportedly maintained relationships with a variety of groups and governments in the Middle East, relationships which included PIRA members training at camps in a number of countries. Organizations cited include al-Fatah in Jordon,[67] the Popular Front for the Liberation of Palestine, and the Palestine Liberation Organization.[68] These links reportedly led to training in Algeria,[69] Libya,[70] and Lebanon.[71]

While many different linkages between PIRA and other entities have been described in a range of published sources, questions have also been raised about the strength of the linkages and the importance of any training provided to the group's capabilities and effectiveness. Glover characterized the links as "elusive" and that "there are no signs that PIRA has either the intention or ability to deliberately foster them."[72] Others have suggested that it is "unclear how useful these links are in operational terms."[73] A group member, interviewed by researcher Tim Coogan,[74] trivialized the contribution the training in Libya made to the group: "Don't mind that talk about Libya. The Libyans were trained in conventional warfare. They couldn't teach us anything." Inferential support for the Volunteer's assessment of the Libyan training can be found in the group's experience with SA-7 surface-to-air missiles. In addition to providing PIRA with the weapons, group members were reportedly trained in their use in Libya.[75] But the group was never able to use the weapons effectively: "[T]he only known deployment of a [SA]-7 in Northern Ireland was against a Wessex [helicopter] at Kinawley on the County Fermanaugh border in July 1991; the missile failed to lock on to the helicopter and exploded on the ground."[76] If training was provided, it was apparently insufficient to provide the group with a sustained capability to maintain and use this particular weapon.

Intelligence and Counterintelligence Training

Identifying targets and planning terrorist attacks requires information. For the clandestine organization, much of the required information must be collected by group members and passed on to the planners and leaders making operational decisions. Recognizing the importance of effective intelligence collection, the topic was included in Volunteer training:

> [R]ecruits are educated and informed of ways in which they are expected to both evaluate information and report it. Recruits are advised that any information may hold potential value to the organisation as "intelligence" which may facilitate or determine the tactics, pace and conduct of operational ac-

tivities. . . . PIRA recruits are reminded that they are not just "soldiers" but the "eyes and ears" for their own comrades. A PIRA intelligence manual states: "H.Q. knows only that which is reported and whatever it manages to glean through independent sources."[77]

The IRA's training manual covers a range of good intelligence practices, including the need for individuals to verify their sources and control access to sensitive information on a need-to-know basis, along with ways to categorize different types of information as it is passed upward in the group, in order to help ensure it was used effectively.[78]

Because of the sensitivity of intelligence knowledge—information on sources' identities, specific methods of gathering critical information, and so on—training new operatives can be difficult. "Intelligence underground . . . rarely leaves records, even for those next in command. Nearly everyone involved prefers to know as little as possible, forego records in return for increased security, and forget as much as possible."[79] This need and propensity for secrecy made it more difficult for the group to broadly develop intelligence collection capacity.

Although collection of intelligence is critical for a terrorist organization to act effectively, without effective counterintelligence practices a group is highly vulnerable to the actions of law enforcement or security forces. For PIRA, counterintelligence and operational security practices were included in *The Green Book* and covered as part of initial training for new Volunteers. Topics covered included teaching new group members to avoid activities that would lead the police to conclude they were Republican sympathizers, warning them of the dangers of drink-induced talk, and providing methods to help them withstand interrogation.[80] The explicit lessons on counterinterrogation techniques were reinforced with simulated interrogations so individuals would become familiar with what to expect.[81] The discussion of counterinterrogation in the manual ends with the succinct: "In conclusion, if and when arrested: SAY NOTHING, SIGN NOTHING, SEE NOTHING, HEAR NOTHING."[82]

PIRA also taught its members techniques and practices intended to blunt the security force's use of forensic science to investigate the group's operations. As the police applied more and more advanced forensic techniques to identify PIRA members and investigate the scenes of attacks, the group developed resources to help its members "break the forensic link to incriminating chemical [and other] residue"[83] tying them to an attack. These included manuals that taught ways to counter law-enforcement efforts aimed at the group: "The IRA, with customary thoroughness, debriefed Volunteers who had gone through the process of detection and trial and produced a 9,000 word document whose title could have been 'How Not to Incriminate Yourself.'"[84] The document describes police procedures during evidence collection and provides Volunteers with advice on minimizing the collection of incriminating evidence in their hair; avoiding and removing gunpowder residues; addressing contamination during explosives manufacture; and minimizing risks from fiber, particle, DNA, and footprint evidence.[85] Some measures that PIRA took, which became a part of the group's overall image—such as the use of rubber gloves and their iconic balaclava facemasks—were partially aimed at reducing vulnerability to many forensic techniques.[86]

Because of the nature of intelligence and counterintelligence activities, objective measures of the effectiveness of a group's training efforts in these areas are even more difficult to develop than for training in more direct military activities. Successes provide anecdotal evidence of effectiveness. For example, PIRA was successful in penetrating some government organizations to help identify targets, gain information, and provide the group warning of security force actions.[87] However, sometimes successes occur by luck rather than skill and, in areas where groups on all sides of a conflict frequently endeavor to hide both their successes and failures, sufficient data to distinguish the two will seldom be available. In counterintelligence and counterforensic activities, the ability of group members to avoid arrest and successful prosecution are clear measures of effectiveness. Information on some parts of PIRA can provide useful insights and suggests that the group's efforts were effective. One example is seen in the South Armagh unit mentioned previously: "This system meant that there were fewer mistakes and therefore fewer arrests in South Armagh than in any other IRA Brigade area."[88] Similarly, the assessment by members of the security forces of the effectiveness of the group's counterefforts—and how much they were forced to adapt as a result—also suggest that the group was successful in these areas.[89]

Conclusions

Over its lengthy operational history, the Provisional Irish Republican Army developed a variety of systems for training its Volunteers in the ways of clandestine warfare. Extrapolating from PIRA's experience, several lessons can be drawn relevant to training by terrorist groups more generally:

- Beginning from a raw recruit, any training—whether transmitting political, organizational, or operational knowledge—is beneficial. The resource constraints for providing such training are minimal.
- A sufficient amount of sanctuary, such as PIRA's provided by the Republic of Ireland, provides better opportunities for realistic and more thorough training, especially for sophisticated weaponry and tactics. However, the specific characteristics of a group's safe haven and available resources will define and may constrain its options.

- Terrorist groups need specialists to provide the expertise needed for specific advanced operations and tasks because even large, well-established groups lack the resources to teach all members every potentially important skill. Groups will need mechanisms to identify potentially promising members for specialized training, and mechanisms to subsequently provide it.

- Cross-training among cells within a group can provide a mechanism for knowledge diffusion throughout an organization, but it does so at a price—such training reduces the security benefits that would come from a tightly compartmented, cellular structure.

- Intelligence and counterintelligence capacities of groups are particularly important. It may only take one mistake by a group member to provide law enforcement or intelligence agencies the opening they need to compromise a terrorist operation or the group itself. To the extent these skills can be provided to group members, an organization can significantly bolster its own survivability.

- In all areas, connections with outside groups or experts can be useful to a terrorist organization—but only if those links are close enough to provide current and useful knowledge support and if the assistance provided to the group is relevant to its operational context.

However, while overarching statements about group training are straightforward to make, understanding the operational relevance of terrorist groups' training programs requires the right information to gauge their actual effectiveness. From the perspective of an outside analyst, a group's training efforts are only of real concern if they are effective. The case of PIRA, a group with a long operational history compared to other groups, and to which considerable analytical attention has been paid, underscores the difficulty of this task: While descriptive information on training is comparatively available—in sources ranging from group publications, manuals, and accounts of group members—the data needed to assess efficacy is much more sparse. In some cases, such as elements of the group's military activities, information is available to assess some elements of group training efforts. Improvements in marksmanship and the group's skills in using explosive devices can be ascribed, at least in part, to the effectiveness of its training efforts. In others, such as initial recruit indoctrination, one can infer that the group felt its training program was successful because of its relative stability over time, though an internal perception of effectiveness does not necessarily mean the effort can be judged effective by external, objective measures. The information needed to assess training in other areas is simply not readily available. As such, beyond providing an example of how to assess a group's training efforts in some areas, PIRA also provides insights into the types of information required to more completely and successfully assess a group's training programs.

Acknowledgments

This project was supported in part by Grant No. 2003-IJ-CX-1022, awarded by the National Institute of Justice, Office of Justice Programs, U.S. Department of Justice. Points of view in this document are those of the authors and do not necessarily represent the official position or policies of the U.S. Department of Justice.

CHAPTER 9

Teaching New Terrorist Recruits: A Review of Training Manuals from the Uzbekistan Mujahideen

MARTHA BRILL OLCOTT AND BAKHTIYAR BABAJANOV

The world of a young man recruited for jihad or holy war is a frightening one.[1] The training he undergoes teaches hatred in the name of religious purification. Colleagues and neighbors are transformed into enemies that he is trained to destroy with deadly weapons fashioned out of simple things from his environment.

This chapter examines the training experiences of a group of Central Asians, mostly Uzbek by nationality, who went through local terror schools during the mid-1990s. From the content of their notebooks, which were discovered in various locations throughout Uzbekistan, it seems that the training went on in the Ferghana Valley of Uzbekistan, a center of Islamic revival in the region. The training site is less important than the content, as these young people could have received virtually identical training in Tajikistan, Afghanistan, or Pakistan during these years.

The blow that the al Qaeda network received through U.S. military actions in Afghanistan diminishes the threat of terrorism, but it does not eliminate it. These notebooks come from the period before the Taliban asserted their control and Osama bin Laden expanded his network. The United States is only one of many targets, and the attacks on U.S. soil are the product of specially trained terrorist groups. Many of the states who have been part of the U.S.-led War on Terrorism are far easier to strike, and may still harbor terrorist cells within their territory.

This is particularly true of the countries of Central Asia, where the United States now has two military bases, in Uzbekistan and in Kyrgyzstan. Both countries are targets of the Islamic Movement of Uzbekistan (IMU). This terrorist group, which developed in the mid-1990s, became part of the al Qaeda network, with camps in Afghanistan and safe havens over the border in Tajikistan. Its founder, Juma Namangani, was reportedly killed during the bombings in Afghanistan, and the whereabouts of another prominent leader, Tohir Yuldashev, are still unknown.

The IMU is credited with masterminding the simultaneous bombings of key government offices in Uzbekistan's capital, Tashkent, in February 1999. Although none of the buildings were destroyed, several people were killed. These attacks came after seven years of harsh surveillance of potential militant Islamic groups by Uzbek security services. After the bombings, Uzbekistan's government successfully pressured the United States to list the IMU as an international terrorist group, and, faced with heightened Uzbek security, the IMU made do with hostage taking and armed forays in neighboring Kyrgyzstan.

The IMU has been largely dormant since the successful U.S.-led bombing campaign in Afghanistan, its capacity to wage terror diminished. While the training represented in these notebooks would be difficult to get in Uzbekistan today, there are many parts of Central Asia where clandestine lessons could be held, and there are still thousands of young people who might be recruited as potential students.

The Origins of Militant Islam in Uzbekistan

The new states that came into being with the collapse of the U.S.S.R. are home to over 50 million people of Islamic heritage, whose religious life had been subject to severe restriction during the seven decades of Soviet rule. These include Tatars, Chechens Azerbaijanis, and nearly 40 million Muslims living in Central Asia, virtually all of whom are Sunni Muslims who adhere to the Hanafi school of law.

Islam first came to Central Asia in the eighth century A.D. and in the period of the Islamic Empire (eighth to thirteenth centuries) the region was a center of Islamic learning, home to Ibn Sina (Avicenna, 980–1037) and al Farabi (259–339 A.H./870–950 A.D.) among others. Several important Sufi leaders, founders of movements of spiritual revival and purification, came from the region, including Ahmed Yasavi and Bahauddin-i Naqshband (1318–1389), whose graves—outside of Bukhara, Uzbekistan, and Turkestan, Kazakhstan, respectively—are still important pilgrimage sites.

The followers of these men, and those of other Sufi leaders, all helped keep the traditions of Islam alive when the teaching of the faith was banned or restricted to a few clerics trained and supervised by the Soviet state. Such activities were also a form of jihad, in which believers struggle for the purification of the faith both in themselves and in others, using words but not arms.

Throughout Soviet rule, and particularly in the densely populated Ferghana Valley, underground mosques and religious "schools" continued to exist. The graduates of these schools played an important role in the revival of Islam that Central Asia experienced beginning in the late 1980s, when political conditions changed and thousands of new mosques and religious schools were opened. At this time it became obvious that Central Asia's Muslims had also been exposed to the teachings of radical Islam. Some of the clerics were Salafiya, people who rejected the dominant Hanafi school of law and believed that Islam had to return to the "purity" of the faith which had been practiced at the time of the Prophet Muhammad. These people were influenced by the teachings of medieval theologians such as Ibn Ahmad ibn Tamiyya and more modern figures like Sayyid Qutb of Egypt (1906–1966) and Sayyid Abul A'la Maududi (1903–1979), the founder of Pakistan's Jaamiat al Islami movement.

The late 1980s and early 1990s were difficult and confusing years for young people living in all parts of the Soviet Union. A seemingly invincible state had collapsed and was replaced by fragile new ones. Conditions were almost apocalyptic, with a formerly commanding economy in disarray, the powerful Red Army in shreds, and those who served it selling off their weaponry.

Muslim activists, claiming that moral turpitude had brought the Soviets down, found it easy to muster arguments to bolster their cause. An Islamic Revolutionary Party (the IRP) was organized in the region. In some places, like Chechnya and Tatarstan, religion and nationalism made common cause, but in most of Central Asia, nationalism became a tool used by the ruling communist élite to preserve their power. The one place where they failed was in Tajikistan, which had a bloody civil war from 1992–1994 and where members of the Islamic opposition were brought into the government as part of a process of national reconciliation in 1997.

Although the Uzbek government refused to register the IRP, a number of charismatic clerics, preaching rejection of the secular state, continued to gain supporters, especially in the Ferghana Valley. And these men in turn developed armed supporters, who in the first months of independence briefly took control of key government buildings in a regional center (Namangan). Fearing that the situation in Tajikistan would be replicated in Uzbekistan, President Islam Karimov authorized a purge of the official Islamic establishment, leading to the arrest or disappearance of prominent unlicensed clerics and leaders of "extremist" Islamic groups.

Several prominent figures escaped the official dragnet, including both Tohir Yuldashev and Juma Namangani (born in 1969 in Namangan). At this time it was still easy to travel between Uzbekistan and Tajikistan, as well as between Tajikistan and parts of northern Afghanistan dominated by Tajiks and Uzbeks—a region that had served for years as a host site for training camps for those interested in making Holy War.

The Terrorist Notebooks

The Islamic Movement of Uzbekistan was born in these conditions, as at a minimum hundreds of young Uzbeks are believed to have passed through the Afghan and Pakistani camps. Some of the Uzbek mujahideen came home to train their countrymen, and set up clandestine terror schools for this purpose.

In 2001–2002, we acquired ten notebooks of students who attended such courses during the period of 1994–1996. These notebooks were acquired through various intermediaries, each unaware that we were collecting material from others, as part of an effort to document the Islamic revival in Uzbekistan. We have no reason to question their authenticity, which the pages reproduced here testify to. Six of the notebooks were obtained in the Ferghana Valley [notebooks 1, 3, and 4 through 7]; three in Tashkent oblast (the capital city region of Uzbekistan) [notebooks 8, 9, and 10]; and notebook 2 belonged to Uzbeks from Khorezm oblast (in western Uzbekistan, near the Turkmen border) and was recovered from an Uzbek village just over the border in Kazakhstan. Some of the notebooks have the names (or pseudonyms) of the fighters in training who wrote them—for example, notebook 6, discovered in the village of Namangan, belonged to a student named "Abdumalik."

Taken collectively, these notebooks allow us to reconstruct the training that the young mujahideen were receiving. While there are similarities between the lessons written up in all of the notebooks, the most complete instruction seems to have been provided in the courses held in the Ferghana Valley. The students seem to have spent the bulk of their time receiving instruction in military subjects. They heard lectures on cartography, artillery, and targeting and then spent a lot of time learning about making and laying mines, as well as preparing and using poisons. When these technical subjects were mastered, the students then went on to learn about when and how to make jihad or holy war. The students also received instruction in Arabic language and in some cases rudimentary instruction in Islam.

Three of the notebooks (two obtained in Namangan, and the last in Kokand) [notebooks 3, 6, 7] are of students who clearly studied together. We have reason to think that they studied in Namangan, possibly in the basement of the Juma Mosque, reopened during these years under pressure from the community after having been used as a storehouse for alcoholic beverages during Soviet time. Juma Namangani, himself, may have served as the instructor for the lectures on jihad; if not Namangani, then one of his close associates.

In several cases, the notebooks were the property of two or more students, who shared materials and studied together. The basic language of instruction for these courses was Uzbek; those who taught the technical subjects knew Russian or Arabic, and in some cases both languages.

We do not know very much for certain about the "mujahideen" who wrote these notebooks. It is our understanding that all were eventually arrested; in the case of those from Khorezm, it was for smuggling light consumables (and "trade" was in fact their livelihood). Most of the others, though, were picked up by Uzbek security forces as suspected terrorists, and their parents, who gave us or our intermediaries the notebooks, were reluctant to talk about them, save to disassociate themselves from their children's "mistakes."

We do not know whether or not the young men who studied in these schools were themselves devout Muslims, living according to the rules of Islam, but it is clear from what they wrote and studied that they were not very knowledgeable about Islam. The same may also be said about their teachers. This is especially apparent in the lessons on jihad, when references to the Koran, offered by chapter and verse, are sometimes to passages which have no relationship to the subjects under discussion. These errors are clearly those of the teachers; most students would not have had their own Korans and also lacked the necessary Arabic language skills to read them in the original.

We can also say with certainty that they were not very educated young people. There were lots of grammatical mistakes in the Uzbek, not just the Arabic or Russian, terminology. Some of the students had very poor attention spans and did a very careless job of taking notes and studying. Others were diligent, and some of the pairings were of stronger and weaker students.

Ayub's Notebook

Ayub is probably a Tajik from Namangan. The text of his notebook [notebook 1] has many grammatical errors (in Uzbek). The lessons begin at the end of the notebook, as is the tradition in Arabic or Persian books. On the inside cover of the notebook is written "military subjects" (*darsi silokh*), part II, and has a drawing of a gun with a flower (Figure 9.1).

All the notes contained in this notebook are from this one person, primarily on military subjects, especially artillery, rules of aiming and calculations of wind direction in launching grenades and other weapons. No humanities, no religion, holy war, or politics are represented in the lessons of Ayub's notebook.

The Course of Study: Military Subjects

One thing is clear, though: These students learned how to make some deadly weapons. All of these were "lab" courses, and the students had hands-on experience. This comes through clearly in the notes; in every field of terror, it was "learning through doing" from instructors who were proficient in their subject matter. Those who used Russian terminology clearly had experience with the Red Army and Soviet system of military instruction, while those who used Arabic terminology likely passed through terror camps in Afghanistan and maybe even those of the Middle East. In many cases, several different instructors taught the various military subjects.

Figure 9.1
Ayub's Notebook

Cartography

The first thing that these students learned was orienting themselves to their surroundings. We showed some of this material to a professor of cartography in Tashkent, not saying where we got it from, and he was able to identify the source and was certain that the person doing the instruction was a cartographer. Given that all high-school students in the Soviet Union were required to receive paramilitary training, there was no shortage of people capable of teaching cartography, or most other military subjects, even in the most remote parts of Uzbekistan. Moreover, with some modification, the textbooks from these courses would have been a good starting point for instruction.

Artillery

The students then went on to study handling small firearms, another topic that Soviet high-school students had always received some exposure to. This was to prepare them for required military service, and during the years of the Soviet occupation of Afghanistan (1979–1989) more local youth acquired combat experience than any time since the end of World War II.

Much of our knowledge about this field of study comes from Ayub [notebook 1], who spent so much time mastering this material that we dubbed him "the gunner." He was also careful to date many of his lessons. Many of the weapons that the students learned to use were common Soviet-era ones, including various forms of the Kalashnikov automatic rifle (the AK-47, AK-56, and AKM). He also, though, was taught to handle several weapons of choice from Afghanistan, including the Egyptian Rocket Propelled Grenade Launcher (see Figure 9.2). "This 82-millimeter version is based on a Russian or Chinese modification of an earlier U.S. weapon," Ayub writes in Arabic, with mistakes. All of these appear in illustrations, with accompanying notes on the functioning and maintenance of these weapons. This lesson is dated 16 January 1995.

Another lesson covered launching mines (see Figure 9.3). The subheading of these notes are in Arabic, suggesting a different teacher from the first two lessons in Ayub's notebook. The description detailed in his notes is that of the Egyptian Minelauncher-27. It is not difficult to see that the student was a beginner in Arabic, because in spelling the title he copied a specially adorned version of the letters, as they appear in slogans, ads, and posters. There is a very detailed description of the mine launcher itself, its characteristics, and the description of the mine (or "load" of the weapon), as well as different ways that it can explode—on the land, in the air, etc, depending upon the objective. There are descriptions of setting up the weapon, calculating the aeronautics of the mine, aiming it, and tables are provided. All of the calculation formulas are in Arabic. The terminology for the most part is in Arabic.

Targeting

Ayub also was diligent in learning how to target the enemy, on the ground and in the air. His notebook includes tables with elaborate calculations on

Figure 9.2
The Grenade Launcher Lesson

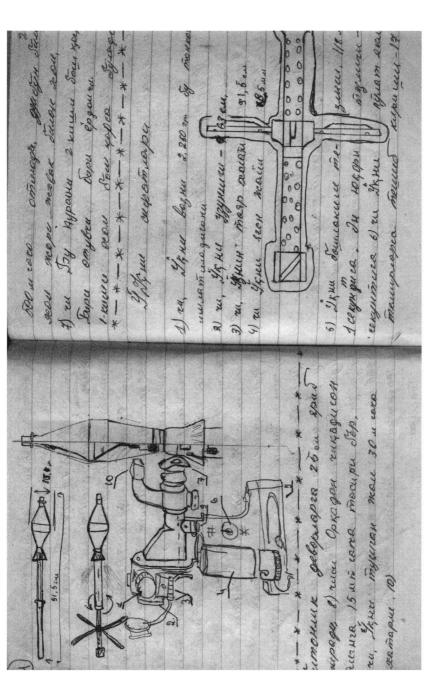

(Ayub's Notebook, Lesson 10)

Figure 9.3
The Mine Launcher Lesson

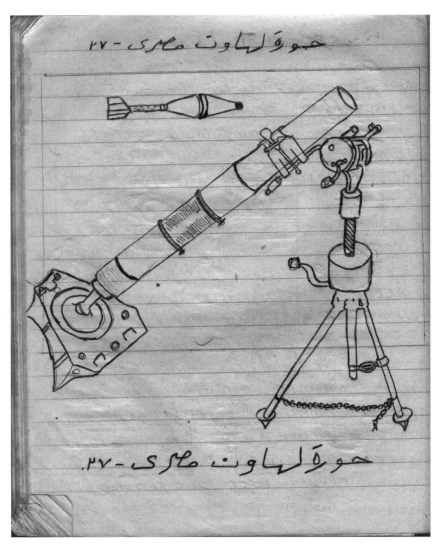

(Ayub's Notebook)

how to target planes and helicopters in varying wind and weather conditions (see Figure 9.4 and Figure 9.5). His teacher used both Arabic and Russian military terminology, and in the course of his lessons Ayub got to handle various forms of sighting instruments, writing in one case "the front glass reflects many colors," and "the plus sign that regulates distance is easily obscured by finger marks."

Figure 9.4
Sighting Moveable and Immoveable Targets

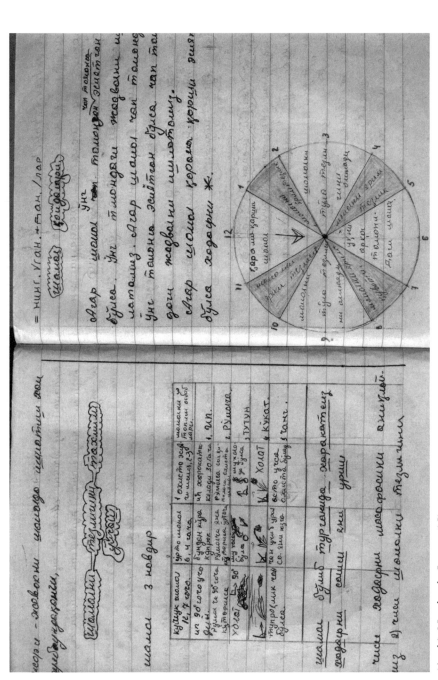

(Ayub's Notebook, Lesson 15)

Figure 9.5
Sighting Moveable and Immoveable Targets

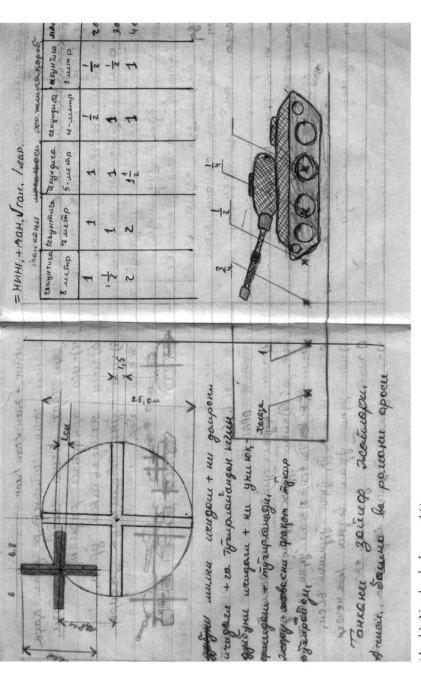

(Ayub's Notebook, Lesson 16)

Mines and Demolitions

This was a basic subject of instruction that all of the young mujahideen in Uzbekistan seem to have been trained in, if our notebooks are at all representative. Many of the mines that the mujahideen learned to make had been commonly used in Afghanistan, and in other guerrilla war settings, including the M18A1 Antipersonnel Mine, which is a plastic-bodied directed fragmentation mine that has ball bearings imbedded in the facing of the target. Variations of this have been produced in the U.S.S.R. (MON-50) as well as in Pakistan, South Africa, South Korea, and Chile. Students also received instruction in the POMZ-2 antipersonnel mine, activated through the use of a tripwire, with a lethal radius of four meters. Variations of it were manufactured in the Soviet Union and throughout the eastern bloc in Europe as well as in China and North Korea.

One notebook [5, from Margilan] includes information on making 15 different kinds of explosive devices, and the two students who prepared this notebook were taught reaction times and temperatures for blowing up buildings, bridges, railroad ties, and electricity relay stations. In fact, they were taught everything necessary to become competent arsonists, including how to escape unharmed, a subject emphasized in some of the lessons. These young men were not being trained as suicide bombers, but as guerilla fighters who would endure a long period of battle.

Almost all the students provided graphic drawings of how the mines should be used, although one of two students who prepared notebook 3, and studied with Abdumalik, offered the most graphic ones. His drawings show American servicemen as well as Russians as the target of attacks.

Poisons

Students were taught how to make poisons with substances that were generally readily accessible, such as tobacco or toxic mushrooms. One illustration in the notebooks featured a substance made from corn flour, meat, fertilizer, alcohol, and water. The student notes that "any dung will do, horse, goat, or even Yak!" Information on the precise amounts of each ingredient, how to mix them properly, and precise reaction times are included. There are also lengthy instructions on safety techniques—for example, when to wear gloves and masks—as well as how to conceal noxious odors so that potential targets are not alerted. Alongside instructions for making and using cyanide, student 2 writes "And the power of Allah is mightier," as if to see off his future victim, as the phrase is commonly used at deathbeds in the region.

Learning Jihad

This is the most terrifying part of the notebooks, for it provides the context for the study of the military subjects, in that their explicit goal was killing people. The lectures on jihad were designed to mobilize the students for battle with the enemy, and this was their final subject of study.

Since Islam was spread by the sword, holy war is an important theme in the Koran, but when it is required and when it is forbidden is a question that theologians have fought over since the time of Muhammad.

The view of jihad represented in these notebooks is both simplistic and uniform, so much so that the students studying in different cities may have been taught by the same person. The teacher was someone who lacked even middling religious education (eight to ten years of study), but rather was a fighter with a religious background, someone like Juma Namangani or Tohir Yuldashev, the leaders of the Islamic Movement of Uzbekistan.

Jihad was depicted as a cleansing act, as Jafar [notebook 7] wrote: "So the old ideology makes way for the new," by which he meant the dominant Hanafi school of religious law makes way for Salafi (or fundamentalist) Islam. Central Asian theologians from the Hanafi school had been preaching accommodation with secular rulers; in fact, most argued that Islamic law demanded this, for to do otherwise was to put the community of believers at risk.

By contrast these students were taught that Uzbekistan's secular rulers were breechers of the faith, and as Jafar wrote in notebook 7, there needed to be a holy war

for our faith of Islam
to make Allah pleased with us
to eradicate oppression against Muslims
to establish Islamic rule in perpetuity

He and his fellow mujahideen were taught that jihad had multiple goals, that economic, political, ideological, and military goals had to be mutually reinforcing. Critical to the effort is the propaganda that precedes military action.

As student 3 writes, the goal of this is to raise popular awareness of the enemies among them:

To make a declaration of the fact that, unbelievers and the government are oppressors, that they are connected with the Russians, the Americans, and the Jews, to whose music they are dancing, and they don't think about their people. We spread true knowledge about Islam in our country [i.e., Uzbekistan], we speak of the fate of faith breachers, according to Islamic law, and about people should distance themselves from those who breach the faith, and should side with the mujahideen. At the same time it has to be announced that jihad is a necessary religious requirement, for all social groups of people, and in the life, everyone must either be a Muslim or a non-Muslim, that is no one can remain in the middle. After this, the declaration will be done, the mujahideen will inform the people of the beginning of Jihad.

The enemies that they were targeting were depicted in political cartoons, which the students appear to have been asked to draw outside of class. Many of these are variants of the kinds of anti-imperialist and anti-Zionist cartoons that Soviet students sometimes drew during their studies, only now they drew caricatures of Russians to go alongside those of the Americans and the Jews.

The anti-Semitism was primitive, based on perverse distortions of history, but effective:

> All the countries of the world are today ruled by Jews. This people who is cursed by God began to rule everyone 120 years ago, at the time of Napoleon. It was so. At the time of the fighting between the armies of Napoleon and the British, the Jews used this to spread rumors among the people of England, that Napoleon won the battle. Hearing it, the British fell into panic, and began to sell their stores, factories, plants, and other kinds of enterprises. They thought as following: "After the victory of Napoleon, he will arrive in England, and we will lose everything." And so lots of enterprises were sold, and very cheaply. The Jews took advantage of the opportunity and starting buying everything very cheaply. A week later it became known that the British won the battle against Napoleon. Hearing this, all the people again began to buy back their things. The Jews sold all this, but for 5–10 times more than they paid, and received enormous profit. That the Jews are cursed by God is demonstrated in Ayat 14 of sura al-Khashr. (59:14)

The first Jews came to Central Asia at the time of the Arab conquests, and anti-Semitism was traditionally much less a factor here than in the Slavic parts of the Russian Empire. The Uzbeks were historically much less positively disposed to the Russians, who conquered their lands and restricted the practice of their faith. The Russians remain a target here, despite their withdrawal from Uzbekistan after the country gained independence in 1991.

Now the mujahideen were determined to rout these enemies out and kill them, as part of their economic, political and ideological goals. Under economic goals were

1. To attack the joint ventures that have been organized by the officials of our city. [Namangan?]. That is, in the first instance, those enterprises with Russians, Jews [presumably Israelis], and American (partners) at the head.

2. To destroy all that is imported from the countries of the enemy, what-ever it may be, food, clothes, etc. This too is an economic and polit-ical blow.

3. To destroy all raw materials that are being exported from the coun-try by unbelievers. This includes fruit . . . one or two cases of fruit should be poisoned, and when this [the poisoned boxes] is discov-ered, it should be announced that all the fruit that was sent (for ex-ample) to Russia, is poisoned. Those who transport things for personal use will be warned once or twice, and then everything will be confiscated from them.

4. Specialists from Russia, Jews (Israelis) and Americans working in the economy will be destroyed.

The same groups were targeted under political goals:

At the time of the political strike against the state, we should also kill Rus-sians, Americans and Israeli citizens. That is, ambassadors, or others of them, who live here, they all must be beaten.

Clerics and missionaries of other faiths were also slated for extermination as part of the ideological program:

From among religious people we will kill:

1. Those who try to gain converts to Christianity on Muslim soil.
2. Spies who work as Christian clerics. We will kill those Christians and Jews, who speak against the mujahideen and those who propagate Islam.
3. Those Christians who collect money for the struggle against Muslims, and those who speak against Muslims. They will be stabbed or shot, or hung, or beaten to death.

Conclusion

The good news is that the young men whose notebooks we have in our possession were never really able to do much with the deadly knowledge they acquired. The bad news is that the threat from groups like the IMU remains a real one throughout most of Central Asia. Large numbers of young people with limited education and diminishing economic prospects living in densely populated communities blame the secular leaders who dominate these countries for their fate. The fact that many of these men were the local masters of the openly atheistic Soviet regime—who many believe have been able to profit from an unprecedented increase in corruption since independence—helps create conditions that are ideal for those preaching the more radical forms of Islam.

Radical Islamic groups have continued to spread their ideas, especially among Central Asia's youth, despite the fact that their activities are usually illegal and their members are subject to arrest. The best known of these groups is the Hizb ut-Tahrir, which continues to attract young people despite extraordinary efforts taken by the Uzbek government to track down and arrest those associated with it.[2] Its numbers are increasing in Kyrgyzstan, but also in Kazakhstan and Tajikistan. This movement is committed to the reestablishment of the Caliphate, of the rule of Islam as it was practiced by the Prophet Muhammad. For now, they maintain, this goal can only be advanced through persuasion, not through force.[3]

Whatever the fate of the Hizb ut-Tahrir, other radical groups seem certain to emerge in the fertile conditions of the economic transitions that the Central Asian states are still undergoing. Moreover, each of these countries must still face serious political challenges, as the Soviet-era élite still in charge are replaced by a new generation.

The use of force alone does not defeat terrorism. A security organization capable of routing out all potential terrorists would inevitably be a source of terror itself. Not only would it tread on the basic civil rights of peaceful citizens, but by targeting "radical" Islam they would invariably make the state organs appear as the enemy of Islam to many loyal citizens who also consider themselves devout Muslims.

For the secular world the enemy is not Islam, but those people who pervert its teachings. Yet it is often hard to convince devout Muslims that this is true, for they believe that only the community of believers can define their faith. Groups that seem extreme to secular regimes may be well within the limits tolerated by those living in more traditional circumstances. A clash of civilizations is not inevitable, but as these notebooks imply, more difficult times may still lie ahead.

CHAPTER 10

Learning to Die: Suicide Terrorism in the Twenty-First Century

ADAM DOLNIK

In recent years, suicide terrorism has become one of the most influential and fastest spreading of terrorist tactics. Since the commencement of the modern practice of suicide terrorism in 1981, there have been over 500 suicide bombings carried out by twenty-five organizations in twenty-four different countries. Further, acts of suicide terrorism are extremely lethal: Of the fifty deadliest terrorist attacks in the last fifteen years, at least 72 percent have involved suicide delivery. This chapter will discuss the motivations of suicide bombers and the trends and prospects of suicide terrorism for the twenty-first century. The first part will concentrate on identifying the key distinction between suicide terrorism and other forms of terrorist violence. Also in this section, the advantages of suicide terrorism as a tactic will be discussed. The second part will focus on the scope of motivations of individual suicide bombers, the organizations that make the decision to employ them, and the process of training to become a suicide bomber. The final section will discuss the contemporary emerging tactical trends of suicide terrorism, and provide an outlook for the future.

Suicide Bombings and Their Advantages

Definitions and History

In order to discuss suicide terrorism, it is extremely important to explain what exactly is meant by this term. There are several difficulties with defining the phenomenon. The first such difficulty concerns the difference between the *readiness* to die and the *desire* to die. For this reason it is useful to define a suicide operation on the basis of the perpetrator's death as a precondition of a successful attack. In other words: If the perpetrator does not die the attack cannot take place. From such a definition, high-risk operations in which the perpetrator has even the smallest chance of surviving are excluded. Another problem is represented by the difficulty in making a distinction between cases in which a terrorist dies willingly and cases in which he or she is unaware of his or her death being a part of the plan.[1] There have been several cases in which the terrorists were fooled into believing that they were only transporting the explosive that was later remotely detonated while in their possession by organizers of the attack. Even though such cases should not be considered, the difficulty of determining the suicide bombers' intentions after their death inevitably results in the misclassification of many such attacks as suicide bombings. For the purposes of this chapter, a suicide terror attack is defined as a *premeditated act of ideologically or religiously motivated violence, in which the success of the operation is contingent on self-inflicted death by the perpetrator(s) during the attack.*[2]

Perhaps the first recorded attack that fits the above stated definition is the biblical story of Samson, who tore down the pillars of the Temple of Dagon, killing himself along with several thousand Philistines. The first modern suicide bombing by a terror group occurred in 1951, when a young communist suicide volunteer assassinated French Brigadier General Charles Marie Chanson in Sadec, Indochina, by detonating a grenade in his pocket. The current wave of attacks, however, began with the 1981 suicide truck bombing of the Iraqi embassy in Beirut by a member of al Dawa, which killed sixty-one people and injured more than 100 others. Over the next ten years, suicide bombings gained notoriety, mainly through high profile operations of the Lebanese Hizballah—such as the 1983 synchronized bombings of the U.S. Marine camp and the French troops' barracks in Beirut, or the two attacks against the American embassy in the same city.

The striking effectiveness of the tactic then resulted in its spread across Lebanon, becoming employed by a number of secular pro-Syrian parties, including the Syrian National Party, Lebanese Communist Party, and the Socialist-Nasserist Party.[3] Further, Hizballah also helped to introduce suicide bombings in Israel, when in 1992 it provided training for exiled Hamas militants who later initiated one of the most prolific suicide bombing campaigns to date. Similarly, al Qaeda—who was encouraged to adopt suicide tactics as one of its principal trademarks by the Egyptian Islamic Jihad and the Lebanese Hizballah—later became instrumental in transferring this capability to groups in Pakistan, Afghanistan, Yemen, the Philippines, Saudi Arabia, Turkey, Indonesia, Morocco, Tunisia, Chechnya, and Iraq.

Of all the groups that have used suicide bombings, however, the often-overlooked Liberation Tigers of Tamil Eelam (LTTE) should be recognized

as the true master of the tactic. Not only has LTTE carried out more suicide bombings than all other organizations in the world combined; the
group has also pioneered many new ideas, such as sea-based and air-based
suicide attacks, as well as the concept of a suicide truck convoy. Further,
LTTE has demonstrated an unparalleled level of organizational sophistication and patience, as exemplified by the assassination of President Pre-
madasa, whose assassin first infiltrated the president's household and
became acquainted with the valet before carrying out the act.[4] Similarly,
the terrorist who used a bomb placed on a coconut cart to blow up Sri
Lanka's Independence Memorial Hall building in 1995 had been selling co-
conuts in Colombo for three years prior to the attack. With the peace negotiations currently under way in Sri Lanka, the epicenter of suicide
bombing campaigns (with respect to the frequency of attacks) remains with
groups in Israel and Iraq, while al Qaeda-affiliated groups and the Riyadus-
Salikhin Reconnaissance and Subversion Battalion of Chechen Martyrs
have become the most proficient at the qualitative level. Overall, suicide
bombing is a truly global phenomenon, as reflected in Table 10.1.

Why Terrorist Groups Use Suicide Bombings

Despite the heightened focus on suicide terrorism in the last two decades,
ideologically and religiously motivated suicide is a much older phenomenon. Throughout history, acts of self-killing have been used as a methodi-
cal demonstration of commitment (samurai *seppuku*), as an effective
military tactic (*kamikaze*), as a tool for preventing the possibility of interrogation of spies and assassins (self-poisoning), and as a persuasive form
of protest (self-starvation, self-ignition). What is crucial to realize is that
the power of the modern act of suicide bombing stems from the fact that
it combines all of the above-stated political purposes of suicide into a single
act.

The first obvious benefit of a suicide operation is its tactical advantage
over other forms of attack. A suicide bomber has the ability to deliver the
payload to places that would be difficult to attack successfully for someone hoping to stay alive. The fact that the bomber also has the capability
of selecting the location, time, and exact circumstances of the attack results
in the remarkable effectiveness of suicide attacks, in terms of delivering a
high number of casualties. Suicide attacks are also attractive for terrorist
organizations because they eliminate the need to the plan an escape route,
and they practically remove the danger of capture and subsequent interrogation of the terrorist.[5]

In some cases, this tactic was also used partly because of its cost-
effectiveness. According to a recent invoice from al-Aqsa Martyrs Brigades
found by Israeli troops at the Palestinian Authority's headquarters during
Operation Defensive Shield, the electrical components and chemical sup-

Table 10.1

Suicide Bombings—Group Overview

Name of Group	Time Period	Approximate Count	Countries
Hizballah	1983–1994	25	Lebanon, Argentina, Panama
al Dawa	1981–1985	3	Kuwait, Lebanon
Liberation Tigers of Tamil Eelam (LTTE)	1987–2004	240	Sri Lanka, India
Kurdistan Workers Party (PKK)	1996–1999	15	Turkey
al Qaeda network	1987–2004	18	Kenya, Tanzania, Pakistan, Afghanistan, Yemen, United States, Saudi Arabia, Turkey, Iraq
Lebanese secular groups	mid-1980s	26	Lebanon
Chechen groups	2002–2004	36	Russia
Islamic Resistance Movement (HAMAS)	1994–2004	50	Israel
Palestinian Islamic Jihad	1994–2003	22	Israel
al-Aqsa Martyrs Brigade	2002–2004	22	Israel
Popular Front for the Liberation of Palestine	2002–2004	5	Israel
Egyptian Islamic Jihad	1995	1	Pakistan
Egyptian Islamic Group	1995	1	Croatia
Babbar Khalsa	1995	1	India
Armed Islamic Group	1995	1	Algeria
Jaish-e-Mohammed	2001	2	India
Ansar al Islam, al Tawheed wa' al Jihad + other groups in Iraq	2003–2005	120	Iraq
Revolutionary People's Liberation Party Front	2001–2003	3	Turkey
Tunisian Combatant Group	2002	1	Tunisia
Assirat al Moustaqim	2003	3	Morocco
Jemaah Islamiyah	2002–2004	3	Indonesia
Vietnamese communists	1951	1	Indochina
Islamic Movement of Uzbekistan	2004	2	Uzbekistan

plies needed to produce a suicide bomb were estimated at about $150.[6] The relatively low expenditures involved in the acquisition of explosives make the costs-per-casualty ratio of a suicide operation a rather favorable one. In addition, suicide bombings are extremely difficult to defend against, and elimination of their indiscriminate use is virtually unattainable without extensive suspensions of civil rights, which in turn can have far-reaching secondary effects on the target population. Finally, the universality of the suicide bomber's possible target causes a widespread feeling of uncertainty and vulnerability among the general public. And even if the local population does eventually become desensitized to the idea of being a target, a well-organized terror campaign can still significantly damage a country's attractiveness for international tourism, resulting in economic harm to the local population.

The seeming irrationality and high casualty rate of suicide bombings are also factors responsible for the extensive media coverage these operations attract. The incomprehensible nature of the attack can also have a legitimizing effect on the cause of the terrorists in the eyes of the international community—the organization gains the status of a resolute actor whose grievances cannot be ignored. As people around the world try fruitlessly to comprehend the motivations of such an act, they are left wondering about the systemic foundations of the enormous dedication and hatred demonstrated by the bomber. The group can then gain the image of committed believers who will do anything to reach their goals, also implying that the present environment is so humiliating that death is preferable to life under such conditions.[7]

Suicide operations also convey an important message to an organization's members and supporters. Organizations such as the Kurdistan Workers Party (PKK) or the LTTE, for example, have initially adopted this tactic with the principal goal of solidifying group morale. An act of self-sacrifice in the name of the organization's cause is a uniting factor. Overt praise of the martyr's accomplishment by prominent members of the group can also increase the self-sense of group prestige and can inspire future volunteers. The willingness to die for a cause is sometimes also used as evidence of superiority of the groups' members over their adversaries, who are portrayed as pleasure-seekers and who—in spite of their military dominance—are essentially weak.[8] The resulting perception among the group is that due to superior determination, their final victory is inevitable.

The tactic of suicide bombings can, of course, have negative effects on the goals of an organization as well. The lack of understanding of "martyrdom operations" in the Western culture can cause the group to be viewed as irrational fanatics, drawing the public opinion closer to the adversary. Further, a prolonged suicide terror campaign against civilians is likely to make the target population more radicalized and less willing to compromise. On the other hand, an emotional military overreaction by the attacked government can suit the terrorists' purposes by providing support for their claims of victimization and injustice. It does not matter who started the circle of violence; as long as innocents suffer from the government's counterterrorism efforts (and they always do), the terrorists have a hope of attracting popular support against their adversary. Finally, establishing a cultural norm in which suicide bombers become idols to be followed may have serious consequences on the psychological health of the society for generations to come. Nevertheless, the organizations that use suicide operations today have come to the decision that the benefits of these operations outweigh the costs.

As demonstrated by this overview, any group that can create a culture of martyrdom within its ranks gains a powerful terror potential. In fact, the advantages of the suicide bombing tactic are so great that a number of groups have attempted to reap its specific benefits without necessarily resorting to the act per se. For instance, the IRA has on several occasions extorted individuals to drive trucks packed with explosives via a certain route, later remotely detonating the explosive while the vehicle was passing near the target location. Comparably, terrorists in Chile have trained dogs to carry bombs to targets, while the FARC in Colombia has used horses and donkeys for the same purpose. The FARC have even gone as far as constructing a remote-control system for delivering moving truck bombs without the need to sacrifice living drivers. Similarly, terrorists in Kashmir have experimented with remote controlled model planes and Unmanned Arial Vehicles (UAV) to deliver explosives from the air. Besides the tactical benefits, some groups in Latin America have attempted to reap many of the political benefits of suicide bombings—in terms of evoking images of desperation and ultimate sacrifice—by including terms such as "suicide command" or "suicide squad" into their names.

What Motivates the Suicide Bombers?

What drives people to strap on an explosive belt and kill themselves in a crowd of civilians? Possibly no terrorism-related question has in recent times been asked with greater frequency. The popular attempts to find an answer have unfortunately focused mainly on extreme positions, with one side pointing to poverty and government policies and the other emphasizing irrational religious fanaticism. Clearly, neither of these viewpoints provides an encompassing explanation. For instance, if socioeconomic reasons provide the answer, why is it that with the exception of three isolated incidents in North Africa, we have not witnessed suicide terrorism on the world's most impoverished continent? And on the other hand, if religious fanaticism is the primary motivation for suicide terrorists, why then has the majority of suicide operations been carried out by secular (as opposed to religious) groups? And why have some of the arguably most fanatical believers aggregated in various religious cults never resorted to outwardly directed suicide operations? The following section will explore the scope of personal motivations of individuals who have carried out suicide operations in the past. It needs to be emphasized up front that the majority of suicide bombers are motivated by a combination of factors, and that none of the factors discussed below have by themselves been sufficient to motivate a person to become a *shaheed* (martyr).

Revenge

In the absolute majority of suicide attacks, the bombers are on a quest for personal revenge; their motivation can be directly traced to either an abstract but deeply felt perception of victimization and injustice or, more often, to a specific traumatic event. In the majority of cases, suicide bombers have witnessed the deaths or repeated abuse of their family members, neighbors, or friends, either directly by the hand of the hated enemy or as a result of denied access to basic medical and social services attributed to government policies (such as checkpoints, curfews, and economic sanctions). Some of the female suicide bombers have also experienced more personal humiliation, having lost husbands, children, or brothers in the conflict, or in many cases having experienced sexual abuse by enemy soldiers. Not in all cases, of course, is it possible to speak of direct victimization. In some instances, suicide terrorists have been driven by an abstract, yet highly compassionate and emotional self-identification with the perceived suffering of members of the perpetrator's own ethnic, religious, language, or tribal community. Either way, one critical component of revenge as a motivation is an unconditional attribution of responsibility for ones suffering; without the effective identification of an enemy, suicide bombings simply do not occur.

Hopelessness

Another factor often contributing to the motivation of a suicide bomber is the perception of hopelessness, defined broadly as an absence of vision for a better future. For someone who lives in a refugee camp in the West Bank or the ruins of Grozny, there may be a dominant perception of limited options, making the individual susceptible to the offer of a "glorious way out." Especially in Muslim communities, where suicide (*Intihar*) is forbidden by the Koran so explicitly that it leaves no room for an alternative interpretation (The Holy Koran 4:29), ending one's life by martyrdom and self-sacrifice in the name of Allah (*Istishad*), as opposed to "suicide," is undoubtedly attractive. A similar argument can be made in the case of nonreligious contexts as well, since suicide is frowned upon in most cultures.

The reason why suicide in the context of *Istishad* is religiously permitted or even desirable is that it does not really constitute an act of self-killing, but rather an act of killing others while dying in the process. In other words, even though the death of the *shaheed* during his mission is by design inevitable, it is not the goal of the operation, and therefore the act is not considered an act of suicide—or at least not the kind of hopeless and impatient suicide that the Koran forbids.[9]

As mentioned above, the source of hopelessness is often socioeconomic in nature: unemployment, poverty, or lack of personal freedoms are all factors that play an important role. At the same time, it would not always be correct to point to these factors as the source of hopelessness and frustration. The absolute majority of people who live in extreme poverty never resort to suicide terrorism, while at the same time it is possible to cite examples of suicide bombers who were relatively well-off. In many cases, the pressures creating a lack of hope come not from the side of the enemy, but from within the *shaheed*'s own community. For instance, female PKK members who have left their families to join the revolutionary struggle are seen at home as outcasts, and thus have no real option of being accepted in their biological family ever again.[10] Perhaps it is not surprising, then, that eleven out of the PKK's fifteen successful suicide bombings have been carried out by women. In other cases in Palestine, several suicide bombers have been independent and ambitious young women who were terrified of the idea of being forced to marry and stay at home with the children, as opposed to pursuing higher education and a career. Also, several suicide bombers in Chechnya and Palestine have come from a population of women who had been divorced by their husbands due to their inability to have children, something that has been deeply stigmatized in their respective cultural context.[11] In this scenario, not only do they fail to fulfill what is perceived as their most important biological role, they also end up becoming an economic burden on their own families after moving back to their original homes. And finally, there have been cases of suicide terrorists who volunteered in order to acquit themselves or their families of accusations of cowardice or collaboration with the enemy. In all of the above-cited scenarios, the person's perception of "no way out" has likely aided in their decision to become a *shaheed*.

Fanaticism

While it could be argued that hopelessness and revenge can provide the motivational push for any potential suicide volunteer, it would be difficult to ignore the ethnonationalist or religious dimension and powerful reward mechanisms that have been invented in order to strengthen the resolve of prospective recruits. In the Islamist context, for instance, a system of rewards has been developed to encourage martyrs, which promises the *shaheed* an eternal life in paradise—described as a place with rivers of milk and wine, services of seventy-two young beautiful black-eyed virgins, and the privilege to "reserve a place" in heaven for seventy relatives.[12] For women, then, this dimension has been modified to promise them even greater beauty and the ability to chose among available husbands in paradise. Arguably, the fascination with this reward mechanism by the media has caused an overemphasis on this "religious" dimension of suicide bombings, resulting in a gross simplification of suicide bomber motivations. At the same time, the sexual dimension can be an important component, as there has been at least one reported case of a suicide bomber who was wearing a towel as a loincloth to protect his genitals for use in paradise. For a poor young male from a refugee camp, the hope of getting married—and thus being able to legitimately engage in sexual activities—is very slim. Under such circumstances, the idea of the promised rewards awaiting in paradise undoubtedly has a strong appeal.

Further, in the Palestinian context, one of the incentives for martyrdom volunteers has been the financial rewards of between $12,000 and $20,000 allegedly given to their families in exchange for their sacrifice.[13] Still, it would be a mistake to conclude that Palestinian suicide bombers are motivated by money. The amount that actually reaches the family is much smaller, usually barely enough to pay for the funeral expenses, the rebuilding of the house which will be torn down by the Israelis in the aftermath of the bombing, and to provide a modest compensation for the bomber's perished income. In this sense, the financial rewards act more as a reparation for the adverse consequences of a suicide bomber's involvement, rather than a reward that can provide the volunteer's family with a better standard of living than before the act.

In addition to the above described "heavenly" rewards, some suicide attackers have been motivated by the promise of status of eternal glory and fame for anyone who sacrifices his or her own life for the cause. Most organizations that have used suicide bombers have been careful to preserve their image as heroes and martyrs, in order to inspire future volunteers. For instance, the funeral service for a *shaheed* in Palestine is a wedding-like ceremony, signified by the drinking of sweetened coffee as opposed to bitter coffee, and by the singing of wedding songs.[14] The "heroic" acts of suicide bombers are also eternalized in history through songs, street names, school textbooks, graffiti, posters, trading cards, and other memorabilia. In Sri Lanka, the prestige and glorification of those who sacrifice themselves is preserved by annual celebrations of the "Martyrs Day," along with the building of monuments such as the one in Puthukuthirippu.[15] Creating a glorified culture of martyrdom is critical for sustaining any long-term suicide bombing campaign. Religion can help in this regard—in terms of providing a concrete vision of an afterlife which makes it easier to prepare oneself for death—but the establishment of a "cult of martyrdom," even a secular one, is arguably more important.

In this regard, it is also imperative to make a distinction between motivation and ideology. As mentioned above, the one feature all terrorists (including suicide terrorists) have in common is that they are incredibly frustrated. Such frustration constitutes an unavoidable prerequisite for an individual's turn to extreme religious belief or active involvement in a struggle for national liberation and independence. Hence the "social/nationalist" or "religious" fanaticism cannot be effectively separated from the core grievances and personal motives described earlier. In this sense, religion and ethnonationalism do not constitute an expressive motivation per se, but rather an instrumental vehicle to mobilize, prescribe, and justify acts of violence by the group of frustrated individuals under the umbrella of a "higher truth." This is why personal and political/religious motivations are inseparable—the latter essentially constitutes a more precisely formulated manifestation of the former. In this sense, it would be incorrect to speak about a religious motivation on the part of a suicide bomber who is avenging a death in the family by participating in a religious organization's suicide operation. That is not to say that for many terrorists, religion does not represent a tremendous legitimizing force and that it does not inspire the perception of enormous gratification and empowerment. The point to make is that without frustration caused by personal or systemic grievances—real or perceived—religion by itself does not typically enough provide adequate motivation for suicide bombers.

Manipulation and Extortion

While it has been emphasized earlier in this chapter that the majority of suicide operations have been the result of voluntary and proactive involvement of the bomber, it should be noted that organizations can also exert serious pressure to attract suitable recruits. Considerable recruitment efforts—concentrating on individuals who have been heard bragging about their desire to be the next *shaheed*, people who have recently suffered a personal loss, or individuals who are seen as particularly susceptible to religious justifications—have been undertaken in the past. There is also a small number of suicide bombers belonging to the category of involuntary involvement: people who have been extorted into participation or individuals who were unaware of their death being a part of the operation they agreed to participate in. In Lebanon during the 1980s, for instance, many of the twenty-five suicide bombers deployed by secular pro-Syrian socialist parties were told that they were only transporting the explosives which were then remotely detonated by another operative.[16] In one case, a man also carried out a suicide bombing in order to keep the group quiet about his father's involvement in a car accident.

Comparably, many of the PKK suicide bombers of the 1990s had been handpicked for the "great honor," as opposed to volunteering. In some cases, appointees who turned down the offer to become a suicide bomber were executed in front of the eyes of the next candidate, leaving little choice for them but to agree.[17] Inside terrorist organizations, where being a traitor is worse than being the enemy, making the decision to die a glorious death, rather than being executed as a defector, is an easy choice to make. Finally, in the contemporary wave of suicide bombings in Palestine, several bombers have been extorted into participation by the threat to publicly release the details of their homosexual or extramarital affairs. Nevertheless, while a considerable number of susceptible candidates made their decision to become *shahedeen* under pressure, bombers who were extorted into participation against their will have been few.

Training Suicide Bombers

The process of becoming a suicide bomber differs considerably depending on the given cultural, regional, and ideological context. In addition, *shahedeen* who volunteer for the operation from the outside as nonmembers require a different training approach than experienced operatives who are recruited from within the group's ranks. For instance, most outside volunteers in Palestine initially go through a short testing period, the length of which usually depends on the demonstrated level of natural skill and commitment, as well as on the political urgency of launching an operation. In the first stage, they are asked to give three reasons for why they want to carry out a martyrdom operation. After their motives are analyzed and confirmed, the bombers are asked to prepare a videotape of their last will, which serves as a propaganda and a recruiting tool for the future, as well as an insurance policy against the bomber's possible change of mind. This practice is somewhat unique to the Palestinian context, although all Jemaah Islamiyah suicide bombers in Indonesia have also left behind a written last will.

The actual training then begins with a period of crystallization, in which the candidate is deliberately placed in surprising and even life-threatening situations in order to test his or her reactions and susceptibility to panic. This period is followed by a segment of ideological and religious preparation, in which candidates watch films depicting the life in Palestine before the occupation, as well as propaganda videos showing the brutality of Israeli soldiers and the glory of past martyrs. During this period, the recruit also commonly undergoes religious indoctrination by spending time with clerics and reading certain passages from the Koran over and over again. As a final test, many Palestinian bombers have been ordered to lie in an empty grave for several hours, in order to examine their determination to meet Allah.[18] Only after the training is completed is the bomber introduced to the plan, the explosive device he or she is supposed to detonate, and to the nature of the target. Immediately thereafter, he or she is sent on the mission. In most cases, the bomber is accompanied all the way until the last possible moment by at least one handler, who provides mental support and encouragement, and also serves as indemnity against a possible change of mind.

In Sri Lanka, by contrast, most of the perpetrators of suicide bombing attacks are not outside volunteers but rather experienced members of the group who have already established their credibility. The LTTE even has a permanently attached suicide squad called the Black Tigers, comprised of the most devoted and able volunteers selected out of the group's toughest combat units.[19] Since LTTE members are routinely issued potassium cyanide capsules (to be consumed when on the verge of capture), the preparedness to die at any given moment is a baseline attribute for all potential volunteers. This has been one of the reasons why the LTTE has not had to lead its bombers "by the hand" throughout the entire process, being able to send self-sustaining suicide attackers on long and patient missions without the fear of failure. A similar observation can be made about al Qaeda suicide bombers, most of whom have not required a great deal of indoctrination to participate in a mission; the individuals who have come to al Qaeda training camps in Afghanistan already had to make extensive sacrifices and had to put their lives at risk in order to get there in the first place. This is one of the reasons why the level of commitment and self-control demonstrated by al Qaeda *shahedeen* has in most instances been outstanding, and why their training has usually been concentrated mainly on the practical skills needed for the completion of the mission, such as martial arts, truck driving, operating boats, scuba diving or piloting aircraft.

On the other hand, in Chechnya—where a culture of celebrating martyrdom has yet to be widely established—the training of suicide bombers has allegedly involved substantial recruiting and indoctrination efforts. In the majority of instances, suicide operations have been carried out by the so-called "Black Widows"—women whose husbands or brothers have been killed in Russian military operations. The widows have allegedly been recruited and trained by Lyuba, a mysterious middle-aged woman with a hooked nose and dark hair, popularly known as the "Black Fatima." The training purportedly involves gatherings in auditoriums, where the women repeat a combination of unfamiliar sounds and words in Arabic, while making very rhythmic body motions with the goal of reaching a state of trance.[20] In addition, one intercepted bomber has claimed in an interview that the Black Fatima repeatedly made her drink orange juice that made her dizzy and gave her a headache. Some witnesses have claimed to have seen Chechen bombers, just moments prior to an explosion, walking with their eyes glazed over and talking on a mobile phone. These observations have quickly led to claims of influence of drugs and hypnotic manipulation. However, it needs to be emphasized that the described symptoms are not dissimilar to the "tunnel vision," a term used by Israelis to describe a bombers' facial expression resulting from their extreme focus on the last moments of their lives.

Organizational Motivations

To sum up individual motivations with a generalization, suicide bombers are frustrated and highly motivated individuals who through their act avenge what they perceive as injustices carried out by their enemy. They are also in essence altruistic individuals who make a deliberate decision to make a personal sacrifice for the "greater good" of others. In most cases, the suicide bomber simply does his or her part to damage the enemy, in a belief that this act will contribute to an eventual victory of his compatriots. That being said, "selfish" motives—such as an escape from hopeless situations, postmortem glorification and emulation, and the visions of a comfortable afterlife in paradise—have also played a role. But in order to understand why suicide bombings have occurred in some contexts but not in others, it is particularly useful to focus on organizational motivations, as opposed to the motivations of individuals.

All suicide bombings to date have been a group phenomenon, and there are no known incidents in which the operation has been initiated, organized and executed by an individual. Further, a suicide bombing campaign can become the instrument of choice in virtually any conflict, given that an organization in that context makes such a decision at the strategic level, along with providing a system of rewards or threats to motivate individual volunteers. In contexts where suicide bombings have not yet taken place, their absence can be more accurately explained by the lack of an organizational perception that such operations would be beneficial to the group's cause or image, rather than by the absence of motivation on behalf of potential individual volunteers.

It is important to recognize that an organization's perception can change over time. In the past, we have seen several factors playing a role in the initiation of suicide campaigns by new organizations. The first such factor has been the creation of a precedent, both at the individual and organizational levels. At the individual level, for instance, the LTTE's first suicide operation was initiated in May 1987 by a man known as "Captain Miller," who volunteered to drive an explosives-laden truck into an enemy military camp following unsuccessful attempts to use this technique with the driver jumping out at the last moment.[21] Miller thus set an example of a martyr and a hero to be followed, creating a breeding ground for the world's most violent suicide bombing campaign in history. A similar assertion can be made in the case of Chechnya, where in June 2000, twenty-two-year-old Khava Barayeva (accompanied by a driver) rammed a car bomb into a Russian military facility in the village of Alkhan-Yurt, killing two servicemen.[22] In this instance as well, the precedent quickly set the stage for the upsurge of suicide operations by Chechen groups. And finally, the possibly accidental demise of Wafa Idris[23]—who now bears the title of the first Palestinian female suicide bomber—triggered a wave of female suicide terrorism in the occupied territories, setting a precedent strong enough to overcome even past religious rulings.

Precedents set by allied or rival organizations have prompted the adoption of suicide tactics by other groups. At the level of cooperation, for instance, the December 1981 suicide bombing of the Iraqi embassy in Beirut by the Iraqi Shia group Al Dawa was followed by a wave of such attacks by other Shia groups in Lebanon under the Hizballah umbrella. Similarly, the Hizballah—along with Egyptian groups—contributed their know-how on suicide tactics to the al Qaeda knowledge base, which in turn has been instrumental in the spread of the method to many other countries. And finally, the cult of the "Black Widows" from Chechnya appears to be spilling into Uzbekistan, where in March 2004, two women detonated suicide belts in separate attacks. At the level of competition, the extreme effectiveness of the Hizballah suicide campaign in Lebanon inspired a number of foe organizations in that country to follow suit, even though most of them frequently suffered from a shortage of volunteers and their attempts had a high failure rate. A similar strategic shift toward the use of suicide bombings as a part of organizational competition can be demonstrated by the Palestinian groups, such as the Islamic Jihad (PIJ)—which competed with the Hamas for the position of the leading Islamist group in the territories—and the secular Fatah-affiliated al-Aqsa Martyrs Brigades, whose adoption of suicide bombings in 2002 was driven by the need to counter the monopoly of both of these increasingly popular religious groups. This shift was further reflected by the adoption of suicide operations by other secular groups who in turn compete with Fatah, such as the Popular Front for the Liberation of Palestine and the Democratic Front for the Liberation of Palestine.

As demonstrated by these examples, the contagion of suicide terrorism is in many cases driven by individual precedent-setting sacrifice from within the group and the aid of allied organizations who embrace this tactic, as well as competition with other groups whose political or operational success can be attributed directly to the use of suicide terrorism. It is likely that these processes, as well as the tactical and strategic advantages described in the beginning of this chapter, will contribute to the further spread of suicide terrorism throughout the twenty-first century.

Emerging Trends

Female Suicide Bombers: The Wave of the Future?

As observed in Keith Stanski's chapter of this publication (see Volume I: *Recruitment*), one of the most glaring trends in suicide terrorism has been

the increasing involvement of female bombers. While the first wave of suicide attacks during the 1980s involved only five women, the LTTE and the
PKK made the use of female bombers a norm during the 1990s, having incorporated them into 40 percent and 65 percent of their suicide operations,
respectively.[24] The beginning of the twenty-first century has been marked
by the emergence of female suicide bombers in additional theaters, including Chechnya, Palestine, and Uzbekistan. There are a number of reasons
why female suicide bombers are an attractive proposition. First, there are
the tactical advantages associated with the disruption of an established profile used by security and law enforcement agencies, as well as the possibility of concealing the explosive device in a fake belly (utilizing the women's
ability to appear pregnant). Another advantage to a group's decision to use
female operatives has been the strong message such a move sends to followers and supporters, triggering a guilt trip among men that they are not
doing enough to fight the enemy and strengthening the pressure to do more.

Female suicide terrorism also has several distinct motivational and operational characteristics. In essence, a woman's motivational route to resort to terrorism is a much longer one than for a man, of whom armed
resistance is expected if not required. Women essentially become involved
as a product of their own decision, often after experiencing a very direct
victimization, as opposed to idealistically following abstract ideological or
religious themes. This is one of the reasons why they are frequently looked
down upon by the male members of the group—especially in Islamist organizations, where additional dilemmas associated with the fundamentalist interpretation of the Koran play a role, such as the restrictions
preventing women from operating freely outside of their homes without
being accompanied by a male relative. Further, there has been a considerable stigma regarding the reliability and determination of women because
of their perceived softness due to motherly instincts. However, women terrorists in general actually tend to be more ruthless precisely because of these
instincts; once they decide that their violent actions will benefit their children and future generations, they will not hesitate to do what they feel is
necessary for the success of the operation. Further, as experience tells us
from left-wing and ethnonationalist organizations' involvement of female
operatives, the desire to prove that they are just as worthy to the organization as men has worked to strengthen their sacrificial resolve even
more.

A particularly important question to ask is why al Qaeda has yet to use
female operatives. One explanation may be associated with ideology: Islamist organizations in general have been rather slow to overcome their
own ideological restraints on using female operatives, and it is crucially important to understand the respective contexts in which this shift has taken
place. In Palestine, the driving force behind deployment of women by PIJ
and Hamas has been the political and operational success of the al-Fatah

controlled al-Aqsa Martyrs Brigades, which started using female suicide bombers in January 2002. Until this point, it had been the Hamas and the PIJ who held the monopoly on martyrdom operations as a symbolic act of anti-Israeli resistance. Al-Aqsa Martyrs' adoption of women suicide bombers not only disrupted this monopoly, but also went further in capturing tremendous media attention and increased funding, especially from the Gulf countries. PIJ and Hamas were then forced to followed suit, in order to remain competitive in their quest to become a viable alternative to the Fatah.

From these and other examples, it seems clear that a few Islamist organizations have shown a sufficient level of flexibility (with regards to violating their own belief systems) in order to succeed operationally. Interestingly, al Qaeda has been the most flexible in this regard, having encouraged its members to shave their beards, wear Western clothes, avoid usual prayer times and locations, drink alcohol, and even spend time with questionable women in order to preserve their plausibility in the land of the enemy. This suggests that we can expect al Qaeda to resort to the use of female suicide bombers at some point in the future, coinciding with the perceived need to introduce another element of surprise.

Tactical Trends

From a tactical perspective, suicide bombings have recently witnessed a number of important trends. First has been the increasing internationalization of the phenomenon, not just in the sense that the tactic has spread to new countries, but also in the sense that terrorist organizations have demonstrated an increasing ability to mount suicide operations outside of their common area of operation. Examples include the operations by Hizballah in Argentina and Panama, the LTTE in India, the Egyptian groups in Pakistan and Croatia, the Chechen groups in the Russian capital, and al Qaeda in a variety of countries on four continents. The second disturbing trend has been the increasing synchronization of suicide bombings, with the clear intention of causing as many casualties as possible. In some instances, suicide bombings have involved secondary and even tertiary devices, the detonation of which incorporated a calculated delay in order to target first-responders and crowds of onlookers. Another recent innovation has been the addition of chemical materials into the explosive devices seen in Israel, where traces of pesticide and even cyanide have been detected on the remains of at least six bombs used in Hamas suicide attacks. In addition, attacks against hard targets such as embassies have recently seen the introduction of suicide truck convoys, which include suicide shooters or bombers whose role is to clear the way for the suicide truck in order to facilitate the explosion of the primary device as close to the target as possible. As a part of this tactic, terrorists have also recently begun using additional bombers in the suicide truck in order to insure that the explosive is detonated, even in the event of the driver being killed by the security guards during the assault. Similarly, the detonation of bombs carried by suicide bombers on foot has increasingly been insured by the inclusion of a remote detonation mechanism, typically two mobile phones. Overall, worldwide suicide bombings have shown an increasing level of organization, planning, patience, synchronized execution, and lethality.

Future Outlook

Suicide bombings represent the ultimate terrorist tactic. Besides their tactical advantages, they also have the capability of satisfying many terrorist objectives in a single attack: demonstration of dedication and capability, attracting attention and media coverage, producing a high number of casualties, and instigating general feelings of vulnerability. Finding recruits for suicide missions is never difficult once a precedent has been established. Suicide attacks can be justified on any religious or ideological grounds in the appropriate historical and cultural context. It is therefore very likely that the use of this tactic will become increasingly frequent in areas where it has already been established, and will be introduced to many other struggles around the world.

At the tactical level, several important scenarios for suicide operations are of particular concern. The first such scenario involves air-based suicide operations involving the flying of aircraft into buildings in order to cause destruction. This tactic, of course, achieved notoriety only after 9/11, but it must be emphasized that while the execution and planning in this case was superb, the idea itself is far from new. Between 1976 and 2001, the plan of flying airplanes into buildings had been cited on at least twenty-two occasions, with two successful incidents actually having materialized (see Table 10.2).

The first of these was a 1976 incident in which a Japanese porn actor crashed his Piper Cherokee into the home of Yoshio Kodama, a rightist leader accused of accepting payoffs from the Lockheed Aircraft Corporation. The pilot wore a kamikaze pilot's headband and shouted the ritual cry over the radio just prior to crashing into his target.[25] The second instance occurred in the United States in 1994, when a heavily intoxicated and drugged suicidal individual crashed a stolen single-engine Cessna 150 onto the South Lawn at the rear of the West Wing of the White House.

A less-frequent means of airborne suicide operations has included suicide bombers on board of civilian aircraft. For example, in 1986 four members of the Abu Nidal terrorist group hijacked Pan Am flight 73 en route from Karachi, with the intention of blowing up the plane over downtown Tel Aviv. In December 1994, Air France flight 8969 from Algiers, Algeria

Table 10.2

Terrorist Incidents Involving the Crashing of Airplanes into Targets

Year	Incident Summary
1945	During World War II, over 4,600 Japanese men die by crashing airplanes into enemy targets.
1973	After shooting down Libyan Boeing 727, the Israelis claim that numerous threats had been made by Black September terrorists to hijack an airliner and crash it into Tel Aviv.
1975	Attempt to seize an aircraft by an individual in the United States, who later claims that he intended to crash an aircraft into a terminal tower as a protest against abortion.
1976	A young star of pornographic films crashes his Piper Cherokee into the home of Yoshio Kodama, a rightist leader accused of accepting payoffs from the Lockheed Aircraft Corporation. The pilot wore a kamikaze pilot's headband and shouted their cry over the radio just prior to crashing into his target.
1984	After intelligence agencies detect the suspicious movement of light planes and helicopters in Iran, Syria, and Lebanon, the Pentagon, fearing kamikaze-type attacks, ships Stinger missiles to U.S. Navy ships in the region.
1984	Interpol reports that an Iranian suicide squad was planning to fly an explosive-laden small airplane into the U.S. embassy in Cyprus. Antiaircraft weapons were installed on the embassy's roof.
1984	The CIA reportedly warns the Reagan administration of a kamikaze-style attack against a U.S. target in the Middle East.
1985	During negotiations, a Lebanese hijacker threatens to crash the plane into the presidential palace in Beirut.
1985	The media in Cyprus report an "unconfirmed rumor" that kamikaze-style attacks are planned for U.S. and Israeli embassies.
1985	Following the Abu Nidal shooting sprees at Vienna and Rome airports, Austrian government reported that the terrorists intended to hijack an El-Al airliner and crash it into Tel Aviv.
1986	The hijackers of Pan American World Airways flight 73 in Karachi confessed that they had plans to blow up the aircraft over an Israeli city, following the completion of the demanded prisoner exchange.
1986	Columnists in the United States report the training of kamikaze pilots in Iran to hit U.S. targets.

Table 10.2 (continued)

Year	Incident Summary
1986	One of the 21 Libyan students being deported from the United Kingdom is found to be a pilot trainee who vowed to carry out a kamikaze raid on U.S. installations.
1988	Brazilian police spokesman announces that during a recent hijacking, the hijacker planned to crash the plane into building in Brasilia.
1989	*The Washington Post* reports that it had received "credible warnings" that Iranian-trained kamikaze terrorists may be planning to dive an explosives-rigged plane into the White House.
1990	Hamburg police report that "the Palestinian Liberation Front of Abu Abbas is preparing an attack with light aircraft."
1994	A heavily intoxicated and drugged suicidal individual crashes a stolen single-engine Cessna 150 onto the South Lawn at the rear of the West Wing of the White House.
1994	After four Algerian Islamic extremists disguised as maintenance men hijack an Air France Airbus 300 jumbo jet on the ground, the authorities received two anonymous tips indicating that the hijackers planned to blow up the plane over Paris. The suicide story was supported by the hijackers' demand to fill the gas tanks of the plane with far more than was needed for the Marseille-Paris flight. Authorities also found 20 sticks of dynamite in the plane.
1995	Philippine police announce that Ramzi Yousef had planned to crash-dive a bomb-laden plane into the headquarters of the United States Central Intelligence Agency in Langley, Virginia. The CIA attack was to be carried out by Saeed Akhman, a Yousef associate.
1998	The Turkish government detains 23 militant Muslims who planned to crash an explosives-laden plane into the Ankara mausoleum of Mustafa Kemal Ataturk, the founder of the state. The suicide attack was planned for the 75th anniversary of the republic.
1999	Mas Selamat Kastari plans to hijack an Aeroflot from Bangkok and to crash it into the terminal tower at Changi airport in Singapore.
2001	Three hijacked airliners crash into both World Trade Center towers and the Pentagon; a fourth crashes in Pennsylvania after passengers stormed the cockpit in an effort to retake the airplane from the hijackers.

(bound for Paris) was seized by four members of the Armed Islamic Group (GIA) during take-off preparations; three passengers were killed before the plane lifted off from Houari Boumedienne Airport. After some negotiations with the terrorists, the flight was allowed to land in Marseilles in order to refuel. The authorities noticed that the plane took on three times the amount of fuel needed, and two anonymous tips revealed that the terrorists' intention was to use the plane as a missile to attack downtown Paris. As a result, a special operations team of the French military stormed the aircraft in Marseille and killed the hijackers. Other cases include the 1994 Ansar Allah attack on a twin-engine plane in Panama, and the infamous attempt in 2001 where passenger Richard Reid attempted to ignite explosives hidden in his shoe. Most recently, on 24 August 2004, two Russian civilian aircraft on domestic flights originating from Moscow crashed within minutes of each other, apparently after female suicide bombers had detonated explosives on board. Clearly, aviation security has now become a critical focus of attention for countries worldwide.

Another source of concern for the future is the possibility of the use of *shahedeen* for delivering chemical and biological agents. A successful delivery of these agents would certainly be more feasible if the perpetrator were indifferent to staying alive. In addition to greater access to the target and enhanced control over the outcome, elimination of protective measures during the attack—such as gas masks, HAZMAT gear, or antiradiation shields—decreases the risk of an early detection and obviation of the attack.[26] Of particular concern should be the possibility of the use of chemical or biological weapons by suicide attackers on board of airplanes in midcourse flight, considering the fact that contemporary airport security measures are not designed to meet this threat. Further, the bodies of terrorists themselves could also be used as crude delivery systems, if the perpetrators are infected with a contagious agent and sent to crowded areas. On the other hand, despite the common tendency to label suicide attacks as irrational, organizations that have perfected this tactic have demonstrated a great level of rationality, patience, and calculation in their attacks. The potential of an uncontrollable spread of the disease by secondary transmission beyond the population that was the intended target of the operation in the event of attacking with contagious agents would be inconsistent with the targeting logic of most groups that have utilized suicide bombers in the past.[27] This does not mean, however, that the possibility of a biological suicide bomber can be discarded completely.

CHAPTER 11

The Terrorist Training Camps of al Qaeda

ROHAN GUNARATNA AND ARABINDA ACHARYA

Two of the main distinguishing characteristics of "New Terrorism" (as compared to its Cold War–era variant) have been the degree of its lethality and persistence. Many of the post–September 11 terrorist attacks— whether targeted against U.S. interests, the interests of its allies (e.g., attacks in Indonesia, Pakistan, or Spain), against Jews (as in Turkey, Morocco), or against Muslims themselves in countries such as Saudi Arabia, Turkey, Tunisia—bear the hallmark of al Qaeda but were perpetrated by many local groups, even new ones, claiming identity of purpose with bin Laden's global jihad. Further, after the U.S. operations began in Iraq in 2003, the threats from terrorism became manifested in newer forms including suicide bombings against a wide spectrum of targets, hostage taking, and the brutal beheadings of hostages in Iraq. Importantly, the terrorist threat seems to have shifted from specific groups to a cadre of highly motivated and resourceful individuals (e.g., Abu Musab al-Zarqawi in Iraq). The significance of emerging trends must be understood within the context that al Qaeda suffered significant attrition in the post–September 11 period in terms of the disruption of its base and training infrastructures, the capture and killing of many of its key leaders, and the restrictions on access to its finances. According to one estimate, about 3,200 out of nearly 4,000 core al Qaeda cadre have been effectively neutralized in the ongoing "War on Terror."[1] However, the terrorist threat remains unabated and is becoming rather more worrisome because of its wider spread and newer manifestations. This chapter will explore the role of training—particularly the training camps established by al Qaeda—in facilitating the spread of the global terrorist threat.

Students and Graduates of Terror Training

While ideology drives the motive of the new terrorists, the high degree of sophistication and professionalism witnessed today in terrorist attacks have been a result of the quality of training and levels of indoctrination. Access to training and weaponry is a significant determinant for the threat projection capability of terrorist groups. Training infrastructure has always been an essential ingredient of terrorist organizations, providing its cadre with capability for armament use and much-needed indoctrination to sustain the ideology that drives the group's members to action. In the lexicon of "new terrorism," religious indoctrination is considered far more important than battlefield or combat training. The focus of al Qaeda's training infrastructure was more on religious indoctrination, for instance, most of the terrorists involved in the September 11 attacks did not undergo extensive military training. Rather, their psychological conditioning and willingness to die for Allah were considered to be the operational priorities.[2] Most of them lived in the United States for over one year without any change in their commitment and mindset, and even though Zacarias Moussaoui, one of the would-be hijackers, was arrested three weeks before September 11, he did not divulge the plans of his organization nor the identity and location of other al Qaeda members in the United States.[3] This was because of their firm belief in (and commitment to) al Qaeda's ideology, inculcated through Osama's special brand of indoctrination.

Similarly, al-'Owhali, the man convicted in the Nairobi embassy bombings, told the FBI after his arrest that he had learned the basics of terrorism at the al Qaeda training camp at Khaldan, where he received military training in light weapons, and, most importantly, had periods of religious instruction—including from bin Laden—which "further solidified his religious feelings."[4] Ahmed Sayeed Omar Sheikh, the man convicted for the kidnapping and killing of American journalist Daniel Pearl in Pakistan, told his interrogators that he received extensive training in urban warfare, use of assault rifles, light machine guns, rocket launchers, night movement, raids and ambushes (including courses on surveillance and countersurveillance), the art of disguise, interrogation, cell structure, cryptology, and codes—all of which took place at a camp in Afghanistan manned by Harakat-ul-Mujahidin and visiting al Qaeda instructors. Letters recovered by U.S. forces from the deserted Khaldan camp in Afghanistan where the September 11 hijackers were trained showed that the hundreds of men who passed through the training camps were angry, motivated, and full of ideas for waging a violent jihad against the West.

All senior al Qaeda functionaries—Mohammed Atta, Ramzi bin al-Shibh, Khalid Shaikh Muhammed, Abu Zubaydah—have trained or received training in al Qaeda training camps. Sahim Alwan, one of six al Qaeda terrorists arrested in Buffalo, New York, received military training at an al Qaeda terrorist training camp in Afghanistan. Many of the Chechen, Taliban, and al Qaeda fighters were trained at a remote wilderness camp in the mountains outside Kandahar.[5] Two senior terrorist figures, Abu Musab al-Zarqawi and Abu Khabab, helped train the people suspected of planning chemical and biological attacks in France and the United Kingdom in early 2003. Abu Khabab's voice has been identified by intelligence sources as the narrator on a videotape showing al Qaeda operatives performing chemical weapons experiments on dogs. He ran the group's chemical and biological weapons testing facility at the Darunta complex near the eastern Afghan city of Jalalabad. Both al-Zarqawi and Abu Khabab also trained at camps in the Caucasus region, particularly the Pankisi Gorge of Georgia and in nearby Chechnya.[6]

Menad Benchellali, arrested by the French in December 2002 in connection with an alleged plot to bomb the Russian Embassy in Paris with conventional explosives, was found to be an expert chemist who was manufacturing ricin in a makeshift laboratory in his parents' spare bedroom in the suburbs of Paris. Benchellali also received advanced training at the Derunta camp. Among the camp's instructors were Yazid Sufaat, a U.S.-trained biochemist who is now in custody in Malaysia, and an unnamed Pakistani microbiologist.[7] One of seven men arrested in London in a ricin poison investigation in January 2003 was also a product of al Qaeda terrorist camps in Afghanistan. Numerous references to making ricin were found in documents produced by the al Qaeda terrorist network. References to ricin were part of the group's training course and in a manual that was spread worldwide.[8]

Some of the Jemaah Islamiyah (JI) members arrested in Singapore in December 2001 had received training at al Qaeda camps in Afghanistan and at Camp Abu Bakar, a Moro Islamic Liberation Front (MILF) training facility which al Qaeda helped establish in Mindanao, Philippines. Seven Westerners were among fifty Indonesians, one of them possibly Australian taxi driver Jack Thomas, arrested in Pakistan on 4 January 2003 who had attended training camps organized and funded by al Qaeda in 2001 on the central Indonesian island of Sulawesi. Singaporean Muhammad Amin Bin Mohamed Yunos, one of several JI members of a group that officials from Malaysia, Indonesia, and Singapore arrested in 2003 (part of the Karachi, Pakistan–based cell code-named "al-Ghuraba" or "foreigners"), also visited the southern Afghan city of Kandahar for full-time military training provided by the al Qaeda network.[9]

A particular type of individual was typically drawn to one of the al Qaeda training camps, as demonstrated by a document found at the Darunta camp complex in Afghanistan. Damir Bajrami, a twenty-four-year-old ethnic Albanian from Kosovo wrote, on his entry application in April 2001, "I am interested in suicide operations. I have Kosovo Liberation Army combat experience against Serb and American forces. I need no further training. I recommend (suicide) operations against (amusement) parks like Disney."[10] Once an individual like Bajrami arrived at a camp seeking terrorist training, he was directed into one of several kinds of training programs, according to his skills and potential for operational effectiveness.

The Curriculum of Terrorist Training

The training needs for various terrorist groups vary according to the nature and the character of the groups. The terrorist groups understand that there can be huge variations in training, especially military training, and a "one size fits all" concept will not suffice. Broadly, training encompasses two areas, physical and ideological. Military- or paramilitary-style training imbues the cadre with a pragmatic approach, with common sense, and with a respect for hierarchy, and readies the trainee for fulfilling a directly assigned mission. Members of terrorist groups receive physical training based on the operational objectives of the groups' leaders. Groups like the LTTE in Sri Lanka—pitted against the regular Sri Lankan armed forces, which have structured training programs and modern armaments—need to train their members to acquire military-style capabilities, through combat drills and courses on endurance and survival techniques. Certain other groups engage in guerrilla operations and emphasize ambush, hit-and-run techniques. Groups that target civilians need expertise in bombing techniques along with skills in disguise and deception. Most groups, however, seek to develop a range of skills, including techniques required to carry out suicide attacks. For example, recruits trained to attack unarmed civilians/noncombatants also need to learn how to engage the security forces if and when confronted.[11]

The duration of the training also varies according to the level of sophistication, available opportunities, and mission objectives of the groups. For instance, groups in the occupied territories in the Middle East lack opportunity for extended periods of training. Further, groups such as Hamas or Palestine Islamic Jihad have adopted the tactic of suicide attacks, in which case the execution phase is relatively short. For these reasons, most of their cadre receive just a few days training before launching their missions. In contrast, Chechen militants tasked to attack targets in Moscow require training for extended periods of time, in order to sustain their operational effectiveness against numerous challenges likely to be confronted in such long-range, deep penetration missions. Without proper training, such missions could result in demoralization and desertion as well as injury and death.[12] The attacks of the type witnessed in Ingushetia (in June 2004) warrant considerably more advanced military training for the Chechen groups than needed by most other groups. The Chechen groups also regularly engage the Russians in paramilitary/guerilla-style operations.

For significantly complex missions, such as the September 11 attacks, recruits require training at various levels of capability, sophistication, and a much longer duration. In such cases the training is mission-specific (also known as "model training"), involving, for example, training to navigate commercial aircraft (as needed by the September 11 terrorists), to drive vehicles (as was the case for operatives tasked to bomb the U.S. Embassies in Africa in August 1998), and to pilot boats (as needed by suicide terrorists who attacked USS *Sullivan* in January and USS *Cole* in December 2000 with explosive-laden boats. Model training helps the operatives acquire stealth, speed, and surprise.[13] It also prepares the cadre for mass casualty attacks, at times even involving chemical, biological, radiological, and nuclear (CBRN) weapons.

For many terrorist groups, the moral/spiritual training has been far more important than physical training. However, the levels of ideological indoctrination also differ from one group to another. Groups militating against the oppression of ethnic minorities, sometimes called ethnonationalists, would require their members to empathize fully with the suffering of their ethnic brethren, embrace the image of the oppressor as subhuman, evil, and destructive, and demonstrate a complete commitment to a sustained terrorist campaign, even at great risks to their own life, in order to ensure the safety and stability of their future generations.[14] Islamist groups—such as those in Palestine, Algeria, Kashmir, Bosnia, Chechnya, Afghanistan, and in Southeast Asia—call upon their fellow Muslims to wage jihad as a religious duty, pledge allegiance exclusively to Allah, and work to establish the Caliphate based on the principles of the Koran and Sunnah. Here, the use of violence and killing of civilians are considered part of the strategy and hence religiously sanctioned. The groups and their ideologues encourage their members to believe that they are fighting on behalf of Islam against the enemies of God, epitomized by Western civilization, and especially the United States—the "Hubal of this age" and literally "Satanic," being in league with the Devil.[15] The goals they pursue are considered higher than life itself and are propelled by a vision that treats Islam as the answer to every conceivable problem.[16] This primes the group's members for mass casualty attacks with catastrophic consequences. The members are led to believe that if they sacrifice their life in jihad, they will be rewarded in heaven.

The curriculum in the training camps varies according to the missions intended. The standard courses are basic (guerilla warfare and Islamic law), advanced (use of explosives, assassination techniques and heavy weapons), and specialized (surveillance and countersurveillance, forging and adapting identity documents, and conducting maritime or vehicle-borne suicide operations).[17] While the curriculum plays an important role in terrorist training camps, perhaps no element is more important than that of the teacher—the knowledge experts who are entrusted by the terrorist groups' leaders to train (and evaluate the learning of) new recruits.

The Role of Experts in Teaching Terrorism

In recent years, training infrastructures and content have become increasingly sophisticated. During the Cold War era, the superpowers at both ends of the ideological divide sponsored many terrorist groups to checkmate each other. These state sponsors provided training to a number of terrorist and guerrilla groups. Nevertheless, they controlled the level of training, access to weaponry, and targeting to keep the threat projection capability of the groups within manageable limits. Today, terrorist groups have access to the same level of training available to security forces personnel. This was facilitated by several factors. The U.S. and allied sponsorship of anti-Soviet *mujahideen* groups included the provision of field manuals reserved for the U.S. military and special forces. For example, in the New Jersey home of Sayeed Nosair, the FBI recovered secret U.S. military manuals originating from the J. F. Kennedy Center for Special Warfare in Fort Bragg, North Carolina.[18] The *Declaration of Jihad against the Country's Tyrants (Military Series)*, the manual that al Qaeda used extensively in its training camps, draws heavily from U.S., British, and other field manuals.[19]

Several former security forces personnel from Egypt, Algeria, and the United States participated in both the anti-Soviet campaign and the subsequent global jihad campaigns that took place during the 1990s. For example, an Egyptian Captain Ali Mohammad, who later joined the U.S. Special Forces as a Sergeant, served as al Qaeda's principal military instructor in Afghanistan, Sudan, Somalia, and Bosnia, and also trained Osama bin Laden's bodyguard contingent.[20] Conversely, many former military and security forces personnel also joined terrorist groups and transferred their acquired knowledge and expertise to other members of the group. For instance, Ahmad Jabril—the leader of the Popular Front for the Liberation of Palestine-General Command (PFLP-GC)—is a former Captain in the Syrian army; Namangani, the founding leader of the Islamic Movement of Uzbekistan, was a former Soviet paratrooper; and Said Bahaji, a member of an al Qaeda cell in Germany, was a former soldier in the *Bundeswehr*. Similarly, the two al Qaeda military commanders Muhammed Atef and Abu Ubadiah al-Banshiri had served in the Egyptian police and the army.[21] Certain intelligence agencies of governments provided (and continue to provide) access to high-quality training—reserved for professional militaries—to foreign terrorist groups, as is the case with Iran's Revolutionary Guards training Hizballah.[22] Similarly, while Omar Sheikh was in Indian custody (prior to his release in December 2000) following the hijacking of the Indian Airlines Flight to Kandahar, he told his Indian interrogators that he had received training from serving members of the Special Services Group of (SSG) of Pakistan.[23]

Other factors contributing to the sophistication of terrorist training have been the privatization of security, proliferation of security companies, and former security forces personnel willing to serve as both trainers and mercenaries (especially at the end of the Cold War). For example, when the Sri Lankan government purchased Medium Landing Craft (LCMs) the LTTE clandestinely hired experts from Swan Hunter, the manufacturer of the LCMs, to understand the vulnerabilities and limitations of LCMs.[24] The use of private security agencies, whose members primarily comprise former security forces personnel, appears to be a growing trend in recent years. For instance, in Iraq nearly 10,000 men and women now perform various jobs under contract to the U.S. military. Even Paul Bremer, America's former civilian administration chief in Iraq, was protected by a private company rather than ordinary U.S. troops. This is an alarming development, especially as governments have little control over those hired. A few people with extensive criminal records have appeared in Iraq under various guises,[25] and it is possible that private sector expertise can also be harnessed by modern terrorist groups such as al Qaeda.

Another area of concern is the ease at which knowledge can be disseminated using modern information technology. There are innumerable instances of various terrorist groups using the Internet as a medium of training and indoctrination.[26] Al Qaeda is known for its extensive use of multimedia means: dramatically choreographed and staged dissemination opportunities and other mass outreach techniques through the Internet and mass distribution of prerecorded videos and audio tapes. In *The Shadow of the Lances*, a series of statements attributed to al Qaeda, Saif al-Adel (one of the group's senior commanders and a former Egyptian Army Special Forces officer) detailed the use of guerrilla warfare tactics against the American and British forces in Iraq.[27] We are now witnessing the manifestation of such tactics in a very lethal manner in Iraq. Many terrorist training manuals, including the ones with instructions for making of chemical and biological weapons and radiological devices, are easily available online. Using widely available technologies for effective, quick and secure communication, propaganda, and instructions, groups like al Qaeda have made terrorism more accessible. This Internet-based "distance learning" is also becoming crucial in building a shared understanding among the cadre.

All terrorist organizations must invest time and effort to refine and transfer operational knowledge, that which provides strategic and tactical capabilities, to new recruits. To this end, al Qaeda developed and used several widely-disseminated training manuals.

- *The Encyclopedia of Afghan Jihad* (7000 pages) covers a wide range of topics such as terrorist tactics, lessons on security and intelligence, topography and land survey, use of handguns, first aid, explosives, grenades and mines, tanks, etc. It is meant to train a new generation of recruits in guerrilla warfare and terrorism, and was compiled, written, translated, and edited over a period of five years by the Egyptian and Saudi elements of al Qaeda. Much of its contents were culled from U.S. and British military manuals.

- *The Declaration of Jihad against the Country's Tyrants (Military Series)* is meant exclusively for terrorist operations. Its eighteen lessons include (among others) how to counterfeit currency and forge documents, the proper organization of military bases, concealment, means of communication and transportation, espionage, and assassination techniques using poisons and cold steel.

- *The al Qaeda Training Manual*, by Dr. Ayman Al-Zawahiri, is a compilation of material drawn from various military, intelligence, and law enforcement manuals for internal security, guerilla, and covert operations.[28]

In many cases, the manuals were adopted to suit the requirements of the particular theater of conflict. For instance, when the Arab trainers who fought in Afghanistan went to Bosnia, they wrote a manual especially for the Bosnian *mujahideen*.[29]

Many recruits also bring special skills they have learned while serving in the regular military or police. Some groups, such as al Qaeda, even encourage their potential recruits to join security forces for the specific purpose of inculcating military, intelligence, and police training. Many of these recruits work in government or private research laboratories and develop specialized skills, including the manufacture and use of chemical and biological weapons.

Al Qaeda's success in conducting well-coordinated guerilla and terrorist attacks has largely been a product of its stringent emphasis on training and retraining.[30] Most of the old and new terror organizations, especially the ones that have waged war against governments and the security and military forces with separatist and or irredentist objectives, used to have some rudiments of training infrastructure to equip their members with necessary skills to carry out attacks against targets in both urban and rural/jungle environments. All this was changed significantly by bin Laden and the al Qaeda network, which transformed the training concepts into something akin to a "terrorist university" unlike any previously seen.

Most of the network's training facilities were in Afghanistan. Al Qaeda was able to set up elaborate training facilities there because of a historically unique set of factors: chaos in Afghanistan; the weakness of its neighbors, especially Pakistan; the emergence of a new, violent ideology with powerful backers in the Middle East—all compounded by a profound lack of interest in the region on the part of Western powers.[31] In subsequent years, al Qaeda was able to rope in various separatist Islamic groups all over the world, especially in Central and Southeast Asia, to establish training facilities within the existing infrastructure of such groups.

Al Qaeda's Training Facilities in Afghanistan

Prior to October 2001, Afghanistan hosted any number of terrorist training camps run, financed, and used by many groups including al Qaeda. The governing Taliban militia had its own training facilities, as did groups like Harkat-ul-Mujahideen, a group fighting for the independence of Kashmir from Indian rule. Most of the camps were set up on sites built by Soviet forces during their occupation of Afghanistan during the 1980s. While scores of young and zealous Muslims graduated from camps run by al Qaeda, only a few thousand—the best of the best, with specialized language, technical skills, and training and assessed rigorously in terms of commitment and dedication—were invited to join al Qaeda itself.[32]

The most important facilities in Afghanistan were the Darunta Complex, housing camps Abu Khabab, Assadalah Abdul Rahman, Hizbi Islami, and the Taliban area near Jalalabad; Camp Farouk at Garmabak Ghar in southeastern Afghanistan near Kandahar; Khaldan at Rishkhor; camp al Sadik; camp Mis Ainac; a camp at Farm Hadda; and the Zawar Kili complex in eastern Afghanistan, southwest of Khowst (the jihad camp).

Darunta

The Darunta complex near the eastern Afghan city of Jalalabad was one of about thirty secret, camouflaged bases set up by bin Laden. The quarter-square-mile terror complex built near Darunta lake dam included:

- the Abu Khabab camp, al Qaeda's chemical-warfare training site;
- the Assadalah Abdul Rahman camp, operated by the son of blind cleric Omar Abdel Rahman, who is jailed in the United States for plotting to blow up the World Trade Center in 1993;
- the Taliban area, run by the religious militia that controlled most of the country, used mostly to house government officials; and
- the Hizbi Islami Camp, operated by a group of Pakistani extremists fighting in Kashmir in India.

Darunta had a network of at least fourteen tunnels that was considered the key to the entire complex. Tunnels were to provide for physical protection from air attacks. They also facilitated the stockpiling of weapons and equipment, as well as training in secrecy. The complex had its own helipad and was surrounded by observation posts and checkpoints on the roads and an elaborate defensive trench network.

The camp Abu Khabab was al Qaeda's secret toxins and explosives laboratory dedicated to the development of (and training with) chemicals, poisons, and other toxins. This camp was named after the sixty-year-old Egyptian chemicals expert who managed it, Midhat Mursi (using the name

Abu Khabab). The camp consisted of three small rooms, the largest of which was the laboratory where Abu Khabab worked. After the camp was abandoned, the makeshift laboratory was found to be packed with chemicals of various types—sulphuric and nitric acid, acetone, and bottles of poisons, including cyanide—along with bomb instruction manuals and documents specifying international money transfers. There was also a thick pile of English-language instruction manuals on chemicals, bomb making, and guerrilla warfare, and instructions on making detonators (including radio detonators) and using household chemicals to make deadly explosives. One of the manuals was titled *Middle Eastern Terrorist-Bomb Designs* and another *Advanced Techniques for Making Explosives and Time-Delay Bombs.*[33] There were also eighty-four pages of bomb-building techniques, involving dynamite and C3 and C4 plastic explosives, that appeared to have been downloaded from the Internet. There was an eighteen-chapter, 179-page training book written by al Qaeda operatives, containing pages identifying "buildings, bridges, embassies, schools, (and) amusement parks" as targets for destruction in the West. There was also some discussion about the destructive potential of "atomic explosions."[34]

From the tapes obtained by CNN, it was revealed that al Qaeda was experimenting with lethal chemicals at the Abu Khabab facility in the Darunta complex. These tapes also revealed images of chemical gas experiments on dogs, lessons on making explosives, and other terrorist training tactics. The chemical tests on the dogs suggested a very strong desire to acquire the capability to use such weapons against human targets.[35] A booklet recovered from the camp, written by Abu Khabab and dedicated to Osama ("our great leader"), talks about chemical, biological, and nuclear (CBN) warfare and how best to protect oneself against chemical weapons, ways to detect a chemical agent and ways to purge chemicals.[36]

Graduates of Darunta included former Boston taxi driver Raed Hijazi, the alleged ringleader in a plot to attack tourist and religious sites in Jordan. Authorities have linked him to some of the terrorists involved in the September 11 World Trade Center and Pentagon attacks. Also trained at Darunta was Ahmed Ressam[37] convicted for his role in a plot to blow up Los Angeles International Airport during the millennium celebrations. During his trial, Ressam described his seven months of training and indoctrination at al Qaeda's basic and advanced training camps. He and other militants from Arab countries (and even Sweden) had learned how to conduct terrorist attacks on a wide range of American targets, from hotels and tourist sites to power plants, embassies, and warships. He was also taught how to assassinate political leaders and disseminate toxins in public buildings.

Camp Farouk: Garmabak Ghar

Camp Farouk at Garmabak Ghar in Southeastern Afghanistan near Kandahar, was one of Osama bin Laden's most important terrorist training camps. The camp, isolated in a rough mountainous region, was home to many would-be terrorists from around the Arab world. The camp reportedly trained some of bin Laden's senior associates, including Mohamed Sadeek Odeh and Mohamed Rashed Daoud al-'Owhali,[38] who were convicted in New York in 2003 of assisting in the 1998 bombing of the American Embassy in Nairobi, Kenya. Odeh and Al-'Owhali admitted to investigators that they learned to use weapons and explosives here before taking part in the 1998 bombings.

According to al-'Owhali's account, the camp held 150 to 200 men at a time, but it was large enough to hold more if necessary. Basic training lasted just one month and included training on the use of light weapons, demolition, communications, and a course on religious ideology. Students at Farouk were divided into groups of twelve to sixteen. After completing his training at Farouk al-'Owhali was transferred to another camp nearby for a month to teach small courses on the AK-47, an assault rifle. Al-'Owhali then graduated to the jihad camp for training in intelligence, information management, kidnappings, and hijackings. Al Qaeda's top-tier camp, which accepted al-'Owhali only after he battled bravely for months alongside the Taliban for control of Kabul, provided an advanced course which was equivalent to terrorist management; al-'Owhali called it "the operation and management of cell training." There he learned skills for target surveys and advanced communications and absorbed lessons on the detailed, four-tiered structure of al Qaeda's terror cells: intelligence, administration, planning, and execution. Towards the end of this training, he met bin Laden several times and expressed to him his interest in missions that he would like to conduct. Bin Laden reportedly told him, "Take your time. Your mission will come."[39]

Camp Farouk at Garmabak Ghar consisted of classrooms and prayer halls, bunkers, testing fields, and firing ranges, and concrete underground stores for weapons and chemicals from which complex tunnels led to concealed entrances. Camp life at Garmabak Ghar had its own rhythm; trainees rose early for prayers, had breakfast on the run, and spent their days in training and classes interspersed with more prayers. Much time in the evenings was spent on the darkened hillsides, some smoking and all drinking sweet green tea.[40]

It was this camp where John Walker Lindh, the so-called "American Taliban," trained before he went to fight for the Taliban in June and July 2001. Lindh first entered Afghanistan with a Pakistani unit, but since he was proficient in the Arabic language he was transferred to one of the Arab "Ansar" brigades. The camp was also the training ground for Wail al-Shehri and Abdulaziz al-Omeri, two of the nineteen hijackers involved in the September 11 terrorist attacks. While at the al-Farooq camp, Lindh was trained in weaponry, orienteering, explosives, pistols, and rocket-propelled grenades. Bin Laden visited the camp on three to five occasions during the time Lindh was there and gave lectures on "the local situation, political issues, old Afghan/Soviet battles, etc."[41] According to a report by the *Sunday Times* (London), al Qaeda trainees "lived in a compound of tents and mud huts surrounded by barbed wire. Each morning, [they] learned the theory of AK-47 rifles and antiaircraft guns. In the afternoons, [they] put the morning's lessons into practice, firing live rounds and learning to throw grenades into the nearby hills."[42]

The al-Farooq camp was featured in a video of bin Laden circulated throughout Muslim countries and on the Internet before September 11, 2001. Hundreds of trainees at al-Farooq, wearing masks and waving black flags, watched as bin Laden told Muslims to travel to Afghanistan and train for holy war against Americans (for occupying the holy lands) and to seek revenge for the killing and imprisonment of Muslims in various countries. Bin Laden's fighters fired antiaircraft guns and rocket-propelled grenades, ran through obstacle courses, blew up buildings, and shot at images of (then) President Clinton.[43]

Farm Hadda

Al Qaeda's camp at Farm Hadda was one of the largest in Afghanistan. The camp was made up of mud and brick buildings. After it was bombed out, copies of a twenty-six-page booklet, *Jihad against America*, were found amid the rubble. The booklet, which intelligence officials say was given to all new recruits to the camp, contains speeches and statements by bin Laden articulating his goals. At the top of the list is the goal to oust U.S. troops stationed in Saudi Arabia. In the book, bin Laden listed various militant groups that he said were "helping Afghanistan in its fight against the infidels" around the world. These include the Egyptian Islamic Jihad, the Libyan Jihad Fighters, the Abu Sayyaf rebels of the Philippines, and what the book called "jihad militants" from Burma, Bosnia, Chechnya, Indonesia, Iraq, Jordan, Lebanon, Pakistan, Somalia, Tajikistan, Turkey, Turkmenistan, and Uzbekistan. These groups also sent their cadres to train at the al Qaeda camps in Afghanistan. "We can defeat the infidels from here," bin Laden wrote. "I will give you the training so you can carry on after we are gone. Our struggle will never end; it will grow stronger and more lethal by the year."[44]

Khaldan

At Rishkhor, in the south of Kabul, camp Khaldan was one of al Qaeda's key installations. Khaldan was a compound of four tents and four stone buildings. Recruits, 100 or so at a time, were grouped by nationality. There were Arabs from Saudi Arabia, Jordan, Yemen, and Algeria, and Europeans from France, Germany, Sweden, and Chechnya. Training was formal. There was a textbook, available in Arabic, French, and other languages. The training incorporated methods that American military advisers had introduced to the Afghans in the 1980s during the war with the Soviets.

Early each morning, the recruits were called to formation, then sent to pray. After a meal, they went through strength and endurance training. Scarred veterans of the Afghan war taught self-defense and hand-to-hand combat, using knives, garrotes, and other weapons. Trainees practiced with small arms, assault rifles, and grenade launchers provided by the Taliban. They learned about the use of explosives and land mines. Representatives of terrorist groups, including Hamas, Hizballah, and Islamic Jihad, gave lectures about their organizations.[45] Several members of the team who bombed the east African Embassies of the United States in 1998 trained in the camp. Ahmed Ressam, jailed for his role in a plot to bomb the Los Angeles airport, also trained here. A key paramilitary trainer at Khaldan was a man named al-Libi, who was captured by the anti-Taliban Northern Alliance in late December 2001.

Zawar Kili

The Zawar Kili complex was a sprawling al Qaeda training camp and tunnel complex in eastern Afghanistan southwest of Khowst in Paktia province. The compound was fairly extensive, including a base camp, a training facility, and some caves. During the 1980s, Soviet forces fought a number of battles in the area, as intelligence reports described the existence of the large cave/bunker complex. Zawar was initially a mujahideen logistics transfer base, which was built up as a mujahideen training center and later expanded into a major combat base for supply, training, and staging. The base was located inside a canyon surrounded by Sodyaki Ghar and Moghulgi Ghar mountains. The canyon opens to the southeast facing Pakistan and is located four kilometers from the Pakistan border and 15 kilometers from the major Pakistani forward supply base at Miram Shah.

To expand the base, bulldozers and explosives were used to dig at least eleven major tunnels into the southeast facing ridge of Sodyaki Ghar mountain. Some of these huge tunnels reached 500 meters and contained a hotel, a mosque, arms depots and repair shops, a garage, a medical point, a radio center, and a kitchen. A gasoline generator provided power to the tunnels and the hotel. This impressive base became a mandatory stop for visiting journalists, dignitaries, and other "war tourists"[46] and was "the place where the al Qaeda members went to regroup."[47] The facility was used for training, storage, and command purposes, and served as a support haven for al Qaeda and the Taliban. Al Qaeda used the camp as a logistics base, a command and control center, and a training ground. The camp was composed of three areas: a set of above ground buildings and two cave and tunnel systems. Overall, the Zawar Kili complex was very extensive, covering an area of roughly three by three miles with more than sixty above-ground structures and at least fifty caves. This camp was the target of the U.S. cruise missile attack following the 1998 bombings of two of its embassies in Africa.

Summary of the Afghanistan Training Camps

Most of the terrorist camps in Afghanistan were abandoned as bin Laden's al Qaeda terrorist network fled the 2001 U.S. assault and Northern Alliance fighters. But what remains of the camps offers clear evidence of the systematic way bin Laden and his lieutenants had been pursuing their efforts to wage jihad. Recruits at al Qaeda's two main camps, the Daunta complex and farm Hadda, were trained in conventional, biological, and even nuclear warfare, according to the aforementioned class manuals. They came from at least twenty-one countries, including Bosnia, Egypt, France, Great Britain, Jordan, Kuwait, Pakistan, Saudi Arabia, and Turkey.[48] The documents recovered from the ruined sites demonstrate the level of sophistication that the training camps in Afghanistan maintained. These documents consist of books, training manuals, student's notebooks, ledgers, inventories, military records, communications and code manuals, and private letters and diaries. Al Qaeda maintained detailed lists of all the trainees in the camps. For example, a document titled "Al Qaeda Military Competence Report" logged the training record, previous experience, and proficiency of the trainees. The report describes a Palestinian, Abu Majid al-Ansari, as having taken courses in infantry tactics, machine-guns, and revolvers, and having conducted several operations, including counterattacks and ambushes. The document also indicated his preference for martyrdom operations and his commander's assessment of al-Ansari as a decent, well-trained and well-mannered individual.[49]

At the camps, every trainee was given an identity card issued by the Office of al Mujahideen Affairs, with information on nicknames or aliases, specialization, the unit to which he belonged, and time spent at the war front. Every trainee was required to register himself by providing personal details such as aliases and their reason for coming to the training. The trainees received personal training kits and were required to write their wills. Then the trainees went through an orientation program, after which formal training—both theoretical and practical—was imparted. The training curriculum was largely scientific and technical in nature, involving electrical and chemical engineering, atomic physics, ballistics, computer science, and communication sciences. The training also involved use of firearms, explosives, unconventional weapons such as chemical and biological weapons, and courses on urban warfare and counterintelligence. During various phases of training, top al Qaeda leaders (including Osama bin Laden) would visit and make personal acquaintance with the trainees. Leaders and commanders made assessments to ascertain the abilities of the recruits and recommended suitable programs for each one.[50] Some recruits were selected to specialize as negotiators, doctors, divers, climbers, and explosive experts.[51]

Through these camps, al Qaeda developed a global cadre of motivated and knowledgeable combatants. Unfortunately, many of them are still at large. Perhaps even more disturbing is the fact that while many of the original camps in Afghanistan are no longer operating, new ones have been founded in various locations, thus continuing the training of new terrorist recruits.

New Camps, New Threats

Despite many significant disruptions to the training infrastructure in Afghanistan, there have been signs of activation of new, albeit simple, training camps in many parts of Afghanistan. Some reports suggest that new volunteers are making their way to these camps, swelling the numbers of would-be al Qaeda activists and enhancing the longer-term capabilities of the network. One or two camps have been discovered near Asadabad, northeast of Kabul and west of the border with Pakistan. The new al Qaeda camps are small, mobile, and regularly dismantled and moved to keep them as discreet as possible. Loosely called "training camps" by Afghan and U.S. military authorities, Sabila—and perhaps a dozen well-defined and named outposts like it along the 1,500-mile Afghan-Pakistani border—have emerged as the new training centers for al Qaeda and Taliban cadres. These camps in desolate and largely unpatrolled tribal areas of Afghanistan are reportedly training "high-level foot soldiers" for both the Taliban and al Qaeda. As reported by a UN Security Council panel, al Qaeda is attracting recruits to new terrorist-training camps in eastern Afghanistan and possibly trying to assemble a "dirty bomb."[52] Members of Kashmiri terrorist groups such as Jaish-e Mohammad, Hizb-ul Mujahideen, Al Badr Mujahideen, Harkatul Mujahideen, and the Afghan-based Islamist party, Hizb-e-Islam, have also visited the new camps.[53]

This type of training at individual/small team level is the most relevant for the decentralized al Qaeda that we are now facing. Individual and small-team training leaves greater potential for variation, innovation, and unpredictability. These traits are of course valuable to terrorists and make life harder for those in counterterrorism. Afghanistan is, however, not the only host to training camps. Indeed, nothing could be farther from the truth; terrorist training is a worldwide phenomenon, with groups and camps spread throughout Central Asia, the Middle East, Southeast Asia, and the Pacific. A review of just small sample of these is instructive.

Pankisi Gorge, Georgia

The Pankisi Gorge in Georgia (in the Caucasus region) emerged as a new and most important terrorist training base following the campaign against the Taliban and al Qaeda in Afghanistan. Here the trainees were mostly from the same region as those in the Afghan camps, though many of them were Algerian. Most of them trained both in Afghanistan (before October 2001) and the Pankisi Gorge, and had similar (if not the same) trainers. The area came to the world's attention following the discovery of plots to attack targets in Britain and in France that were foiled by law enforcement officials in late 2002. Police investigations unearthed a network of Algerian extremists with connections in Afghanistan and Chechnya. Intelligence sources indicated that Pankisi Gorge "was used by al Qaeda units fleeing Afghanistan to set up a new training camp."[54] Abu Musab al-Zarqawi and Abu Khabab, who ran al Qaeda's chemical and biological weapons testing facility at the Darunta camp in Afghanistan, trained at a camp in the Pankisi Gorge. However, the formulas for chemical weapons found during the searches appeared to be different from the formulas in al Qaeda's *Encyclopedia of Jihad* and other training manuals for developing bombs and chemical and biological agents that were recovered from abandoned camps in Afghanistan. The materials discovered here suggest that those being trained in the Caucasus region may also be receiving instruction from men who had experience with chemical and biological weapons in the Russian army. Until February 2002, fighters of Arab origin had built and equipped a military hospital in the area with funds received "directly through Al Qaeda channels." Large amounts of cash were smuggled into the area on orders of people close to Osama bin Laden. The money was reportedly used to set up training camps and a firing range.[55]

Training Camps of Ansar al Islam, Northern Iraq

Ansar al Islam, a religious militant group, took hold of a small corner of Kurdish-controlled Iraq and established harsh Islamic order over a wild, isolated land beneath the Shinerwe Mountain. Ansar was accused of dispatching assassins and suicide bombers, of harboring al Qaeda fighters from Afghanistan and of training several hundred local fighters. Ansar al Islam—whose name means Supporters of Islam—was formed in 2001 when several splintered parties in the region merged into one and joined the international jihad. The group operated on several levels. It ran training camps with lessons on infantry weapons, tactics, suicide bombing, and assassination. It videotaped combat operations and battlefield operations and put them up on a web site (www.ansarislam.com). It also sent copies on compact discs to al Qaeda at an undisclosed location. The group was also host to Arab fighters who left Afghanistan as the United States routed the Taliban. According to Kurdish intelligence officials as many as 150 foreign fighters were in Ansar's ranks. The group operated in deep geographic and political isolation. Villages under its control were nearly impenetrable to outsiders.

Among the leaders of the group were Mullah Namo and Omar Barziani, two Kurds who met with al Qaeda in Afghanistan; Abu Zubair al-Shami, an Arab who was Osama bin Laden's representative; and Ayub Afghan, a Kurdish explosives specialist who fought alongside Afghans against the Russians and was an expert in making suicide bomber's belts.

Ansar collaborated directly with al Qaeda, a claim also confirmed by al Qaeda documents found in Afghanistan by reporters from the *New York Times*. According to some Kurdish officials, this region was infiltrated by al Qaeda in 2001 in order to set up an alternative to the group's Afghanistan headquarters. According to Nisherwan Mustafa Amin, a senior member of the Kurdish politburo in northeastern Iraq, Beyara was the "command center of the Middle East." Documents that were found by a *Times* reporter—along with bomb manuals and al Qaeda ammunition inventories—in an al Qaeda guest house in Kabul also establish a connection between the Islamists in this valley and al Qaeda's international jihad. The documents include a memorandum from the "Iraqi Kurdistan Islamic Brigade" listing several Iraqi villages beneath the Shinerwe Mountain's ridges, including Beyara, and declaring that the Islamists should be urged to unite and apply the Taliban's style of civic order there.[56]

The existence of this camp, which contained the headquarters of what Ansar called its "Victory Brigade," was disclosed in a presentation to the UN Security Council by Secretary of State Colin L. Powell, who described it as a poisons training camp and factory supported by both Baghdad and al Qaeda. Powell said a terrorist network run by Abu Musab al-Zarqawi, an operative of al Qaeda, had "helped establish another poison and explosive training center camp, and this camp is located in northeastern Iraq." A photograph with the caption "Terrorist Poison and Explosives Factory, Khurmal" was also displayed during the presentation. There were indications that al-Zarqawi might have spent time in Ansar's territory in 2002.[57] Kurdish leaders also claimed that they have eyewitness accounts, prisoners' confessions, and seized evidence to support claims by Secretary Powell. Sadi Ahmad Pire, a high-level official of the PUK, pinpointed the village of Sargat near the Khurmal district as the site of the chemical-weapons plant.[58]

Indonesia

Al Qaeda's activities in Southeast Asia were part of a larger plan to move al Qaeda's base of operations from Afghanistan to Southeast Asia. Ayman al-Zawahiri, Osama bin Laden's right-hand man, and Mohammed Atef, al Qaeda's former military chief, visited Indonesia in 2000. The visit was a fact-finding mission to assess the possibility of moving al Qaeda's base of operations to Southeast Asia. Southeast Asia's political-geographical peculiarities, including porous borders and slack immigration controls, were of particular advantage. For example, Indonesia—the sprawling archipelago of more than 13,000 islands—has relatively porous borders and plenty of potential hiding places beyond the routine control of any of the security agencies that made it ideal for establishing training bases. Al Qaeda operatives from all over the world (especially from Europe) had traveled to the region for training.

Osama bin Laden wanted to move the base of operations for his al Qaeda network from Afghanistan to Southeast Asia in 2000 and was particularly interested in Aceh in Indonesia, where members of the Free Aceh Movement (GAM), fighting for a separate Islamic state, were working with al Qaeda. When Ayman al-Zawahiri and Mohammed Attef (accompanied by Kuwaiti Omar al-Faruq and Indonesian Agus Dwikarna) visited Aceh in June 2000, they were impressed by the lack of security as well as the extent of support from the Muslim population.[59]

In December 2001, Indonesia's intelligence claimed that training camps organized and funded by al Qaeda existed in Sulawesi. Al Qaeda provided funds, along with weapons and explosives expertise, for at least ten camps in the jungles near Poso in Central Sulawesi province. These camps operated between March and November 2001, and were located deep in the forests. Each camp had two or three trainers, one of whom was the son-in-law of the late Indonesian Abdullah Sungkar, believed to be one of the founders of the Jemaah Islamiyah terrorist network. The instructors were experts in the use of explosives and weapons. Reports of the Poso camp first publicly surfaced in November 2001 in court documents in Spain after the arrest of an al Qaeda leader. His group, the documents say, allegedly sent hundreds of al Qaeda operatives from Europe to Indonesia for training.

The Poso camp was set up by Agus Dwikarna, who commanded Laskar Jundullah, an extremist militant group based in Sulawesi. Dwikarna's connections with al Qaeda in Europe went to the highest levels. He allegedly helped bring hundreds of operatives from Europe for training in Indonesia. Dwikarna also used the training camp to help fuel sectarian violence in Indonesia. He was connected to the al Qaeda cell in Spain whose leader, Imad Eddin Barakat Yarbas, was in frequent contact with Mohammed Atta, the suspected leader of the September 11 hijackers. Parlindungan Siregar was the go-between man for Dwikarna, and arranged for several hundred al Qaeda operatives from Europe to travel to Indonesia for training.[60] In a report in June 2002, the Singapore intelligence agency also said that al Qaeda was training militants in Indonesia—particularly in the areas of Poso and Ambon, both of which are flashpoints for Muslim-Christian violence.[61]

After the December 2002 bombings of a McDonald's restaurant in Makassar, Indonesian police uncovered a military-style training camp in South Sulawesi near the Towuti Lake area in Luwu regency, some 500 kilometers from Makassar. It is suspected of belonging to the group of Agung Abdul Hamid, the alleged mastermind of the bombing in Makassar. The camp was allegedly used by the Makassar bombing suspects for training in shooting and the assembling of bombs. The police had earlier found four similar camps across South Sulawesi in the regencies of Enrekang, Palopo, Luwu, and Bulukumba, about 250–500 kilometers from Makassar, which they also believed belonged to the Agung-led bombers. Their investigations revealed that the instructors for the camps were brought in from the southern Philippines and Afghanistan.[62] Key suspects in the Makassar attacks allegedly had links with the suspected Bali bombers, who had ties with Jemaah Islamiyah.[63]

The Philippines

During the 1990s, Osama bin Laden asked the chairman of the Moro Islamic Liberation Front (MILF), Hashim Salamat, to set up training camps in the Philippines for al Qaeda because it was becoming harder for his operatives to travel secretly to Afghanistan for training. MILF set up three training camps for the al Qaeda terrorist network in Mindanao inside its former sprawling base, Camp Abubakar, in Maguindanao.[64] Of the three, Camp Vietnam and Camp Palestine were used by the al Qaeda cadres and the other, Camp Hudaybiyya, by JI militants from Southeast Asia.

Camp Abubakar was the MILF's main headquarters and was also used for terrorist training along with Bushra in Lanao del Sur and a host of other satellite camps scattered throughout Central Mindanao. Militants from all over the world, including those from the Middle East, had explosives training in MILF camps until as late as 2002.[65] Up to 1,000 Indonesians members of Jemaah Islamiyah also trained in these camps, in particular, camp Hudaybiyya. In 1994, MILF established the Abdul al-Rahman Bedis Memorial Military Academy in the Camp Abubakar complex to commemorate the return of Moro veterans of the Afghan war. MILF had a core group of arms experts, who had been trained in Afghanistan, Pakistan, and even Germany. Donors supporting MILF operations were mostly from Saudi Arabia, including Muhammad Jamal Khalifah, a brother-in-law of Osama bin Laden.[66]

In 2000, the Philippine military captured all of the MILF's camps in Mindanao, including Camp Abubakar.[67] The military confirmed that "terrorists with connections to al Qaeda" did train in MILF camps before they were shut down in a military offensive.[68] However, training continued in makeshift complexes at least up to early 2002, until the arrests of Indonesians Fathur Rohman al-Ghozi and Agus Dwikarna. In early 2003, the Philippine military in North Cotabato arrested Sulayman Ismael alias Abu Hashim, an Afghanistan-trained bomber who had served as an instructor at the MILF military academy in Camp Abubakar.

In an eyewitness account, reporter Azhar Ghani of *The New Paper*, Singapore, tells how the camp was a well-organized community, with an arms factory capable of making rocket-propelled grenades (and accompanying launcher tubes). The explosives were unsophisticated, made of materials like the fertilizer-based chemical ammonium nitrate, with crude timing and activation devices. Inside the complex there was a two-story building which used to be part of a college that the MILF ran. Other buildings housed MILF schools and a hardware store. Some of the trainees were foreigners with Arabic features.[69] A Saudi national allegedly led MILF members in a suicide attack on the headquarters of Army's 6th Infantry division in 1997.[70] When the camp was overrun by the military, the rebels left behind a lot of foreign passports—evidence of the presence of foreigners, mainly Indonesians and members of GAM.

In May 2002, police in the Philippines raided a suspected al Qaeda terrorist training camp in an Islamic school in a mountainous area in Tarlac province, bordering Pangasinan, and seized high-caliber firearms, grenades, and a grenade launcher, along with documents.[71] In November 2002, the armed forces overran the MILF's abandoned camp Ibnu Abbas in Lanao del Sur, in Darul Internal, in the vicinity of Upper Maganding, Sultan Gumander town. The terrorists left behind bombing and demolition implements consisting of two rounds of 60-millimeter mortar, a locally made rocket-propelled grenade, two kilograms of ammonium nitrate, twenty-one dynamite sticks, six blasting caps with detonating cords, and an electric tester—all of which, the military said, would have been used in terrorist attacks. The troops also seized a wooden paper printer, forty-four disposable syringes, three units of clamp assemblies, a quarter-wave VHF antenna, two empty shells of unknown caliber, five sets of magazine pouches, assorted military uniforms and various documents. The abandoned camp had eleven semipermanent structures consisting of a brigade headquarters, communications center, a training area, a madrasa (or Islamic school), an armory, a mosque, personnel quarters, a multipurpose hall, and a kitchen. Underground bunkers were also found.[72]

The arrest in October 2003 of Taufik Rifki from Jabal Quba, on Mount Kararao, revealed the presence of new training locations in Mindanao. Rifki was an instructor at the new JI camp and worked with Fathur Rohman al-Ghozi. In April 2004, the Philippine authorities arrested Sammy Abdulgani, an alleged JI member from Buliok complex in Pikit, North Cotabato. Sammy claimed that he was trained by Indonesian JI members in the making of car bombs.

The training camps in Southeast Asia ran almost like their counterparts in Afghanistan, imparting training in firearms and explosives. In addition, recruits studied Islam intensively, receiving up to four hours a day of religious indoctrination. The training facilities in Indonesia and the Philippines served many strategic interests of the groups. Apart from replicating the Afghan combat experience, these camps also imparted a sense of exclusive and esoteric "in-group" Islamic brotherhood, bonded through a common understanding of practical violent jihad. Further, these centers became the catalysts for extensive personal linkages among the members of various groups which later became the hallmark of terrorist networks in Southeast Asia.

Myanmar

Among the videotapes that the CNN obtained from al Qaeda's archives in Afghanistan, one titled "Burma BUGGED" was about Muslim "allies" training in "Burma" (Myanmar). The training camp purportedly was run by the Rohingya Solidarity Organization (RSO). RSO was founded by Rohingya Muslims from Myanmar's Rakhine State during the early 1980s, when radical elements among the Rohingyas broke away from the more moderate, main grouping, the Rohingya Patriotic Front (RPF) led by Muhammad Yunus. Following the breakup of the Arakan Rohingya National Organization (ARNO) in 1999–2000, three new factions emerged, all of them reclaiming the old name RSO. Traditionally, the RSO had linkages to Jamaat-e-Islami and Islami Chhatra Shibir in Bangladesh, Gulbuddin Hekmatyar's Hizb-e-Islami in Afghanistan, Hizb-ul-Mujahideen (HM) in Jammu and Kashmir, and Angkatan Belia Islam sa-Malaysia (ABIM), the Islamic Youth Organization of Malaysia. During the early 1990s, RSO had several military camps near the Burmese border, where cadres from the Islami Chhatra Shibir were also trained in guerrilla warfare.[73] Afghan instructors were seen in some of the RSO camps along the Bangladesh-Burma border, while nearly 100 RSO rebels were reported to have undergone training in the Afghan province of Khost with Hizb-e-Islami Mujahideen. The tape presumably dates from the early 1990s, since by the late 1990s the RSO's training camps were taken over by Bangladeshi Islamist militants from the Hakrat-ul-Jihad-al-Islami (HuJI), which was formed in 1992, allegedly with financial support from Osama bin Laden.[74]

Australia

Islamic extremists linked to JI have even conducted combat training in a remote forest outside Melbourne in Australia. The camps were run for almost five years. Extremist Indonesian political movement Ahlus Sunnah wal Jammah, a close-knit group known for its secrecy and fundamentalist ideology and based at the Preston Mosque was believed to have organized the camps. Ahlus Sunnah wal Jammah was known to be associated with Indonesian terrorist group Laskar Jihad.

Abu Qatada (alias Omar Mohammed Othman), a senior al Qaeda operative based in the UK and accused of being a key figure in the September 11 attacks, was a spiritual guest speaker at one of the camps. Although Australian law enforcement officers maintain that Qatada was refused entry as he tried to enter Australia during the 1990s, Sheik Taj el din Al-Hilaly, Australia's most prominent Muslim leader, maintains Qatada not only entered the country in the 1990s but engaged in a speaking tour as well. Fehmi Naji El-Imam, the imam of Melbourne's Preston Mosque, also confirmed that Qatada spoke to his congregation. Abu Qatada is now in police custody in Britain.

According to some reports, the camp's attendees came from all parts of Australia, but had Algerian, Somali, Lebanese, Palestinian, and Philippine backgrounds. Members of the Sydney-based extremist group Islamic Youth Movement, which publishes a pro-terrorist magazine, had also attended the camps. Training in these camps was provided by Islamic militants who fought in Afghanistan or Somalia. Training sessions involved target practice and a walk-through combat shooting range, as well as spiritual discussions. The Australian Security Intelligence Organization found spent cartridges at the undisclosed state forest training camp.[75]

Conclusion

"It is from these camps that much of the world's terror has originated."[76]

—Haji Abdul Qadir

The training camps set up by al Qaeda and its associates became the lifeblood for the groups, providing indoctrination and training for foot soldiers, go-betweens, planners, document forgers, communications specialists, scouts, technicians, bombers, and even hijackers. According to some estimates, many militant Muslims from more than fifty countries have passed through the camps, spending from two weeks to more than six months learning the general and specific skills that modern terrorism requires. In addition to bin Laden's training camps, the Taliban and other militant Muslim groups affiliated with al Qaeda have also trained thousands in similar facilities in Afghanistan as well as other parts of the world. Some estimates put the total veterans of these camps at more than 70,000. Many veterans of the camp remain unaccounted for.

Given the importance of training facilities—in terms of armament use, research in CBRN weapons and indoctrination, as well as in providing a valuable link between various terrorist groups—the necessity of locating and disrupting terrorist camps can hardly be overemphasized. As former militant Liaqat Ali (who trained in Afghanistan) puts it, "if you don't hit terrorist camps, you are going to have lots and lots of terrorists over the world."[77] Jalalabad's Governor Qadir nicely summed up the enormity of the challenge: "I fear there's a lot more out there that we just don't know about. I'm afraid what happened at the World Trade Center and Pentagon was just the beginning. The worst terror may be yet to come."[78]

CHAPTER 12

The Mujahideen of Bosnia: Origins, Training, and Implications

EVAN KOHLMANN

In September 2004, U.S. warplanes bombed a convoy of suspected al Qaeda fighters traveling through the suburb of Abu Ghraib west of the Iraqi capital Baghdad. Among those killed in the Abu Ghraib air strike was Abu Anas al-Shami (a.k.a. Omar Yousef Jumah), a Jordanian insurgent commander considered to be the right-hand man of most-wanted terrorist leader Abu Musab al-Zarqawi. Shortly thereafter, al-Zarqawi's organization in Iraq lamented their loss in a commemorative video recording of the life and times of the late Abu Anas. But according to the video, it was not Iraq where Abu Anas had "begun his journey in jihad," but rather the unlikely land of Bosnia-Herzegovina, where he had first worked as "an Islamic missionary and a fighter . . . for a year and a half" during the early 1990s.

The same can be said for Khalid Sheik Mohammed (the admitted terrorist mastermind behind the September 11, 2001 suicide hijackings) and Abdul Aziz al-Muqrin (the slain Saudi al Qaeda leader who personally beheaded U.S. hostage Paul Johnson on camera in June 2004)—both of whom experienced their first tastes of post-Afghan jihad while alongside the Arab mujahideen battalion hidden in the Balkans during the disastrous Bosnian civil war. When U.S. investigators discovered a videotape in December 2001 apparently showing Osama bin Laden and a cohort gloating over their involvement in the 9/11 suicide hijackings plot, they were shocked to learn the identity of bin Laden's mysterious confidant: Abu Sulaiman al-Makki (a.k.a. Sheikh Khalid Harbi), a former teacher at the holy mosque of Mecca who had fought in Afghanistan alongside bin Laden and was later paralyzed from the waist down in October 1992 during combat with ethnic Serb forces near Tesanj, central Bosnia. In the tape, Abu Sulaiman—who remained an influential terrorist figure in the Balkans long after the end of the Bosnian war—crowed his enthusiastic approval of 9/11:

> That day the congratulations were coming on the phone nonstop. . . . No doubt it is a clear victory. . . . Thank Allah America came out of its caves. We hit her the first hit and the next one will hit her with the hands of the believers, the good believers, the strong believers. By Allah it is a great work. Allah prepares for you a great reward for this work. . . . I live in happiness, happiness, I have not experienced, or felt, in a long time. . . . In these days, in our times, that it will be the greatest jihad in the history of Islam.[1]

These examples give some evidence of the importance of the Bosnian civil war to the early development and history of the al Qaeda terrorist organization. Many of al Qaeda's most important military and leadership figures, both past and present, were catapulted forward on the world stage as a result of their early involvement with the mujahideen in Bosnia. But simply because the militant fundamentalist minority finds the subject noteworthy does not necessarily make it so. This will perhaps raise the basic question: Of all the places that al Qaeda has extended its influence to, why is Bosnia so important? The answer to that question is not so simple; it stems from a number of interrelated factors. First, the deployment of Arab fighters to Bosnia, who were generally loyal to the jihadi leadership in Afghanistan, exploded during the mid-1990s into numbers sometimes estimated even to exceed 5,000. Second, this massive and significant migration of Arab Afghans to Bosnia occurred at an early stage of the al Qaeda movement, meaning that the experience had long-lasting effects, both practically and ideologically, on the terrorist group. Third, Bosnia's unique geographic position directly between Western Europe and the Middle East was the ideal jumping-off point for organizational expansion of the movement into Italy, France, Germany, Austria, Canada, and the United Kingdom. It provided an environment where trained foreign Muslim fighters arriving from Afghanistan could mingle with (and help teach) unsophisticated but eager terrorist recruits from Western Europe and could form new plans for the future of the jihad. No such contact had ever occurred before in the short history of al Qaeda, and it provided the organization and its radical membership limitless possibilities for development and growth.

Al Qaeda: From Afghanistan to Bosnia

Many years of research on Osama bin Laden and al Qaeda led me to understand that the particularly enduring influence of the legends of jihad and martyrdom from—of all places—the Bosnian civil war was inescapable. Looming larger than the writings Sheikh Omar Abdel Rahman or even

Osama bin Laden, the stories of the men who lost their lives fighting in a supposed Muslim "holy war" against Eastern European "crusaders" are much more telling of the history and goals of al Qaeda, not merely to the organization's followers, but to the world at large. These men epitomized the sacrificial ideology pioneered by bin Laden and his henchmen that would lead them to enthusiastically offer their lives in exchange for paradise, serving as quixotic "armed humanitarians" and defending the Muslim ummah against a host of real and imaginary enemies. Thus, the importance of the conflict in the Balkans has been repeatedly and unfortunately understated. Americans and Europeans often wonder how al Qaeda has so effectively penetrated Europe and the West, establishing terrorist cells across Italy, France, Denmark, Austria, Germany, Sweden, Spain, the United Kingdom, Canada, and even the United States. Some of the most important answers can be found in Bosnia, where the cream of the Arab Afghans tested their battle skills in the post-Soviet era and mobilized a new generation of hardened guerilla zealots with only two unswerving priorities: armed combat and Islamic fundamentalism.

Moreover, the influence of European culture and technology also gave the Arab-Afghan movement a big boost: according to representatives of the mujahideen, the influx of Westernized European Muslims to the fundamentalist movement

> was instrumental to, not just the jihad in Bosnia, but the world-wide jihad, for what they managed to achieve. And you think this is an exaggeration, but by the hands of the brothers they did many things that you wouldn't believe. Books were translated and produced, in the front-lines, because you had the English brothers that could speak English and the Arab brothers that could speak Arabic and a bit of English, and they go together and translated books about jihad. Now, these books are guiding other brothers back to the jihad again. They've computerized whole computer networks because of their computer knowledge.[2]

Perhaps what is most striking about the story of the jihad in Bosnia is that, unlike Afghanistan, it did not take place in a region far from the reach of American influence—quite to the contrary, these mujahideen were able to organize and prosper right under the nose of U.S. and United Nations troops in the midst of an abortive international peacekeeping mission. The Bosnian war happened to occur at a convenient time for the Arab Afghans. In January 1993, the Pakistani government, eager to put the Afghan jihad in the past, ordered the closure of Arab mujahideen offices in the country and threatened official deportation to any illegal foreign fighters who attempted to remain in Pakistan. A month later, the FBI secretly recorded a senior Egyptian jihad leader offering over the telephone to send new volunteers to the Arab-Afghan training camps in Pakistan. He was told, "All of them [are] closed, Sheik, nothing is left open . . . even the Base [al Qaeda] is closed completely and they all departed from here . . . except for special situations."[3] Many of these displaced men faced a serious problem, because returning to their countries of origin meant certain arrest, torture, and likely death. At the time, a Saudi spokesman for the Arab Afghans in Jeddah explained in the media, "The Algerians cannot go to Algeria, the Syrians cannot go to Syria or the Iraqis to Iraq. Some will opt to go to Bosnia, the others will have to go into Afghanistan permanently."[4] His assessments were predictably accurate, and a number of prominent Arab guerillas left South Asia destined for a new life of asylum and "holy war" amidst the brutal civil conflict in the Balkans.

Following the mujahideen conquest of Kabul in April 1992, a Saudi al Qaeda envoy known as Sheikh Abu Abdel Aziz "Barbaros" traveled with four other unidentified veteran Arab-Afghan commanders to Bosnia-Herzegovina to "check out the landscape" and determine if the Balkans would serve as fertile ground for the displaced Arab-Afghan movement, which was no longer officially welcomed in Pakistan.[5] However, unlike other remote stops in their worldwide tour of Muslim "hot spots," Bosnia was truly a foreign land to the Islamic extremists of the Middle East. Prior to the Western media coverage of the expanding civil war there, many had admittedly never even heard of the place. In an interview with *Al-Daawah* magazine, Abu Abdel Aziz confessed that, at this point, "We were unable to understand where Bosnia was; was it in America or in the southern hemisphere or in Asia? We had no idea where it was. When we found out that it is a part of Yugoslavia in Eastern Europe, we still had no idea how many Muslims were there and we had no idea as to how and when Islam reached there."[6]

But after witnessing the injustice of the bloody conflict, the Saudi jihadi swiftly concluded that this was indeed a legitimate holy war. "All Muslims should participate," he suggested, "either by contributing money, caring for orphans and widows, taking in refugees or fighting in the jihad."[7] Abu Abdel Aziz had no illusions about his mission in Bosnia. Though he spent part of his time encouraging *da'wa* (Islamic missionary work), he cautioned "We are not here to bring supplies like food and medicine. . . . There are a lot of organizations that can do that. We bring men."[8] Upon his arrival, the mujahideen leadership in Bosnia and Afghanistan designated Sheikh Abu Abdel Aziz as the first *Amir*, or commander-in-chief, of the Bosnian Arab-Afghans. The new Amir quickly established his first headquarters at the Mehurici training camp, near the central Bosnian town of Travnik.

In the fall of 1992, Osama bin Laden personally ordered a former key Sudanese member of al Qaeda—Jamal Ahmed al-Fadl, who later turned government informant—to travel to nearby Zagreb, Croatia, for consultations with key Arab-Afghan leaders operating as al Qaeda emissaries in Bosnia.[9] According to briefs published by the U.S. Attorney's office in Chicago, during that conference, Abu Abdel Aziz[10] advised Jamal al-Fadl that "al Qaeda was seeking to establish training camps in Bosnia, forge relations with relief agencies in Bosnia and establish businesses to support al Qaeda economically."[11] He also discussed the purchase of weapons from Germany destined for the mujahideen in the Balkans and stressed the need for a *fatwa* (religious edict) permitting al Qaeda members to dress and act as Westerners while in Bosnia in order to conceal their presence and "blend in."[12]

Once these housekeeping issues had been taken care of, Abu Abdel Aziz proceeded to elaborate further on Osama bin Laden's master plan for Bosnia. He told al-Fadl without hesitation that al Qaeda's primary goal in Bosnia "was to establish a base for operations in Europe against al Qaeda's true enemy, the United States." Not long afterward, Abu Hajer al-Iraqi (Mamdouh Mahmud Salim, one of the original founders of al Qaeda in Afghanistan) confirmed to al-Fadl that Abu Abdel Aziz had spoken the truth and Osama bin Laden's interest in Bosnia was largely as a staging area from which to strike at America.[13] Consequently, al Qaeda representatives arranged for nine élite instructors from the Al-Sadda terrorist training camp in Afghanistan to be immediately imported into central Bosnia.[14] Within a month of the landmark meeting in Zagreb, a Saudi cousin of Osama bin Laden who had fought and distinguished himself during the Afghan jihad was killed in a sudden shootout with United Nations peacekeepers near the Sarajevo International Airport.

Mujahideen Recruitment from Europe and North America

Despite a series of near catastrophic human setbacks, the mujahideen had nevertheless established themselves as a viable and respected fighting force in Bosnia by the end of 1992. While relatively small in number, they had proven on occasion to be more courageous and capable in the heat of battle than their Bosnian counterparts. Their reputation grew in importance despite the fact that they had achieved no clear victories against the Serb enemy. Meanwhile, the stories of dramatic "martyrdom" emerging from the Balkans were generating tremendous interest throughout the larger international Islamic community. Spreading word of the sacrifices made by these early "martyrs" was a compelling tool to lure future would-be jihadis. A broad collection of young men from across the Muslim world, dreaming of similar glory, would seek to emulate this example, even if it meant certain death—and with the Arab foreign legion in Bosnia gaining recognition from the highest circles, these militants saw a bright future for themselves on the horizon.

Amongst the nations of Western Europe, the Bosnian war caused a particularly strong backlash in the prominent and outspoken British Muslim community. Educated and idealistic youths angrily protested against the persecution of fellow Muslims in Bosnia. One college student, a classmate of several men who had left to seek training in Afghanistan and Bosnia, saw nothing wrong with taking up arms against the "enemies of Islam": "You cannot turn a blind eye when Muslims are being massacred, because what will you do when it is happening on your doorstep?"[15] In Bosnia, amateur mujahideen cameramen interviewed several British volunteers, including a masked man who identified himself as "Abu Ibrahim," a twenty-one-year old third-year medical student at Birmingham University living in Golders Green, London. Abu Ibrahim criticized the hypocrites among his peers in the United Kingdom who swore revenge on the Serbs and Croats, yet were too afraid to join the jihad in Bosnia: "What we lack here is Muslims that are prepared to suffer and sacrifice. There in Britain, I see Muslims, every medical student is saying that my third year is for Islam, my third year is for the Muslims. They get their job, they get their surgery. Fifty, 60, 70,000 pounds a year they're earning. And then, no struggle, no sacrifice." Abu Ibrahim spoke of the intense sense of satisfaction he felt fighting in the Bosnian war, as compared to the apathy of the secular Muslims who remained in London. In Britain, "I watch the TV and tears roll down my face when I see the Muslims in Bosnia, Muslims in Palestine, Muslims in Kashmir. And then I come [to Bosnia] and you feel a sense of satisfaction. You feel that you are fulfilling your duty. You feel that you are doing what the Prophet and his companions done [sic] 1,400 years ago."[16]

Abu Muslim al-Turki, of an older generation, was originally of Turkish descent but had lived most of his life in Britain as a secular Muslim. Until he was in his late forties, he was not an avid follower of Islam and was in fact married to a non-Muslim. However, after witnessing the dramatic Muslim-Serb struggle in Bosnia, Abu Muslim experienced a reawakening of religious idealism. During the physical endurance part of the training, special amenities were in place for him "due to his old age and the difficulties he would have." However, firmly set on the path of jihad, Abu Muslim survived and eagerly battled first the Serbs and, later, the Croats. Reportedly, he had to plead his case every time with the military commanders to allow him to join the fighters. Hesitant about Abu Muslim's advancing age and wounded state, they reluctantly agreed to put him in battle and it was not long before Abu Muslim was cut down by enemy gunfire.[17]

Apparently as the result of the same 1993 battle in central Bosnia, another British Muslim, this time a convert named David Sinclair, was also "martyred." Sinclair (a.k.a. Dawood al-Brittani) was a twenty-nine-year old employee of a computer company in the United Kingdom. After suddenly converting to Islam and adopting traditional Muslim dress, Sinclair ran into problems with senior management at his company. Within a week of wearing his new clothes to work, he was reportedly terminated. He thereupon decided to travel to Bosnia and join the Islamic military organization based there. In the midst of his training, he generously gave away his two British passports to Arab-Afghan "brothers in need." Dawood refused to return to the United Kingdom, evidently out of a determination to avoid living the life of a *kafir* (infidel). During combat with the Croats, he was shot and killed near an enemy bunker.

The unusual case of David Sinclair is a reminder that Arab-Afghan mujahideen volunteers active in Bosnia came from virtually everywhere, even the United States. A Bosnian mujahid interviewed years later by an Associated Press reporter discussed how "a mosque in Newark, New Jersey" had sponsored "Project Bosnia": an undertaking whereby fourteen Americans claiming to be veterans of U.S. special forces were sent to help train Arab and Bosnian fighters near the town of Tuzla. The foreign instructors had themselves been initially trained by veterans of the Afghan jihad and Egyptian Islamic militants at secret paramilitary camps in Pennsylvania, where they were educated in the "firing of semi-automatic assault rifles, commando style shooting exercises, intense physical fitness training, hand-to-hand combat techniques, martial arts instruction, pepper mace training, and mock nighttime assaults on a nearby electric power substation." The camps were funded by a $150,000 promised donation from the Saudi Arabian embassy in Washington, DC.

In a wiretapped conversation with an FBI informant, one of the camp organizers explained, "Our goal is that these people get extensive and very, very, very good training, so that we can get started at anyplace where jihad is needed. . . . And after they receive their training, they go to Bosnia, I mean, they depart. . . . And whoever survives, I mean, could come and . . . [instruct] somewhere else, or Egypt, or any other place, etc."[18] Within two months in the winter of 1993, the group of U.S. nationals had trained twenty-five more mujahideen in central Bosnia—including at least eight Sudanese Islamic militants—in "insurgency warfare."[19] Despite their professed mission as "armed humanitarians" protecting innocent Bosnians, twelve of the American instructors and all of the Sudanese fighters involved with "Project Bosnia" inexplicably departed the combat zone following completion of the brief guerilla warfare course.

By December 1995, Pentagon spokesmen were publicly accusing a U.S. national and alleged veteran of "Project Bosnia" of stalking U.S. troops in the Balkans while in the midst of preparing a terrorist attack. Isa Abdullah Ali (a.k.a. Kevin Holt), a former groundskeeper at Howard University in Washington, DC, was an eccentric and enigmatic figure who had thoroughly tested the patience of the Pentagon and the U.S. State Department.[20] Ali had received his initial military education serving as a U.S. Marine in Vietnam, yet turned down a different path in the early 1980s. A former co-worker of Ali's at a bar in Washington, DC, offered an equally curious portrait of the eccentric American mujahid:

He certainly looked the part of the doorframe heavy, showing up for work in biker leathers or military fatigues. A pair of goggles strapped around his balding head gave him the air of somebody who was always combat-ready; through the thick lenses, his small brown eyes looked like floating saucers. A mole on his right cheek came into focus whenever he leaned forward, either to make a point or to shift his weight off a bullet fragment still lodged in his left thigh, a souvenir from his final gunfight in West Beirut. Isa told me his Creator had put him on Earth to defend innocent Muslim civilians.[21]

By the closing months of the Bosnian war in 1995, Isa Abdullah Ali was clearly less concerned with the atrocities committed by the Serbs than with scheming to disrupt the U.S.-led peace process in the Balkans. Ali quickly aroused the suspicions of U.S. and NATO troops across the region soon after the signing of the Dayton Accords. A number of sentinels and junior officers distributed at various checkpoints in northern Bosnia reported that they had seen him several times during January and February, near a U.S. base adjacent to the northern Bosnian town of Orasje. Other sightings placed Ali not far off in the Lasava River Valley. According to the American soldiers, he was traveling around in a "beat-up" Humvee and deliberately harassing them. One sergeant at a NATO checkpoint said that Ali had driven right up to the base near Orasje before concealing a booby-trapped device under a glove on the ground and then driving off again. As he had previously been cited for falsely posing as an authorized military member, American officials worried that, with "the proper uniform and equipment, he could easily disguise himself as a U.S. soldier."[22] At the Pentagon, spokesman Lt. Col. Arnie Owens would only say that Ali was "regarded as a potential security threat to American personnel."[23] He was the perfect operative to scout potential American targets in Bosnia and to evade NATO security cordons setup to deter terror attacks.

By this time, the U.S. government began emphatically insisting to the Bosnian Muslim President Alija Izetbegovic that the remaining foreign fighters present in the Balkans would need to leave immediately after the signing of the landmark Dayton Peace Accords. While many Arab Afghans simply went underground in postwar Bosnian Muslim territory, others gleefully complied with the orders of America. Their terrorist commanders had decided to ironically profit from the U.S. interest in expelling the mujahideen from Bosnia. Hundreds of veteran fighters, accused of brutal wartime atrocities and expertly trained in urban warfare, were readily granted political asylum in a collection of European countries, Australia, and Canada. Canada, particularly, was favored among North African ex-fighters because of its lax immigration laws and Quebec's eager preference for francophone speakers. It was a devious tactic that allowed al Qaeda to infiltrate key Western democracies with skilled and well-motivated terrorist sleeper cells. A French report written by the highly esteemed French counterterrorism magistrate Jean-Louis Bruguière later concluded that the "exfiltration" of significant numbers of veteran fighters from Bosnia was beneficial for al Qaeda in the sense that it enabled the mujahideen "to be useful again in spreading the jihad across other lands." In fact, "among the veterans of the 'Moudjahiddin Battalion' of Zenica, many would go on to carry out terrorist acts following the end of the Bosnian conflict."[24]

The 1993 World Trade Center attack and the 1995 Paris metro bombings had proved the particular strength of the al Qaeda–linked North African mujahideen organizations such as al-Gama'at Al-Islamiyya and the Armed Islamic Group (GIA). The Egyptian and Algerian Islamic militants gained a distinct reputation among their comrades for employing fanatical methods and fielding a relatively impressive international sleeper cell network. During the Bosnian civil war, an unusually large number of foreign Muslim fighters claimed an affiliation with these Maghribi groups, including jihad training camp managers, frontline unit commanders, élite bodyguards, and volunteers for suicide missions. Conversely, in Afghanistan, Osama bin Laden surrounded himself with predominantly Egyptian advisors and appointed them to senior positions in al Qaeda—even to head its prestigious military committee. In February 1998, bin Laden publicly formalized his partnership with al-Gama'at and al-Jihad during the inauguration of the World Islamic Front Against Jews and Crusaders. The Egyptian extremists eagerly signed on to bin Laden's edict advocating the murder of American civilians as an individual religious duty for every Muslim.

Fateh Kamel and the Al-Kifah Refugee Center

For the radical North African mujahideen fighters educated and headquartered in the Balkans, the campaign of terror targeting France, the United Kingdom, Italy, and the United States had already been initiated years earlier. The Arab-Afghan wave of terror directed from central Bosnia, starting in 1996, bore the distinct characteristics of traditional al Qaeda operations, including the use of Islamic charitable front groups. In this case, the notorious al-Kifah Refugee Center office in Zagreb, Croatia, served as the initial rendezvous point for many of the eventual conspirators. The al-Kifah office in Zagreb was run by a collection of unusual employees, mostly of Algerian origin, including a hardened Arab-Afghan veteran named Fateh Kamel (a.k.a. "Mustapha the Terrorist," "El Fateh"). Kamel, who had lived in Canada since 1988, was a sadistic genius with a dangerous propensity for violence. As an Algerian who had been trained early at al Qaeda's camps in Afghanistan, his slick, polished exterior boasted a professionalism that was matched only by his pure cold-bloodedness. French intelligence determined that Kamel and his associates had "multiple links" with "diverse Islamic terrorist organizations around the world, and particularly in Bosnia, in Pakistan, in Germany, and in London."[25] Kamel was not permanently based in the Balkans, but instead would travel frequently across the world in order to traffic in illegal passports and other documents and overall to maintain the widespread terrorist network of the Afghano-Bosniak disciples.

Fateh Kamel drew particularly close to a loose network of units of North African immigrants and European converts to Islam who had come to aid the mujahideen during the early stages of the Bosnian war. For all intents and purposes, he became their handler, giving assistance and issuing orders directly on behalf of the two most senior European al Qaeda leaders still active in Bosnia after the 1995 Dayton Peace Accords. Over a nine-month period in 1996, Kamel suddenly began activating a number of his "Bosniak" terror units implanted in Europe at the apparent behest senior representatives of the GIA and Al-Gama'at Al-Islamiyya, instructing them to prepare for new jihad operations to take place inside France, Italy, and the United States.

In the Roubaix-Lille region of northeastern France, Kamel allegedly activated a particularly eager terror cell led by two native Frenchmen who had fought with the foreign mujahideen in Bosnia: Lionel Dumont (a.k.a. Abu Hamza) and Christophe Caze (a.k.a. Abu Waleed). According to French judicial officials, the most senior Algerian military commander in central Bosnia "exerted a lot of influence" on both Dumont and Caze "which led them to commit . . . violent actions under the cover of Islam."[26]

Dumont grew up in a family with a Christian background, and studied history in hopes of becoming a journalist. In 1992, he suddenly dropped out of his French university to volunteer for mandatory French army service, resulting in a stint as a UN peacekeeper in Somalia. There, he was a firsthand witness to the collapse of the international humanitarian effort and the U.S. military debacle in Mogadishu. He brooded in a local church bulletin, "The sight of such poverty strangles me." He was shaken by what he had seen in Africa and was unsuccessful in finding any employment at home when he returned to France.

The prolonged experience in East Africa had also radically changed Dumont. He became a convert to fundamentalist Islam who refused to consume alcohol or pork and insisted that his friends call him "Abu Hamza." His sister attempted to explain the cryptic personality of Dumont: "He is a sincere person. . . . Anyone who hasn't been in a war can't imagine what derailed him."[27] Determined to act as an "armed humanitarian" on behalf of Islam, Dumont traveled to Bosnia and, at the end of 1993, volunteered as an aid convoy driver for the Al-Kifah Refugee Center in Zagreb, known to be affiliated at that time with a group of "militant Algerians."[28]

Dumont bonded closely with one of the men he met there: Christophe Caze, a French medical student who was likewise an extremist convert to

Islam. Caze had first gone to Bosnia to offer his services to the mujahideen near the end of 1992.[29] In Zenica, he worked in the local hospital where other Arab fundamentalist volunteers gathered. It was the same hospital where Fateh Kamel later spent time recuperating from a battlefield wound to his foot.[30] By most accounts, Caze also participated in military actions and was trained in advanced guerilla warfare skills at the battalion's headquarters at the Vatrostalno factory complex. His combat experiences pushed him further along the path of radical Islam and its calls for the shedding of blood.[31]

Christophe Caze came home to France a changed man when his tour of duty with the mujahideen ended in the early months of 1993. He would incessantly speak of his combat experiences and try to convince his friends to leave their "worldly" lives and join the "heroic" jihad in Bosnia.[32] Caze's return to Western society had clearly not been a step towards resuming his mundane past life as a medical student. Rather, as a result of his training in Bosnia, he was now dead-set on a path to construct a network of like-minded Muslim militants in his locality (Roubaix) in immediate preparation for military operations aimed at "infidel" targets in France. The plot would succeed in inspiring terror among the French and any financial proceeds would be further donated to help support the GIA in Algeria. To obtain the necessary heavy weapons, Dumont and Caze relied on the hidden stockpiles in Bosnia presided over by remaining mujahideen leaders hiding there. Once in Bosnia, the two would amass a formidable collection of AK-47s, pistols, grenades, RPGs, and more. These men were preparing themselves for much more than a mere life of crime; they were mobilizing to take part in a larger suicidal holy war.

The Roubaix Group

Between January and March, the Roubaix Group lived up to its (limited) vision, and was the prime suspect in at least six holdups of vehicles carrying cash deposits from supermarkets along the French-Belgian border, as well as a botched attack with an RPG on a Brinks armored car. Police were at first baffled, because the trucks carrying the supermarket money were considered low-value targets, especially given the amount of firepower involved. The modus operandi of these criminals was quite distinct and they seemed to be more interested in creating chaos and taking innocent life than actually stealing anything valuable.[33] In one incident, Caze and his men shot and killed a French Muslim who did not hand over the keys to his prized Mercedes-Benz fast enough. In total, for all their hard work, the gang only netted about $10,000—not a very impressive take for a risky career robbing armored cars.[34]

The Roubaix conspirators, including Dumont and Caze, unwisely traveled around openly in their vehicles, flaunting their freedom, even as they knew police were eyeing them suspiciously. Indeed, at some point in mid-March, the cell became aware that a number of its members were under direct surveillance by local French police, who considered them the prime suspects in the chain of robberies. Infuriated that the authorities would even dare to pursue them (much like the attitude of the mujahideen towards British peacekeepers in Bosnia), the Roubaix Group swore that they would punish the meddling of the infidels. On 29 March 1996, a small blast went off in a white Peugeot 205 parked outside police headquarters in the nearby city of Lille, 10 miles southwest of Roubaix. Inside the car, authorities found three 28-pound gas canisters (eerily similar to the devices used by the GIA the previous summer) that had failed to explode when their detonator, a smaller explosive with a simple remote transmitter, was successfully ignited.[35] What really worried the French government was that, two days later, French President Jacques Chirac was scheduled to open a major G-7 international diplomatic summit less than 200 meters away from the ill-fated Peugeot.

Police quickly suspected the inhabitants of 59 Henri Carette, especially after two suspected members of the Roubaix gang (identified as the owners of the car) were witnessed driving it in the Lille area on the day of the bombing.[36] The men chose to deliver the weapon themselves and made remarkably little effort to conceal their tracks, especially in light of their supposed "élite military training" in Bosnia. Police called the failed car bombing a "provocation"—this was a deliberate challenge to authorities from an egotistical crew of dangerous hoodlums.[37] It was almost as if Dumont and Caze were daring the police to try and fight it out with them: "They acted out of pure hatred of cops," stated judicial policeman Bernard Gravet in the *Voix du Nord* newspaper.[38]

If this was indeed a dare, than it was graciously accepted by the French police, who did not take being targeted lightly. The mujahideen hideout was already under scrutiny stemming from the robberies, and now police carefully surrounded the house with snipers and GIGN counterterrorist commandos. The fanatics inside opened fire first, unloading the heart of their in-house armory of between six and eight AK-47 assault rifles, hand grenades, boxes of ammunition, and other equipment.[39] The firefight became so fierce that French officials were forced to evacuate the entire neighborhood. The GIGN commandos eventually attempted to storm the house amid a hail of gunfire, wounding two policemen.[40] Either as a deliberate act of arson by the suicidal terrorists or simply as the result of the sheer amount of bullets and grenades flying through the walls, the sagging house finally burst into flames. The roof and the upper floor of the structure caved in and collapsed on top of its stubbornly resisting occupants.[41] Investigators found three very badly charred bodies inside: two Moroccans, Rachid Souindi and Said el-Laihar; and, an Algerian, Teli bel Hachem.[42] They also came across an impressive collection of Islamic fundamentalist magazines, including several tied to radical Algerian terrorist groups, in the remains of the house.[43]

Simultaneously, in the suburbs of Lille, police attempted to separately arrest Christophe Caze and an additional suspect by constructing a roadblock. The two opened fire on authorities and forced their way through the barricade in a stolen car. Caze aimed to flee France and took the E17 motorway towards the Belgian border. Police closed in and finally intercepted the vehicle on the E17 bridge between Mouscron, France, and Kortrijk (Courtrai), Belgium. Motorists fled in panic as Caze fiercely battled his pursuers and bullets whizzed across the bridge, eventually leading to his unceremonious death in the crossfire.[44] More magazines, weapons, and grenades, were found in the car alongside the limp body of Christophe Caze.[45]

Yet astonishingly, Lionel Dumont and another co-conspirator were able to somehow escape their pursuers, spirited by Egyptian and Algerian terrorist ringleaders through Italy and then back to the underground mujahideen network hiding in postwar central Bosnia. It did not take long for French police to discover that the Roubaix Group had strong connections to the GIA and Al-Gama'at Al-Islamiyya, as particularly evidenced by the involvement of foreign mujahideen veterans from the Bosnian war. In Caze's electronic address book, investigators found extensive contact information for both Fateh Kamel and an Algerian commander in Bosnia.[46] The address book also contained telephone numbers for another alleged member of the Roubaix Group, master document forger Zohair Choulah— a commander of the Bosnian mujahideen and key associate of Fateh Kamel deemed "officially unwelcome" in France since 1995. Choulah's alias "Abdul Barr" was printed in Caze's organizer along with a corresponding Sarajevo number linked to alleged members of Al-Gama'at Al-Islamiyya.[47] A high-ranking French police official admitted that they were studying the Afghano-Bosniak phenomenon very closely: "It was enough here that one person served in Bosnia. This sort of thing will repeat itself."[48]

For his part, Fateh Kamel was mysteriously absent from both the Middle East and Europe at this time. In the lingering wake of the March 1996 Roubaix debacle, French intelligence tracked Kamel as he returned to Canada and started recruiting a new group of young, willing, North African terrorist accomplices, many of whom were tied (like Kamel) to the Bosnian war. Judge Jean-Louis Bruguière, who witnessed the development of Kamel's network in Canada, argues that Kamel's sudden interest in North America heralded a dangerous new era for these Afghano-Bosniak terrorist disciples: "The structure of the organization and the targets had changed. The targets weren't just in France or Europe [anymore]."[49] Unbeknownst to most Americans, al Qaeda and its international terrorist foreign legion were now taking determined aim at the homeland of their most powerful and hated enemy: the United States.

From Bosnia to North America

In Montreal, Fateh Kamel worked closely with another Bosnian mujahideen veteran living illegally in Canada: Karim Said Atmani (a.k.a. "Abu Hisham"), born in Morocco in 1966. He was widely reputed to have "considerable jihad experience in Algeria . . . he was a leader, and he was a veteran of fighting in Algeria during the 1990s."[50] One U.S. official has since called Atmani a "crazy warrior with a nose so broken and twisted that he could sniff around corners."[51] In particular, Atmani had previously served as part of an infamous GIA terror cell, known as the Mansour Meliani Commando Group, responsible for the 26 August 1992 bombing of the Algiers International Airport, killing nine and wounding 123.[52]

Afterwards, for roughly five years between 1994 and 1999, Atmani worked as Fateh Kamel's "right hand" man among the Bosnian mujahideen.[53] Atmani's links with the Arab fighters based in the Balkans were long and substantial; throughout 1994 and 1995, Atmani was officially tasked with organizing the transfer of foreign guerillas to Bosnia from staging points in Milan and elsewhere in Europe. Atmani, though perhaps only a midlevel operative in the loosely-organized international jihad network, has a fearsome reputation in the counterterrorism community. However, despite his undeniable years of terrorist "expertise," Atmani was not a terribly original thinker. Once in Canada, true to form, he began scheming a Roubaix-style "armed robbery of the bureau of exchange in Montreal" and a GIA-signature "terrorist attack on a U.S. airport."[54]

In Canada, Fateh Kamel and Atmani befriended a mixed group of other young, unemployed, and restless North African immigrants, including recent arrival Ahmed Ressam.[55] Ressam was a native of Algeria, where it did not take long for him to get in trouble with local authorities. Fed by his parents on stories of the 1962 independence war, the unemployed Ressam grew bored of his comparatively meaningless existence and quickly became "fascinated by [television] shows about 'unsolved' conspiracies like the Kennedy assassination."[56] In the early days of the Algerian civil war, Ressam fled his homeland after he was accused by Algerian authorities of arms trafficking for Islamic fundamentalists in North Africa. He traveled first to France and then to Montreal in 1994. Ressam had come to Montreal for nightclubs and Armani suits, not jihad and Osama bin Laden. However, unable to find employment, he turned to petty crime as a means to finance his desired lifestyle in the West.

He developed his skills enough to gain the attention of a wealthy and influential member of the Montreal Muslim community who was working closely with Ressam's roommates: Fateh Kamel. At the time, Kamel was using his storefront business in Canada as a cover for his growing role as an international terrorist mastermind. He employed the promising Ressam as an invaluable source of passports, credit cards, petty theft, and the other necessary functional tools of terrorist activity.[57] Once again, as French Judge Jean-Louis Bruguière would later testify in U.S. court, Fateh Kamel had become the leader of yet another "conspiratorial cell," this time based out of Montreal.[58]

Kamel, Atmani, and the others in Montreal drew Ahmed Ressam deep into their world of radical Islam. Several members of the Malicorne gang quietly left Montreal in March 1998 on a quest to seek military training in Afghanistan. Ressam flew to Karachi, Pakistan, where he was given a new identity, Afghan clothes, and an authorized letter of transit to a guest-house in Jalalabad. Shortly thereafter, Ressam was moved on to the nearby Khalden training camp.[59] The camp had about 100 total men, divided into cells of between six and fourteen recruits each. The cells were taught to exist and operate independently of any central command structure. According to Ressam, at Khalden, they learned "how to blow up the infra-structure of a country . . . electric plants, gas plants, airports, railroads, large corporations . . . hotels where conferences are held."[60] While in Afghanistan, Ressam also participated in gruesome chemical weapons experiments on dogs and learned "how to mix poisons with other substances, put them together and smear them on doorknobs . . . designed to be used against intelligence officers and other VIPs."[61]

In late 1998, Ressam met with several other cell members and al Qaeda representatives in Afghanistan. They agreed to return to Canada in three carefully programmed phases. Atmani, mostly likely back in central Bosnia during the summer of 1998, was scheduled to arrive in Montreal in the third and final phase. Upon the successful return of all the cell members, Atmani, Ressam, and the others were planning to commit a series of Roubaix-style operations (mainly bank robberies) in order to finance a major terrorist strike against the United States; specifically, a massive bomb explosion at Los Angeles International Airport coinciding with the start of the new millennium. The choice was made because "an airport is sensitive politically and economically."[62]

Despite Karim Said Atmani's failure to re-enter America himself, other members of the cell already positioned inside the United States were reassured by their handlers based in Montreal that Ressam "used to be in Afghanistan and Bosnia" and that "the fire is on."[63] They referred to Ressam's imminent solo arrival as "a great blessing"; one conspirator later admitted that he knew exactly what this meant: "[t]his guy was coming for some violent act."[64] On 14 December 1999, Ressam was stopped by U.S. border patrol agents at the Port Angeles crossing near Vancouver. In his car, investigators found the precursors to terror: 100 pounds of explosives and simple timing devices. Ressam made a bold effort to escape, reminiscent of the slippery Lionel Dumont; one Customs agent recalled, "I was looking right at him, had my weapon pointed in his direction. . . . He quickly darted into traffic, bounced off a car, continued to run hard. And that was what really triggered me, caused me to get very nervous, when he came up to a passenger vehicle and tried to commandeer it or open the car door. I thought, 'This guy really wants to get away, and he's dangerous.' "[65]

Conclusion

In sum, for al Qaeda the real value of Bosnia-Herzegovina was as a step in the ladder towards its enemies in Western Europe and North America. It was a place, with proximity to London, Riyadh, and Cairo, where terrorist recruits could train, coalesce into cells, and seek shelter from prosecution by foreign law enforcement. Especially for North African militant groups like the Algerian GIA, Bosnia was the best uncontrolled war zone where they could set up nearby overseas operations. According to one unnamed former State Department official, "[t]hey come to Bosnia to chill out, because so many other places are too hot for them."[66] Bosnia's key role was in drawing together the various components of an amorphous group of disaffected, unemployed European-North African youths who were susceptible to the same stories of jihad and martyrdom that had lured so many Saudis and Kuwaitis to Afghanistan in the 1980s. Bosnia was also ideal for some of the economic projects of al Qaeda, particularly revolving around the Islamic charitable organizations mostly based from and heavily funded by the Kingdom of Saudi Arabia.

Amazingly, it took many years for global intelligence agencies, particularly in Europe, to recognize the new emerging threat from North African Islamic exiles and sleeper cells. An anonymous Spanish security official admitted to *Time* magazine reporters, "In Europe we were too preoccupied with our own terrorist problems—ETA in Spain, the IRA in the U.K., the Corsicans in France and so on—and we devoted our resources to these threats. . . . Even after the attacks on the U.S. embassies in Kenya and Tanzania, the Islamic threat seemed distant." According to the Spaniard, "Everything changed after September 11. Before then we looked on bin Laden as someone from another planet, like a Martian."[67]

Bosnia provided the ultimate meeting ground for the mostly Saudi, Egyptian, and Yemeni lieutenants of Osama bin Laden and the North African jihadi foot soldiers (a good number of whom were European citizens). Bosnia was the link that tied the European and Canadian terrorist networks of men like Fateh Kamel to the senior mujahideen leadership in Afghanistan. Though these men were adherents of the Algerian GIA, they were receiving their marching orders directly from the al Qaeda terrorist masterminds at the behest of bin Laden. It was almost as if bin Laden had "contracted out" a terror campaign to a generic GIA sleeper cell.[68] Even some Saudis themselves, such as journalist Jamal Kashogji, had predicted that "allowing [Islamic militants] to go to Bosnia and get military training there will make them good prospects for something else later on."[69] Stefano Dambruouso, a prosecutor in Milan investigating local al Qaeda links, now admits, "The real problem in Europe before 1998 was Algerian nationals, who were involved in mostly single episodes that weren't coordinated. . . . After that, bin Laden began to connect and coordinate all these cells that already existed, rendering the phenomenon much more radicalized and potent."[70] In other words, the spark met the powder keg when the intricate network of would-be international terrorists in Europe and Canada who had fought and sacrificed together on the battlefields of the Balkans met the growing financial and political influence of the Saudi exile and prince of the fanatics, Sheikh Osama bin Laden.

CHAPTER 13

Indoctrination Processes within Jemaah Islamiyah

KUMAR RAMAKRISHNA

The Jemaah Islamiyah ("Islamic community" or JI) radical Islamist terrorist organization has emerged as the biggest threat to Southeast Asian security. JI, which has Indonesian origins, seeks to establish a *Daulah Islamiyah Nusantara,* or an archipelagic Islamic Southeast Asian state incorporating Indonesia, Malaysia, the southern Philippines, and inevitably, Brunei and Singapore.[1] What sets JI apart from other violent radical Islamic Southeast Asian groups is its transnational aspirations: Over and above establishing ties with regional entities such as the Moro Islamic Liberation Front (MILF), JI has also had contact with Osama bin Laden's al Qaeda. JI has been responsible for a series of bombings in Indonesia, the latest being the September 2004 bomb attack outside the Australian Embassy in Jakarta. Nine people were killed and more than 180 injured. Reports suggest that the attack on the embassy was planned by a senior Malaysian JI bomb maker Azahari Husin, at large in Indonesia, and executed by a squad involving a "new generation of JI cadres" from South Sumatra.[2] The fact that new recruits were involved in the latest major strike suggests that the organization—despite vigorous counterterror action by regional governments—is regenerating. Clearly, JI indoctrination processes have continued to be effective in ensuring fresh recruitment.[3]

This chapter seeks to examine the processes by which JI indoctrinates new militants. In this respect, it can be argued that against the necessary wider historical, sociocultural, and political backdrop of indigenous militant strains of Islam in Indonesia, the key to JI indoctrination involves three intersecting factors: first, the deliberate exposure of recruits to the radical Islamist ideology of Qaedaism; second, intensive psychological programming aimed at engendering hatred for Westerners in particular; and third, the existence of an isolated "ingroup space" within which both ideological and psychological programming can be carried out with maximum efficiency.

The Wider Historical-Political Context

Radical Islam is not a new phenomenon in Indonesia. In the eighteenth century, the Wahhabi-like Padri movement that emerged in West Sumatra sought to introduce a harder, fundamentalist edge to the syncretic, softer forms of Islam that had long been in existence in the country. Similarly, after World War II, the fledgling Indonesian republic was confronted by the Darul Islam (DI) rebellion, led by a charismatic Javanese activist called S. M. Kartosuwirjo. Kartosuwirjo violently rejected the secular state vision and religiously neutral *Pancasila* ideology of secular Indonesian nationalists such as Sukarno and Mohammad Hatta. Kartosuwirjo proclaimed instead an Islamic State in Indonesia (NII) based on *sharia* law in August 1949, and the DI/NII forces waged jihad against the Republican regime throughout the 1950s. By 1962 however, the DI revolt that had spread from its West Java epicenter throughout the country was crushed, while Kartosuwirjo was captured and executed. DI thereafter splintered into several underground factions. While DI failed to attain its political goal of an Indonesian Islamic State, it nevertheless "inspired subsequent generations of radical Muslims with its commitment to a *sharia*-based state and its heavy sacrifices in the cause of jihad."[4]

The cofounders of JI, Abdullah Sungkar and Abu Bakar Ba'asyir, were strong DI sympathizers who were committed to keeping the vision of *Daulah Islamiyah* (Islamic State) in Indonesia alive. Following the October 1965 coup that eventually led to the emergence of Suharto and the New Order regime in Indonesia, Sungkar began campaigning openly with Ba'asyir for an Islamic state in Indonesia. Among other things, Sungkar and Ba'asyir oversaw the establishment of the Pondok Pesantren al-Mukmin Islamic boarding school in 1971, which later moved to the village of Ngruki, east of Solo. Influenced by the Egyptian Muslim Brotherhood, Sungkar and Ba'asyir sought to create extended families of morally upright al-Mukmin alumni (*usroh*). Ultimately they intended to forge networks of *usroh* into the wider Jemaah Islamiyah (or Islamic community) as the necessary penultimate step toward the realization of the Islamic state.[5] Being themselves sympathetic to the older and wider DI ideological diaspora, Sungkar and Bashir decided subsequently to affiliate the early JI network of ideological communes with the already existing DI. Consequently, JI officially became part of the Central Java DI in Solo, in 1976.[6] While part of DI, Sungkar and Ba'asyir became involved in the activities of a violent underground movement called Komando Jihad. Somewhat like JI today, this organization sought to set up an Islamic state in Indonesia and carried out bombings of nightclubs, churches, and cinemas. Ironically, Komando Jihad was to a large extent a creation of Indonesian intelligence and was set up to discredit political Islam in Indonesia and legitimize the New Order's subsequent crackdown on "less radical and non-violent Muslim politicians."[7]

In 1978 both Sungkar and Ba'asyir were detained for their involvement in Komando Jihad. They were released by the New Order regime in 1982, but following the Tanjong Priok incident two years later—in which the security forces killed scores of Muslims—both were charged yet again for subversion. This prompted them and several of their followers to flee to Malaysia in 1985. While in Malaysia, Ba'asyir adopted the pseudonym Abdus Samad and Sungkar took on the *nom de guerre* Abdul Halim.[8] Over the years, both men, through the financial support base generated by their effective preaching activities, were able to buy property of their own in other parts of the country. Wherever they went, they set up Koran reading groups and were invited to preach in small-group settings in both Malaysia and Singapore. In 1992, Sungkar and Ba'asyir set up the Luqmanul Hakiem pesantren in Ulu Tiram, in the southernmost Malaysian State of Johore. Luqmanul Hakiem was a clone of al-Mukmin back in Solo. Ba'asyir later told the Indonesian magazine *Tempo* that in Malaysia he set up "As-Sunnah, a community of Muslims."[9] In this way the original Sungkar/Ba'asyir network of *usroh* communities spread outward from Indonesia, sinking roots in Malaysia and Singapore.

The Role of Ideology

By the time Sungkar and Ba'asyir arrived in Malaysia in 1985, it could be said that they had become committed "radical Islamists." Before proceeding with this discussion, terms such as these must be explained. Islamic fundamentalism (or Salafi Islam) is no monolithic phenomenon. Salafi Muslims, who take the injunction to emulate the Companions of the Prophet very seriously, may express this piety simply in terms of personal adherence to implementing *sharia*-derived standards of worship, ritual, dress, and overall behavioral standards. The majority of Salafi Muslims, in fact, may be considered as "neofundamentalists" who possess "neither a systematic ideology" nor "global political agenda."[10] Islamism, on the other hand, "turns the traditional religion of Islam into a twentieth-century-style ideology."[11] To put it another way, when Salafi Muslims see it as an added obligation to actively seek recourse to political power in order to impose their belief system on the society at large, then they become not simply Muslims but rather *Islamists*.

Despite regional variations, Islamists worldwide share the common belief that seeking political power—in order to Islamize whole societies—is the only way Islam as a faith can revitalize itself and recapture the former preeminent position it enjoyed vis-à-vis the West. Modern Islamist movements include the Muslim Brotherhood in the Middle East and the Jama'at-I Islami in the Indian subcontinent, as well as many of the Iranian ideologues of the 1979 Revolution that brought down the Shah. These Islamists sought to construct "ideological systems" and "models" for "distinctive polities that challenged what they saw to be the alternative systems: nationalism, capitalism and Marxism."[12] In short, while the average, neo-fundamentalist Salafi Muslim emphasizes individual spiritual renewal as the key to Islamic civilizational renaissance, the Islamist, as American scholar Daniel Pipes suggests, seeks power as the superior approach.[13] It is entirely possible, moreover, that in pursuing political objectives Islamists—like other political activists seeking to implement an ostensibly religious agenda—may lose touch with the ethical core of the very faith they are seeking to preserve and champion. This process of ethical or moral disengagement facilitates terrorist acts, as described in this chapter and elsewhere in this volume.[14]

For years, both Sungkar and Ba'asyir had been Islamists in the sense that they ultimately sought to set up an Islamic state based on the *sharia* in Indonesia. But a latent ambiguity existed within their ideological systems over the role of violence. Both men had been aware of the potential of *dakwah* (proselytization) for gradually Islamizing Indonesian society from the bottom up; Sungkar had after all been the chairman of the Dewan Dakwah Islamiyah Indonesia (the "Indonesian Islamic Propagation Council" or DDII) Central Java branch, while Bashir had majored in *dakwah* at the al-Irsyad Islamic University in Solo.[15] This belief in *dakwah* had also led them to establish the al-Mukmin school in Solo in 1971. At the same time, however, they were not demonstrably opposed to Kartosuwirjo's argument that Islamizing the polity by force was the better approach. They even affiliated the nascent JI movement with Hispran's DI, and were involved in the Komando Jihad. Their incarceration in 1978 and subsequent targeting by the New Order regime may have been the "tipping point" in terms of providing them with the final insight that *dakwah* in the absence of jihad would be an exercise in futility. In other words, they became not merely Islamists but *radical* Islamists who believed in jihad as the means to actualize an Islamized Indonesia.

The Indonesian journalist Blontank Poer observes that the jihadi emphasis in the overall strategy of Sungkar and Bashir became more developed after the shift to Malaysia in 1985.[16] In this sense, the Sungkar-Ba'asyir radicalization experience brings to mind the Egyptian Muslim Brotherhood activist Sayyid Qutb, who was increasingly radicalized by the Egyptian government's clampdown on the Brotherhood. Cairo's repression prompted Qutb to transform "the ideology of [Muslim Brotherhood founder Hassan] al-Banna and [Jama'at-I Islami founder Mawlana] Mawdudi into a rejectionist revolutionary call to arms."[17] By the 1980s, Islamist ideas from the

Middle East and the Indian subcontinent had been translated and were in circulation in Southeast Asia.[18] These mingled and fused with the individual experiences, ideas, and impressions of Sungkar and Ba'asyir. Thus the injunctions of al-Banna and Mawdudi to set up a "vanguard" community to serve as the "dynamic nucleus for true Islamic reformation within the broader society"[19] were long accepted by the Indonesian clerics. Furthermore, Sungkar and Ba'asyir would have viscerally embraced Sayyid Qutb's polarized view of the world as irrevocably divided into "home of Islam" where "the Islamic state" exists and the "home of hostility" where the writ of Islamic law is not recognized.[20]

Thus it could be said that in the latter half of the 1980s and into the 1990s, the Indonesian émigré community in Malaysia believed in several core tenets. Some of these tenets would not have been unusual to mainstream Salafi Muslims:

- Islam possesses exclusive authenticity and authority;
- Committed Muslims must keep God at the center of every aspect of life;
- God loves but tests his truest followers; he also reserves for them eternal rewards in the life to come;
- Science and technology must be harnessed, but within an Islamic rather than a Western context; and
- The profane world is an abomination to God; he only accepts the prayers and good works of Muslims who adhere strictly to the demands of the *sharia*, the Quran and the Sunnah.

Other Sungkar/Ba'asyir precepts, however, clearly shaded into politically driven Islamist thinking:

- Deviation from the path of true Islam and emulation of Western models has resulted in worldwide Muslim weakness;
- *Sharia* provides the ideal blueprint for a modern, successful Islamic society capable of competing with the West and restoring Muslim identity, pride, power, and wealth;
- Alternative systems—such as democracy, socialism, *Pancasila*, capitalism, other religions, and Islam as practiced by the majority of the Muslim community—are not acceptable to God and are destructive; and
- True Muslims cannot with good conscience accept a political system that is not based on the *sharia*.[21]

Finally, by the early 1990s, the Sungkar-Ba'asyir ideological framework represented a radical Islamist vision because it included the explicit willingness to resort to jihad in pursuit of the goal of an Islamized Indonesia. It should be noted that apart from the DI legacy as well as the more recent radicalizing effect of direct New Order repression, Sungkar, Ba'asyir, and others in their immediate circle were also likely exposed to the ideas of the Egyptian radical Mohammad al-Faraj, executed by Cairo in 1982 for his role in the assassination of President Anwar Sadat.[22] Faraj, himself influenced by the works of al-Banna, Mawdudi, and Qutb, brought their incipient absolutizing ideas to their ultimate extremist conclusion. Unequivocally rejecting the efficacy of *dakwah* as a means of Islamizing *jahili* (un-Islamic or immoral) society,[23] Faraj argued that the decline of Muslim societies was due to the fact that Muslim leaders had hollowed out the vigorous concept of jihad, thereby robbing it of its "true meaning."[24]

In his pamphlet the *Neglected Obligation*, Faraj asserted that the "Koran and the Hadith were fundamentally about warfare" and that the concept of jihad, in contrast to the conventional wisdom, was meant to be taken at face value. It was not allegorical. According to him, jihad represented in fact the sixth pillar of Islam and connotes physical confrontation. Faraj held that not just infidels but even Muslims who deviated from the moral and social dictates of *sharia* were legitimate targets for jihad. He concluded that peaceful means for fighting apostasy in Muslim societies were bound to fail, and ultimately the true soldier of Islam was justified in using "virtually any means available to achieve a just goal."[25] Given their own recent experiences at the hands of the Suharto regime, Sungkar and Ba'asyir would have endorsed, at some deeper level, the ideas of Faraj on the necessity for a literal understanding of jihad, as well as his wider argument that jihad represented the highest form of devotion to God. This is precisely why, in 1984–85, when the Saudis sought volunteers for the jihad in Afghanistan against the invading Soviets, Sungkar and Ba'asyir willingly raised groups of volunteers from among their following.[26]

Al Qaeda's Ideology and Training for Jihad

The Afghan theater was seen as a useful training ground for a future jihad in Indonesia itself.[27] As it turned out, however, rather than Afghanistan being seen as a training ground for a jihad aimed at setting up an Indonesian Islamic state, that conflict became the source of ideas that transformed the original Indonesia-centric vision of Sungkar and Ba'asyir. To be sure, prior to the 1990s, the radical Islamist ideology driving JI may be termed (following American scholar Marc Sageman's analysis) as "Salafi Jihad."[28] The aim of the Indonesian émigré community in Malaysia, led by Sungkar and Ba'asyir, was ultimately to wage a jihad against the Suharto regime— in Faraj's terms, the so-called "near enemy"—and set up a Salafi Islamic state in Indonesia. However, returning Indonesian and other Southeast

Asian veterans of the Afghan jihad exposed Sungkar and Ba'asyir to fresh thinking on this issue.

In Afghanistan, the Southeast Asian jihadis were inspired to think in global terms by the teachings of the charismatic Palestinian *alim* (singular for *ulama*) Abdullah Azzam. Azzam, a key mentor of Osama bin Laden, had received a doctorate in Islamic jurisprudence from al-Azhar University in Cairo, had met the family of Sayyid Qutb, and was friendly with Sheikh Omar Abdul Rahman. Sheikh Omar Abdul Rahman—better known as the "Blind Sheikh"—was the spiritual guide of two key Egyptian radical Islamist terrorist organizations, the Egyptian Islamic Jihad (EIJ) and the Egyptian Islamic Group (EIG) and would later be implicated in the 1993 World Trade Center bombing in New York. When the Soviets withdrew from Afghanistan in 1989, Azzam, who had played a big part in recruiting non-Afghan foreign mujahideen worldwide, including from Southeast Asia, for the anti-Soviet jihad, began to set his sights further. He argued that the struggle to expel the Soviets from Afghanistan was in fact the prelude to the liberation of Palestine and other "lost" territories such as "Bukhara, Lebanon, Chad, Eritrea, Somalia, the Philippines, Burma, Southern Yemen, Tashkent and al-Andalus."[29]

Unlike Faraj, however, Azzam did not sanction jihad against "apostate" Muslim governments in Egypt, Jordan, and Syria. His understanding of jihad was a traditional one in the sense of evicting infidel occupiers from Muslim lands. He did not wish to see Muslim wage jihad against Muslim. But after his death in a car bomb explosion in Peshawar in November 1989, the Afghan Arab mujahideen community, and Osama bin Laden in particular, again accepted the Faraj argument that targeting Muslim governments seen as apostate was perfectly legitimate. Moreover, at the beginning of the 1990s, once American troops arrived in Saudi Arabia and in Somalia, both Muslim territories, it was argued in certain radical Islamist circles that local apostate Muslim governments were in fact pawns of a global power, the United States. This in effect reversed Faraj's strategy, and now the priority was jihad against the "far enemy" over the "near enemy."[30]

These shifts in global radical Salafi ideology post-Afghanistan were not lost on Sungkar and Ba'asyir. In addition to their discussions with returning Indonesian veterans of the Afghan war, both men also met with international jihadi groups in Malaysia. Consequently, by 1994, Sungkar and Ba'asyir were no longer talking about establishing merely an Islamic state in Indonesia. Over and above this, they were now talking of establishing a "world caliphate uniting all Muslim nations under a single, righteous exemplar and ruler."[31] It is no coincidence, then, that at about that time Sungkar and Ba'asyir reportedly made contact with Egyptian radicals associated with the Blind Sheikh.[32]

In the early 1990s, Sungkar and Ba'asyir also disassociated themselves from the Central Java DI movement because of serious doctrinal differences with regional DI leader Ajengan Masduki, who had apparently embraced Sufi teachings on nonviolence and tolerance. Sungkar and Ba'asyir, casting off the overarching DI appellation, resurrected the name Jemaah Islamiyah. This is the JI, infused with the post-Afghanistan neo-Faraj ethos of Global Salafi Jihad, that henceforth took it upon itself to wreak vengeance against perceived Western aggression and brutality toward Muslim communities. By the turn of the century, the virulent ideological strain of Global Salafi Jihad infusing JI had matured, and radical Islamist writers like Azzam, Qutb, and Faraj featured prominently on JI reading lists.[33]

Broader Social Psychological Factors Underpinning JI Indoctrination

Mere exposure to Qaedaist ideology, however, while important in and of itself, is insufficient to produce the fully indoctrinated JI militant. Ideological programming needs to be reinforced by broader social psychological processes. Unfortunately, such processes reinforcing ideologies of hatred readily exist. Social psychologists explain that the human mind groups people into categories to simplify information processing. However, such categorization tends to produce stereotyping of other social groups and worse, favoritism for one's own group. In a nutshell, "taken to extremes," ethnocentrism and stereotyping can foster prejudice.[34] All individuals, unfortunately, are prejudiced to some extent toward various "outgroups"; that is, the prejudiced individual is coolly dismissive of and indifferent to the sensibilities and sufferings of outgroup members.[35]

More disturbingly, within the larger pool of prejudiced individuals there is a smaller and more problematic number, the *bigots*. Bigots are those who are strongly biased in favor of one's own group, religion, or race. Importantly, rather than being passively indifferent like the simply prejudiced, bigots are actively intolerant of individual members of the disliked outgroup. The bigot would have little problem supporting legislation and social conditions that deprive outgroup members of their basic dignities and freedoms. Finally, it is from the smaller sociocultural pool of bigots that the *haters* emerge. While a bigot may feel resentment whenever he thinks of members of the despised outgroup he is not obsessed with them. On the other hand, hatred requires both passion and an obsessive focus on the outgroup. In truth, prejudice and bigotry expedite the destructive attitudes and behavior of the haters.[36]

This short exposition on prejudice, bigotry, and hatred is important for understanding JI. Ba'asyir once told an Indonesian intelligence official that as a preacher he likened himself to a "craftsman" who sells "knives," but is not responsible for what happens to them.[37] As the foregoing analysis suggests, however, Ba'asyir's remarks are disingenuous, as rhetoric matters a very great deal. One analyst illustrates this point with an acute observation:

> As recently as the summer of 2002, the *New York Times* reported an interview in which a professor of Islamic law explained to a visiting reporter: "Well of course I hate you because you are Christian, but that doesn't mean I want to kill you." Well, the professor may not wish to kill the reporter, but the students he instills with his theological justifications of hatred may have different ideas about the proper expressions of hatred.[38]

In fact, what Sungkar and Ba'asyir have done through their preaching in Indonesia and elsewhere in Southeast Asia, therefore, has been to generate pockets of sociocultural space that breed the prejudice, bigotry, and ultimately hatred that can be exploited to fuel JI extremism and violence. For example, Singaporean Malay/Muslim journalists who managed to visit the al-Mukmin school in January 2004 noted how anti-Western—and more specifically anti-American—sentiment was woven into the daily routines and instruction of teenage students. In particular, students were programmed to believe that Americans and Jews were infidels and so were Muslims who stood by and did nothing to prevent alleged Jewish-American aggression against Muslims everywhere. Significantly, posters and signs proclaiming jihad, spouting messages like "Jihad, Why Not?" and "No Prestige without Jihad," were prominently displayed on lockers, walls, and walkways leading to classrooms. Students, moreover, were spotted wearing T-shirts with images of Osama bin Laden, Saddam Hussein, and the Chechen militant leader Shamil Basayev.[39] Al-Mukmin was clearly acting as a dissemination center of Global Salafi Jihad or Qaedaist ideology, shaping a burgeoning culture of hatred.

While not all JI supporters or sympathizers may be directly involved in the planning, support, and/or execution of terror attacks, in truth they have a place somewhere along the continuum of prejudice described earlier: starting initially with prejudice, progressing to bigotry and then to hatred as an extreme. Under certain circumstances, prejudiced Islamists may well transition toward bigotry and even hatred, embrace Qaedaist worldviews, and become full-fledged, hate-filled terrorist operatives quite capable of killing so-called Western infidels. This final step in the JI indoctrination process must occur within the confines of what we may term "ingroup space."

The Decisive Contribution of "Ingroup Space"

In essence, wider sociocultural pockets of prejudice in Indonesia and the region, especially the particular *usroh* communities linked to Sungkar and

Ba'asyir, may produce a number of individuals who have been mentally conditioned to embrace Qaedaist dogma. This may compel them to transform from bigots into relatively obsessed haters of Westerners, which may in turn prompt some of them to seek entry into the actual JI organization. However, even within a small community of haters, there can be degrees of antipathy. For instance, within the Singapore JI cell, not all members were willing to engage in suicide or "martyrdom" operations against U.S. interests.[40] Hence, a relatively hate-dominated affective state may help explain why an Islamist from the wider population of al-Mukmin alumni, for instance, may decide to join a terrorist outfit like JI, but it does not necessarily explain how that individual can be psychologically prepared to engage in activities designed to physically obliterate the hate object. An additional set of psychic forces, operating within the framework of a clearly defined and sharply demarcated ingroup space, generates the psychological capacity to kill.

When one scans the backgrounds of members of the actual JI terrorist organization, one is immediately struck by the fact that many of them had backgrounds in which religion played the dominant role in identity formation. Mukhlas, a key operational JI leader, for instance, grew up in Tenggulun village, in Lamongan East Java, a very religious region of Indonesia, and was deeply immersed in an Islamic medium of education throughout his upbringing. He studied at al-Mukmin and Universitas Islam Surakarta and trained as a religious teacher at Payaman in Solokuro in East Java.[41] For his part, the fiery Bali bomb-field coordinator Imam Samudra attended a religiously conservative high school in Serang in Banten province in West Java. Like Mukhlas, he was deeply immersed in an Islamic medium of education, and spent time in Koran-reading sessions under DDII auspices, gradually imbibing a deeply anti-Christian worldview.[42] The intense religious insularity of the backgrounds of JI militants such as Mukhlas and Samudra is significant. Psychological research shows that intense religiosity tends to generate a strong sense of moral superiority as well as deeply ethnocentric, prejudiced, and discriminatory attitudes toward the outgroup.[43]

Furthermore, during intergroup contestation, crisis, and conflict, overarching group identity becomes much more important than individual identities; concern with in-group welfare replaces individual preoccupations; there is a heightened sense of shared, collective grievances; and importantly, members of the in-group tend to become behaviorally aggressive and engage in outgroup stereotyping.[44] In addition, "an attack or affront is personal when directed not only against one's physical self," but the wider in-group, or one's "collective self."[45] Because the collective self is important to the psychic well-being of individual in-group members, any serious threat to the collective self—whether physical or even metaphysical, involving power or honor—is likely to generate an intensely primal reaction comprising "hasty generalizations, stereotyping, us-them distinctions, and raw emotions—particularly anger and hate."[46] Hence if in-group members, despite their assumed innate moral superiority, are led to feel that the out-group enjoys greater power and status resources, and worse, is holding back or even physically harming the in-group through nefarious means, out-group hatred—possibly murderous hatred—could result. In the specific case of JI—which, as observed earlier, is shaped cognitively by Qaedaist fantasy war constructs—"in-group members' perceptions of outgroups and relevant external events" have been heavily "distorted, causing them to view the outgroup as an enemy."[47] Hence, the net effect of the deeply insular, religiously-driven life experiences of Mukhlas and Samudra, including their respective training and operational stints in Afghanistan, had endowed them with a religiously legitimated bigotry that ultimately became transmogrified into hatred toward the outgroup, especially Westerners in general and Americans in particular.

In concrete terms, nurturing the out-group hatred legitimated by the virulent Qaedaist worldview requires deliberate in-group isolation. Deliberately self-isolating communities place huge reliance on "alternative news sources," "home schooling," and "closed religious/ritual systems." These may "pull one away from competing social networks and constructions of reality."[48] In this regard, it is worth noting that in January 2004, al-Mukmin students were warned not to talk to strangers and were punished if they did.[49] In addition, following the August 2003 J. W. Marriott attack in Jakarta, a radical pamphlet entitled "Marriott Conspiracy Theory," blaming "Israeli and U.S. intelligence agents" for the incident, were readily accessible to al-Mukmin students.[50] The Singapore White Paper notes that JI as an organization deliberately policed its boundaries:

> After their induction into JI, members stayed away from mainstream religious activities and kept to themselves. Keeping together as a closely-knit group reinforced the ideological purity of the group and kept them loyal to the teachings of their foreign teachers.[51]

Similarly, JI training facilities in Mindanao in the southern Philippines—first Camp Hudaibiyah within the MILF's Abubakar complex, and since 2001, Camp Jabal Quba on Mount Kararao—have been extremely remote localities. These have not only facilitated extensive training courses in weapons and explosives; more importantly, they have facilitated ideological programming of new batches of young Indonesians and other Southeast Asians, designed to deepen their motivation for jihad.[52]

Intensive ideological programming aside, deliberate in-group isolation also expedites the amplification and focusing of out-group hatred. Some social psychologists argue that humans in all societies are socialized into accepting socially mandated "self-sanctions" that regulate their behavior. They point out that "to slaughter in cold blood innocent women and children in buses, department stores and in airports," requires "intensive psychological training" in the "moral disengagement" of these self-sanctions. One powerful way to relax self-sanctions is by "cognitively restructuring the moral value of killing" so that the killing can be done free from guilt.[53] JI leaders, as we have seen, deliberately portray their attacks on Western targets as part of a fully justified and legitimate defensive jihad. For example, some Singapore JI members who took part in Muslim-Christian fighting in Ambon in the Maluku archipelago in eastern Indonesia regarded their activities as justified, seeing themselves as defenders of fellow Ambonese Muslims who were in danger of being killed by Christians. The September 2004 attack on the Australian Embassy in Jakarta, furthermore, was presented as an attempt to compel the Australian "crusaders" to leave Iraq.

A second mechanism for disengaging the inner restraints against killing is euphemistically relabeling otherwise reprehensible activities so as to confer a respectable status on them.[54] We have seen how JI, like violent Islamist groups elsewhere, has exploited the term "jihad"—which has a very respectable pedigree in Islamic history—to justify bomb attacks on civilians. In addition, Sungkar justified criminal activity on the part of his followers by recasting them as *fa'i*—"robbing the infidels or enemies of Islam to secure funds for defending the faith."[55] Third, it can be said that people may well behave in ways they normally reject if a perceived external legitimate authority both authorizes and accepts responsibility for the consequences of their conduct. In this respect, several Malaysian and Singaporean JI terrorists have mentioned Osama bin Laden's February 1998 *fatwa* declaring jihad on the Jewish-Crusader alliance as justification for their own terror activities, while it is clear from interrogation reports that JI terrorists took special care to seek spiritual sanction for key operations from JI leader Bashir. Finally, self-sanctions against "cruel conduct can be disengaged or blunted by divesting people of human qualities."[56] In this respect it is noteworthy that Mukhlas himself declared that all Westerners were "dirty animals and insects that need to be wiped out."[57]

The final element that marks the transition of the JI hater into the JI killer is that the existing hate obsession of the JI terrorist must be deliberately manipulated immediately prior to recruitment and/or embarking on an operation. This is why JI leaders have relied heavily on atrocity propaganda in the form of homemade video compact discs (VCDs). The Maluku conflict of 1999–2000 in eastern Indonesia, for instance, provided much raw material for JI leaders, who made VCDs and distributed them across Southeast Asia, from Indonesia to the southern Philippines. These were shown during informal teaching sessions by JI clerics, and the "eager young men in attendance, duly incensed by what they had witnessed, were then briefed on how they could join the jihad."[58]

Taking Stock

This chapter has attempted to lay bare the complex processes by which ordinary young Muslims in Southeast Asia become indoctrinated JI terrorists, capable of killing in cold blood. It has been noted that while the ideology of Qaedaism is important, it is by no means the only factor influencing the transformation process. Sociocultural pockets of prejudice shaped by history and politics, intense in-group cognitive restructuring, and emotional conditioning processes all play their part as well. As the latest JI terrorist outrage in Jakarta illustrates, the threat from this organization has yet to abate despite counterterrorist successes. Significantly, the evidence indicates that losses are being replenished by fresh recruitment. This is important because it means that the JI network is self-regenerating and therefore enduring.

Clearly, while improving law enforcement, military, intelligence, and judicial measures domestically and internationally are important for dealing with the real-time threat of JI, they are powerless to prevent JI from gradually becoming a self-regenerating, existential threat. What is needed is fresh thinking on a whole range of issues that are not amenable to "hard" military/law enforcement solutions. While programs designed to improve regional state capacities to deal with the real-time threat of terrorism and ameliorate poverty and unemployment should continue to be pursued by regional governments with the assistance of the international community, this analysis suggests that other problems are in need of closer analysis and engagement.

First and foremost, one cannot ignore the wider communities of religious prejudice from which JI terrorists ultimately emerge. Second, ostensibly nonviolent leaders like Ba'asyir—who nonetheless preach polarized, absolutist ideologies that nudge impressionable individuals along the continuum toward hate obsession and potential terrorist recruitment—are clearly a cause for concern. It would be folly for such entrepreneurs of hate to be given free rein. Third, certain educational environments that deliberately limit contact with the outside world and appear to propagate alternate constructions of reality should be spotlighted and their managements urged to expose their student populations to wider informational and intellectual vistas. And of particular salience, the continuing inability of either liberal Muslims or Islamic modernists to devise and propagate modern interpretations of the faith that trump the simplistic, "us-versus-them" radical storylines in the estimation of the Muslim ground is a problem that urgently needs redressing.

Finally, it is not yet fully appreciated that in an era of globalization, what the United States does or does not do in the wider Muslim world can be selectively filtered through Qaedaist ideology to both strengthen JI and justify the most heinous of terrorist atrocities against civilians.[59] The analysis of the JI indoctrination process provided herein cannot be accepted without the concomitant recognition that as far as Southeast Asia is concerned, the real war on the roots of radical Islamist terrorism remains very much in its infancy.

CHAPTER 14

Christian Militia Training: Arming the "Troops" with Scripture, the Law, and a Good Gun

CINDY C. COMBS, ELIZABETH A. COMBS, AND LYDIA MARSH

The militia movement, one of three major right-wing antigovernment movements in the United States, is both fairly old and very new. It has deep roots in the Constitutionally-ingrained belief in the right to bear arms and the need for a "civilian militia" and a unique modern persona which often finds itself linked, in membership and ideals, with fundamentalist Christian organizations. In order to assess the training in the modern Christian militia movement, it is important to carefully define this modern phenomenon, clarifying the difference between movements in militia and Christian fundamentalist groups and identifying the relationship that clearly exists between these two movements and modern terrorism.

A brief analysis will show that this relationship began with a shared leadership cadre of Christian fundamentalists who helped to initiate the rebirth of the militia movement during the 1980s. Three important aspects of the relationship continue to shape the training of the Christian militia today: the Biblically-based theology which seeks to rationalize the preparation for violence by members of militia groups; a fervent belief in the Bill of Rights, particularly the right to bear arms and the right to generate an "unorganized militia"; and a commitment to a loose, virtually leaderless membership structure, with members trained to act alone or in small groups to "take back" the government, through force if necessary. This chapter will explore these aspects, beginning with the overlapping leadership and history of militia and Christian fundamentalists groups in the United States.

Shared History and Leadership Cadre

The militia movement today is heir to the antigovernment ideology of groups like the Posse Comitatus. This group, and others like the Silent Brotherhood, the White Patriot Party, and the Covenant, the Sword, and the Arm of the Lord, were early militia-type organizations united by a racist form of Christian fundamentalism and by the belief that the legitimate government of the United States had been subverted by conspirators. Most notable among the early leaders of these groups was William Potter Gale, a Christian Identity movement minister in the 1980s who was also one of the founders of the Posse Comitatus.

Gale, a former aide to General Douglas MacArthur, articulated the claim—later espoused by many militia proponents—that these "ungoverned militia" were not only legal, but also designed by law to oppose the government if it should become necessary. This claim was based on the U.S. Code, Title 10, subtitle A, Part 1, Chapter 13:

311. Militia: composition and classes

   (a) The militia of the United States consists of all able-bodied males at least 17 years of age and, except as provided in section 313 of title 32, under 45 years of age who are, or who have made a declaration of intention to become, citizens of the United States and of female citizens of the United States who are members of the National Guard

   (b) The classes of the militia are:

      (1) the organized militia, which consists of the National Guard and the Naval Militia; and

      (2) the unorganized militia, which consists of the members of the militia who are not members of the National Guard or the Naval Militia.[1]

Under Gale's leadership, many Posse members engaged in paramilitary training, and the training manual for "free militia," which will be examined later in this chapter, reflects the effort to organize and train members of the militia movement in cells with rudimentary military structure.

It is important to remember here that Gale was a Christian Identity minister as well as a militia leader. The Christian Identity movement links individuals by opposition to gun control, the federal government, taxes, environmental regulations, homosexuality, racial integration, and abortion, as well as by support for home schooling, states' rights, and a shared belief in an international one-world conspiracy that, led by the United Nations, is preparing to take over America and the world.[2] Christian Identity teaches that white Christians are God's chosen people, that Jews are the offspring of Satan, and that minorities are not human. Many Identity adherents are driving forces in the militia movement and believe that the "system" no longer works, because it has been taken over by the "New World Order," a secret group which actually runs the world. The membership of this secret group is less clearly defined; for some it is "the Jews," for others, the United Nations.

Many Identity members, particularly those in militias, define the enemy as the U.S. government, which is recast into the role of a tyrant or despot, with members of the Movement defining themselves as true "patriots." They reject the normal democratic processes of change, including election, petition, assembly, and constitutional amendment, believing instead that they alone are the defenders of freedom in their country.

Because so many leaders of the modern militia movement have also been Christian Identity leaders, the Identity theology permeates many of the right-wing groups, militias, and their proponents. For example: Robert DePugh, millionaire founder of the ultrarightist Minutemen; Glenn and Stephen Miller, organizers of the White Patriot Party; Jim Ellison, founder of the Covenant, Sword and Arm of the Lord; and James Wickstrom, former Posse Comitatus leader, were all fervent Identity believers.[3]

In order not to unfairly vilify the religious right in this country, it is important to note that there are important differences between membership in the Christian Coalition, a political alignment of the religious right, and the Christian Identity Movement. It would be a large step for those who would go from the Christian Coalition—which from its position on the religious right of the political spectrum wants to impose its ways on American society within the rules, not by breaking them—to a militia movement, which rejects the rules and flouts them with enthusiasm to "save" America. It is a much smaller step to go from the Christian Identity Movement to the militias, since CIM also despises much of what comprises the system today and can rationalize, by religious doctrine, the death/destruction of "children of Satan" and other non-Aryan types.[4] It is as unlikely that a militia leader will be elected to the U.S. Congress as it is that a Christian Coalition leader will consider poisoning a town's water supply. The Christian Identity Movement members could do either.[5]

A Christian Identity Movement pastor, Peter Peters, who also had links to the former Silent Brotherhood, the Posse Comitatus, and to the Aryan Nations, convened a meeting in 1992 in Estes Park, Colorado. Held shortly after the surrender of Randy Weaver at Ruby Ridge, the meeting attracted a vast array of leaders from the white supremacist world. Louis Beam (Aryan Nations leader) and Richard Butler (Aryan Nations founder); Larry Pratt, of Gun Owners of America (who wrote *Armed People Victorious*, a blueprint for the "well-armed local militia" for which he had called in 1990); Frank Isabell, Christian Patriot leader; and many other leaders of the Identity and patriot movements attended this "summit," and researchers believe that this 1992 meeting was the "birthplace" of the modern-day militia movement.[6]

At this gathering—now known as the Rocky Mountain Rendezvous, held on 23–25 October 1992 at a YMCA in Estes Park, Colorado—plans were developed for a citizens' militia movement that exceeded anything the United States had yet experienced. The group of 160 white men who gathered there were white supremacists and pro-gun extremists meeting at an invitation-only gathering two months after FBI attempts to arrest Randy Weaver, a Christian Identity as well as a survivalist militia member, resulted in the deaths of Weaver's wife and son on 19 April at Ruby Ridge in Idaho. This was the most significant meeting of the extreme right in recent U.S. history, and from it exploded the growth of the modern militia movement. Within five years of this important gathering, the number of militias and militia support groups had grown from perhaps a dozen to over 800.[7]

A series of events, beginning with the FBI attempt in 1992 to arrest Weaver at Ruby Ridge, and culminating in the cataclysmic bombing of the federal building in Oklahoma City three years later, focused and enervated the Christian militia movement, providing inspiration and martyrs. Exactly one year after Ruby Ridge, on 19 April 1993, a fifty-one-day siege by agents of the Federal Bureau of Investigation and the Bureau of Alcohol, Tobacco, and Firearms ended in a tragedy which included the death of seventeen children at Mount Carmel in Waco, Texas, where David Koresh and his followers had stockpiled a large supply of illegal weapons.

For many of those drawn into the Christian militia movement, these events were examples of a government willing to take extraordinary measures to stamp out people who refused to conform or to surrender their weapons. This anger toward a government seen increasingly as an enemy produced, two years later on 19 April 1995, the most destructive act of domestic terrorism in U.S. history (prior to the events of September 11, 2001): the bombing of the Alfred P. Murrah Federal Building in Oklahoma City, where 168 people were killed and 850 others were injured. This spectacular act of violence was carried out by a man whose family was involved in the Christian Identity Movement and who had himself been a member of a militia group.

It is ironic to note, in passing, that many militia groups have adopted 19 April the anniversary date of the Battle of Lexington in 1775 that launched the American Revolution, as a special date, since militia personnel consider themselves as instrumental in restoring the pristine values that the Revolution fought to protect. It has certainly proved to be a bloody date in the history of the modern Christian militia movement.

From a Shared Heritage and Leadership to a Shared Vision

This shared heritage of leadership and history helps to explain at least three important aspects of the modern Christian militia movement: the wide-

ranging geographical dimensions, the diversity of causes its adherents espouse, and the overlapping agenda among its member groups. There are
militia groups from Idaho to California, Arizona to North Carolina, Georgia to Michigan, and Texas to Canada. Almost every state has at least one
such group, and most have several. These groups share motivations span-
ning a broad spectrum: antifederalism, sedition, racial hatred, and religious
hatred. Most have masked these unpleasant-sounding motives under a
rather transparent veneer of religious precepts.

Training manuals, articles, and books generated by members of these
groups indicate that they are bound together by a number of factors, including shared hostility to any form of government above the county level
and even an advocacy of the overthrow of the U.S. government (or the
Zionist Occupation Government, as some of them call it). Vilification of
Jews and nonwhites as children of Satan is combined with an obsession
with achieving the religious and racial purification of the United States and
a belief in a conspiracy of powerful Jewish interests controlling the government, banks, and the media.

Although there has not been extensive research into the context of terrorist belief systems, studies have offered insights into the framework by
which individuals willing to commit terrorist acts view their world. A quick
look at the elements suggested in several recent studies helps to suggest how
the vision of the world shared by members of Christian militia may facilitate a willingness to commit such acts.

One of the significant components of a terrorist belief system is the image
of the enemy held by the individual and the group. Dehumanization of the
enemy is a dominant theme. It is not human beings whom the terrorist
fights; rather, it is this dehumanized monolith.[8] It is easy to make war, even
illegal, "unthinkable" war, on an "inhuman" enemy. As one researcher
noted, when the enemy does not have a face, a wife or child, a home, griev-
ing parents or friends, the destruction of that "enemy" is a simple matter,
requiring little or no "justification" beyond the "enemy" status.[9]

Also of interest in this belief system is the self-image of the person carrying out the terrorist act. Individuals of both the left and right ends of the
political spectrum who carry out acts of terrorism tend to think of themselves as belonging to an élite, a small group chosen to fight the inhuman
enemy, often seeing themselves also as the victims, rather than the aggressors, in the struggle. The struggle in which they are engaged is an obligation, a duty; they are the enlightened citizen-soldiers seeking to protect the
mass of unenlightened citizens from the enemy within, or the religious
zealot, "chosen" by a supreme being to lead the struggle and to be a martyr in confronting the "monster" which threatens the world of the "faithful."

Studies suggest that people carrying out terrorist acts tend to view themselves as *above* the prevailing morality. Normal standards of behavior do
not apply to them. They do not see themselves in any sense bound by con-

ventional laws or conventional morality, which they often regard as the corrupt and self-serving tools of the "enemy." Thus, it would be useless to condemn as "immoral" an action by a terrorist, since the person embracing terrorist tactics no doubt believes that the morality condemning his action is inferior to his own morality.

This view of morality is integral to the terrorist' vision of the nature of the conflict in which they are engaged. Not only is this a "moral" struggle, in which good and evil are simplistically defined, but terrorists tend to define the struggle also in terms of elaborately idealistic terms. Terrorists seldom see what they do as murder or killing of innocent persons. Instead, they tend to describe such actions as "executions" committed after "trials" of "traitors."

It is also useful to understand the world of the would-be terrorist in terms of the image they have of the physical victims of the violence. If the victims are fairly easily identifiable with the "enemy," then as representatives of the hostile forces, they are despised and their destruction easily justified, even if such victims have committed no clear offense against the terrorist or his group. Innocent victims, persons whose only "crime" was in being in the wrong place at the wrong time, are generally dismissed as, in military terms, "collateral damage"—unimportant by-products of the struggle. "Fate," rather than the acts of man, is often blamed for the deaths of such persons. Thus, the persons in the child-care center at the Murrah building in Oklahoma City were only victims because they were in the wrong building at the wrong time, while those killed in the federal offices were "enemies" of the people.

There is at least one more important dimension of terrorist visions of the world to consider: the predominant theme of millenarianism. Personal redemption through violent means is a millenarian theme found in many extremist belief systems. Violence is often viewed as being essential to the coming of the millennium, an event which may be hastened by the actions of believers willing to violate the rules of the old order in an effort to bring in the new order (often conceived of in terms of total liberation).

This "millennialist" view is supported by the Christian Identity Movement's theology, which purports that the world is in its final days. Identity adherents hold that Jesus will not return until after the Tribulation, and many believe that they are in, or are about to enter into, the time of Tribulation, a great battle between good and evil in which they will take part. They view the coming battle as a race war, as made clear in the writings of William Pierce in *The Turner Diaries*. Timothy McVeigh's bombing of the Murrah building in Oklahoma City was, by his own statement, an act described in the *Diaries* as a part of this millennial conflict.

These elements of Christian militia ideology give useful insights into the ability of the members of such groups to carry out acts of terrorism. Individuals carrying out terrorist acts, then, often have "images" of their world, their victims, and themselves which enable them to kill people whom they do not know, and feel justified in doing so. To view the "enemy" as a "child of Satan"—as the Identity theology permeating much of the Christian militia movement advocates—allows the person carrying out the violent act of terror to dehumanize the victims, as researchers suggest terrorists must in order to kill.[10] To view the struggle of the group as an effort to "purify" the nation is to view it as a battle between good and evil, which again fits the "images of the struggle" essential for terrorists.[11] A "Warrior" fighting in a cause to "purify" a state from the "children of Satan" will have little problem in justifying the use of lethal force.

Clearly, it is essential to understand the ideology, or theology, which shapes the Christian militia movement today. Perhaps the best source for building an understanding of this is offered in the *Field Manual for Free Militia*, which is available on the web and which is cited or quoted in most militia group literature. This manual offers insights not only into the theology of this particular type of militia, but also into the training of individuals and cells within this "leaderless movement. Sold by the United States Taxpayers Party—organized by Howard Phillips, who attended the 1992 meeting in Estes Park—this manual contains a section on "Principles Justifying the Arming and Organizing of a Militia." Since its publication in 1994, the *Field Manual for Free Militia* has become a staple within the militia movement, setting out in specific detail not only the principles/theology "justifying" the militia, but also the command structure of militia and detailed instructions for countermeasures against the "enemy" who would be trying to subvert their actions. An analysis of this manual is essential to gaining an understanding of the recruiting, training, and arming of the Christian militia in the United States.

Theology: Recruiting and Training Tool

According to the *Field Manual of the Free Militia*, the first and arguably most important step towards training new members of the Christian militia entails persuading novice associates to wholly accept the theological foundations prescribed in this manual, because this acceptance serves as a vital connecting link between militia members and cells. For example, this theology connects cells of Christian militia in Montana to cells in California, Texas, or North Carolina, whether or not any personal contact has been made between members of the different cells. Militias ostensibly operate within the context of a "leaderless resistance," meaning that groups and individuals conduct activities separately, without reporting to, or receiving orders from, a center of operations.[12] Leaderless resistance aimed at achieving a common goal becomes possible through the use of theology as a first-step training tool, since it builds upon commonly held belief systems in a predominantly Christian society.

Theological foundations of the Christian militia movement can be found in detail in Section I, Subsection 1.1 of the *Field Manual of the Free Militia*, entitled "The Morality of Arming and Organizing," which lays out, step-by-step, a biblical justification for the ideals and goals of the Christian militia movement. The biblical foundations for the militia movement are broken down into four primary theological pieces: biblical inspiration and authority, continuity of the Old and New Testaments, the premise that Jesus Christ was not a pacifist, and the principles of just war.

According to the Free Militia manual, the New Testament scripture found in II Timothy 3:16 establishes both the divine inspiration and the divine authority of the Bible, stating that all scripture is "God-breathed." Using other scriptures to substantiate the "errorless truth" of the Bible, the manual is written in a manner designed to lead followers to accept that the Bible in its entirety must be believed, obeyed, and followed. The "leader" of the leaderless resistance may then be said to be the word of God and not of man. For new and old members alike, the God factor lends legitimacy and justification to their cause and actions, enabling people to participate in illegal activities they might otherwise avoid. This section concludes: "We must make sure that whatever we do in any department of life, including the use of force, conforms to the truth and moral principles of the Bible."[13] If the new recruits accept the premise that the leadership of the militia is in the word and hands of God, then they can believe that nothing they are asked or trained to do for this leadership can be wrong, even if the actions break the laws of the land, since, according to the precepts urged in the manual, the laws of God take precedence over the laws of man.

Following the primary theological basis, the authors of the manual next attempt to negotiate the age-old conflict of Old Testament law versus New Testament law for militia members by arguing that the New Testament does not replace the Old Testament laws but rather builds upon, enhances, clarifies, or fulfills the Old Testament. For example, rather than eliminating the law against murder, the manual contends that in Matthew 5:21–22, Jesus extends the law to prohibit hatred as well. Instructing the appropriate theological perspective for militia members on the issue of Testaments is crucial to arguments concerning the use of force to which militia members may expect to be called. The Old Testament contains detailed laws by which people were to abide, laws which would be rendered invalid if movement members believed the New Testament law abolished the Old Testament law. Furthermore, the Old Testament abounds with examples of violence and war that are condoned rather than condemned by God, wars in which people fought against invaders and tyrannical rulers. This justification of the use of force is critically important to the training of new members in the militia.

The third theological basis addresses the nature of Jesus Christ, who emphasizes love throughout the New Testament, thus leading some contemporaries to argue that Jesus was himself a pacifist. The Free Militia's manual claims that Jesus was *not* a pacifist for the following reasons: Jesus did not condemn soldiering, only the abuse of power; Jesus allowed, even directed his people to carry swords; Jesus used force when he cleared out the temple, as well as on other occasions; Jesus will, it is prophesied, one day use excessive force to separate the wicked from the righteous; and Jesus taught his disciples to use force, albeit as a last resort. Most of the points are certainly backed by carefully selected scriptures, except the idea that Jesus taught followers to use force as a last resort, which is instead inferred from various other scriptures. Again, the focus of this scripture "lesson" in the manual is clearly to justify, morally, the use of force.

Finally, the manual describes the biblical principles of "just war" to help members understand that it is not only acceptable to use force, but the use of such force may even be "commanded" by God, in order to prevent or redress a "wrong." Just war principles include the use of self-defense to protect one's life, the application of capital punishment for serious crimes, and the use of force for resistance to tyranny. Resisting tyranny applies to government institutions or leaders who commit murder, curb liberties, and/or impose a tyrannical regime. In these instances, people—according to the manual—must resist, including the use of force. In order to participate in a "just war," the warriors must ensure that the war is in the name of justice rather than revenge and that it is a collective action, not personal.

Understanding these four basic theological principles of the Free Militia manual makes clear the manner in which theology becomes a training tool and in which the militia movement in the United States today is becoming the "Christian militia movement." Members first become versed in the ideals and justifications of the group, using Section 1 of the manual; only after accepting the theology in this section are members fully integrated into the movement, which in some groups entails paramilitary training.

Theology acts as both a recruiting and a training tool in another manner as well. Individuals who have been raised in Protestant churches, or at some point in their lives have become familiar with Protestant theology, are prime targets of recruiting efforts. People falling into this category have been in a sense "pretrained" to accept the ideals and goals of the Christian militia group. The primary theological points rely heavily on biblical scripture and resemble the theological beliefs of many churches which are entirely unrelated to the militia movement. These similarities may lead to the membership of individuals in militia groups who would otherwise not have joined such an organization.

The Constitution as a Training Tool

Militiamen are also reminded not to forget the biblical command to obey authority, as prescribed in Romans 13:1, which states that "everyone must submit himself to the governing authority." According to the theology in the manual, the highest authority in the United States is the Constitution, not elected officials. Indeed, the manual claims that "Jesus Christ is the ultimate authority and the Constitution is the real governing authority."

While theology provides moral approval for militia activities, the U.S. Constitution provides legal justification. As noted previously, the militia manual maintains that the United States Constitution comprises the highest authority in the land, and the Constitution must be upheld either by the government officials in power or laymen if circumstances require. One of the unifying ideas of militia members is any threat to the violation of the Bill of Rights, the Second Amendment:

"Article II: A well regulated Militia, being necessary to the security of a free state, the right of the people to keep and bear Arms, shall not be infringed."

Militia members cite U.S. Code, Title 10, Section 31 as containing the legal definition of "militia," thus interpreting the first phrase to mean a "well-organized citizens' army."[14] The necessity for a well-organized citizens' army to the security of a free state means, to militia, the ability of the citizenry to overthrow a tyrannical government if the government cannot be held in check peacefully. By their logic, without the ability to rise against an oppressive regime, the "free" status of a state cannot be guaranteed because the oppressive forces can proliferate unbridled.

Militia theology interprets the Constitution to be the ultimate authority next to God, thus the "right" to bear arms cannot be altered through the use of new legislation requiring licenses, special taxes, and other restrictive measures. The current government must enforce the right to bear arms rather than hinder the ability to access weapons. Furthermore, the constitution protects the rights to both "keep" and to "bear" arms, indicating two separate liberties. First, people have the right of gun ownership, under the right to "keep" arms. Secondly, people have the right to carry guns when they leave their property, under the provision of a right to "bear" arms. The right to bear arms may only be overruled when one person's right to bear arms infringes with another person's right to ban weapons from entering personal property, according to the militia manual.

"Weapons" more accurately describe the "arms" the militia believes are protected under the Second Amendment. The "right to bear arms" entailed, in the view of militia adherents, the implicit right to bear the best available guns at the time that the amendment was written, and remains a right to the "best available guns" today. Arms, in their view, may not constitutionally be limited by the number of rounds that can be fired in a minute or the characteristics of the bullets. Thus, all guns, ranging from fully automatic to single-shell shotguns, ostensibly fall under the protection of the Bill of Rights. To strengthen this argument, the expansion of gun technology and its protection by the constitution is compared, in the manual, to the development of the television and radio, both of which fall under the first amendment right to freedom of speech and of the press.

A final arena of contention concerning current gun policies and the ideals of gun ownership (as they are interpreted by the militia) concerns the last phrase of the Second Amendment—the phrase "shall not be infringed." Militia organizations, as well as other pro-gun organizations, define infringement as any encroachment upon full access to obtain and carry weapons of choice. The training manual suggests that laws concerning licenses, permits, registration, prohibition, taxation, and the like explicitly violate the Second Amendment by infringing upon the rights of citizens. Attempts to reduce gun manufacturing and availability also infringe upon the rights of citizens and thus also illustrate violations of the Constitution, according to the militia leadership.

The first part of the "training" offered in this important militia literature, then, includes a strong theological statement of beliefs, which serves to both link and bind members in a "just cause," and an equally strong adjuration to firmly demand the rights guaranteed by the Second Amendment to the Constitution. The moral and legal premises on which the militia may then call upon its membership is based on recruits reading and accepting these basic tenets, before full membership in a militia cell is granted. Thus, instruction in a core ideology and in the laws which could be interpreted to support the actions taken are the first critical steps in the training process offered by the widely-used manual.

Arming the Troops

To most American citizens, it would seem obvious that raising arms against the U.S. military would be a futile effort. The leaders of the free militia would be inclined to agree. In the second part of the *Field Manual of the Free Militia*, the emphasis is not on taking up arms to defend freedom against the U.S. military or even the local police; instead, the "enemy" is suggested to be the federal agencies and their agents. While this enemy may seem to be less formidable than the entire U.S. military, federal agencies would still be better trained and equipped than a small militia unit. So what gives these individuals the incentive to believe they can defeat this enemy? There are at least three basic principles outlined in the field manual that give militiamen confidence of victory. First, the manual outlines the advantages of being a nontraditional military force, and explains how those advantages will overcome the obviously superior forces. Next, the manual outlines the equipment that is considered necessary for properly arming a militiaman. Finally, there is an outline of the psychological mindset that the men must have to overcome their enemies.

Advantages of a Non-Traditional Force

The manual refers to three specific points that will allow militia groups to triumph over seemingly superior forces: Their people are willing to defend their freedoms, they have a cause to fight for, and they have specific advantages within their own militias. First, the writer of the manual clearly understands that the militia would face superior numbers in a large "federal" enemy; however, the manual suggests that superior numbers do not spell victory. The basis for this point is simple: The writer of the manual suggests that any event that will cause the militia to come to arms—standing up to fight the "enemy" (the government)—will also cause millions of Americans to rebel against that government and fight as well on the militia's side. So while their numbers may seem less now, once the fighting begins, the free militia will, according to the manual, be joined by all the ordinary Americans out there who will also want to fight to defend their freedoms.

The second point about the "cause" for which they fight is equally significant. When examining the "cause" mentioned in the field manual, it is important to understand all the influences that are a part of that cause. Militia members are encouraged to have not only the religious beliefs and the theological premises noted earlier on which to base their actions; they should also be guided by a fundamental belief in their right to defend themselves and their freedoms. The militia are instructed, in this manual, to believe that they have a responsibility to uphold the Constitution and defend the rights listed in that document to the best of their abilities, including a responsibility to take up arms and fight for those rights. In the manual, there is a quote explaining what sets the militia soldiers apart from the normal soldier: "The drafted soldier is motivated to survive until his tour of duty is up. The career soldier is motivated by promotions in rank and higher salaries. The patriotic volunteer is motivated to win for the sake of a higher cause." Following this line of reason, the premise seems to be that people who fight in a militia group would win because they have a compelling reason to fight, whereas the soldiers in the U.S. military do not have a reason to fight other than strict personal gain and thus will not fight as well or as long. To the men of the Christian militia, might does not make right; on the contrary, right makes might, so they train their soldiers to believe they will win because they fight on the side of a good cause, on the side of the righteous, and that puts them above the normal laws of war.

Finally, the authors outline the advantages of a militia, advantages that would be able to balance out any obstacles they may face with an enemy that has superior numbers, training, and organization. While there are several advantages listed in the manual, a few are worth special attention, as they are of particular importance. First, the authors of the manual understand the "enemy" will have superior numbers, and although they believe they will only have those numbers initially, they do acknowledge the larger force. They point out that the militia will counter that with the advantage of having more dependability among their men. Since the men in the militia are fighting for a cause they believe in, they will not face the attrition of men to moral objections, as the manual predicts the enemy will.

The next important advantage noted in the manual focuses on the superior training of the enemy forces, which the authors also acknowledge as an obstacle to be overcome. To defend against that training, the manual suggests that the militiamen will have a superior motivation; that is, since the men in the militia are patriots, they will be expected to have a higher motivation to fight and therefore they will fight better.

In some of the other advantages pointed out in the manual, the authors speak about the basics of combat and explain how the militiamen will be better equipped to handle the fighting. In terms of the advantages of the enemy to be overcome, the authors of the manual acknowledge the superior firepower, mobility, and supplies. Their arguments to counter these superiorities seem to be based on the same principles by which the minutemen of the American Revolution fought. The Americans who fought in the Revolution understood that they were facing a bigger, stronger military; understanding this, they still fought the British because they had some of the same advantages that the manual points out will be enjoyed by the militiamen. For example, the Revolutionaries were fighting on their home terrain, so they were extensively familiar with their fighting ground, in theory more so than their enemy. Another premise suggested is that the Revolutionaries, who were fighting to free the people, enjoyed the help of the "friendlies" (people not involved in the fighting), who provided simple aid and assistance to the "rebel" troops. This, according to the manual, would also be an advantage which militia would enjoy.

A final point made by the authors regarding the militiamen's advantages over the enemy focused on their ability to fight directly with the enemy. During the American Revolution, the minutemen seldom won battles by direct face-to-face combat; instead, they fought what could only be considered guerrilla warfare. They fought from the concealment of the land in nonconventional ways, ways for which the British troops were unprepared and with which they were not familiar. These "unconventional" ways are the ways the authors of the manual suggest the militias will be fighting: They do not suggest open warfare with the enemy; rather, they suggest subversive and nonconventional tactics, like those used in the American Revolution.

Equipment for a "Prepared" Militia Member

Following the development of a cause and a reason to fight is the introduction of suggestion of what militia should be prepared to fight with in the forthcoming battles. The manual outlines extensively the weapons and other equipment considered necessary to be a genuinely ready and armed militiaman. This begins with the choice of weapons, which they advocate should ideally be a medium- to high-power semiautomatic rifle with a magazine that is detachable. After listing several different types of weapons and the reasons for and against each for use in the militia, the authors then move onto the other types of equipment that would be needed to set up a fully armed and prepared cell of militiamen. Much of what they list next is basic military equipment, from the clothing to be inconspicuous (like camouflage) to the protective gear needed in direct combat (like helmets and flak jackets) to the basic radio equipment that would be necessary to keep a small force of men in contact during a battle. In this section of the manual, the authors are very detailed about what is needed and what it will probably cost them to fully prepare themselves for battle with the enemy, as well as how to conceal oneself from the outside authorities. They point out the importance of not making it known that members possess all the weapons and equipment they do, because then they will be an obvious target of the enemy when the time comes. They give suggestions like buying weapons from private dealers and paying for equipment in cash so there are no records of the materials purchased. In a time and age of computers, practically anyone can get access to any number of weapons online, with little to no checks on background and culpability.

In the next section of the field manual the authors describe how the cells will be organized and included in the cause. Like most known terrorist organizations, the emphasis in the Christian militia groups is that the individual cells be small and be able to operate independently of any larger organization. The cells are designated to be only eight men, who are capable of acting without the direction or resources of any larger group of people, much like the al Qaeda groups are organized around the world. They use the small groups, or cells, of eight men to encourage camaraderie and to ensure the group's ability to operate independently, since they would need more then just a few men to carry out any real military operations. While they do not encourage coordination between the cells for operation, they do encourage diversifying the cells to include different primary functions for each cell. The four different cell structures that are listed in the manual are the command cell, the combat cell, the support cell, and the communiqué cell. While each cell would have a specialized function to perform, the emphasis of the militia is that they all should still be able to perform without each other, so if one group is cut off, the others can and will still fight. Much of their structure within the larger groups, or multiple cells, is very similar to the way the traditional army is organized. They have a commander (a General) and ranks that follow all the way down to a Private. One of the things that is unique about the structure and set-up of the cells and the militia as a whole is that it includes no women. In the last section of the manual, it is even specified that members' wives and children are to be left out of any planning or knowledge of the free militia completely. They are to know as little as possible beyond the basic principles of the Second Amendment; they are not to know the names of the other members of a cell and they are not to know of any of the plans with that cell.

Psychological Mindset of a Militiaman

The last part of the militia training, which should be considered as important as the arming of the soldiers, is the development of the mindset that is believed to be necessary for a true militiaman. This is beyond the mindset of being right and fighting for a cause; this deals with how militiamen are going to live on a daily basis, how they will live normal lives outside of the militia. Reading the last part of the field manual, one can grasp an effort to ingrain a sense of paranoia. Here, the reader is taught methods for protecting oneself from any outside "enemies" who may be trying to spy or to bring down their cause. The authors of the manual describe several ways that the "enemy" may chose to spy on members of the militia, dividing those ways under the headings of eavesdropping, surveillance, snooping, and infiltration. Under each of these headings, they describe several ways that the enemy could be working against them, and suggest what the militia soldiers should do to prevent these things from occurring.

This final section of the manual also contains instruction on how to protect one's equipment, the way one should train, and the steps that should be taken to ensure no government involvement. It is recommended that every member of the militia maintain an extremely low profile, including not keeping the weapons and equipment in the house, not training where it would be possible for others to see, and not speaking about militia business to anyone except those in the cell. Most of what happens in the militia is to be kept minimal, according to the manual, which has special warnings regarding large meetings and information spreading. Militia members are instructed to keep information about events to a very small number of people, and they are rarely, if ever, to hold meetings to discuss upcoming militia business. Clearly, the idea is to be and to stay inconspicuous, to the government and to a large extent to the public eye. The implication is that, when the time comes for the battle with the government, the public will decide to stand and fight with the militia, but the militia cannot afford to have the public aware of what is going on now.

The authors of this manual understood, when it was written in 1994, that the militia might not be accepted and appreciated in society as a whole; they understood that they could and probably would be labeled as conspirators and fanatics. Understanding those concepts, they also were aware of the need for secrecy and knew that with extreme secrecy comes the need for a certain degree of paranoia, which they clearly try to ingrain on the militiamen in the last section of the manual. They even suggest words that should not be mentioned when talking in public places or over the phone, lest they arouse suspicion in the wrong people.

Five "key principles" of secrecy and security are offered at this point in the training manual, each of which reinforces the paranoia suggested earlier. These points, briefly stated are:

- Keep a low profile,
- Keep your mouth shut,
- Be as decentralized as is possible,
- Be as transient as possible, and
- Protect all records and information.

The focus on remaining as separated as possible, being quiet, staying "below radar" and moving as often as possible strongly suggest that, although a leadership structure is clearly outlined in the manual, there is greater emphasis on the ability to act alone or with a very small group of cohorts. This does not necessarily imply a built-in weakness or inability to act, but does suggest that militia today are evolving into a networked structure that is very difficult to oppose or suppress, since it lacks a central command structure or clear chain of authority linking all cells and members. It also encourages members to arm, train, and plan alone or with only a small amount of assistance, as Timothy McVeigh did, and to be prepared to act alone if the opportunity is given, as McVeigh was clearly able to do. Using this type of individualized, "train yourself and stay only loosely connected" approach, modern militia are at once hard to rapidly mobilize in an organized fashion but also quite capable of unilateral actions of widely divergent types in many different locations, making them a serious challenge for law enforcement today.

Conclusions

The Christian militia offers a significantly different challenge to government efforts to provide security than did the left-wing "college radicals" of the 1960s and 1970s. Unlike the isolated, crudely unsophisticated pipe-bomb manufacturers who dominated most of the U.S.-based terrorist groups for at least two decades, members of militia groups are often well trained in the use of arms and explosives. Some militia groups even have skilled armorers and bomb makers and members with outdoor survival skills who are adept at guerrilla-warfare techniques.

Militia groups in the United States are widespread, intricately linked by overlapping memberships, and bound together in a political and religious doctrine which defines the world in terms that make the use of violence not just acceptable but necessary and offers an apocalyptic vision of eminent war. Since many of the members of these groups are skilled in the use of weapons, and utilize survival training in camps throughout the country, planning for an "inevitable" racial war, the impact of these groups may well be formidable in the twenty-first century.

Although the United States has produced many different types of right-wing extremist groups, particularly last two decades of the twentieth century, Christian militia group cells share striking similarities in ideology and overlapping membership which help to explain several important factors: the broad popular base enjoyed by militia groups, the assumption on the part of the general public—and much of the law enforcement community, until the Oklahoma City bombing—that such groups are nonthreatening as a whole, and the festering of support for hatred which such groups provide to individuals seeking someone or something to blame for the loss of jobs, income, family farms, and other problems.

As Abraham Foxman, National Director of the Anti-Defamation League (ADL), noted in 2004, "While less vocal, less public and less visible, the militias are quietly attempting to retool, restructure and reorganize and are still players on the extremist scene."[15] Foxman noted in his ADL report several significant trends in the modern militia movement which reflect some of the training discussed in this chapter. These include, but are not limited to:

- Maintaining a low profile: While militias have begun to increasingly connect with each other and to seek recruits, this has been done in low-profile arenas, such as online discussion forums and mailing lists from websites. This fits with the psychological training in the manual discussed earlier.

- Fear of the government: Militias have been re-energized by post–September 11 fears of conspiracies and government power, viewing the "war on terrorism" and the Patriot Act as being directed at them. This also fits the "paranoia" pattern suggested in the manual.

- The perception that "time is running out": Militia members are unifying around the idea that the country is headed toward a violent confrontation between its citizens and "the government." This anticipation of a millennial conflict between "good" and "evil" has also been noted as fundamental to the worldview of someone willing to carry out a terrorist act.

Militia groups in the United States today fit easily into the all-channel network pattern of groups, with no specific "group leader" or hub; each cell is capable of acting independently, with varying degrees of skill and success, against a common target—frequently a government individual or facility. When an individual like Timothy McVeigh has membership in both the religious right (in the form of the Christian Identity Movement) and a militia group, his ability to act independently is enhanced but it is also more likely that he would be see himself as a "holy warrior" in a good cause supported by his religious beliefs. This combination of independence, military expertise, and religious zeal can clearly be quite lethal.

One last conclusion is relevant here. McVeigh proved that militia groups, while not directly responsible for the actions of their members, may offer social and psychological support which will enable individuals to carry out lethal acts on their own. However, since the training materials of militia groups today stress paranoia and a lack of overt leadership structure, it is unlikely that the militia movement will be responsible for an event on the scale of the September 11 tragedy. This is not particularly encouraging, since the Oklahoma City bombing was incredibly destructive. But compared to that of 9/11 it was a modest effort. The danger may lie in the ability of individuals, motivated by militia propaganda, to launch unilateral attacks on disparate targets, coordinated only by timing—and that danger remains clear and not yet preventable.

CHAPTER 15

The Hizballah Training Camps of Lebanon

MAGNUS RANSTORP

Since its inception in 1982, following Israel's invasion of Lebanon, the Hizballah movement has occupied a central position as *the* "A-team"[1] of terrorist organizations with a global reach for successive American administrations. Prior to 9/11, Hizballah was charged with being responsible for the greatest number of American casualties worldwide in terrorist attacks following the April 1983 suicide attack against the U.S. Embassy in Beirut and the simultaneous suicide attacks against the U.S. and French contingents of the Multinational Force (MNF) on 23 October 1983, killing 241 U.S. Marines and fifty-six French paratroopers. This latter incident revealed a remarkable degree of operational innovation in fusing suicide attacks into a synchronized attack mode, a tactic that would later serve to inspire the al Qaeda hijackers on 9/11. It also underscored the close operational logistical support that the Iranian clerical establishment—and the Iranian Revolutionary Guards Corps (IRGC) in particular—had extended from 1982 onwards in the establishment of Hizballah in the Bekaa Valley and in their provision of a matrix of crucial guidance in the fields of recruitment, ideological indoctrination, material support, and military training in specific terrorist training camps.

The Complex Matrix of Hizballah Terrorism

A multitude of Iranian clerical personalities and institutions were instrumental in the actual formation of Hizballah and in providing logistical assistance in rapidly building a sophisticated terrorist capability. A series of contingents of the *al-Qods* (Jerusalem) forces within the Iranian Revolutionary Guard Corps were immediately redeployed from the Iran-Iraq battlefield following Israel's invasion of Lebanon in 1982. Their headquarters was established in the Syrian border village of Zebdani, with an 800-man-strong contingent deployed in Baalbek and with a further 700 distributed in smaller villages in the eastern Bekaa region, most notably in Brital, Nabisheet, and Baalbek. These élite military units provided not only the organizational basis and infrastructure for the formation of Hizballah but also imparted religious indoctrination, military training, and guidance for the terrorist active-service units, eventually crystallizing into three divisions of the Special Security Apparatus responsible for security and intelligence matters. These clandestine units within Hizballah were further supported by a range of Iranian clerics and institutions, from Iran's personal representatives in Damascus and Beirut to the Office of Islamic Liberation Movements with the Iranian Ministry of Foreign Affairs and the Iranian Ministry of Intelligence and Security (MOIS).[2]

Throughout the 1980s, the Hizballah's clandestine security wing, the so-called Special Security Apparatus (SSA), with close Iranian coordination and Syrian patronage, abducted numerous Western hostages in Beirut between 1984 and 1990. These human pawns were used skillfully for years as a coercive leverage against the American, French, and British governments to affect change in their foreign policies against Iran and Syria.[3] In addition, Hizballah applied further punitive pressure on the French government outside Lebanon in a series of deadly bombings in Paris between February and September 1986. A year earlier, members of Hizballah's SSA, most notably Muhammad Ali Hamadi, Hasan Iz-el-Din, and Ali Atwa—working under Imad Mughniyeh's supervision—had hijacked TWA 847, commandeering it to Beirut and forcing Israel to eventually release 766 Lebanese and Palestinian prisoners in exchange for the release of the passengers. All these terrorist incidents revealed a close operational relationship to varying degrees between Hizballah operatives and Iranian clerics and select Iranian security institutions, most notably the Iranian MOIS.

The fusion of active and passive Iranian assistance to Hizballah at multiple levels has assisted both Iran and Hizballah in efforts to obscure and conceal its clandestine activities, especially in ensuring "plausible deniability" in more complex operations overseas. It has also led to the common perception that the state-sponsor relationship is conceptually one-dimensional, occurring through one or a few channels in a linear fashion from sponsor to proxy. The realities on the ground are much more complex and fluid, changing over periods of time and according to context, operation, and security circumstances. A key senior Hizballah SSA operative, Imad Mughniyeh, exemplifies the complexity in deciphering the exact contours of whether the organization's principal terrorism architecture is primarily located within Hizballah's leadership or within the Iranian MOIS, or both. This complexity, combined with a highly secretive command structure, has made identifying the operational nerve center very difficult, particularly in terms of whether it is located in Beirut or in Teheran at any particular time. Imad Mughniyeh is by some accounts reporting directly to Hizballah's Secretary-General and serves as a conduit to Iran's MOIS operatives, operating under cover at the diplomatic missions in Beirut and Damascus and relaying instructions directly to the MOIS headquarters in Teheran. Some argue that the appointment of Jawad Nur-al-Din to the seven-member *Shura al-Qarar*, the highest-ranking elected leadership body of Hizballah, was indeed a cover name for Imad Mughniyeh himself.[4] It is believed that Mughniyeh travels on an Iranian diplomatic passport and always travels to Lebanon via Damascus airport to avoid being intercepted and arrested by the CIA's clandestine CTC unit, which is monitoring and tracking his potential movements worldwide.

Equally, it has been very difficult to identify with any degree of certainty the exact operational activities in Hizballah-run terrorist training camps, since relatively few operatives captured over the years have revealed their nature in interrogations. An exception to this is the 1996 case of Muhammad Hussein Mikdad, an accountant to one of the social services managed by Hizballah's spiritual leader (described later in this chapter). Mikdad was recruited for his foreign-language abilities and his Western looks and was trained in the Hizballah-run Janta training camp before being deployed from Lebanon, via Geneva, with a mission to infiltrate Israel and conduct a terrorist operation involving a sophisticated improvised explosive device concealed in a Sony radio.[5]

Another difficulty in pinpointing terrorist training camps has been the vast expansion of Hizballah's activities in the political, social, and military domains since the early 1990s. Unlike many other terrorist organizations, Hizballah is horizontally and vertically integrated within Lebanon and its large Shia community as an Islamic social resistance movement with hundreds of thousands of members and sympathizers. Apart from undertaking major structural reforms in the early 1990s with the creation of the *Shura al-Tanfidh* (Executive Shura) for deliberating strategic matters—operating in parallel to the supreme national *Shura al-Qarar* (Decision Shura) at the helm of Hizballah's command decision making—the movement established a "Politburo" (*Maktab al-Takhtit*), a supervisory committee in charge of coordinating Hizballah's recruitment, propaganda, and support services on the regional and local levels, and *al-Majlis al-Jihadi* (Jihad Council), responsible for all military matters.[6] These structures are often overlapping with each other, as operational members are recruited from the social wings into the military units and may provide further opportunities for concealment. As such, the social and military aspects of Hizballah are not separated by firewalls but serve to mutually reinforce each other in many spheres.

Another complicating factor in locating terrorist units is the evolution of

Hizballah's early terrorist training camps into full-fledged guerrilla and military camps designed to train fighters for combat in southern Lebanon and across the border into northern Israel. With the end of the Lebanese civil war in 1989/90, Hizballah worked hard to progressively entrench its position as a major political, social, and military resistance movement and, as such, reoriented its energy and attention towards militarily confronting Israel's continued occupation of southern Lebanon. The presence of smaller units from the Iranian Revolutionary Guard Corps in mobile training camps in the Bekaa Valley continued to be instrumental in providing advanced operational advice and material assistance to Hizballah's military wing—the Islamic Resistance (*al-Muqawama al-Islamiyya*)—on the battlefield in its guerrilla campaign against the Israeli Defense Forces (IDF) and its proxy, the South Lebanese Army (SLA). Supervised by senior Islamic Resistance commanders, groups of twenty Iranian training officers of the Iranian Revolutionary Guard Corps, each a specialist in various aspects of guerrilla warfare techniques, were deployed to various Hizballah training and bivouac camps in the Bekaa region.[7] In these camps, Islamic Resistance fighters were provided advanced logistical and technical assistance with a focus on infiltration techniques, explosives, and intelligence operations. As such, advanced guerrilla (and terrorist) training was extended to a highly compartmentalized core of 500 fighters in active-unit service strength and 3,000 part-timers.[8] This has provided Hizballah with a large potential "reserve" corps to recruit from for various missions requiring advanced terrorism and intelligence skills. Evidence exists that more novice operatives have received technical terrorist training from some of these Hizballah-run camps in Janta, Baalbek, and mobile guerrilla units in southern Lebanon. The more senior members of the small and compartmentalized SSA have longstanding security training both within Lebanon and Syria and probably from MOIS-operated camps within Iran.

The release of the final Western hostages in December 1991, masterfully brokered by UN negotiator Giandomenico Picco,[9] seemed to conclude a long, dark, and murky chapter of Hizballah's extensive involvement in terrorism both within Lebanon and on foreign soil. Although Hizballah focused on transforming itself into a major and permanent political, social, and military movement within Lebanon's post–civil war environment, the killing of Hizballah's Secretary-General, Sheikh Abbas al-Musawi in February 1992, by Israeli missile-firing helicopters in southern Lebanon, provided the catalyst to retaliate with a major terrorist attack against Israeli targets overseas. A month later, Hizballah cells in Buenos Aires deployed a car bomb against the Israeli Embassy, killing twenty-nine civilians and wounding over 300. Two years later, with Iranian assistance, the Hizballah carried out another car-bomb attack on the main building of the Jewish Community Center (AMIA) in Buenos Aires on 18 July 1994. The Argentine investigations into these two attacks revealed not only official

Iranian involvement but also the existence of an extensive Hizballah net-work in Latin America, stretching from Colombia to the Triborder area (where the borders of Argentina, Brazil, and Paraguay meet), primarily tap-ping into the Lebanese expatriate community for logistical support, fundraising, and financial support primarily through illicit trade in coun-terfeit property.[10] Again, the identity of the infamous Imad Mughniyeh sur-faced and was named as a principal architect for both attacks, with extensive Iranian involvement ordered by the then–Intelligence Minister Ali Fallahian (who was later indicted by German courts for his involvement in the murder of four leaders of the Kurdish opposition to the Tehran regime, known as the 1992 Mykonos affair).[11] In other areas of the world, Hizbal-lah operatives were intercepted in a plot to bomb the Israeli Embassy in Bangkok, Thailand, in 1994. Less-publicized joint Hizballah-MOIS logis-tical activity overseas has been alleged by Matthew Levitt of the Washing-ton Institute, cataloguing instances of Hizballah reconnaissance in Malaysia, Singapore, and Thailand, as well as auxiliary logistical and fund-raising activities in Sierra Leone and Liberia (conflict diamonds), Uganda, Canada, South Africa, and the United States.[12]

Although Hizballah has acquired a "global reach" through its close re-lationship with the Iranian MOIS, its primary focus has been to combat Is-rael along its northern border and to extend logistical assistance to Hamas and Palestinian Islamic Jihad members inside Gaza and the West Bank. The closeness of this relationship was forged with the Israeli expulsion of 415 Hamas and Palestinian Islamic Jihad activists to southern Lebanon in De-cember 1992. The extensive contact between Hizballah and Hamas lead-ers directly facilitated the transfer of the suicide tactic as a method to be used in the Palestinian theatre. The level of unity and support between Hizballah and Hamas solidified further following the Israeli withdrawal from southern Lebanon in May 2000, and accelerated dramatically fol-lowing the Israeli targeted assassinations of Hamas leaders Abu-Shannab, Yassin, and Rantisi in 2004. A priority for Hizballah was to logistically as-sist Hamas and other factions in qualitative strategic operations or "spec-taculars" inside Israel. As publicly promised by Sheikh Hassan Nasserallah to Hamas leader Khalid Mishal, "Consider us in Hizballah, from the secretary-general and leadership down to our fighters and women, mem-bers of Hamas, and our soldiers under your command."[13]

Imad Mughniyeh and other key SSA members are suspected of playing a key role in finding avenues to circumvent Israeli security measures by re-cruiting foreign operatives abroad. Iranian involvement in facilitating this close-knit cooperation between Hizballah and Hamas has not been absent, as Hojjatoleslam Ali-Akhbar Mohtashamipour is spearheading these efforts in his capacity as the Secretary-General of the International Conference to Support the Palestinian Uprising (*intifada*) and as a member of the Com-mittee to Support the Palestinian Revolution.[14] It is interesting to note that the role of Ali-Akhbar Mohtashamipour mirrors his critical past and personal role in the actual creation and growth of the Hizballah movement in Lebanon during his tenure as Iran's ambassador to Syria between 1982–85. According to a U.S. National Security Agency intercept, Iranian intelligence headquarters in Teheran relayed a message to Mohtashamipour to contact Hussein Musawi, the leader of Islamic Amal in charge of the Sheikh Abdallah barracks in Baalbek, and instruct him "to take spectacular action against the United States."[15] According to U.S. intelligence, this message culminated in the 1983 U.S. Marine barracks attack.[16]

In many ways, the Hizballah-Iranian relationship has come full circle as many of the movement's command leadership and Iranian clerical personalities and institutions are almost the same in 2005 as they were in 1982–83. Some of the Iranian clerical personalities have rotated positions within the security establishments over time, while a few Hizballah leaders have been killed and its SSA operatives have blended further into the shadows. Most of the principal Hizballah leaders received their early formative clerical schooling in the Iraqi holy city of Najaf during the 1960s and 1970s, studying under the future Iranian clerical establishment as their disciples and forging close personal and trusted friendships. Some Hizballah operatives like Imad Mughniyeh worked closely with the Palestinian Fatah Force 17 as security personnel before joining Hizballah and came into contact with many Iranian clerics, who in turn received armed training from Palestinian militant factions during the 1970s. This has meant that parallel webs of personal relationships exist informally between Hizballah's clerical command leadership and the Iranian clerical establishment ensuring loyalty, trust, and security. For Hizballah's SSA, the role of clan and family affiliation became vital early on to avoid hostile penetration by enemy agents.

The Early Days: Arrival of the Iranian Revolutionary Guards

The arrival of 1,500 IRGC units from Iran after July 1982 came in response to Israel's full-scale invasion of Lebanon, and was formalized in a joint Syria-Iran military agreement. However, it was decided early on in both Teheran and Damascus that any direct IRGC engagement alongside Syrian military forces was politically unwise and logistically impractical, as the relatively small size of the IRGC units would be too small for a direct combat role against the technologically superior and rapidly advancing IDF. Instead the IRGC focused on ensuring the survival and growth of Hussein Musawi's newly created militia, the Islamic Amal, basing itself at the Sheikh Abdallah barracks at the heart of the Bekaa Valley town of Baalbek (under Syrian military control). Alongside its support and patronage of Islamic Amal, the IRGC units, spearheaded by religious and military instructors, were deployed in late 1982 to smaller villages along the eastern Bekaa Valley to recruit and indoctrinate potential members into the newly formed Hizballah movement.[17] Iran actively supervised this solidifying process by merging together the Lebanese al-Da'wa, the Association of Muslim Students, defectors from the Amal movement, and other radicalized Shiite associations—all of which had a commonality of having leaders who received clerical training in Najaf, Iraq, by senior Iranian clerics.[18]

Besides the IRGC units, who provided military training and ideological guidance and imposed its control over residents to adhere to more strict Islamic behavior, Ali-Akhbar Mohtashamipour, Iran's ambassador to Damascus, played a critical role in the formation of the Hizballah. He had himself been pursuing theological studies in Najaf under the supervision of Ayatollah Ruhollah Khomeini, the founder of the Islamic Republic of Iran, alongside future Hizballah leaders. He had also established extensive contacts with Lebanese and Palestinian elements engaged in "anti-Zionist" armed activity during the 1970s, and, in fact, in 1971 he had graduated from a military training course supervised by Palestinian groups. These early close connections between Iranian clerics and Palestinian factions, who provided military training within Lebanon in the early 1970s, influenced the recruitment of future Hizballah operatives from Fatah Force 17, Arafat's élite bodyguard unit.[19]

In the early days of Islamic Amal and Hizballah, the IRGC units played an all-service role in the recruitment of new members and in the provision of logistical assistance and military training.[20] This recruitment drive was aided by financial inducements in the form of a monthly salary, and fighters were offered special privileges, including cost-free education and medical treatment for themselves and their families.[21] The IRGC was supported by large Iranian funds to finance arms shipments, training, and infrastructure, and in July 1984 it had established six military centers in the Bekaa region to train Hizballah and Islamic Amal fighters.[22] The most notorious of these was the Sheikh Abdallah barracks in Baalbek, made famous as the operational nerve center for Hizballah's kidnappings and later as a known storage facility for some of the Western hostages. It had also an important role to play in the planning of the October 1983 bombing of the U.S. Marine barracks outside Beirut airport.

Islamic Amal's Husayn al-Musawi (a former school teacher and defector of Amal) had played an instrumental role in seizing the Sheikh Abdallah barracks from the Lebanese army in November 1982 before handing it over for operational control to the IRGC.[23] Husayn al-Musawi, together with his security chief, Husayn al-Khalil (the brother-in-law of Hizballah Politburo Member Ali Ammar and current close adviser to Sheikh Hassan Nasserallah) were identified as the principal operatives in an initial secret directive from MOIS to Ali-Akhbar Mohtashamipour, Iran's Ambassador to Syria, instructing them to instigate attacks against the Multinational

Force coalition in Lebanon.[24] Instead, Mohtashamipour contacted Ahmad Kan'ani, the IRGC commander in Lebanon, instructing him to put the operation in motion, and a meeting was convened, attended by Sheikh Subhi al-Tufayli (Hizballah's first Secretary-General between 1982–91) and Sheikh Abbas al-Musawi (Tufayli's successor until he was killed in 1992). In this meeting they collectively devised the plan to synchronize the twin suicide bombings using a water-delivery truck. According to testimony of one of the Hizballah operatives present, the trucks were built and equipped in an underground warehouse in the Hizballah-dominated southern suburbs of Beirut (*al-Dahiyya*), known as the *Bir al-Beid* neighborhood. The 19-ton water delivery truck packed with PETN (a bulk form of pentaerythritol tetranitrate) was driven by Ismalal Ascari[25]—importantly, an *Iranian* rather than a Hizballah or Islamic Amal member, which again underlines the extremely close operational relationship between Iranian military and intelligence and Islamic Amal and Hizballah in the planning as well as the execution of operations. The Iranian fingerprints were obvious given that the time scale from directive to conception and execution took less than a month. According to anonymous security officials, the Italian contingent of the MNF had also been initially selected as a potential target, but reconnaissance determined that the operation would be less effective, as some of the soldiers were housed in tents rather than collectively in a building. The exact contours of Hizballah or Iranian responsibility in this operation remains murky, especially when one considers that a Hizballah youth from southern Lebanon, inspired and directed by Sheikh Raghib Harb, had carried out a suicide attack a year earlier when the Hizballah was in a rather embryonic stage.

On 11 November 1982, a day later than planned, Ahmad Qassir launched a suicide mission against the eight-story Israeli military headquarters in Tyre, killing seventy-five soldiers and wounding twenty-eight others.[26] For Hizballah, Qassir's action was pioneering, as it represented the first official suicide attack launched by the organization. More importantly, it symbolically represented the "spirit" of martyrdom in showing and paving the way for future Hizballah resistance against its enemies. As such, 11 November of every year is designated "Martyr's Day" by the Hizballah movement. However, the Hizballah leadership concealed the identity of Qassir until 19 May 1985 in order to avoid any direct reprisals on his family or the emergent public Hizballah leadership.[27]

In parallel to the consolidation of Hizballah in the Bekaa region under Iranian and Syrian patronage and supervision, the movement gradually spread to other areas heavily populated by Shia, including the southern suburbs of Beirut and the villages and towns in southern Lebanon. Hizballah was practically aided by the financial assistance received from an array of Iranian institutions, operating side by side with Hizballah-run social, charitable, and religious institutions, as well as by the expansion of some

IRGC units from Baalbek into Beirut after April 1983. Soon, Hizballah controlled the southern suburbs of Beirut with a network of neighborhood informants and security personnel to protect its senior leadership. This security blanket was assisted by continuous support and advice from Iran's intelligence operatives based in its Beirut embassy, and functions today both visibly and covertly in many places of *al-Dahiyya* (the Hizballah-dominated southern suburbs of Beirut). In many of these areas, Hizballah operates with complete autonomy in terms of security, as neither the Lebanese army nor Syrian intelligence are allowed to operate here without prior permission. This iron-clad security matrix rests on the meticulous files collected on all past, present, and new members by Hizballah's internal security branch, making it obligatory for all members to report on any meetings or contacts, especially with any "outsiders."[28] Any security breaches are investigated and handled by Hizballah's so-called "Engagement and Coordination Unit," headed by Wafic Safa (who acts also as the chief negotiator in prisoner exchange processes with Israel).[29]

Although Hizballah continued to expand its influence over the economically disenfranchised and politically marginalized Shia community, the issue of security for Hizballah members increased, especially following the 1984 killing of Sheikh Ragheb Harb in the southern Lebanese village of Jibsheet, and the 1985 failed assassination attempt on Sheikh Muhammad Hussein Fadlallah, Hizballah's spiritual leader.[30] However, security concerns had always been paramount for both Hizballah and Islamic Amal in a civil war milieu, and special attention was given to carefully concealing the multiplicity of Iranian agencies at work within Hizballah and the Lebanese theater, especially Iranian military and security structures. Therefore, according to Nizar Hamzeh, the Hizballah has invested heavily in the growth and size of its internal security branch consisting today of over 5,000 personnel.[31]

Hizballah's Special Security Apparatus and the Imad Mughniyeh Factor

The decision to create a specialized élite clandestine unit within Hizballah, the so-called Special Security Apparatus, was made early on to protect emerging senior clerical figures and leaders as the organization crystallized, as well as to safeguard Iranian security and military involvement. Like Mughniyeh, Husayn al-Khalil had spent his formative experience with Fatah during the 1970s and had defected to join Islamic Amal as chief of security, basing himself at the Sheikh Abdallah barracks. Here, al-Khalil assumed responsibility for Hizballah's security and intelligence, while other trusted operatives were recruited into the SSA's three subgroups: the central security apparatus, the preventative security apparatus, and an overseas security apparatus.[32]

The composition of these units was primarily made up of operatives who had distinguished themselves as possessing special security and intelligence skills harnessed during their involvement with Palestinian and other militant groupings before and during the civil war. The recruitment of SSA operatives was also based on clan and family affiliation, in order to ensure secrecy, loyalty, and protection against hostile penetration. An example of this family-based structure is the case of the two Hamadi brothers: Muhammad Ali Hamadi, who participated in the 1985 hijacking of the TWA 847 plane, and Abbas Ali Hamadi, who kidnapped two German citizens in 1987 in retaliation for the arrest of his brother at the Frankfurt airport. Similarly, the Musawi clan, from the village of Nabi Sheet, became influential with three members involved.[33] Other SSA operatives were recruited because they were trusted close or extended family members of senior Hizballah clerics and officials or because they had worked closely with these leaders in a security capacity or even trained Iranian clerical leaders in the past. This was the case of Imad Mughniyeh, who had spent his early years with Fatah Force 17 before allegedly becoming a bodyguard to Hizballah's spiritual leader, Muhammad Hussein Fadlallah.[34] All these SSA operatives had some autonomy or operational freedom according to security circumstances, but all were ultimately answerable to Sheikh Abbas al-Musawi, the overall head of SSA between 1982–85, and Sheikh Subhi al-Tufayli, the then Secretary-General of Hizballah. This became increasingly clear as these SSA units were tasked to kidnap select Western nationalities to suit Iranian and Syrian interests and also as they relied on official Hizballah-channels to Iranian and Syrian intelligence in order to monitor the passenger manifestos of incoming flights to Beirut airport.

The concept of kidnapping foreign nationals was originally Iranian-inspired and operationally driven following the 4 July 1982 kidnapping by Lebanese Forces of four Iranians, two of whom were diplomats, at the Barbara checkpoint en route from Tripoli to Beirut. Two weeks later, David Dodge, the acting president of the American University of Beirut, was kidnapped by Iranian agents and transported across the Lebanese-Syrian border before being flown in a box to Teheran. According to Robert Baer, the IRGC intelligence chief based in Baalbek was instructed to create a layered "cut-out" structure with local trusted operatives, as Iran had been implicated through tracing Dodge's movement out of Lebanon.[35]

A favored and trusted instrument for the Iranians' devious policy designs became the creation of the SSA from primarily within the ranks of Islamic Amal in early 1983, which could perform multiple clandestine functions to ensure Iranian plausible deniability. Operational efficiency required Iranian collusion in the provision of high-grade intelligence on targets and financing of these kidnappings, providing assistance in the establishment of secret safe houses and hiding locations in the southern suburbs of Beirut and in Baalbek (Sheikh Adallah barracks) with loyal guards and secret modes of periodic transport. For example, U.S. hostage Terry Anderson testified that he was held for a period of his captivity in the sub-basement of military barracks occupied by IRGC units.[36] Similarly, suspicion of Iranian collusion came with the precision kidnapping of CIA-chief William Buckley in Beirut on 16 March 1984; he was allegedly transferred to Iran, interrogated under torture, and returned to Lebanon.

It was in connection to the Buckley case that Imad Mughniyeh's name first surfaced on the intelligence radar screens provided by the Algerians to the CIA.[37] It was probably provided earlier with the overlapping and complimentary interests between Hizballah and Iran, which motivated many of these types of kidnappings. The abduction of Buckley served Iranian intelligence interests, while Imad Mughniyeh and the Musawi clan had a personally vested family interest to create maximum pressure on Kuwaiti authorities, who had arrested two of their relatives for involvement in a group known as the *al-Da'wa 17*, which was implicated in multiple terrorist attacks against U.S and French targets in Kuwait City. These two arrested operatives in Kuwait were Hussein al-Sayed Yousef al-Musawi (first-cousin to Islamic Amal leader Husayn al-Musawi) and Elias Fouad Saab (brother-in-law and cousin to Imad Mughniyeh).[38] The *al-Da'wa 17* prisoners held in Kuwait brought Imad Mughniyeh to U.S. intelligence attention, and the case would precipitate more acts of terrorism, including the 1984 hijacking of Kuwait Airlines 221, the 1988 hijacking of Kuwait Airlines 422, and kidnappings of foreigners within Lebanon. However, this case illustrates that the Iranian intelligence machinery would assist in select operations, but it would equally provide a degree of autonomy for SSA operatives to pursue terrorist actions in consultation. Timing and operational procedures were all underpinned by a developed intelligence liaison and command structure between senior SSA members—through the *al-Qods* forces within the IRGC contingent based in the eastern Bekaa—and Iranian intelligence personnel based in both Beirut and Damascus, themselves receiving instructions, assistance, and directives from the Teheran-based MOIS machinery. These channels occurred through the intelligence officer of the IRGC contingent in Baalbek, and were later formalized as Hizballah developed and incorporated two Iranian representatives into its seven-member supreme decision-making body, *Shura al-Qarar*.

The Hizballah SSA-MOIS relationship increased in scale and depth with the practical complexities of terrorist operations, most notably when SSA's security branch operated overseas and in Europe. Muhammad Mouhajer (a nephew of Hizballah leader Sheikh Ibrahim al-Amin) and Fouad Ali Saleh (the principal leader of Hizballah's network in France), along with Iranian Embassy officials, jointly coordinated the 1986 bombing campaign in Paris. The MOIS also provided logistical assistance to senior SSA operatives, helping them avoid detection during traveling; aiding in the procurement of weapons, identities, and money; and providing local liaison assistance by identifying Lebanese expatriates as potential recruits. Talent spotting for new "foreign" recruits became a skill Mughniyeh specialized in to circumvent Israeli security. These operatives also specialized in conducting reconnaissance, searching for security weaknesses in Israeli diplomatic missions abroad. For Hizballah, MOIS represented indispensable operational support, as it was one of the largest intelligence services in the Middle East, with fifteen departments and over 30,000 employees.[39] This auxiliary support continues to provide Hizballah with indispensable force projection capabilities far from the Lebanese theater.

Closer to home, MOIS provided the protection for operatives traveling through Syria, seeking refuge in Teheran for security reasons and for further experience in operational tradecraft. It is alleged that Imad Mughniyeh (and one of the Hamadi brothers) spent long periods in Iran (October through December 1987 in northern Iran, and January 1988 through July 1990 in Qom) and sought refuge there for security reasons following the Israeli kidnapping of Mustafa Dirani in May 1994 and following the assassination of Imad's younger brother Fuad in Beirut in December 1994.[40] This security threat to its members was constant and real, as illustrated by the August 2003 killing of Ali Hussein Salah (from the Bekaa village of Brital), who was believed to be a seasoned explosives expert and worked as a security guard at the Iranian Embassy in Beirut.[41]

Hizballah's primary intelligence support outside MOIS channels (and its associated closer links with SSA) was through the well-oiled channels established with the local *al-Qods* forces within the IRGC contingent based in the eastern Bekaa region and across the border inside Syria. These *al-Qods* units operated alongside Iranian representatives of the Foundation of the Oppressed and Dispossessed (*Bonyade-e-Mostafazan*), the Martyrs Foundation and other charitable bodies to provide Hizballah from the outset with the necessary financing to spread its religious and political appeal and influence. These charitable contributions from Iran lessened over time as Hizballah developed self-sufficiency through a vast social network and a myriad of foundations and charities. However, the primary purpose of the IRGC expeditionary force was to act as a conduit for arms shipments for Hizballah and provide advanced guerrilla training to fighters and specialized terrorist tradecraft to some of its operatives.

While Hizballah had little difficulty in securing weapons during the civil war from indigenous Lebanese sources, many arms shipments with more sophisticated weapons were transported from Iran via air to Syria (especially through Damascus airport or military-controlled airfields).[42] These were then shipped over land across the Syrian-Lebanese border and redistributed to protected and concealed Hizballah-controlled arms depots. From small arms to standoff weapons, Hizballah gradually acquired an impressive arsenal, from over a thousand 122mm Katyusha rockets, AT-4 antitank missiles, and rocket-propelled grenades (RPG's) to mortars and antiaircraft batteries. This made it among the most sophisticated and well-armed guerrilla/terrorist groups in the world. The types of weaponry supplied by Iran reflected the shift of Hizballah's own priorities after 1991, with the end of the Lebanese civil war and the release of the Western hostages, the latter of which was facilitated by the release of the *al-Da'wa 17* prisoners following Iraq's invasion of Kuwait in 1990. Instead, the focus and priority became to equip its forces to fight a complex, effective and sustained guerrilla campaign against the IDF occupation in southern Lebanon and its proxy militia, the SLA.

Hizballah's Centers of Learning: Tactical Agility and Innovation

The presence of IRGC-Hizballah training camps in the eastern Bekaa region served not only to provide the Islamic Resistance fighters with necessary weapons training and guerrilla techniques, but also served as a gateway to select recruits with potential for regular Hizballah infantry battalions, higher-ranking officers, or even for special operation selection. These fighters went through rigorous family background and screening checks by the (counter)intelligence units within the Islamic Resistance in concert with Hizballah's internal security wing. In exceptional circumstances, this was a potential pathway into service with SSA, initially as protective detail or technical specialist. The emphasis was naturally on patient and controlled talent spotting of trusted and exceptionally gifted individual operatives who had successfully passed through Hizballah's two-year stages of recruitment.[43]

For security reasons, the command structure of the Islamic Resistance was effectively compartmentalized from field operations in the seventy-five different sectors comprising the three regional commands in southern Lebanon, the Bekaa region, and the southern suburbs of Beirut.[44] Hizballah's combat units were almost impossible to infiltrate, as its squads were composed of no more than three to four members deployed on infiltration missions in southern villages from rear bases in the Bekaa region or in other areas adjacent to southern Lebanon. A senior Islamic Resistance official headed many of the training and bivouac camps in the Bekaa region and supervised groups of twenty IRGC training officers in each camp, each providing specialist expertise in different aspects of guerrilla warfare.[45] This tactical training embraced studying and learning ambush techniques, concealment and detonation of roadside bombs, mortar attacks, advanced reconnaissance and intelligence, infiltration methods, and aspects of psychological warfare.[46] Some of the more battle-hardened and seasoned fighters assessed each mission with their Iranian advisers to bolster the degree of surprise and effectiveness in preparation for the next one. Reconnaissance work, planning, and intelligence gathering meticulously under-pinned Hizballah's combat missions.

The Islamic Resistance fighters were highly skilled at reconnaissance and intelligence gathering in the field, often remaining invisible from Israeli un-manned aerial vehicles (UAVs) and managing in the wadis and hills of south Lebanon to evade ground surveillance radar, infrared sensors, motion de-tectors, and roaming Israeli special forces (*Egoz*) units along guerrilla-infiltration routes. These fighters were also highly innovative in using roadside bombs—the deadliest weapon employed by the Islamic Resistance as it claimed over half of all IDF and SLA casualties annually. These road-side bombs grew in technological sophistication and innovative conceal-ment. Hizballah developed sophisticated electronic remote-detonation devices using photocell and mobile phone technology and often disguised these bombs inside fiberglass garden rocks to make them "invisible" in the surrounding countryside.[47] Iranian assistance in driving technological and tactical innovation was even extended to the sea and air, as diving equip-ment and eight Iranian-produced unmanned airborne vehicles were pro-vided to Hizballah in August 2004.[48]

Auxiliary channels for the procurement of dual-use technology by Hizbal-lah extended even to the United States. In 2002, Hizballah members Mo-hamad and Chawki Hammoud, based in Charlotte, North Carolina, were convicted of providing material support to Hizballah through a multimillion-dollar cigarette-smuggling operation. In this case, the Hammoud brothers re-ported to Haj Hasan Hilu Laqis (Hezbollah's chief military procurement officer) in diverting the profits from the cigarette-smuggling operation in order to acquire night-vision goggles, global-positioning systems, advanced aircraft-analysis and -design software, stun guns, nitrogen cutters, naval equipment, ultrasonic dog repellers, and laser range finders from U.S. and Canadian retail and military supply stores.[49] Much of this material arguably was designed to enhance the organization's guerrilla activity in southern Lebanon, but this example provides a rare "snapshot" insight into the range and level of ingenuity and sophistication of Hizballah's tactical thinking and adaptation to a constantly changing security environment. This versatility cascaded throughout the entire structure of Hizballah, especially in security and intelligence matters.

As a complement to Hizballah's primary focus on accelerating its guer-rilla warfare in southern Lebanon against Israel and in the sphere of infil-tration, Imad Mughniyeh and the SSA wing began studying weaknesses in Israel's border security in the early to mid-1990s. This option had been el-evated following Israel's decision to expel 415 Palestinian Islamic Jihad and Hamas activists to southern Lebanon in December 1992. As several Hamas leaders from Gaza and the West Bank told this author in interviews, they immediately forged internal tactical and strategic relationships between members (as many had worked within Hamas and PIJ but had never personally met before) and more broad relationships with Hizballah command leadership and members. In turn, this encounter influenced the decision by Hamas and PIJ to gradually adopt suicide operations as a preferred method.

The priority to assist the radical Palestinian Islamist organizations logistically to amplify their violent campaign led the Hizballah, after Iranian consultation, to adopt the decision to find suitable candidates for infiltration missions into Israel beginning in 1996. During that year, Hussein Muhammad Hussein Mikdad, from the Lebanese village of Farun, was recruited as an operative primarily on the grounds of his foreign-language abilities and his Western appearance, enabling him to pass as a British national. Mikdad, an accountant in one of Sheikh Fadlallah's charitable foundations, received instructions in terrorism tradecraft and counterinterrogation techniques at the Janta military training camp in the eastern Bekaa region, along with seven other terrorist candidates. After receiving a stolen British passport in the name of Andrew Jonathan Charles Newman and spending a few days at the Iranian Embassy in Beirut, Mikdad was routed to Geneva, Switzerland, before arriving at and passing through the Ben-Gurion Airport in Tel Aviv, Israel. After renting a car in Tel Aviv, Mikdad proceeded to travel to east Jerusalem and checked into the Lawrence Hotel on Salah Eddin Street. Spending three days in the hotel, Mikdad began assembling an improvised explosive device (with less than a kilogram of the chemical cyclotrimethylenetrinitramine, or RDX), to be hidden inside a Sony multiband radio with the detonation switch in the antennae. The explosives prematurely detonated in Mikdad's lap, causing him to lose both his legs and one arm.[50]

After extensive hospitalization and subsequent interrogation by the Israeli Shin Bet—during which he revealed that he had planned to detonate the device either onboard an El-Al flight departing from Tel Aviv or in a crowded Israeli market—Mikdad was imprisoned and later returned to Lebanon in a prisoner-exchange deal. Although the high-risk operation ultimately failed and would have likely been detected in El-Al's special security screening procedure at Tel Aviv's airport, it nevertheless illustrates the meticulous planning and preparation undertaken by Hizballah's SSA with likely Iranian MOIS assistance. As Israel heightened the security at its border and port entry points, Hizballah revised its infiltration techniques by recruiting and harnessing foreign nationals for actual suicide missions or for auxiliary reconnaissance in support of future terrorist operations occurring inside Israel. The Mikdad incident had taught Hizballah operational planners that foreign nationals who had converted to Islam, if properly screened and indoctrinated, would be ideal to target as recruits, as they reduced the risk of detection. These recruits also increased the organization's mobility within Israel, and logistical assistance could be provided from inside Israel by Hamas or PIJ rather than brought in from outside the country.

The next opportunity to find this type of foreign recruit came in Germany, one of Imad Mughniyeh's favorite recruitment grounds, when Hizballah talent spotters identified Steven Smyrek at a mosque in Braunschweig. After four years in the German Bundeswehr before entering crime and serving a short prison sentence as a drug courier, Smyrek had converted to Islam in 1994 and adopted the name Abdel Karim while working in a Turkish-owned pizzeria and becoming involved with an Egyptian Muslim woman. His virulent hatred for Israel was quickly noticed, and two Hizballah contact men, Fahdi Hamdar and his cousin Mohammad, eventually approached him and suggested a visit to Lebanon to join Hizballah and undertake military training. To show his level of commitment (and prove that he was not an informer) the Hizballah handlers insisted he visit them. In August 1997, Smyrek arrived in Beirut where he was extensively interrogated and pressured before being sent to a terrorist/military training camp in southern Lebanon. After two months of training, Smyrek was sent back to Germany to receive a new clean passport. In November, he purchased a ticket on El-Al to Israel from Amsterdam. Dutch authorities detained him briefly on departure, as the German security service had him under surveillance following intelligence received by the Israelis. Smyrek was released after questioning, but missed the original El-Al flight and reportedly contacted his handlers, who instructed him to board the next available one.[51] On arrival at Ben-Gurion, Smyrek was arrested by Israeli intelligence and found to be in possession of $4,000 in cash and a camera provided by Hizballah to conduct surveillance photographs on key potential Israeli targets. Smyrek confessed in his interrogation that the second part of his mission was going to be a suicide mission against civilian targets in Tel Aviv or Haifa. Hizballah had requested that he videorecord a "martyrdom" message where he announce his desire to be a *shaheed* (martyr) and denounce the Zionist enemy.[52]

The arrests of Mikdad and Smyrek did not deter the Hizballah SSA from identifying other suitable operatives to deploy on infiltration missions. In early January 2000, another Hizballah operative with dual Lebanese-British nationality was arrested in Jerusalem, close to the residence of the Israeli Prime Minister. Jihad Aya Latif Shuman, a graduate of the American University of Beirut in computer studies, had routed himself through London before entering Israel. In London, Shuman had acquired a mobile phone enabling him to communicate from Israel to his handlers in Lebanon on a regular basis. It is unclear whether Shuman was purely on a reconnaissance mission, as he had a *kippah* (a traditional head covering) and several cameras and a video camera in his possession, was on an attack mission involving the assassination of an Israeli politician, or was preparing a suicide attack.[53]

Mikdad was released in a 1998 prisoner-exchange deal between Israel and Hizballah, brokered by German intermediaries and Wafic Safa (Hizballah's chief prisoner negotiator), while Smyrek and Shuman were returned in a similar exchange process in 2004. These three cases of recruitment of "foreign" operatives for infiltration, reconnaissance, and attack missions inside Israel revealed that Hizballah placed a high priority on developing an advanced intelligence gathering capability inside Israel. For Hizballah, according to Daniel Sobelman's incisive study, this priority reflected broader sophisticated strategic planning on developing a "databank" on future potential military and infrastructure targets inside Israel. It also reflected a contingency measure, as an Israeli withdrawal from southern Lebanon would constrict "legitimate" areas of Hizballah's military engagement with Israel.[54] This alternative channel was not just limited to infiltrating its own operatives into Israel, but also involved the development of a network of indigenous collaborators, extending from increased cooperation with Palestinian militants in Gaza and the West Bank to the recruitment of Israeli Arabs. Often Hizballah utilized monetary incentives to recruit operatives for conducting reconnaissance missions. It also utilized drug smuggling channels on the Israeli-Lebanese border to supply arms to Palestinian or Israeli-Arab agents of influence. In addition, Hizballah intensified efforts to provide logistical assistance and arms to a variety of Palestinian factions, ranging from the notorious Karine-A affair (when an investigation into a ship carrying weapons revealed Iranian-Palestinian collusion to smuggle 50 tons of weapons into the hands of the Palestinian Authority through the offices of Hizballah) to providing the blueprints for the development of the al-Qassam rockets to the military wing of Hamas.[55] Some Palestinian operatives have received extensive training in Hizballah-run military training camps, usually for three-month courses, teaching them how to operate small arms and explosives and conduct intelligence and countersurveillance.

Hizballah's focus on developing an operational terrorist infrastructure inside Israel and the Palestinian territories has revealed three emerging patterns. First, Hizballah's SSA has prioritized finding new and ingenious methods of kidnapping Israeli citizens abroad, following the successful abduction of retired IDF officer Elhanan Tannenbaum in October 2000, who was lured to Beirut via Brussels and Abu Dhabi under false business pretences. The principal architect of this operation was Kais Obeid, an Israeli Arab hailing from one of the wealthiest families in Taiba, and whose grandfather served as Labor Member of Knesset (Israel's parliament) from 1961 to 1973. Obeid's father and two brothers had been arrested during the 1980s and sentenced to prison for smuggling drugs from Lebanon to Israel. Obeid's close friendship with Tannenbaum provided the vehicle of trust for the kidnapping operation, and he left Israel in September 2000 for Beirut and resurfaced as a close adviser to Hizballah leader Sheikh Hassan Nasserallah.[56] It is alleged that Obeid is in charge of "Israeli" affairs within Hizballah and is tasked with providing liaison between Hizballah and Tanzim/al-Aqsa Martyrs Brigades, Hizballah's financial connections to the Palestinian territories, and the recruitment of Israeli Arabs.[57] It is also believed that Obeid has become Hizballah's chief "abduction agent" of Israelis. This suspicion was elevated when reports emerged that Kais Obeid had contacted a number of Israeli citizens in 2002, attempting to lure them with business ideas to travel to the Lebanese border and to Europe.[58] The successful series of prisoner exchanges, following the 2000 abduction of three IDF soldiers and the Tannenbaum kidnapping, made this option attractive for the Hizballah, who drew up a target priority list of Israelis, among them the former Israeli Energy Minister Gonen Segev.[59]

Second, Hizballah is investing a great deal in increasing its capacity to infiltrate its own agents inside Israel and in cultivating collaborators for reconnaissance missions and the establishment of sources capable of acquiring weapons and explosives inside Israel. This forward contingency planning enables Hizballah to compress the time from when decisions for terrorist missions are taken by the leadership to when it is carried out by its operatives.[60] Towards these ends, the Hizballah has specialized in recruitment of "foreigners" with European Union passports as demonstrated by the January 2005 arrest of a Lebanese-born Danish citizen, who allegedly was tasked to document and photograph security installations, IDF troop movements and in identifying potential recruits. According to this operative, if successful he would have been given a more complicated future task.[61]

A third pattern emerging is seen in the desire by Hizballah to acquire high-grade intelligence on military and critical infrastructure inside Israel, to monitor IDF troop movements, and to develop a targeting matrix of gas and electricity installations. This was underscored by the Israeli indictment of Nissim Musa Nasser in June 2002, charging him with acquiring detailed maps of some of Tel Aviv's gas storage facility and electricity substations on behalf of the Hizballah. This followed closely the May 2002 failed operation by Hamas against the Pi Glilot petroleum and gas storage facility in the densely populated area of Herzeliya, narrowly averting a major catastrophe as a bomb, planted on the undercarriage of a fuel tanker and activated by mobile phone, exploded but failed to ignite other storage facilities. The Pi Glilot facility supplies over 70 percent of gasoline and diesel fuel to Israel's gasoline stations and is situated at the busiest highway juncture in the country. Similar efforts were made by Hamas in a foiled plan to target one of Tel Aviv's skyscrapers, and in the March 2004 Ashdod port incident, in which two suicide bombers using high-grade plastic explosives may have intended to target chemical storage facilities.[62] All these incidents, combined with Hizballah efforts to acquire intelligence on Israel's critical infrastructure, have elevated fears of a "megaattack" in the future. Hizballah will continue to collect intelligence on these types of targets, in order to evaluate and identify potential vulnerabilities as a contingency for future operations in case the organization's leadership and position is comprehensively targeted, severely pressured, and existentially threatened. An attack of this nature will only be activated as a means of last resort and if Hizballah could manage to reduce or conceal its operational signature.

Conclusion

Since its foundation in 1982, Hizballah has developed a highly complex and multifaceted terrorist infrastructure under Iranian guidance and support and with Syrian patronage. In many ways Hizballah has been pioneering the tactical repertoire of terrorist groups worldwide, and few can match the complexity as well as the concealment of its overall command structure and terrorist missions. Like a spider's web, Hizballah's operational contacts stretch far and wide into the inner vortex of Iran's security establishment, through individual Iranian clergy and multileveled relationships with Hamas and the Palestinian Islamic Jihad. Few Hizballah SSA operatives have ever been caught and brought to justice for alleged terrorist atrocities stretching back over two decades, despite massive U.S. intelligence investment of resources towards these ends (at least prior to 9/11). Underpinning this difficulty in locating operatives has been the absence of actionable intelligence and human intelligence sources, compounded by the killing of Robert Ames, the CIA's station chief, in the 1983 U.S. Embassy bombing in Beirut and the lengths to which Iranian intelligence have gone to ensure plausible deniability in its involvement with Hizballah's SSA.

Another difficulty in understanding the contours and structure of terrorism within Hizballah has been its ability to conceal and embed this architecture within crevasses of its massive social and military infrastructure and its political legitimacy within a large proportion of Lebanese society, suffering from a longstanding civil war (1975–90) and successive Israeli military occupation of Lebanon. Although Hizballah has gone to extraordinary lengths to ensure continued asymmetric confrontation with and within Israel, it has also exercised a degree of self-imposed constraint, as its terrorist violence is carefully calibrated to suit the political interests and calculations of its own position as well as that of its two major patrons, Iran and Syria. This balancing act between contending interests has been a hallmark of Hizballah's unparalleled sophistication and ability to maneuver.

As demonstrated in this chapter, Hizballah's training camps within Lebanon have served multiple political and operational purposes over time, extending from solidifying its structure in the early 1980s to providing very advanced guerrilla and terrorist training to its own and other selected fighters from Palestinian factions. Gradually, Hizballah has acquired an impressive weaponry arsenal and a high degree of interoperability between its military and terrorist wing, especially with the expert assistance of Iranian military advisers and instructors. This interaction drives innovation and agility in learning from past missions and mistakes towards constantly devising new operational terrorist methods with a highly developed degree of surprise and impact. In this lethal enterprise there are few organizations as capable, precise and dangerous.

CHAPTER 16

The Human Factor in Insurgency: Recruitment and Training in the Revolutionary Armed Forces of Colombia (FARC)

ROMÁN D. ORTIZ

As with any other type of organization, the strategic path of a terrorist or guerrilla group is dependent upon its effectiveness in the reception and management of human resources. To begin with, the social and demographic profile of the armed militants determines the pattern of political-military action of the organization, the social sectors against which the violence is deployed, and the ultimate ends of the struggle. Furthermore, the group's operational capabilities depend directly on the political and military training received by militants. Finally, in time, the group's survival options and success opportunities are a result of the movement's chances of enlarging its recruitment niches and of improving formulas for the insertion of new militants in the operational dynamic of the insurgent organization. In other words, the human factor determines the shape assumed by political violence in a given scenario.

This principle is perfectly applied to the case of the Revolutionary Armed Forces of Colombia (FARC). It is impossible to understand the longevity of this guerrilla group—prior to the transformation of its strategic scenario and the increase of its financial and military power—without taking into account the changes in its militants' profile as well as the modification of its recruitment and training mechanisms. However, it is also necessary to consider changes in the nature of FARC's human resources in order to understand its organizational weaknesses and the strategic obstacles which the group has been unable to overcome. Consequently, an adjusted view of the evolution prospects of Colombian insurgency requires an analysis of its human component.

The Membership of FARC

As with any other armed group, a precise estimate of FARC's membership is an almost impossible task for two reasons. On one hand, the underground nature of the organization makes determining the human volume of insurgency extremely challenging. On the other hand, it is very difficult to agree on how to define a guerrilla militant in order to assess the full scope of insurgent forces. This difficulty may seem surprising, but it responds to the features of the force structure of a group that has embarked upon an insurgent campaign. In fact, any guerrilla movement has a hard-core of full-time militants, as well as several layers of collaborators who are involved in support tasks of more or less importance in political or military terms. Finally, there is a social base (varying in size and breadth) composed of civilian populations under the orders of insurgents resulting from the guerrillas' use of terror as a tool for social control. The boundaries between these categories are not absolutely rigid, as an individual could easily move from one to another, either escalating or decreasing his or her involvement in the armed movement.

At first glance, it is clear that it is not possible to automatically qualify as insurgents the whole sectors of the population under the organization's rule. In many cases, they accept the insurgent domain only because they are living in areas where the group has intimidation capacity. Likewise, there is no doubt that full-time combatants should be considered as militants in the organization. The problem emerges with individuals moving in the grey area between the hard-core militants and the civilian population merely obliged to obey insurgent orders; this category includes people engaged with the organization at levels ranging from individuals under coercion to sporadic collaborators, as well as recruits under training before becoming full-time combatants. The question is how far these sectors can be considered as part of the political and military power of the armed organization.

In FARC's particular case, the organization counts among its members a certain number of full-time militants who make up the hard-core combat units (guerrillas, companies, columns, and so on) as well as two categories of part-time militants. In one category are the so-called Bolivarian Militias, individuals who have received a basic military training. They are usually armed, giving support to the main combat units and executing minor scale actions. In the other category are the Popular Militias, individuals like the elderly or handicapped who cannot take part in combat. They occasionally carry weapons and are involved in surveillance, intelligence, and logistical support tasks. Taking into account this categorical difference, it should be noted that the assessment of FARC's membership has usually been focused on the full-time fighters—in other words, the full-time armed members of the group. From this point of view, it should be noted that during its four decades of history the organization has experienced an amazing growth in the number of its combatant figures. In May 1964, Pedro Antonio Marin, alias "Tirofijo," as leader of the insurgent stronghold of Marquetalia could not gather more than forty-eight fighters to face the Colombian army's assault (an event which is considered the beginning of the armed struggle of FARC). Almost four decades later, when the peace negotiations between the guerrillas and President Andres Pastrana's administration collapsed in February 2002, the organization's numbers added up to almost 17,000 combatants (according to calculations of the Colombian Ministry of Defense). During the last couple of years, the pressure exercised by a new counterinsurgency strategy implemented by President Alvaro Uribe Velez—known as *Política de Defensa y Seguridad de Democrática* (PDSD or Defence and Democratic Security Policy)—may have reduced FARC's membership to between 13,000 and 14,000 combatants. In addition to these figures, the guerrillas could also count on receiving assistance from a number of collaborators (precise numbers are hard to estimate) belonging to militias and to the *Partido Comunista Colombiano Clandestino* (PCCC or Clandestine Colombian Communist Party), the political wing created by FARC to give ideological support to the armed struggle and to serve as a reserve from which to recruit new combatants for the guerrilla movement.

In general, the organization's enlargement did not follow a linear trajectory, but instead alternated between phases of stagnation and slow growth and stages of accelerated increases in manpower. During the 1960s and 1970s, FARC grew very slowly while spreading from its stronghold on the Andean central mountain range (where the organization was founded) towards the eastern Andean mountain range and towards Tolima, Caldas, Quindio, Cauca, and the central riverbed of the Magdalena River. It took the organization fourteen years to reach 1,000 militants (in 1978), but then FARC went through two periods of rapid growth during which it reached its current size. The first stage, during the mid-1980s, coincided with an attempt to increase the political projection of the organization through two main channels; on one side, a peace negotiation with President Belisario Betancourt's administration was opened, and, on the other, a political coalition known as the *Unión Patriótica* (UP or Patriotic Union) was formed with the official *Partido Comunista Colombiano* (PCC or Colombian Communist Party) in order to complement the armed struggle with legal political activism. Both channels failed to increase FARC's political power because of the collapse of the negotiations and the split of the UP due to contradictions between the official Communist Party and the guerrillas as well as an overwhelming wave of extreme right-wing terrorism against coalition members.

These events led to an exponential growth in FARC's human resources. According to Colombian army data, FARC's membership grew from 1,800 to 4,000 combatants during the regime of President Betancourt (1982–86), an increase of 133 percent.[1] However, the organization's growth seemed to decelerate during the next several years, and by the end of President Virgilio Barco's administration in 1990, the guerrilla movement had grown to 5,800 men, a modest increase of only 45 percent compared with the previous period.

During the 1990s, however, the pace of the organization's growth accelerated again. By the end of President Cesar Gavira's administration in 1994, an assessment of the Colombian Ministry of Defense placed the membership of FARC at around 9,500. The end of the 1990s witnessed another exponential expansion of the guerrilla movement. By the year 2000, a new estimate by the Defense Department indicated FARC's manpower was nearly 16,500 men. This second quantitative jump in membership was the result of a combination of changes in the Colombian strategic scenario and political and military innovations tested by the organization. Since the end of the 1980s, the Colombian state was forced to divert its security resources to face other insurgent organizations, the drug cartels, and the growing paramilitary movement. Consequently, the means available to combat FARC's expansion were reduced considerably. In this context, during the early 1990s, the rebels tried to strengthen their own capacity to mobilize the masses by breaking their last links with the official CCP and creating a political structure under their direct control, called the Clandestine Colombian Communist Party (CCCP). For this purpose, the guerrillas created a base for this new political organization, bringing together its own militants with splinter groups of the youth organization of the official Colombian Communist Party. The outcome was a moderate enlargement of the social base of insurgent recruitment.

At the same time, FARC made a qualitative jump in its military capabilities, implementing the so-called New Operational Way (NOW), which involved the development of mobile warfare and the putting into practice of complex operations (such as strikes against military bases or large ambushes). The result was the expulsion of the Colombian security forces from wide areas of the country and the consolidation of insurgent control over substantial amounts of population and territory. This process allowed FARC to access additional human resources. Finally, between 1998 and 2002, the recruitment of new militants was facilitated by the negotiation process held between the insurgents and the Pastrana administration. In fact, the creation of a demilitarized region of 42,000 square kilometers (known as the Distension Zone) to host the negotiations offered the guerrillas an enormous safe haven. Inside this area, the insurgents could move freely without the pressure of the Colombian military forces, making the recruitment and training of new militants notably easier. Further, the powerful public image of a guerrilla organization negotiating face-to-face with a government stimulated a large number of youngsters to join a movement they thought was close to achieving victory. This combination of factors led to an exponential growth in the insurgent organization during the 1990s.

At the beginning of the new millennium, the new counterinsurgency strategy developed by the Uribe administration began to address the factors which facilitated the recruitment and development of new militants by FARC. Consequently, the insurgents have faced an increasing number of obstacles to replacing their casualties. In fact, the progressive restoration of state control over the majority of Colombian populated territory has significantly hindered the insurgents' recruitment activities. At the same time, the chain of successful operations by the military and police has eroded the image of the guerrillas as an invincible organization, reducing the enthusiasm of potential recruits. Finally, the inability of insurgents to force President Uribe to release hundreds of guerrilla fighters held by the government in exchange for a group of kidnapped politicians and soldiers has demonstrated the incapacity of FARC to aid its imprisoned militants, leading to a sharp image of weakness. As a result of these factors, the guerrillas have lost their ability to attract disenfranchised young people in rural areas, and thus the aforementioned decrease in FARC membership during the few last years.

FARC Recruitment

When depicting a sociodemographic profile of FARC beyond the total figures of militants, it is clear that the organization is still a peasant movement. In fact, the members of rural origin prevail in the organization in contrast with other Latin American insurgent groups, whose leadership comes from urban middle class sectors. In this sense, FARC is an exception since its founders, starting with the almost fifty original fighters who faced the Colombian Army in Marquetalia, were peasants. This tendency has been maintained, with the majority of guerrilla militants coming from the countryside. Representing one of the sociodemographic features commonly associated with rural culture, the bulk of FARC members are men with a low educational level. In fact, the predominance of males with little or no education is a consequence of the social conditions in the regions where the guerrillas operate and recruit.

Also, as a reflection of the patriarchal character of Colombian rural communities, females have a subordinate role among the insurgents. Thus, a woman has never been appointed as part of the leadership organ of FARC known as the Secretariat. Likewise, the low academic level of militants reflects the shortage of educational opportunities among the rural populations that form the social base of the guerrilla movement. However, this educational deficiency has had mixed consequences for the organization: On one hand, it has made the recruitment of new militants easier, using extremely simple political messages, and on the other hand, it created enormous obstacles to providing political education to militants who lack enough intellectual skills to understand the ideological principles of the organization and are prone to purely military action.

In any case, while keeping in mind the predominant rural composition of FARC, it must be noted that the enrollment of members of urban origins has played a strategic role in the expansion process of the organization. In fact, it is impossible to explain FARC's evolution without taking into account the contributions of these urban militants, who brought with them a higher cultural (and sometimes educational) level and a modern concept of politics. When the Marquetalia insurgent group and communist leaders Jacobo Arenas and Hernando Gonzalez joined forces in 1964, this alliance played a decisive role in abandoning the former self-defense strategy and beginning to operate as a mobile guerrilla organization under the denomination of the Revolutionary Armed Forces of Colombia.[2] Fifteen years later, the enrollment of communist militants of urban origins—inspired by the Nicaraguan revolution experience—was critical to boosting the political and military modernization of the guerrilla movement. In fact, people belonging to this group—such as Luis Edgar Devia Silva, alias "Raul Reyes," or Guillermo Leon Saenz Vargas, alias "Alfonso Cano"—would reach the top ranks of the organization, becoming innovators of the political-military strategy of the group.

Taking into account these previous experiences, during the late 1990s FARC's leadership detected the lack of middle-rank commanders as one of its main weaknesses when controlling an organization considerably enlarged after a period of accelerated growth. Accordingly, it was decided that recruitment in state universities should be intensified in order to gather an urban group of militants with a higher education level who could hold the mid-level leadership positions in the organization's structure. This decision gave rise to the creation of an insurgent unit known as the Company of Bachelors, which would serve as a training detachment for the formation of future insurgent leaders. Thus once again, the organization tried to solve a bottleneck in its process of growth by enrolling urban militants capable of supplying new political and strategic skills.

Regarding FARC's recruitment in rural areas, it must be noted that the insurgents have focused their efforts on attracting new militants in areas of Colombia where the political and social conditions have facilitated their penetration. Consequently, the organization has incorporated a remarkable number of new militants from areas where the communist movement has had a notably historic presence, such as the Sumapaz region near Bogotá or in some areas of the Tolima department. In these areas, the insurgent presence and its recruitment activities have profited from an extensive guerrilla tradition associated initially with the existence of liberal armed groups and then with the self-defense communist movements of the 1940s and 1950s.

The rural communities have tended to weave personal relations with FARC militants present in their regions. In this context, a certain number of families have become used to their youngsters joining the guerrilla movement. On the other hand, the insurgents have found another main recruitment niche in the so-called colonization areas.[3] These regions have traditionally been characterized by recent settlement associated with agricultural exploitation of virgin territories by settlers migrating from other parts of the country. Throughout this socioeconomic scenario, the presence of state administration has always been weak, practically excluding these social sectors from the influence of Bogotá's governance.

Under these conditions, a series of factors have combined to facilitate the insurgent recruitment tasks in these areas, including the existence of an uprooted population suffering severe social problems such as family disintegration and high levels of crime. Furthermore, the lack of basic public services—a result of the state's absence—ranging from justice to educational infrastructure has facilitated FARC recruitment, while the political and military predominance of guerrilla groups has transformed membership in an armed organization into an attractive option for many youngsters without any other labor prospects. The outcome of these conditions has been the conversion of colonization areas into one of FARC's main recruitment grounds. This tendency is particularly salient in regions where colonization processes were associated with the development of illegal drug crops. There, settlers combined the dimension of uprooted populations with the practice of an illicit labor activity which obliged them to live illegally. Under such circumstances, these sectors could not turn to the state to obtain such public services as security or basic healthcare. Consequently, they were forced to accept the guerrillas as a political-military power capable of replacing the state.[4]

However, a series of social and political factors have forced FARC's recruitment capacity into a sudden crisis. To begin with, recent demographic changes in Colombia have reduced the proportion of the country's population suitable for becoming guerrilla fighters. Particularly, the rapid nationwide urbanization process, which began in the 1960s, has brought a large flow of migrants from rural areas to the cities. The result has been a massive population relocation from the country to the cities, which gradually reduced the volume of social sectors accessible to the recruitment strategy of FARC. The percentage of Colombia's population classified as "urban" grew from 57 percent in 1970 to 74.5 percent in 2002, with equivalent decreases in the population of rural areas.[5] The impact of these tendencies on guerrilla recruitment opportunities is particularly salient when taking into account that migration to cities was particularly strong among age groups most suitable for the workplace (that is, young males—the same demographic group which potentially could be recruited for violent activities). As a result, insurgents over time had a smaller audience for their rural revolutionary project and a shrinking quantity of potential recruits.

Moreover, the emergence of the paramilitary movement during the end of the 1980s affected FARC's opportunities for enrolling new militants. Indeed, the paramilitary's terrorist strategy increased the organization's difficulties in carrying out its recruitment campaigns in rural areas by scaring away their potential social base and increasing the risks faced by farmers and their families willing to accept the organization's calling. In addition, as illegal self-defense groups sought to expand their manpower, they created an alternative demand for recruitment among the same peasant population that had previously nourished the FARC's ranks. Since paramilitary groups were looking for new members as well, a youngster willing to follow an illegal career found that FARC was no longer his only option. In fact, groups such as the *Autodefensas Unidas de Colombia* (AUC or United Auto-Defense of Colombia) represent a far more tempting offer than the guerrillas. The insurgents demand a lifetime commitment to the organization, pay no wages to their militants—although sometimes they promise wages to the new recruits—and deny them any chance of gaining personal wealth. In contrast, the paramilitary movement demands an initial enrollment of only one or two years, pays wages of around US$200 per month, and allows its militants to accumulate a personal fortune through their participation in drug trafficking, extortion, and other forms of illicit business. In this sense, peasant youngsters perceive their enlisting in illegal self-defense organizations as a far more attractive option than joining the guerrillas. The result has been a decrease in the volume of potential recruits available to the FARC.

Undoubtedly, FARC's recruitment problems have accentuated since the beginning of President Uribe's term and the implementation of the Defense and Democratic Security Policy. In general terms, the military pressure exercised by the state against the guerrillas has created an unfavorable environment for the organization's recruitment activities. Moreover, in many municipalities the setting up of local security forces known as *Soldados de mi Pueblo* (Soldiers of my Town) or *Soldados Campesinos* (Peasant Soldiers) has created additional barriers for insurgent attempts to enroll new militants. These kinds of local security units are composed of young men of military age who maintain their civilian labor activities and render military service by providing security to the communities to which they belong. Under this scheme, *Soldados Campesinos* have created a protective screen that has reduced FARC's capacity to approach rural populations, to intimidate them, and to place them under the organization's control. Furthermore, the creation of these detachments has generated a demand for recruits among the same population from which the guerrillas and the paramilitaries used to draw their militants. In other words, the state has decreased the recruitment pool for these insurgent and self-defense groups by creating opportunities for peasants within its own security forces.

The growing difficulties for recruitment have obliged FARC to broaden the scope of the population they seek to enroll. The result has been a growing incorporation of minors and women, which is gradually changing the sociodemographic profile of the guerrilla movement. In the case of underage militants, the truth is that FARC—as is the case with many other insurgent groups—has never respected international laws prohibiting the recruitment of minors. In fact, guerrilla leaders have openly advocated the legitimacy of recruiting fifteen-year-olds. This insurgent tendency to recruit minors reflects cultural factors as well as convenience. Usually, the incorporation of men into the workforce comes earlier in rural areas than in cities. In this sense, FARC's propensity to recruit minors would be a military reflection of this rural custom. Moreover, enrolling minors is convenient for an organization which demands a lifetime commitment without any economic compensation. In fact, minors are easier to attract without pecuniary incentives because of their relish for guns or the social recognition enjoyed by the organization among certain rural populations. Furthermore, they can be completely molded by the organization to the point of not being able to understand life away from the guerrilla movement. In this manner, FARC hopes to form generations of loyal combatants, safeguarded from temptations to desert their comrades-in-arms. However, beyond this recruitment strategy the truth is that the scarcity of peasants willing to join their numbers has forced the guerrillas to enroll a growing number of minors. As a result, the enlisting of militants under fourteen, thirteen, or even twelve years of age by FARC is not unusual.

Regarding women, recruitment has been enlarged to reach a significant percentage in the organization—by some accounts, up to 40 percent.[6] During FARC's first two decades of history, the female presence within the organization was reduced to assistance, labor, and support, and they were excluded from the top ranks of the command structure of the guerrilla movement. However, beginning in the mid-1980s the group began to recruit women for combat.[7] This decision was motivated by the need for militants within a context of the depopulation of rural zones, which hampered traditional recruitment efforts. Since then, women have achieved some degree of influence within the insurgent movement. A good example would be the case of Anayibe Rojas Valderrama, alias "Sonia," who was responsible for the finances of the regional command in charge of operations in the southern parts of Colombia, and who was captured by Bogotá authorities in February 2004. Nevertheless, a female presence in command positions should be interpreted as an exception rather than the rule; the FARC leadership remains in male hands. As a reflection of this, it should be noted that women were absent from the guerrilla delegation which held negotiations with the Pastrana administration between 1998 and 2002.

Beyond the sociodemographic profile of its militants, FARC has become an efficient machinery of political and military training. The organization has the capacity to enroll recruits from different origins, develop them in accordance with the organization's principles and transform them into components of a solid insurrectional machine. Youngsters enrolled in the guerrilla movement enlist for a wide variety of reasons. Certainly, there is a percentage of forced recruitment carried out by different units of FARC, depending on their replacement needs and the recruitment opportunities in each area, with the intimidation ability of FARC overcoming the village's resistance to the group's recruitment activities. However, it is hard to imagine the majority of people joining the guerrilla movement because of mere coercion.

It is also common for those in charge of recruitment to resort to false promises of economic rewards in order to encourage hesitant potential recruits. Still others factors come into play in driving a certain number of youngsters to join FARC. A social environment in crisis, broken homes, and acute labor prospects tend to drive out potential recruits from their places of origin and encourage them to see the armed struggle as a possible way of life. In this context, a broad variety of individual reasons may provide the ultimate stimulus required to make up one's mind to join FARC. Amid these motivations is found, for instance, the desire for social prestige among communities that view the guerrillas with both amusement and fear. The youth's fascination for weapons and the power associated with them may work in a similar manner. The desire to exact revenge on local power holders for real or imagined grievances should also be included.[8] Finally, emotional and family ties with members of the organization also play a role in FARC's recruitment. Overall, the majority of recruits enroll in the organization because of a combination of social factors and personal aims, where the ideological principles of FARC and the identification with the organization's political objectives become absolutely secondary.

FARC Training

After becoming a member of FARC, the organization assumes the task of transforming the recruit into a revolutionary combatant. To move forward in this process, the insurgent group uses a three-part strategy that includes the development of an extensive political-military education plan, the imposition of rigid discipline, and the establishment of absolute control over its members. The combination of these three tools allows the organization to absorb the individual, secure his loyalty, and place all his personal resources in the service of the cause. In other words, by subordinating all dimensions of militants' lives to its political objectives, FARC acts as a totalitarian organization. This approach to the management of human resources, common among terrorist organizations, has at least two rationales.[9] First, the organization's ideology, which is based on Marxism of a Stalinist nature as well as radical agrarianism with deep totalitarian roots, denies any space to the individual in favor of the common good.[10] Second, the logic of insurgency demands the subjugation of militants to a rigid discipline in order to achieve revolutionary victory. On this basis, FARC has developed an extremely oppressive organizational culture for its militants, which has ensured a noteworthy internal coherence and military effectiveness.

Concerning the political-military education of its members, FARC considers that training should be a permanent process extending throughout the militant's membership in the organization. In this sense, the guerrillas have established a series of political and military training courses that combatants are required to take while ascending the organization's ranks. Furthermore, the group maintains educational and self-criticism formulas that work as effective control procedures. For instance, militants hold periodic cell meetings to analyze and criticize the functioning of their own unit. Likewise, the members of guerrilla units hold daily meetings—called *relacion* (review)—where daily events are reviewed and solutions to the problems identified are suggested.

Theoretically, the insurgent leadership grants equal importance to military training and political indoctrination, yet a series of events has elevated training in military matters over ideological instruction. In the first place, the confusing and complex nature of FARC's ideology creates enormous problems for its internalization by militants. In fact, given the combatants' low educational level, they are not usually well qualified to assimilate a political ideology based to a great extent on theoretical concepts drawn from Marxist thinkers. Finally, the demands generated by an increased pace of military operations have reduced the available time and resources for political instruction. In spite of all these factors, starting in the late 1990s, the insurgency's leadership has stressed the importance of the ideological education of its members, calling attention among its units towards this task. This emphasis on political training responds to two phenomena that are threatening the armed group's political identity. To begin with, an increased involvement in criminal activities such as drug trafficking and kidnapping are weakening discipline and stimulating corruption within the organization. Moreover, the addition of a new generation of militants, who are more concerned with power and enrichment than committed to the ideological objectives of the group, is cause for increasing concern among FARC's senior leadership.

In the meantime, FARC has used a good deal of its economic resources and international connections to improve its combatants' military training. The organization functions as a modern military machine, offering a series of training courses and programs which combatants are required to take throughout their life in the guerrilla movement. Basic military training is provided by the recruit's arrival unit. In addition, instructional centers and training units have been created for the development of more complex educational programs. The establishment of the Hernando Gonzalez Military School in the Yari plains (Caquetá department) is the best example of this commitment. This school trained the generation of guerrilla commanders who put into practice the mobile warfare strategy deployed by the organization from the mid-1990s until the beginning of the year 2000. Likewise, the creation of the aforementioned Company of Bachelors (to form middle-rank commanders) is further evidence of the robust military training system developed by FARC.

The organization has also looked to its international connections with other armed groups as a source for improving their military training. In this regard, FARC has brought to Colombian territory foreign instructors to impart specialized courses to its members. For example, in 1997, the presence of Japanese Red Army (JRA) members in the northern part of Colombia, believed to have been training the guerrillas in terrorist tactics, was denounced by Colombian intelligence community sources. Along the same lines, the arrest of three Provisional Irish Republican Army (PIRA) militants in the Bogotá airport in 2001 indicated that FARC had enlisted the services of this European terrorist group in order to improve its explosive management skills and its urban tactics.[11]

The insurgent organization has also sent its members abroad to receive training in specialized matters. In fact, during the 1990s some militants are believed to have traveled to Vietnam to receive training in Special Forces operations. Also, according to some sources, beginning in 2002 a group of FARC militants traveled to Libya to receive training as plane and helicopter pilots. All these military training programs at home and abroad have evolved alongside the modification of the organization's military strategy. In other words, the insurgency's leadership has adapted FARC's recruitment and training efforts to meet the organization's changing strategic needs. In this sense, the decision to jump into mobile warfare during the mid-1990s was preceded by programs for the training of militants and commanders to accomplish complex operations such as large ambushes and military base assaults. Likewise, FARC's return to guerrilla warfare in 2002 brought along an increase in sniper and mine warfare and special operation tactics training. Overall, military training has been conceived by FARC as an essential form of preparation to carry out the appropriate tactics in accordance with the general strategy developed by the group for various occasions.

Beyond the substantial military sophistication achieved by FARC, the fragile ideological training of its militants should have brought serious problems to the organization's internal coherence and combative capacity. Nonetheless, internal divisions are practically absent from FARC's history, apart from the splinter group of the mid-1980s that was opposed to the dialogue established by the rebel leadership with the Betancur administration. Furthermore, throughout its four decades of armed activity the group has suffered a limited volume of desertions when compared to other armed organizations such as the Ejército de Liberación Nacional (ELN or National Liberation Army) and paramilitary groups. In fact, FARC has demonstrated a remarkable ability to endure and expand its membership despite the military pressure of the state.

The paradox of an ideologically weak organization with enormous internal coherence is explained by the totalitarian nature of the living conditions inside the group. In fact, FARC members depend on the organization for all aspects of their daily existence, which leads to their complete subjugation to the group's guidelines. For example, commanders take care of their subordinate's food and clothing. Furthermore, the organization controls and filters the information received by its members, providing a distorted perception of reality. Likewise, the combatants' personal and family lives are subject to the leadership's will.

FARC militants also require authorization to establish love relationships.[12] In fact, commanders have the power to determine if a relationship is harmful for the revolutionary cause and can order its break-up accordingly. Likewise, female guerrilla fighters need their commander's permission to give birth, being forced to abort if consent is not granted.[13] But even when approval is obtained, the newborn is separated from the mother at birth in order to allow the mother to return to her duties in the organization. The whole control system is backed up by a draconian discipline. For instance, the punishment for a desertion attempt is the death penalty, regardless of whether the member in question is a minor. Even small acts like stealing food rations entail extreme punishments, such as engaging in armed combat without a weapon. This disciplinary regime has a demolishing impact on the psyche of youngsters who join the group. After some years in the bosom of the guerrilla movement, and having established not only material but emotional dependence upon the group, it is extremely hard for combatants to remove themselves from the organization.[14] In this manner, the totalitarian character of life inside FARC transforms the organization into an extremely efficient military machine.

Conclusion

The question now is whether the combination of rural recruitment, depleted political education, and rigid internal discipline, which has allowed FARC to endure successfully for four decades, will work in the future. Theoretically, even today, this guerrilla organization stands as a colossus with military and financial power unprecedented in Latin American history. However, the evolution of the Colombian strategic scenario and the international context are dissolving the pillars upon which the organization built its power. The depopulation of the countryside is reducing the bulk of potential active or passive supporters of the agrarian revolution promoted by FARC. Consequently, beyond the strategic mistakes made by the group, Colombia's own social evolution has radically downsized the potential social base for rural insurgency.

In the meantime, the ideological approach used by the organization to attract new militants has become old fashioned amid the cultural changes associated with the urbanization of Colombian society. Inhabitants of the cities have individualistic values distant from the collective, totalitarian nature that has historically been the guerrilla movement's social offering. In fact, this enormous gap between the political platform of FARC and contemporary urban values explains to a large extent their considerable difficulties in attracting new militants from Colombian cities. Finally, the ideological fragility of FARC has become an additional obstacle for the group's exploration of strategic options, such as urban terrorism, which could increase the organization's capacity to pressure a country whose political and economic axes remain in the urban areas.

Terrorists need a solid political grounding in order to operate individually under the pressure of secrecy in a hostile environment. However, Colombian insurgents seem to lack the fanatic conviction required to effectively practice this form of political violence. In this sense, the political-military strategy that for four decades guaranteed the guerrilla movement's expansion is doomed to fail, a victim of the Colombian massive urbanization process that has transformed the agrarian revolutionary project into an impractical anachronism. Thus, FARC seems close to being defeated by the unstoppable evolution of history—a paradoxical end for a group convinced that its victory was written in the future.

CHAPTER 17

The Making of Aum Shinrikyō's Chemical Weapons Program[1]

JOHN V. PARACHINI

In 1995, a group known as Aum Shinrikyō used sarin nerve agent in an attack on the Tokyo subway; this attack marked a fundamental shift in the perceived danger posed by terrorist groups. Prior to this event, terrorists had rarely crossed the threshold of using toxic chemicals as weapons. Equally surprising, the group responsible for the attack was not a recognized terrorist group, but an obscure religious group. There are a number of unprecedented aspects to Aum's development as a subnational group, its willingness to use chemical weapons, and its efforts to acquire the capability to do so. In the decade since the Tokyo subway attack, there have been several other unprecedented and largely unanticipated terrorist acts. Most important have been the September 11th attacks and the anthrax letters.

Despite considerable concern that other terrorist groups would repeat Aum's effort to develop unconventional weaponry or seek such capabilities from around the globe, fortunately none have done so with the same degree of success. Osama bin Laden, al Qaeda, and the global jihadist movement have certainly expressed interest in such capabilities and sought them in a variety of ways. Yet, they seemed to have followed a "portfolio management" approach to weapons development and procurement; bin Laden and his followers have pursued lots of options and have tended to focus their energies on those that rendered desired outcomes via simpler means. Since the possibility that some group of jihadists may dedicate more effort to acquiring unconventional capabilities, examining the Aum case with an aim to understanding how the group evolved and assembled the capabilities to wage attacks with chemical agents is valuable for the current situation.

Shoko Asahara, Aum's self-proclaimed guru, preached a bizarre philosophy that combined elements of Buddhism, Hinduism, scientific fascinations, Nostradamus, and millennialism. Over the course of eight years, Aum Shinrikyō evolved from a small organization offering yoga and meditation classes to a multinational entity with hundreds of million of dollars and programs to procure and develop weapons often found in the arsenals of states. Aum transformed from a mere religious group to a terrorist group proselytizing apocalyptic Armageddon and willing to commit violence against its critics, law enforcement authorities, and ordinary Japanese citizens.

Aum's evolution and use of chemical weapons is a case example of how a terrorist group may develop a capability to cause catastrophic violence. Fortunately, the incident has thus far not been repeated in scale or scope, although since the 1995 subway incident there has been an increased interest in chemical agents on the part of some terrorist groups. This chapter will focus primarily on the evolution of Aum's chemical weapons program. Aum engaged in several other weapons development programs and nefarious activities, but they will only figure in this chapter to the extent that they illuminate an aspect of the group's chemical program. Aum is important because it is one of the few cases where a terrorist group sought chemical weapons, obtained them, and used them to inflict mass and indiscriminate casualties.

The success of Japanese authorities in arresting and prosecuting key Aum members has produced a public record of many of the group's activities. However, even though the attack occurred more than a decade ago, a number of aspects of the group's activities are still not well understood. Focusing on the group's chemical weapons program helps put in perspective some of the group's activities that many feared would be copied by other terrorists. Understanding the making of terrorists interested in chemical weapons will help law enforcement and intelligence authorities to assess other groups and individuals who may have similarly dangerous inclinations and capabilities.

Finally, when a group leader or an entire organization believes they are charged with a higher mission, anything may seem justified to further a sanctified mission. The Aum case is important because of the insights it may offer on how a religiously motivated organization might seek to harness the unique qualities of unconventional weapons to pursue the violent fulfillment of its divinely inspired worldview.

This chapter is organized into four sections. The first section outlines a few elements of Aum's organizational structure and associated business. The second section describes the evolution of the group over the course of a decade, with particular attention to events that influenced the development of the group's motivations and chemical weapons capabilities. The third section focuses on the development of the group's chemical weapons capability and the key personnel involved in the program. The fourth section examines some of Aum's activities abroad that contributed to the development of its chemical weapons capability. Emerging from these four sections are several conclusions that should help put terrorist use of unconventional weapons in perspective, highlight factors influencing and impeding terrorists' pursuit of these unconventional capabilities, and suggest some indications and warnings that law enforcement and intelligence authorities should note.

Aum's Organizational Structure

The organizational structure and leadership style of the Aum Shinrikyō profoundly influenced the nature and operations of the group. At the pinnacle of the organization's structure was Shoko Asahara, the group's founder and "ultimate liberated master."[2] Asahara's religious vision and leadership style were critical to the evolution of Aum from a small meditation sect to an organization with 10,000 followers in Japan and more than 30,000 followers in other countries. He was charismatic, paranoid, and had delusions of grandeur.[3] These personality traits combined to make him a domineering and controlling leader. His leadership style shaped the evolution of the group's organizational style. He was the guru, and group members were devoted to him above all else. As the organization grew in size, a small group of close associates formed around the guru and aided in the management of the group. Asahara, however, reigned supreme in the organization, and all others were his subjects, even those who formed the core of his closest associates.

In addition to Asahara as founder and guru, the next levels of organizational leadership were also defined by religious achievement as defined by Asahara. Members wore different-colored clothes to highlight different levels of religious attainment. Members could rise up the ranks of the organization by paying initiation fees to participate in certain levels of training. To enter the highest rank of Aum culture, members paid a fee and had to reject all connections to their previous lives. At this stage, members were frequently urged to give all their assets to Aum. Out of the 10,000 members in Japan, approximately 1,100 had ascended to the stage of a "renunciate."[4]

As the movement grew in size and evolved in character, two classes of members emerged. One class was composed of new recruits drawn to the organization for psychological and religious reasons. Another class of members developed an affinity for Aum beyond the religious and meditation practices and became totally devoted to Shoko Asahara. The guru and their devotion to him became the dominant factor for their membership in the organization. This class of members was called "renunciates" because they renounced their previous life and dedicated themselves to Asahara's service.

The consequence resulting from these two broadly defined class of members was that those totally devoted to the guru could exploit the financial resources, skills, and mere membership of those drawn to the organization on personal spiritual quests. Meanwhile, those intensely devoted to Asahara, the renunciates, were willing to do anything for him, including kill other members and perceived group adversaries.

Even within the group of renunciates, a small circle of long-term followers of Asahara served as the key members of the group. In 1994, during the fourth phase of the group's evolutionary history, Aum established an organizational structure that mirrored the ministry system of the Japanese government.[5] All of Aum's "ministry leaders" were long-time followers who had demonstrated their devotion to Asahara. This small circle, and those who worked with them, most closely comprised the body of people that acted as Aum's organizational unit to develop and procure weapons and conduct the group's violent attacks.

Aum's business activities began as modest endeavors related to the group's religious work, and over time extended into a variety of other sectors. These business activities were critical to Aum's evolution because they served as important sources of revenue and covers for procurement activities related to its weapons programs. Aum's publishing activities and medical clinics were transparent about their relationship to the group. Other business activities that the group wished to hide were conducted through separately incorporated companies or in the name of individual group members. Hasegawa Chemical and Tokyo and Beck, Inc., were two businesses the group established in Yamanashi Prefecture that purchased the chemicals the group used in its weapons program.[6] These companies eventually purchased precursor chemicals the group used in its sarin attacks in Matsumoto and Tokyo.

Most of the international procurement for Aum's computer business and its international activities was conducted via a company named Mahaposya.[7] The group also used businesses established in foreign countries to facilitate local purchasing of equipment to export back to Japan. Much of this equipment contributed to Aum's weapons programs in one way or another. Most of these businesses were established in countries like Australia, Taiwan, and the United States, where it was easy to set up businesses. In the United States, Aum first established a nonprofit and later set up several for-profit entities (all at the same location as the nonprofit). Aum's business activities importantly contributed to the organization, achieving a scale that allowed it to take on scientific projects of a size that eventually led to the production of military-grade chemical agents. Its ability to swell its membership with foreign adherents, boast an organizational presence in several countries, and enjoy financial strength that enabled it to operate in many countries outside of Japan (and often meeting with senior foreign leaders) all augmented the organization's perception of what it could achieve.

Evolution of Aum as a Violent Subnational Organization

The Aum Shinrikyō began as a fifteen-person meditation group in 1984 and grew into a movement with almost 50,000 members. At its peak, Aum's financial assets amounted to hundreds of millions of dollars, and it had facilities in several different countries, including the United States, Germany, Russia, Taiwan, and Sri Lanka. It also engaged in assassinations, assembled unconventional weapons programs, plotted to overthrow the Japanese government, and contemplated how to start a cataclysmic war with the United States. The chronology of Aum's evolution as an organization reveals a number of insights about its aggressive and delusional tendencies as well as its particular fascination with poison. Its evolution into a group willing to use chemical agents indiscriminately results from a combination of peculiar personalities, motivations, capabilities, and the circumstances in which it operated.

The evolution of the Aum Shinrikyō can be divided into four periods that stretch from its creation to the attack on the Tokyo subway. In each of these phases, a complicated set of factors combined to influence the organization and its activities. Most of what is known about Aum and its guru Asahara comes from Aum statements and publications; post–Tokyo subway accounts by members and their trial testimony; scholarly books, and articles; and journalistic reporting throughout the life of the group. Despite all these sources, many aspects of Aum's evolution remain unclear. Part of the difficulty in comprehending many of the bizarre aspects of Aum is the cultic nature of the organization. Despite the many public sources available on the group and its activities, its closed nature and delusional worldview obscure many aspects of its existence.

In the first period of Aum's evolution, Chizuno Matsumoto experimented with different new religions and eventually started his own. He changed his name to Shoko Asahara and anointed himself as the leader. Asahara attracted Japanese adherents who were mostly young and seeking spiritual and personal fulfillment. His persuasive power and ascetic meditation practices drew members in a remarkable fashion. When asked about the initial appeal of Aum, one follower indicated that "everyone in Aum was aiming for the same thing—raising their spiritual level—so we had lots in common."[8] Aum members were seeking a more peaceful state of being and freedom from earthly troubles. Members attained this heightened level of spirituality through an ascetic lifestyle and meditation. Part of the freedom members felt they obtained resulted from their devotion to Asahara as their guru. Members were freed of decisions and responsibilities, as they followed whatever he proscribed. All they needed to do was follow the ascetic practices defined by the guru, who they believed could help liberate them from negative karmic energy and achieve a higher state of existence. The extreme control Asahara exercised over members' lives is an important factor that led to the group's violent activities. Members were willing to kill in order to please Asahara. This formative period lasted until the group's first known killing.

During this initial period, Asahara had an encounter with authorities that provided a first indication of his interest in chemicals. At the age of twenty-seven, Asahara supported his new wife and child by making and selling "healing and alternative medicines."[9] He ascribed all manner of healing and restorative powers to his brews. In June 1982, authorities arrested Asahara for making these potions without a license. This incident led him into bankruptcy and created considerable turmoil in the life of his young family. His intense interest in religious practices began after this incident. As one religious scholar observed, it was as though he took solace from his predicament by concentrating on religious practices.[10]

Two observations about this incident are relevant for Aum's chemical activities. First, it may reveal how Asahara became acquainted with practices of mixing chemicals and other ingredients to synthesize substances. Synthesizing sarin nerve agent is obviously a very different task than producing some alternative medicines and potions. Yet, there are common practices of procuring precursor ingredients, experimenting to get the right combinations, and producing enough to serve some larger purpose. The second noteworthy aspect is that he ascribed fictional powers to the healing potions and medicines, just as he later justified the production and use of sarin nerve agent in part as a means for freeing people from the bad karmic energy their earthly bodies contained. In both cases, Asahara deluded himself about the power of the mixtures he produced or directed others to produce. The similarities should not be overdrawn, but in order to discern why and how Asahara became fascinated with poison, his early experience as a producer of alternative medicines is noteworthy.

The second phase of the group's evolution is characterized by an increasing alienation from society and inclination to use violence against those who impeded the fulfillment of Asahara and his close associates' delusional objectives. This period began in the fall of 1988 and continued until the group's complete failure in the 1990 national election. In October 1988, a young group member died during a harsh initiation ceremony in front of Asahara and a number of other group members. For some members, this death called into question the legitimacy and safety of some of the organization's practices. Aum leaders, in contrast, feared the death might adversely influence government authorities who were considering an appeal of their decision to delay granting Aum certification as a religious organization. To cover up the incident, Aum leaders clandestinely disposed of the deceased member's body, which only added to the discomfort of members who witnessed the death. Asahara sought to recast the tragic incident as being in the benefit of the victim, arguing that he had, in the end, obtained greater spiritual fulfillment. A few months later, in April 1989, Asahara's most devoted followers killed a group member who had witnessed the earlier fatal incident and wanted to leave the organization. Once again, Asahara justified this killing as necessary to allow Aum to flourish and ful-fill its mission of spiritual salvation. Asahara's righteousness and the divine destiny that he prophesied Aum would reach enabled them to justify violence to achieve this higher state of being. This murder and its justification paved the way for more murders to follow.

A number of other developments followed these two deaths that served to undermine the group's grandiose vision and foster feelings of paranoia about being prevented from achieving its higher ends. First, the group's membership growth slowed. Second, the group faced considerable unfavorable media coverage, which probably further diminished growth in membership. And finally, relatives of Aum members organized an Aum Shinrikyō Victims' Society in order to try to free their loved ones from the group—a group that was increasingly being viewed as a religious cult which brainwashed members and also held some against their will. The Society retained representation from Sakamoto Tsutsumi, a civil rights attorney, who began to investigate a number of Aum activities that he found suspicious. All of these developments combined seemed to confirm for Asahara, his close associates, and other group members that there was a conspiracy against Aum.

In response to these negative developments, Asahara ordered a small group of his most devoted followers to engage in violence. Sakamoto Tsut-sumi not only led the family group, but he also appeared in the media regularly criticizing Asahara and the validity of Aum's practices. Asahara subsequently ordered a small team of his most devoted followers to kill Sakamoto. Later, in court testimony, Aum members described the killing of Sakamoto as "salvation activity."[11] Aum members broke into Sakamoto's house and strangled him to death. In the course of killing Sakamoto, the Aum assassins also killed his wife and fourteen-month-old son. Several Aum members were disturbed to learn about the murder of Sakamoto's son, who surely was not a threat to the group. Aum's violence had a gallop effect: A first killing made the next easier to do and easier to justify. Killing the Sakamoto family was a tragically natural progression from how the organization dealt with members who Asahara feared might get in the way of Aum's higher purpose.

The third phase of Aum's evolution followed the group's resounding defeat in the February 1990 elections, and was marked by an increasing sense of paranoia and the development of an even more delusional worldview. Asahara believed that the Aum slate of candidates would be elected. When it garnered an embarrassingly small number of votes, he envisioned a variety of conspiracies to explain the devastating defeat. His sense of alienation and rejection increased dramatically following the election. The group's problems were compounded by a further decrease in the number of new members and an increase in the number of members who sought to leave. Asahara's rhetoric became increasingly apocalyptic and violent. Some reports indicate that in April 1990, at a seminar on Ishigakijima Island in Okinawa Prefecture, Asahara "instructed those with special expertise and knowledge to take up residence at Aum facilities right away."[12] In many ways, the events of this period established the ideological justification for Aum's increasingly confrontational view of all individuals and entities outside of it, and its robust weapons development and procurement programs.

Aum's experimentation with biological weapons began in this third period.[13] According to confessions from an Aum member, the group attempted to cultivate botulinin toxin and distributed what they produced around Tokyo and outside a U.S. naval base. Biological weapons experts believe that they failed to produce a toxic agent because they were unable to prepare the agent in a fashion that released the agent's toxic material. Failure with biological weapons may have contributed to the group's interest in pursuing chemical agents, which were comparatively easier to synthesize and produce in quantities. While this activity has been widely reported as part of Aum's history, there is no forensic evidence that these events actually occurred. Aum members' confessions have been the primary source of information on these activities. Given the number of contradictions between Aum members and the imperfection inherent in the process of extracting confessions prior to trial, some skepticism is warranted. If true, however, these activities simply add to the picture of Aum's gathering interest and capabilities to develop or acquire poisons for use as weapons.

The fourth phase of Aum's history began sometime after the elections 1990 and continued until the 1995 Tokyo subway attack. In this phase, Aum pursued chemical agents via a variety of pathways, all of which culminated in two sarin attacks: one in Matsumoto in July 1994 and the other in Tokyo in March 1995. In the years before these attacks, Asahara made a number of statements that, in retrospect, reveal the organization's interest in chemical weapons, particularly sarin. Asahara first mentioned sarin in a sermon in 1993, when he alleged that the United States attacked Aum with chemical weapons dispersed from planes flying over Aum compounds. It was as though Asahara created a pretext that justified Aum's own military preparations, particularly its development of chemical weapons agents. He projected onto a perceived adversary precisely the evil he and his associates were undertaking as a justification for doing it themselves.[14] Another explanation for Asahara's statement is that since not all Aum members were aware of the secret weapons-development activities, Asahara made the allegations as an explanation for accidents that occurred at Aum's chemical agent production facilities.

The group progressed from killing members to assassinating outside critics and, eventually, to larger and less-focused attacks. In July 1994, Aum members released sarin near a dormitory that housed three judges who were to rule on a land dispute between Aum and local citizens in Matsumoto who sought to prevent the group from entering their community. The attack killed seven people and injured several hundred, including the judges. The legal case involving Aum was postponed, providing yet another example for Asahara and his key associates of how violent methods in service of its cause could work. Less than six months later, Aum members released liquid sarin nerve agent on several different Tokyo subway lines. While the attacks fit into the broader apocalyptic vision Asahara had articulated over the course of the previous five years, the proximate cause was the group's desire to attack Japanese National Police Agency personnel. The group sought to disrupt and distract law enforcement authorities from an investigation into the kidnapping of an elderly man, who had a relative in the group who sought to escape. The police investigation into the kidnapping risked exposing Aum's clandestine chemical weapons program by giving them a clear basis for searching the group's facilities for evidence.

The Development of Aum's Chemical Weapons Capability: Personnel, Infrastructure, and Critical Knowledge

Aum embarked on a full spectrum of weapons programs in the early 1990s, but they developed their chemical weapons capabilities to the fullest extent. Producing chemical weapons proved much easier than producing either biological or nuclear weapons, because the skills to do so were easier to master and the availability of dual-use chemicals that could be fashioned into weapons made them easier to obtain.

Accounts vary on the exact number of key people involved in developing Aum's chemical weapons program. The structure of the program can be divided into roughly three different subsets of people. Estimates of the number of people involved in the construction of weapons production facilities and agent production ranges from 30 to 80 people.[15] The key people driving the program, conducting key experiments, buying equipment, planning attacks, and carrying them out, were approximately a dozen people. How many other key members knew about these activities, but did not participate in the production of weapons agent or the attacks, is not clear. The small size of the key chemical cadre undoubtedly contributed to the organization's ability to maintain operational security. Yet, even with a small number of people, the organization built up a substantial capability and evaded detection until it attacked the Tokyo subway. Thus, even a small group of people, if they have sufficient resources and are able to maintain tight security, can pose a catastrophic danger.

Key Aum members included the heads of Aum's "Ministries" and those involved in the group's "Household Agency."[16] A U.S. Senate committee report identifies six people who served as "ministry" heads as the key leaders.[17] In the same report, Senate investigators identify twelve people as being "Key Aum Members" out of a listing of sixty-five noteworthy members. In 1990, the group's electoral slate included twenty-five people, but none of these candidates were later named group ministers.

Six Aum members were particularly important to the group's development of chemical weapons. The most important was the group's chief chemist Masami Tsuchiya. At his court sentencing on 30 January 2004 the judge reportedly said, "Without the defendant, the cult would not have been able to pull off a crime that used chemical weapons."[18] Tsuchiya received a master's degree in organic chemistry from Tsukuba University. He left the university's doctoral program to join Aum. Given these modest formal credentials, his abilities were quite remarkable, as he was able to develop military-grade chemical agents sarin and VX as well as hallucinogenic drugs (such as LSD) for group rituals and illicit sale. During an earlier trial, Tsuchiya reportedly exhibited his devotion to Asahara when he remarked, "My faith in Aum leader Shoko Asahara has never changed and I believe I should die after completing what I should do for him."[19] At approximately the same time, Kayoko Sasaki, a former member of Aum's "household agency," testified in court that Tsuchiya confided to her that he "did not feel any reluctance when . . . [he] was told by Asahara to produce LSD." Yet, he "did feel resistance in the case of sarin."[20] Given the sophisticated chemistry involved in producing sarin and VX and the size of Aum's production facilities for sarin, his claimed "reluctance" represents extreme naivety or self-delusion.

Seiichi Endo, nominally Tsuchiya's superior as Aum's minister of Health and Welfare, also played an important role in Aum's chemical program. He served as the group's leader in developing biological weapons, but his failure to produce lethal biological agents led to a decline in his stature within the organization. In the end, despite being Tsuchiya's superior, Endo was assigned to assist him with the chemical program.[21] While Endo is more associated with Aum's efforts to develop biological weapons, he was deeply involved in Aum's chemical agent production and the major chemical attacks.

Tomomasa Nakagawa was another important member of the Aum core involved in the organization's chemical program. Trained as a medical doctor at Kyoto Prefectural University of Medicine, Nakagawa left a medical residency at Osaka hospital to dedicate himself to Aum. He allegedly was one of the approximately ten Aum members involved in the synthesis of sarin. He was also involved in several of Aum's murders. Despite his training as a medical doctor, Nakagawa was so devoted to Asahara that he expressed great pride when he was selected to kill in support of the guru.

Hideo Murai, Aum's Minister of Science and Technology, rose to be Asahara's second in command until he was stabbed to death shortly after the Tokyo subway incident. He oversaw Aum's weapons development programs, which included the construction of the chemical production facilities. A graduate of Osaka University, Murai worked as a scientific researcher at Kobe Steel prior to joining Aum.

Kiyohide Hayakawa, who served as Aum's Minister of Construction, was the organization's key link to Russia. His importance to Aum's chemical weapons program is hard to evaluate, but if Aum received a recipe or blueprint from Russian sources on how to make sarin, he is likely the connection. The importance of this external assistance is critical.

Finally, Etsuro Ikeda led a group of Aum members in the construction of the chemical production facilities. His engineering talents were critical to Aum achieving an industrial scale of production that made the group truly dangerous. Not often deemed a key leader in various accounts of Aum's activities, Ikeda rises in importance when one focuses primarily on how the group amassed the capabilities to produce significant quantities of chemical agent.

An English language translation of the Japanese National Police Agency annual "White Paper" describing its activities for 1996 indicates that Aum's chemical weapons program began in earnest in March 1993. Asahara apparently "directed followers who had majored in chemistry at graduate school to research and develop toxic gas, and those who had studied pharmacology to establish a dummy company, from which they could purchase chemicals needed to make toxic gases."[22] Aum's main chemical agent production effort was located in a facility entitled Satian 7 in Kamikushiki near Mount Fuji. Nearby in Tomizawa was another Aum two-story building that allegedly "housed Aum's chemical research group."[23] One account argues that the "sarin used in Matsumoto city was made in a prefabrication facility called Kushitigalva."[24] What is not clear is how the group's alleged earlier attempts to distribute biological agents and its production of illegal drugs influenced the development of its chemical program.

Aum's chemical weapons activities involve two agents—sarin and VX. Sarin, the easier of the two agents to synthesize, was the main chemical agent in Aum's program. It was produced in limited quantities on a few occasions and the agent was used for assassinations. The following discussion of Aum's chemical program will focus separately on the group's activities with each of these two chemical agents.

Sarin

The chronology of Aum's production of sarin reveals that the group started small and worked their way up to a larger scale effort over time. Asahara ordered the construction of a production facility and the procurement of enough precursor chemicals to produce 70 tons of sarin at a rate of 2 tons per day.[25]

The production facility named Satian 7 was completed in June 1994. According to reports from court testimony, Tsuchiya and his team initially produced 600 grams of sarin. By November 1993 they had produced another 3 kilograms.[26] According to a senior Japanese law enforcement official, ten months after Asahara called upon members with special expertise to take up residence at Aum facilities, they "had produced about 30kg of sarin."[27]

As Aum sought to establish a capability to produce sarin in the volume Asahara commanded, members began to make mistakes. In hindsight, these mistakes were early warning signs of Aum's pernicious activities. A former Aum member who was asked about the construction of Aum's chemical production complex recalled, "Asahara gave the order to finish everything by May 1994."[28] In order to meet this deadline, Aum members without the appropriate skills were pressed into service. The Animation Department from Aum's publishing group was assigned to be apprentices with more experienced welders. However, a number of people made mistakes and burned themselves. Ultimately, a series of chemical releases at the facility attracted the attention of law enforcement authorities. Unusual injuries or reports of environmental accidents are just a few of the types of less-obvious indicators of clandestine weapons development.

Aum's release of sarin in Matsumoto proved to be a much more sophisticated and tragically successful attack than the attack on the Tokyo subway. Not only did the Aum members participating in the attack succeed in injuring three judges slated to hear a legal case against the organization, but Aum attackers did so without fatal injury to themselves, and they evaded detection by law enforcement authorities. On 27 June 1994, seven senior Aum members traveled in a "specially converted refrigerator truck" to Matsumoto, a city located 125 miles northwest of Tokyo.[29] During the night, Aum members used a heat-sprayer device to disperse sarin towards a dormitory where the judges slept. The attack dispersed the agent over a 500- by 100-yard space, killing seven people, injuring 144, and causing 264 to seek medical attention.[30] Probably because Aum feared an imminent raid from law enforcement authorities, the group's preparation for the 20 March 1995 Tokyo subway attack was not as great. One account of the material used in the Tokyo subway attack asserts that Aum synthesized the agent just two days prior to the attack.[31] Instead of an effective device for dispersing the agent, Aum members placed bags of liquid sarin on the subway cars and punctured the bags with the tips of umbrellas that had been sharpened specifically for this purpose. The result was the agent leaked out in liquid form and vaporized comparatively slowly. In Matsumoto, the Aum attackers were able to disperse the agent in a wider area. The key factor that accounted for the different casualty level and media attention was the concentration of people in the subway of the nation's capital and not the sophistication of the attack.

The success of Aum's attack in Matsumoto undoubtedly added to the group's confidence about using chemical agents to achieve Asahara's "holy" objectives. However, in mid-July, on more than one occasion, accidents at the Satian 7 facility created noxious odors, prompting local residents to notify police.[32] While law enforcement authorities did not immediately investigate the complaints, these accidents eventually fit a pattern of reports that prompted Japanese authorities to collect forensic evidence to verify the complaints of local residents and raise suspicions about the group's possible involvement in the incident in Matsumoto. In January 1995, a major Japanese newspaper reported that Aum was the target of law enforcement investigations relating to Matsumoto. Asahara and his close associates thus sought to hide the evidence of the group's chemical activities. The sarin the group had on hand was destroyed and preparations were made to hide the activities of the facilities. In March 1995, when the police raided Aum facilities in response to a kidnap case, Tsuchiya and his team rushed to produce a new batch of sarin, which ultimately was the agent used in the Tokyo subway attack.

VX

Aum also used the chemical agent VX in assassinations in Japan. Presumably, they made the agent themselves, but not in the same quantities as sarin. VX is much more difficult to produce. The quantity of VX the group produced is not known, but the production process is much more difficult. Lab bench–scale quantities seemed to have been the extent of the effort. Japanese National Police Agency experts believe that Tsuchiya began researching how to make VX in January or February 1994.[33] Tsuchiya used foreign books to guide his research, but his initial attempts were not successful. NPA experts reported that he was able to develop his own synthesis pathway which was different than that described in the foreign texts, when he discovered the formula for a VX precursor in a chemistry magazine. Sometime prior to July 1994, he informed Asahara that he could produce the agent, but that it would require a different facility than the one used to produce sarin. In late July, Tsuchiya produced 1 kilogram of VX and Asahara named the agent *Jintsuriki*, meaning "divine power." By early September, he had managed to produce 20 grams. The purity of the agent was still not very high, which accounts for the group's failed assassination attempt using VX in November 1994. A month later, using VX, Aum killed one of its members, whom they believed to be a spy.[34]

Aum Shinrikyō International Activities and Its Chemical Weapons Program

Aum's development of chemical weapons raised the concerns that officials harbored about weapons of mass destruction (WMD) proliferation throughout the 1990s and up to the current day. The fear was and remains that terrorist groups can procure unconventional weapons capabilities by purchasing them on the black market from unsuspecting or unscrupulous officials. This danger seemed particularly acute in the aftermath of the collapse of the former Soviet Union, a former superpower—with the world's largest unconventional weapons complex—that became economically weak and politically unstable in a matter of months. The status of the once tightly guarded laboratories, weapons production facilities, and weapons scientists and technicians who worked in them, was unclear. The economic turmoil that ensued following the end of the Soviet Union sparked concern that underpaid former Soviet scientists would sell their expertise to the highest bidders. In addition to the weapons expertise of the former Soviet scientists, many feared they might also help rogue nations, criminal groups, or terrorists get the materials and equipment for unconventional weapons for the right price.

Aum's activities in Russia are the most widely known example of how a well-funded, nonstate actor could exploit the political and economic instability of a state to procure unconventional weapons capabilities. Much of Aum's activities in Russia were disclosed during a U.S. Senate committee staff investigation and Senate hearings entitled "Global Proliferation Threats."[35] Despite Aum's extensive activities in Russia, what they gained was quite limited compared to what was feared could occur. Legitimate concerns about the proliferation of materials, weapons, and expertise remain, but the nature of the danger is much less. The Aum experience is a useful example of the type of proliferation that might occur, as well as the limitations that groups face. As will be discussed below, in many respects, it is surprising that Aum did not get more from its Russian and global procurement activities.

Aum's involvement in Russia is one of the most spectacular aspects of the group's evolution. Its leaders met with the Russian vice president, the head of the Russian parliament, and the Secretary of the security council, a close ally of President Boris Yeltsin. Aum's greatest membership recruitment occurred in Russia. A combination of post-Soviet experimentation in new and exotic Eastern religions and Aum's financial power catalyzed the group's activities in Russia. In 1992, Shoko Asahara and an entourage of several hundred Japanese members made a "Salvation Tour" of Russia, which sparked a tremendous surge of interest in Aum. Over the course of the eighteen months following Asahara's tour, the group's Russian membership surged. Estimates vary, but Aum's largest membership amounted to approximately 30–40 thousand people, including several hundred who renounced their previous lives and devoted themselves to Aum.

Aum used its tremendous wealth to gain access to high officials and buy weaponry, weapons production plans, and military training. Some estimates suggest that Aum paid "$12 million in payoffs to well-placed officials."[36] Russian press reports allegedly estimated that Aum's overall investment in Russia "amounted to some $50 million."[37] Oleg Lobov, then Secretary of the Security Council in Russia and a close associate of Boris Yeltsin, significantly facilitated Aum's entry into Russia. Lobov promoted Russian-Japanese business contact via a leadership role he had at Russia-Japan University. Russia had several quasi-educational institutions such as this that built upon the Soviet practices of using these institutions to interface with foreign organizations, but, in the dawn of the new Russia, every contact with a foreign organization with money was a business opportunity. Lobov encountered Aum leaders in Japan and seized upon their eagerness to use their money to build alliances in Russia. While Lobov met with many organizations in Japan, few were as ready and willing to put cash into a relationship.

Aum's most significant transformational learning occurred when it obtained the Soviet formula for synthesizing sarin. Like a number of the details of Aum's sarin program, it is not clear when Aum obtained this information, but a number of different sources suggest that this knowledge transfer occurred.[38] Given Aum's access to officials and large membership in Russia, the idea that this knowledge came from Russia seems credible. The most telling evidence is that the samples of sarin examined by Japanese Defense Agency chemical weapons experts revealed that it was synthesized in a fashion that is unique to the Soviet arsenal of chemical agents.[39] In the turbulent times of the early 1990s, it is possible to imagine Russians exploiting access to critical knowledge for personal gain. According to Russian news accounts of the court hearing of Yoshihiro Inoue, Aum's "Chief of Intelligence," Ikuo Hayashi identified Lobov as the source of the documentation Aum followed to produce sarin.[40] Russian authorities denied that Lobov was the source of this critical information and they asserted that the process for making sarin is widely known.

Aum's activities in Russia declined as swiftly as they rose. In August 1994, the Russian government revoked the group's status as a religious organization. A few days prior to the group's sarin attack on the Tokyo subway, Russian authorities raided its Moscow offices, confiscating much of the group's property to reimburse for damages determined during the course of several legal cases.[41] A small group of devoted followers continued the organization, but in a greatly diminished fashion. The influence of Aum's Yen investments in Russia in the early 1990s could start the organization in Russia, but it could not sustain it. Moreover, the sarin attack on the Tokyo subway so stained the group's reputation that the small number of people who sought to continue the organization essentially went underground.

Aum's activities in Australia rivaled contacts in Russia in terms of importance to the group's development of chemical weapons. In May 1993, Aum established two Australian companies. The operations included the purchase of a 500,000-acre ranch in the outback, almost 400 miles north of Perth. While this property may have contained some uranium, which interested Aum, the organization ultimately used the property for testing chemical agents on sheep.[42] In addition to Aum's feeble attempt to use their wealth to purchase a nuclear weapon or material in Russia, the group was willing to spend considerable sums to search for the radioactive ore on their own. When uranium proved too hard to develop, the group instead sought to use the vast expanse for other deadly purposes. Aum was flexible as an organization to the extent that when members encountered obstacles, they devolved their activities back to something easier and that they could manage; they did not keep pursuing something endlessly. When they encountered insurmountable technical obstacles, the group refocused its efforts and pursued an easier option.

In September of 1993, Asahara and twenty-five other followers traveled to the group's ranch in the outback. The entourage had to pay a huge sum for excess baggage. Additionally, Australian authorities fined two of the travelers for clandestinely attempting to ship toxic chemicals in containers marked "hand soap." With Asahara dressed in brightly colored robes, traveling with five young women under the age of fifteen and carrying excess baggage, some of which contained highly toxic chemicals, the group drew the attention of Australian authorities. Despite their nefarious activities, Aum did not seem to adopt even modest operational security procedures during this trip. Either Aum members believed that the rightness of their mission would safeguard them from the authorities or they were incredibly naïve. Both explanations may account for how they operated. Two members of the group were fined for not declaring these dangerous chemicals to customs officials. They drew so much attention that the next time members of the group sought to travel to Australia they were denied visas. A couple of group members eventually did succeed in obtaining visas and proceeded to the ranch to conduct a series of tests of toxic agents on sheep.

Australian authorities who conducted a forensic investigation of the ranch after the 1995 Tokyo subway incident discovered that sarin was the agent used to kill the sheep. The investigation by the Australian Federal Police revealed that Aum was able to test chemical agents in a large-scale fashion.[43] The ability to conduct such tests in such a remote location without drawing attention to their activities likely enabled Aum members to learn things that would be difficult to obtain from mere lab bench tests. Aum sought to produce chemical weapons in a quantity that could produce mass death. Batch processing entails scaling of chemical engineering processes that pose different challenges than production experiments at the lab bench level. An analogy is how cooking a recipe for two people is a different challenge when one attempts the same recipe for a group of fifty people. Thus, while Aum may not have obtained the nuclear material it sought, it advanced their chemical weapons program by conducting larger scale open tests of chemical agents on sheep. Its activities in Australia are yet another example demonstrating that, while the group simultaneously pursued more than one area of interest, it was able to make more progress with chemical agents than with other means of destruction.

Conclusion: Was Aum a Precedent or an Aberration?

Aum's experience with chemical agents illustrates the opportunities and limitations nonstate actors encounter when they attempt to develop an unconventional weapons capability on their own from scratch. Thus far, Aum is the one subnational group to develop chemical weapons on its own and successfully deliver them to a target causing mass and indiscriminate casualties. Many officials and scholars fear it is just a matter of time before more groups go down this path themselves. Many assert that because of the wide availability of dual-use chemicals—some of which could be used as weapons without any further chemical synthesis—and common knowledge of formulas for chemical weapons that require only modest skill to produce, it is inevitable that other groups will follow Aum's precedent. Yet, what Aum achieved was tragic but comparatively modest. Aum killed far fewer people with toxic chemicals than a host of major bombings in the last twenty years.[44]

A combination of factors enabled Aum to inflict the mass and indiscriminate attacks in Matsumoto and Tokyo. First, the organization achieved a financial and organizational scale that enabled it to acquire materials, fashion them into weapons, and test them in remote locations. While some individuals and groups may be able to acquire or produce chemical agents like Aum, few have the resources and the organizational scale to do so in a way that might produce a catastrophic result. Second, not only could Aum operate in a grand fashion; Shoko Asahara and many of his closest followers believed they were divinely permitted to operate in such a fashion. Moreover, their activities—including violence against innocent people—served a greater good. Third, Aum may have sought and received assistance from unscrupulous Russians at a unique time in the history of Russia. While Russian concern about terrorist acquisition of unconventional capabilities is not as acute as American official concern, the ongoing struggle with Chechen separatists and the September 11th attacks have caused them to be much more security conscious than was the case in the early 1990s. Whether Aum was reluctant to seek outside expertise in Russia or Russian experts were not willing to provide it to a strange religious group from neighboring Japan is unclear. Both are possible. Finally, Aum's intense determination to acquire chemical weapons and willingness to use them was unprecedented. Japanese authorities and intelligence services of many other countries should have been more attentive to warnings and proactive to investigate Aum's activities. But like the September 11th attacks, unprecedented events are difficult to anticipate and difficult to detect. Aum's fascination with poisons and willingness to produce them and use them as weapons was just bizarre enough to be discounted. Not any more.

While Aum Shinrikyō's attack on the Tokyo subway with sarin fundamentally changed the U.S. government's perception of the threat from terrorist use of unconventional weapons, in Japan the attacks were not universally viewed as terrorist acts. Some Japanese officials and a significant portion of the Japanese public viewed Aum as a bizarre religious cult and not necessarily as a terrorist group. Aum's acts were perceived as so far outside the norm of anticipated behavior that they were discounted. This view has changed somewhat since September 11, but nonetheless, the societal reaction is noteworthy and suggests that the Japanese body politic sees Aum and what it did as an aberration. To date, fortunately, this view matches the empirical record. Unlike Aum, whose leader was obsessed with sarin in a fashion akin to a serial poisoner, jihadists are motivated to achieve catastrophic outcomes with whatever means they can exploit. If a sufficient chemical weapons capability was easily obtainable, they would use it. Otherwise, simpler and more readily available means are suitable for the catastrophic outcomes they desire.

Many of Aum's bizarre and violent activities stimulated concern about the prospects that subnational groups would be the new frontier of unconventional weapons proliferation. While the concern endures, the novelty and the potential danger of so many of Aum's activities has obscured the fact that what they actually achieved was crude, and fortunately caused far fewer fatalities and serious injuries that most large conventional bombings. A considerable gap existed between what they envisioned and what they were actually capable of doing.[45]

Appreciating their mistakes is as important as understanding their successes. Insights about these failures provide insight about the hurdles future terrorist groups must overcome and help guide law enforcement and intelligence authorities to recognize signs regarding potentially successful terrorist acquisition and development programs. Had Japanese authorities appreciated the implications of some of these learning mistakes, they might have had a basis to intervene before the Tokyo subway attack. Aum's accidents provided telltale signs of their activities.

Given Aum's Russian membership base, political connections and the economic weakness of Russia at the time, it is surprising Aum did not get more than it allegedly did from Russian experts. Instead of seeking outside expertise to develop these capabilities, Aum sought to develop its capabilities in-house. Reliance on its own personnel may be an indication of the group's hubris. Alternatively, the group may have consciously sought to avoid contact with outsiders regarding the development of unconventional weapons fearing their own intentions might be discovered. It is also possible that Aum members did not seriously consider how outside experts could have aided their program. Whatever the case, the story of Aum Shinrikyō is a story of terrorist learning and knowledge transfer of a most lethal kind. Preventing future tragedies like the 1995 Tokyo subway attack will benefit from a richer understanding of how terrorist groups learn and early detection of their activities to escalate to new levels of violence.

Acknowledgments

The views expressed here are the author's and do not represent those of the Rand Corporation or its research sponsors. An earlier version of this chapter was supported in part by Grant No. 2003-IJ-CX-1022, awarded by the National Institute of Justice, Office of Justice Programs, U.S. Department of Justice. Points of view in this document are those of the author and do not necessarily represent the official position or policies of the U.S. Department of Justice.

CHAPTER 18

Terrorist Training Centers Around the World: A Brief Review

JAMES J. F. FOREST

The most common and important places where indoctrination and operational teaching for terrorism (on strategic and tactical levels) takes place are the various training camps scattered throughout the globe. These are places where a new terrorist recruit travels to learn (for example) how to mount rocket launchers in the beds of pickup trucks; how and where to launder money; how to successfully conduct a kidnapping; how to conduct target identification, surveillance, and reconnaissance; how and where to build camouflage-covered trenches; and how to covertly communicate with other members of a group or network—for example, using personal messengers (particularly on horseback, motorcycle, or bicycle) rather than electronic communications, or changing frequencies when using electronic communications in battle.

Ahmed Ressam, an Algerian who intended to set off a suitcase bomb at Los Angeles International Airport around New Years' Day 2000, admitted at his trial that he received training at the Khaldan camp in Afghanistan, learning how to fire handguns, machine guns, and rocket-propelled grenade launchers, as well as how to assemble bombs and TNT from the plastic explosive C4.[1] He also talked of studying urban warfare, "how to block roads and storm buildings" and "how to blow up the infrastructure of a country . . . such installations as electric power plants, airports, railroads, large corporations, and military installations."[2] At the trial in Hamburg, Germany, of Mounir al-Motassadek, a Moroccan man accused of involvement in the 9/11 attacks, German police claimed that upwards of 70,000 militants received weapons training and religious instruction in al Qaeda's training camps in Afghanistan.[3]

According to research conducted in the 1990s by a member of the U.S.

Marine Corps, a typical day at a PLO training camp began with early morning physical fitness exercises, and as the day progressed, students generally conducted a parade. Daily instruction included education in explosives and detonators, the art of setting mines in munitions dumps and on bridges and vehicles, the rudiments of chemical and biological warfare, field command and escape tactics, marksmanship and camouflage, and the use and employment of Soviet RPG rockets and shoulder-borne Strela missiles.[4] Clearly, life in a terrorist training camp was not your ordinary Boy Scout campfire outing.

In 2002, *New York Times* reporters C. J. Chivers and David Rohde examined hundreds of documents collected from "terrorist training schools" during the U.S. military assault on the Taliban and found "signs that in developing martial curriculums, the [terrorist] groups were cannily resourceful in amassing knowledge."[5] The documents included student notebooks, instructor lessons plans, course curriculums, training manuals, reference books, and memorandum—collectively, the same sorts of materials one would expect to find at a conventional military academy. Analysis of the documents revealed that students began their training by learning all about Kalashnikov rifles, the ubiquitous Soviet-era weapon used by many insurgent organizations around the world. Once the history, design, and operation of these weapons were mastered—mainly through rote memorization—students turned their attention to "PK machine guns, 82-millimeter mortars and the RPG-7, a shoulder-fired rocket effective against armored vehicles and trucks."[6] In this program of study, a sort of "infantry weapons 201," some students learned sniper rifle skills and how to fine-tune a rifle sight at short range to ensure accuracy at longer distances, while others studied how to direct weapon fire at targets on the ground and in the air. Training in four-man unit deployments and formations, including wedges, columns, echelons, and lines, reflected similar techniques used by U.S. Marines and Army Rangers.[7] Demolition instruction was also provided, covering mines and grenades, pressure and trip-wire booby traps, and the basic knowledge of electrical engineering that would allow students to figure out "the wiring, power sources and fuses required to spark an explosive charge."[8]

According to an archive of videotapes obtained by CNN in 2002, al Qaeda has also trained recruits in urban guerilla tactics. These tapes show how the group "replicated a small Western-style city on a hillside in eastern Afghanistan, using canvas and stone" and how trainees used explosives to destroy simulated houses, office buildings, and bridges.[9] Also included on the tapes were "step-by-step instructions on how to use a surface-to-air missile" and "lessons on complex hostage taking techniques and assassination operations."[10] And according to terrorist trial testimony and other sources, many training camps offer instruction in basic hand-to-hand combat skills, including the use of knives and martial arts.[11]

In addition to strategic and tactical learning, terrorist training camps incorporate a number of psychological development processes—as described in the earlier chapters of this volume—which advance the ideological motivations that brought the students to the camps in the first place. The physical isolation of the training camps is an important aspect to this process, in part because members come to rely on each other for success and survival and thus build bonds of mutual trust within the organization. In sum, training camps for terrorism are obviously places of great concern for the civilized world, because they bring enthusiastic learners with a willingness to kill together with experts who teach them how to kill.

The Geographic Diversity of Terrorist Training Camps

It is important to recognize that the training centers covered in the chapters of this volume are but a small sample of the impressive array of terrorist facilities that exist throughout the world. Indeed, contrary to the mainstream media's focus on the training camps of Afghanistan (and to a lesser extent Indonesia), terrorist training facilities can be found throughout the world. The geography of former and current terrorist centers of learning includes the following, listed alphabetically rather than by order of importance:

Afghanistan and the Anti-Soviet Jihad. By some estimates, several thousand camps were established throughout Afghanistan between 1980 and 1989, providing military training and seminars in Islamic history and theology to Afghanis, Arabs, and others committed to the goal of driving Soviet forces out of the country. Training was provided by seasoned veterans from other armed services. For example, in 1986 Osama bin Laden established a base camp for non-Afghan fighters in the mountains southeast of Jalalabad, at which two former Egyptian servicemen and senior Egyptian Islamic Jihad members (Abu Ubaydah al-Banshiri and Abu Hafs al-Masri) led combat training and operations.[12] Other camps for the mujahideen were established across the Pakistani border, in and around the city of Peshawar and the tribal region of Waziristan. The curriculum at these camps typically included a broad range of learning objectives, including the operation of Stinger missiles, the production of explosives and poisons, vehicle driving and maintenance, basic engineering, farming, and even urban guerilla tactics.[13] These were harsh learning environments: mud huts, dusty classrooms, obstacle courses, mazes of barbed wire, trenches, and of course, no basic utilities.[14] Once the Soviets withdrew from Afghanistan, thousands of the combat-trained veterans returned home, some to comfortable environs and regular lifestyles, others to join Islamist groups elsewhere in the world, including the Chechen Mujahideen, the Armed Islamic Group in Algeria, the Abu Sayyaf Group in the Philippines, and Jemaah Islamiyah in Indonesia.

Algeria, the Armed Islamic Group, and the GSPC. Beginning in the 1960s, Islamists in Algeria began training in urban guerilla tactics, for the purpose of driving the French colonial government out of the country. Political developments after Algerian independence eventually marginalized the extremists, who formed a number of organizations such as the Armed Islamic Group (GIA), the Salafist Group for Preaching and Combat (GSPC), and the Al Takfir wal Hijra (Excommunication and Migration) movement (one of the most extreme jihadi groups, whose members seek to identify and target Muslim civilians and regimes that do not meet their standards of piousness). In the early 1990s, particularly with the return home of many veterans of the Afghanistan jihad, attacks against the government began to increase in number and lethality. Training camps both in Algeria and across the border in Tunisia were used to teach combat tactics, explosives production, and weapons handling to new recruits. After a decade of open civil war with the government, the Islamic radical organizations in Algeria have recently begun to abandon the cities in the north of the country and head south in search of opportunities to regroup, establish new training camps and plan new attacks.

Bosnia and the Balkan Mujahideen. The war in Bosnia played an important role in providing training to members of the global Islamic jihad network. During the early 1990s, thousands of mujahideen left Afghanistan and other parts of Central Asia to fight alongside Bosnian Muslims against the Serbs. Weapons and fighters were smuggled through Croatia and other locations to support the Muslims in their struggle, and "on the job" combat training for new fighters was common. By 1994, major Balkan terrorist training camps included Zenica, Malisevo, and Mitrovica in Kosovo, where experienced veterans taught new recruits.[15] In February 1996, NATO forces conducted a raid at a former ski chalet located about six miles south of Fojnica, in central Bosnia, and found it was being used as a training camp, complete with classrooms and an extensive armory, explosives, handguns, sniper rifles, rocket and grenade launchers, and assault rifles.[16] Some of the explosive devices found were built into small plastic toys for children, including a toy car, an ice cream cone, and a helicopter. NATO officials said that they also found extensive instructional materials on explosives and conducting ambushes and sabotage. Students were apparently being trained to attack both military and civilian targets, conduct covert bombings, and lay booby traps. After the war, many foreign Islamic extremists chose to become Bosnian citizens, establishing normal lives (and, incidentally, providing convenient safe havens for the movement of jihadi elements to and from Europe), while others took their experience in search of a new place to continue the jihad.

Chechnya and Anti-Russian Separatists. In 1995, a group of veterans from the Afghanistan conflict, led by a Saudi citizen named Samer ben Saleh ben Abdallah al Swelem (known locally as Amir Khattab), arrived in

Chechnya to assist the out-gunned Chechen separatists in their struggles against Russian Federal Forces.[17] Khattab's so-called International Islamic Battalion (IIB) were instrumental in aiding local Chechen commander Shamil Basayev's ability to facilitate the withdrawal of Russian forces a year later. Khattab married a local woman from neighboring Dagestan and established a series of training camps in southeastern Chechnya, largely with funding from Saudi charities like the Al Haramein foundation. As with other centers of learning, the precise number of jihadis trained at these camps remains unknown, but their contribution to the ongoing conflict in the region is widely accepted.

Egypt, EIJ, Jamaat al Islamiyaa, and the Muslim Brotherhood. During the 1990s, alumni of the Afghan jihad were blamed for a series of attacks in Egypt, including the 1997 attack in Luxor by Jamaat al Islamiyaa ("the Islamic Group"), which killed fifty-eight tourists and four Egyptians.[18] The November 1995 attacks on an Egyptian diplomat in Switzerland and the Egyptian Embassy in Pakistan were also attributed to Egyptian-born alumni of the Afghan training camps. However, most observers point to the much older Muslim Brotherhood as a prominent ideological source of Islamic extremists movements in Egypt and elsewhere. Founded in 1928, the Muslim Brotherhood produced the likes of Sayyid Qutb, who wrote the influential jihadist pamphlet *Ma'alim* (Guideposts), as well as many members of Egyptian Islamic Jihad (EIJ)—including al Qaeda members Ayyman al-Zawahiri (Osama bin Laden's deputy) and Mohammed Atef (believed by many to be the strategic architect behind the attacks of September 11th).[19] As early as 1940, the Muslim Brotherhood's militant wing, increasingly disenchanted with perceived corruption throughout the country's political system and thus committed to armed revolutionary struggle, established guerilla training camps in the Mukatam Hills overlooking Cairo. Graduates of these camps then conducted a series of attacks, including the 1948 bombing of the Circurrel Shopping Complex and the assassination of Prime Minister Noqrashi Pasha, Judge Ahmed al-Khizindaar, and several internal security officials.[20] After decades of mass arrests and financial crackdowns by the government's security forces, there are no longer any known terrorist training camps in Egypt, although the Muslim Brotherhood has continued to play a vital role in the spread of global jihad.

Indonesia and Jemaah Islamiyah. Jemaah Islamiyah (JI) is a religious extremist organization which seeks to create a pan-Islamic state uniting Indonesia, Brunei, Malaysia, Singapore, and the Southern Philippines. Some estimates suggest that more than a thousand Southeast Asian Muslims were trained by (and fought with) the Afghan mujahideen during the 1980s, returning home afterward with valuable combat knowledge, experience, and the belief that they contributed to the fall of a world superpower. JI's own training facilities include several camps located in the southern Philippines (see below) and Camp Jabal Quba on Mount Kararao, which provides courses in weapons and explosives.[21]

Iraq and the Anti-Coalition Insurgency. Since May 2003, parts of Iraq have become new centers of terrorist learning, much of which could be called "on the job training." Indeed, according to Robert Hutchings, director of the National Intelligence Council, post-Saddam Iraq has become "a magnet for international terrorist activity."[22] A mix of Sunni extremists, foreign regime elements, and foreign fighters have caused a significant number of deaths (the majority of them Iraqi civilians) throughout the country, primarily through the use of explosives and light weaponry. While ideological support varies from group to group, and little strategic coordination is likely between the groups, the ongoing conflict is providing a forum for new terrorist recruits to gain tactical and operational learning, particularly in the area of urban guerilla warfare. Indeed, one could argue that al-Tahir—the terrorist group established by Abu Musab al-Zarqawi, which claims responsibility for many of the explosions, beheadings, and other attacks in Iraq—might not exist without the opportunity to gather motivated individuals who could subsequently gain operational knowledge in the Iraqi theatre of combat.

Japan and the Aum Shinrikyō. In 1993, the Japanese cult Aum Shinrikyō (or "Supreme Truth") built Satian 7, a nondescript building within the Aum complex at Mt. Fuji, which housed one of the most sophisticated chemical manufacturing facilities in the world. While new recruits were brought to the Aum complex (as well as Aum monasteries and other locations in Japan) mainly for ideological indoctrination, this particular building had only one purpose: to develop the group's capacity to manufacture sarin gas (a deadly nerve toxin), as well as VX, mustard gas, and phosgene gas, which the group used in several attacks on individuals and the general public around Japan.[23] Under the leadership of Masami Tsuchiya, a gifted chemist, the lab was capable of producing two tons of liquid sarin a day, and on 20 March 1995 the group released sarin in the Tokyo subway system, killing twelve people and injuring more than 5,500. When police raided Aum properties two days later, they found enough chemicals to kill 4.2 million people.[24] In 1998, Satian 7 became the first chemical production facility destroyed under the United Nations Chemical Weapons Convention.[25] While this unique center of operational knowledge transfer was used exclusively by members of Aum, its development and use certainly provides a model for other like-minded organizations.

Kashmir and Pakistani Terrorist Groups. The main Pakistani terrorist organization, Lashkar-e-Taiba, is mostly active in and around the northern region of Kashmir and receives local support for their fight against the Indian police and soldiers in the southern part of Kashmir. Kashmir has also been an important center of learning for al Qaeda, primarily because of the specialized training experience available there. For example, while the Afghanistan camps offered training for a guerrilla fight against conventional military forces, terrorist training in Kashmir has included actual penetration across the Indian border, sabotage actions, assassinations, and urban guerilla warfare.[26]

Lebanon, Amal, Hizballah, and the PLO. Between the founding of the state of Israel in 1948 and the Six Day War in 1967, the Palestinian refugee population in Lebanon grew to 350,000, providing an important recruiting ground for the recently-formed Palestinian Liberation Organization (PLO). In 1968, the PLO began to launch guerrilla raids against Israel from bases within Lebanon. Israeli reprisals against the PLO led to increasing Lebanese casualties, and a political rift between supporters and critics of PLO's presence in the country contributed to ongoing religious tensions (particularly between Shia Muslims and Maronite Christians), which erupted into civil war in 1975 (a war which continued until 1990). For their part, the PLO provided arms and training to militias who supported their cause, the most prominent of which was Musa Sadr's Shiite group *Afwaj al-Muqawama al Lubnnania* (Amal), or Lebanese Resistance Detachments.[27] In 1982, after several years of internal chaos and cross-border attacks, Israeli Defense Forces crossed into Lebanon and began occupying the southern part of the country, resulting in a Shiite resistance force that came be known as Hizballah.[28] This group—along with others, like the so-called Islamic Jihad—began using suicide bombers (often driving cars packed with explosives) to attack convoys of Israeli soldiers. Young men from the Palestinian refugee camps and other places in the north of the country were trained and brought into the theatre of conflict for such operations.[29] Several of the these training camps have been established in the Bekaa Valley (in eastern Lebanon), which has been under the control of Syrian forces since it intervened in Lebanon's civil war.[30]

Libya and State-Sponsored or Sanctioned Training Camps. Until very recently, Libya's leader Muammar Qaddafi has viewed his country's destiny as a revolutionary catalyst, a guide to the future that should sponsor every one of the faithful (particularly those faithful to Islam) as well as those opposed to imperialism.[31] Thus, since the early 1970s, Libya has provided a safe haven for a variety of terrorist training camps, and particularly for groups committed to the spread of Islam. According to Israeli terrorism expert Boaz Ganor, Libya opened its military bases to terrorist organizations and provided a variety of courses in military expertise to members of the PFLP and other Palestinian groups at Sinawin, Zuwarah, and Tubruq, and the Ras al Hilal facility, among other locations.[32] The group responsible for the May 1990 seaborne attack against Israel were trained at the Bilal Port Facility near Sidi. Bin Ghashir, just south of Tripoli, is said to have been used to train dissidents from Africa, Asia, and Latin America in terrorist/guerrilla tactics. In addition to Palestinian and Islamic terrorists, groups that have received training in Libya (particularly at the Seven April Training Camp) include the Irish Republican Army, the Basque separatist group ETA, Sierra Leone's Revolutionary United Front, the Ecuadorian Alfaro Vive, Carajo organization, Colombia's M-19, the Haitian Liberation Organization, the Chilean Manuel Rodriguez Patriotic

Front, the Armenian Secret Army for the Liberation of Armenia, and the Japanese Red Army.[33]

Northern Ireland and the IRA. The Irish Republican Army (IRA) was founded on an island where weapons, even sporting guns, are closely controlled, licensed, and monitored, and where no great war has left the countryside littered with discarded military gear.[34] Nonetheless, through the cooperation of the Irish diaspora, and especially Irish Americans, a variety of weapons were imported, including the civilian version of the military's M-16, the Armalite, that could be purchased in America as a deer-hunting rifle. Used on semiautomatic, the weapon proved ideal for poorly-trained gunmen, and the .223 cartridge could pierce the shell armor of British personnel carriers. Training for the IRA took place in a small number of locations in Northern Ireland, and more commonly in locations scattered throughout the Irish Republic. According to one account, IRA training was "carried out in most parts of the republic, even as far south as Cork. . . . Training camps [were] of various types: a deserted farmhouse, a beach or remote wood, dependent mainly on the security of the area."[35] At firing ranges constructed in isolated places, including abandoned mines and convenient cellars, new IRA recruits were trained on the Armalite—along with the AK-47, during the 1980s—as well as how to properly handle the explosive compound Semtex.[36] Although the IRA did not really use anything dramatic—no heavy weapons, no exotic explosives, no high-tech equipment that could not be bought at Radio Shack—they did prove ingenious in creating all sorts of explosive devices and traps, in the use of high-tech monitoring equipment, and in adapting their weapons to rural and urban conditions.[37] Many members improved their bomb manufacturing skills through knowledge acquired in their civilian occupations as electricians, and surprisingly, as pinball machine repairmen.[38]

Peru, Sendero Luminoso, and Tupac Amaru. One of the most ruthless terrorist groups in the world, Sendero Luminoso (the Shining Path) is based in the Peruvian countryside. Its forces have occupied villages, established revolutionary governments, and organized schools through which they have indoctrinated locals and evaluated their potential as new recruits. Training in and outside the schools has included guerilla strategy, the use of firearms and explosives, and on-the-job training in militant action against government forces, organized peasants, or collaborators with rival organizations.[39] Tupac Amaru (officially, the *Movimento Revolucionario Tupac Amaru*) was founded on many of the communist principles that led to the Cuban revolution. The group wants to rid Peru of all imperialist elements and is best known for its 1996 takeover of the Japanese ambassador's residence in Lima. The group is estimated to have only a few hundred members at present and operates mainly in the upper Huallaga Valley, a vast jungle area in eastern Peru controlled by guerrillas and drug traffickers. For both groups, the dense jungle canopy and wide-open spaces of the Peruvian countryside allow for a significant amount of guerrilla warfare training to take place undetected.

The Philippines, the MILF, and the Abu Sayyaf Group.   Three major JI terrorist training camps—Camp Vietnam, Camp Palestine, and Camp Hudaibiya—were located in the Moro Islamic Liberation Front's (MILF) Camp Abu Bakar complex in Mindanao, the Philippines.[40] Research has pointed to al Qaeda involvement with both organizations; both JI and MILF camps have, according to Philippine military intelligence, played host to several hundred trainers from the Middle East.[41] Abu Sayyaf, an organization with more criminal tendencies than jihadist sentiment, established a central base on Basilan's Mohadji mountain called Camp Abdurajak—one of at least nine Abu Sayyaf camps hidden in the jungles of the Philippines.[42]

Somalia and Islamic Terrorist Groups.   Because it is a chaotic, poor, battle-weary Muslim country with no central government, there is great concern that Somalia will become another Afghanistan-like safe haven for Islamic fundamentalist terrorism.[43] In fact, Al Ittihad Al Islamiya (AIAI), a Muslim radical organization in Somalia that was recently designated as a terrorist organization by the U.S. Department of State, is reported to have once hosted Osama bin Laden and had, during the 1990s, militia training camps set up in the southeastern corner of the country.[44] As noted in a recent USIP report, "With 2,000 members, AIAI is the most powerful radical band in the Horn of Africa, and it has been funded by Al Qaeda in the past. Other reports have identified the Dabaab refugee camp on the Somalia-Kenya border as a training ground for Islamic extremists, through a Muslim charity, al Haramain, that has established religious schools and social programs. In 1998, Kenya revoked the registration of Muslim NGOs, including al Haramain, because of their links to terrorism."[45] According to U.S. government allegations, AIAI camps in Somalia were used by al Qaeda members in preparing and executing the attacks on the U.S. Embassies in Kenya and Tanzania in 1998.[46] Investigations into the 1993 shooting down in Mogadishu of two U.S. helicopters (as featured in the movie *Black Hawk Down*) suggested that members of Mohamed Farrah Aidid's militia reportedly trained in al Qaeda camps.[47] However, despite these observations, it is widely believed that Somalia's role as a safe haven for training camps is limited, largely because the lawlessness that exists throughout the country—extortion, kidnapping, betrayal—creates conditions of insecurity that constitute a risky environment for terrorist operations.[48]

Spain and the Basque Homeland and Freedom (ETA).   Founded in 1959, the aim of ETA (an acronym for the Spanish phrase *Euzkadi Ta Askatasuna*) is to establish an independent homeland, based on Marxist principles, encompassing the Spanish Basque provinces of Vizcaya, Guipuzcoa, and Alava, as well as the autonomous region of Navarra, along with the southwestern French Departments of Labourd, Basse-Navarra, and Soule.[49]

Since the 1960s, ETA has been accused of, and often taken credit for, more than 1,000 deaths, including a number of bombings and assassinations of Spanish Government officials, security and military forces, politicians, and judicial figures.[50] ETA's most notorious attack was the assassination in December 1973 of Admiral Luis Carrero Blanco, who was seen at the time as Franco's most likely successor. In the early 1960s, they also attempted to derail a train transporting politicians and army veterans. While ETA is believed to have received training at various times in the past in Libya, South Yemen, Lebanon, and Nicaragua, more recently ETA activities have been coordinated from France. For example, in February 2003, French police discovered a training area in the secluded Landes forest in southwestern France which had been used to teach ETA activists how to use homemade grenade-launchers capable of piercing armored cars.[51]

Sri Lanka and the Tamil Tigers.   Since the 1970s, one of the world's most fearsome organizations has been the Liberation Tigers of Tamil Eelam (LTTE), a guerrilla/terrorist group representing the minority Tamil community, fighting for an Eelam (or homeland) in the northern and eastern provinces of Sri Lanka. This separatist-terrorist organization is widely viewed as being at the cutting edge of insurgent and terrorist technology, military adaptation, and innovation—credited with, among other things, the invention of the speedboat suicide attack.[52] A unique, if macabre feature of its tactics has been the use of suicide commandos, both men and women, some in their early teens, for individual assassination as well as mass attacks.[53] Through intense training and conditioning, as well as societal isolation, the LTTE camps, many of them located in Jaffna and remote areas in the northern part of the Sri Lanka, provide important centers of operational knowledge transfer. While several LTTE training camps are known to have existed in India—particularly in the state of Tamil Nadu— there are as yet no indications that this group has provided training for anyone other than Tamils committeed to the goal of establishing a separatist state.

Sudan and Islamic Terrorist Groups.   During the early 1990s, Osama bin Laden was exiled from Saudi Arabia and settled in Khartoum, the capital of Sudan. He brought with him a number of seasoned veterans from the Afghan conflict and established military training camps throughout the country. Some reports say more than twenty camps were built near Khartoum, Port Sudan, in the Damazin areas of eastern Sudan, and in the southern Equatoria Province, near the Ugandan border.[54] A recent report by the U.S. Institute of Peace indicates that

the Sudanese government has used its territory to provide safe haven, training bases, and staging areas to numerous terrorist organizations, including Al Qaeda, Egyptian Islamic Jihad (EIJ), Hizballah, Hamas, Palestinian Islamic Jihad (PIJ), Abu Nidal, and Gama'at al Islamiyya. Operatives not only moved freely in and out of Sudan, but also established offices, businesses, and logistical bases for operations. Training camps were opened in the east of the country, which sent fighters from Lebanon, Afghanistan, and Algeria across the border into neighboring Eritrea and Ethiopia.[55]

Syria and Palestinian Terrorist Organizations. When Lebanon's civil war erupted in 1975, Syria (a predominately Sunni Muslim country) came to the aid of the Christians, who were being pounded by Shiite Muslim groups like Amal.[56] According to the U.S. Department of State, several radical terrorist groups have maintained training camps or other facilities on Syrian territory in the last 20 years, including the Turkish separatist group PKK and Palestinian groups like the Popular Front for the Liberation of Palestinian (PFLP), the Abu Nidal Organization, and the Palestine Islamic Jihad (PIJ).[57] Many of the training camps have been located in the Syrian-controlled Bekaa Valley, in eastern Lebanon. One notorious example is the Ayn Tzahab terrorist training camp in Syria, allegedly supported by Iran and used for operational training for Palestinian terrorists, including Hamas and Palestinian Islamic Jihad operatives.[58]

Turkey and the PKK. According to Ely Karmon (1998), Islamic terrorist groups in Turkey—including the Hizb ut-Tahrir (Islamic Liberation Party)—have been active since the 1960s, recruiting new members from poor towns and villages with a large Kurdish population (Dyarbakir, Silvan, Cizre, Kiziltepe and others), especially among the young and unemployed.[59] He notes how in 1993, a Turkish minister of interior declared at a press conference that members of radical Islamic organizations underwent months of military and theoretical training in Iranian security installations, traveled with Iranian real and forged documents, had weapons and explosives of Iranian origin and participated in attacks on Turkish citizens and also Iranian opposition militants.[60] However, while some Turkish terrorist organizations may have profited materially from Iranian backing in training, logistical support, weapons, and explosives, the more worrisome centers of terrorist knowledge are found among the training camps of the PKK.[61] Aside from the previously mentioned training camp in Lebanon's Bekaa Valley, the PKK has maintained centers of learning throughout southern Turkey and northern Iraq.

The United States and Extremist Groups. In addition to far-away places like Indonesia, Sudan, and Uzbekistan, the United States has also played host to several terrorist training camps in recent decades. From Alabama to Montana, centers of motivational, and sometimes operational, knowledge transfer are cause for increasing concern. In Northern Idaho, the Aryan Nations Church's 20-acre, gated fortress with guard towers provided a sanctuary in which Christian Identity adherents received weapons training, combat tactics, and indoctrination. According to James Aho, the closely-related Covenant, Sword and the Arm of the Lord, headquartered on the Missouri-Arkansas border, amassed one of the largest private arms caches ever uncovered in American history on its 224-acre base, Zarepath-Horeb, consisting of a 30-gallon oil drum of arsenic, at least one improvised armored vehicle, facilities for retooling machine guns out of semiautomatic weapons, grenades, RPGs, silencers, and thousands of rounds of ammunition.[62] Another U.S.-based extremist group, the Christian Patriots Defense League, established a perimeter of armed encampments around the American heartland to protect it from a planned incursion of troops from Africa, allegedly stationed on America's borders awaiting orders from the UN to invade.[63] And Timothy McVeigh, who was convicted and executed for his deadly 1995 attack on the Murrah Federal Building in Oklahoma City, was a frequent visitor to Elohim City (literally, the City of God), a Christian Identity enclave located nearby.[64] These and other "centers of learning" have played an important role in transforming motivated individuals into dangerous terrorists. Without violating the crucial civil liberties of the United States (such as the freedom of association), widespread community vigilance must play a vital role in identifying and closing or preventing future training camps in this country.

Uzbekistan and the IMU. During the Soviet era, the Fergana Valley of Uzbekistan became host to a number of underground mosque and religious schools, and over time, a supportive environment for Islamic radicalism allowed the establishment and maintenance of jihad terrorist training camps.[65] From this environment was launched the Islamic Movement of Uzbekistan (IMU), the most active group of its kind in Central Asia. While the IMU purportedly has used training camps and military bases in Afghanistan, Pakistan, and Tajikistan, as well as a "forward base of operations" in Batken, Kyrgyzstan, the group operates largely in the Ferghana Valley on the Uzbek-Kyrgyz border, where it receives support and some protection from local inhabitants.[66]

Yemen and the Training of Political and Religious Terrorists. Located at the southern tip of the Arabian Peninsula, Yemen is a poor Muslim country with a weak central government, armed tribal groups in outlying areas, and porous borders, which makes it fertile ground for terrorists.[67] During the Cold War, the Soviets and their satellites from East Germany and Cuba established a network of training facilities in South Yemen for members of national liberation movements from Palestine, Somalia, Oman, and some other Arab countries. By one account, during the 1970s and 1980s there were at least 1,000 active Soviet military personnel in South Yemen, together with some 3,000 Cuban advisors in militia and terrorist training camps.[68] For example, Cuban instructors trained members of the People's Front for the Liberation of Oman in a training camp located in the region of Shabwah. The Shabwah town of El-Geida served as the major hub for the Front. Al Qaeda reportedly had several major training camps in Yemen until the late 1990s, when the Yemeni government uprooted them.[69] However, recent signs of activity indicate that Yemen is still seen by some as a safe haven for terrorism. For example, in June 2001, local authorities arrested eight Yemeni veterans of the 1979–89 Afghan mujahideen in connection with a plot to blow up the U.S. Embassy in Sanaa, Yemen's capital, and in July 2002, an accidental explosion that killed two al Qaeda operatives led to the seizure of 650 pounds of plastic explosives from a Sanaa warehouse.

Conclusion

While this brief overview is clearly not inclusive of all countries in which terrorist training camps have existed, it is representative of the multifaceted and geographically diverse world of training for terrorism. Many of these training camps have a good deal in common. To begin with, geographic isolation is needed in order to foster group identity formation and group cohesion; it is also important to avoid disturbing one's neighbors with the sounds of live combat training. Obviously, there are many good reasons why almost all terrorist training camps are located in areas of low population density. Another element that is common to most of these camps is the lack of a state government with the will or ability to close the camps down or prevent new ones from forming. Further, as seen in the extreme cases of Afghanistan, Libya, Syria, and Sudan, state sponsorship is obviously a beneficial element for the establishment and maintenance of terrorist training camps.

These centers of terrorist learning also require easy access to weapons and ammunition, including mortar rounds for heavy weapons training. Members with military combat experience play a critical role as the knowledge experts upon whom the students rely. And given the absence of municipal services in these places, a large amount of food, water, and shelter is obviously needed. To sum up, at a minimum an operational center of learning needs operational space (preferably isolated), teachers (experts in professionally relevant knowledge), committed learners, time, money, and basic necessities.

It must be noted that several of the countries mentioned above (like Northern Ireland) may no longer be considered centers of terrorist learning. Further, as the astute reader will notice, training camps are not always necessary for a country to become a place of operational knowledge transfer; as recent events in Iraq have clearly shown, a good deal of operational knowledge is (perhaps by necessity) acquired "on the job." As terrorism scholar J. Bowyer Bell observes, "it is impossible to simulate the impact of driving a live car-bomb; the anxiety generated that determines operational parameters must be experienced, not imagined."[70] Thus, when new recruits join an ongoing insurgency (such as the group in Iraq led by Abu Musab al-Zarqawi), their training for terrorism is most likely limited to watching the more seasoned veterans carry out a particular attack.

As the chapters in this volume have demonstrated, training for terrorism is a multifaceted process which takes place at a significant number and variety of locations throughout the world. Also, while the majority of effective terrorist training takes place in a face-to-face setting, an important role is played by print and online information resources, although much of it is of questionable value to improving an individual terrorist's operational capabilities. For example, real training for explosives requires experienced teachers and well-prepared students. Too many idle followers of website bomb-making instructions are likely to blow themselves and their families to bits. Thus, training camps and "on the job" training will continue to play a crucial role in developing the operational capabilities of terrorist groups for the foreseeable future. Our ability to identify future centers of terrorist learning will thus prove vital in the global war on terrorism. To this end, the chapters in the third and final volume of this series will address political, social, and environmental dimensions of countries, particularly weak or failing states, which could become new safe havens for terrorist training camps, and thus warrant considerable attention.

Acknowledgments

The views expressed herein are those of the author and do not purport to reflect the position of the United States Military Academy, the Department of the Army, or the Department of Defense.

APPENDIX

Examples of Training Manuals for Terrorism and Guerilla Warfare

Sample #1. Encyclopedia of Afghan Jihad

The Associated Press acquired an eleven-volume Encyclopedia of Jihad, reputedly stolen from the headquarters of bin Laden's fighters in Kandahar, also the home base of Afghanistan's Taliban rulers. Here is an overview of the index to that encyclopedia:

	Principal subjects addressed	The book includes
Book 1: Explosives	Eight chapters with diagrams and formulas to handle, manufacture, and detonate explosives	How to disarm explosives, scientific theories, industrial terror, the use of liquid explosives
Book 2: First aid	Methods of first aid including the handling of psychological shock, the treatment of burns, and electrical shock	The handling of several medical needs including delivering a child
Book 3: Pistols, revolvers	Illustrated guide to the care and use of pistols, revolvers, and specialized handguns	Where to keep guns in the house and how to use silencers
Book 4: Bombs, mines	Illustrated manual on grenades, bombs, mines, mine fields, and mine war	Recipes for mines made of raw materials, how to pass through a mine field

	Principal subjects addressed	The book includes
Book 5: Security, intelligence	How to spy, kinds of security, military intelligence, sabotage, communications, security within Jihad, secret observation, assassination, brainwashing, protection of leaders, laws of sabotage, arms use	Punishment of spies, Muslim and non-Muslim; interrogation; analyzing information; psychological war; poison use; opening locks; U.S. military training; assassination by riding a motorcycle
Book 6: Tactics	Principles of war including battle organization, reconnaissance, infiltration, ambush, elaboration on incursion	Urging Muslims to follow the jihad established in Afghanistan against un-Islamic states and states where true Islam is not practiced
Book 7: Weapons making	Diagrams of machinery for the manufacture of arms	On the manufacture of bullets and silencers, metal casting, the use of a steel file
Book 8: Tanks	The anatomy and history of tanks, their effectiveness, and descriptions of different types	Cost of maintenance of tanks, how to drive a tank
Book 9: Close fighting	Physical fitness, aikido and other forms of self-defense, how to overcome a rival	How to attack with knives or chairs, methods of releasing oneself from a grip
Book 10: Topography area survey	Natural directions, using a compass, topography, following directions on maps, military area survey, area survey apparatus	Estimation and measurement of distance, height, and speed for military use
Book 11: Armament	Use of small arms including antiaircraft arms, machine guns, rifles, antitank arms, and artillery	Reviews mostly Russian weapons; offers practical details on the assembly, cleaning, and use of weapons

Source: Kathy Gannon, "Jihad Manual a Testament of Death," Associated Press (2 October 2001).

Sample #2. Excerpts from al Qaeda Training Manuals

The following excerpts are from *The Declaration of Jihad Against the Country's Tyrants* (Military Series), a terrorist training manual found by the Manchester (England) Metropolitan Police during a search of an al Qaeda member's home. The manual was found in a computer file described as "the military series" related to the "Declaration of Jihad." It was subsequently translated into English and was entered as evidence in the New York City trial of four men accused of plotting the 1998 bombings of American Embassies in Kenya and Tanzania. Several portions of this manual are available online at the website of the U.S. Department of Justice: http://www.usdoj.gov.

First Lesson: General Introduction

Principles of Military Organization:

Military Organization has three main principles without which it cannot be established:

1. Military Organization Commander and advisory council
2. The soldiers (individual members)
3. A clearly defined strategy

Military Organization Requirements:

The Military Organization dictates a number of requirements to assist it in confrontation and endurance. These are:

1. Forged documents and counterfeit currency
2. Apartments and hiding places
3. Communication means
4. Transportation means
5. Information
6. Arms and ammunition
7. Transport

Missions Requires of the Military Organization:

The main mission for which the Military Organization is responsible is the overthrow of the godless regimes and their replacement with an Islamic regime. Other missions consist of the following:

1. Gathering information about the enemy, the land, the installations, and the neighbors

2. Kidnapping enemy personnel, documents, secrets, and arms

3. Assassinating enemy personnel as well as foreign tourists

4. Freeing the brothers who are captured by the enemy

5. Spreading rumors and writing statements that instigate people against the enemy

6. Blasting and destroying the places of amusement, immorality, and sin; not a vital target

7. Blasting and destroying the embassies and attacking vital economic centers

8. Blasting and destroying bridges leading into and out of cities

Second Lesson: Necessary Qualifications and Characteristics for the Organization's Member

Necessary Qualifications for the Organization's Members:

1 –Islam: The member of the Organization must be Muslim. How can an unbeliever, someone from a revealed religion (Christian, Jew), a secular person, a communist, etc., protect Islam and Muslims and defend their goals and secrets when he does not believe in that religion [Islam]? The Israeli Army requires that a fighter be of the Jewish religion. Likewise, the command leadership in the Afghan and Russian armies requires that any one with an officer's position to be a member of the communist party.

2 –Commitment to the Organization's Ideology: This commitment frees the Organization's members from conceptual problems.

3 –Maturity: The requirements of military work are numerous, and a minor cannot perform them. The nature of hard and continuous work in dangerous conditions requires a great deal of psychological, mental, and intellectual fitness, which are not usually found in a minor. . . .

4 –Sacrifice: He [the member] has to be willing to do the work and undergo martyrdom for the purpose of achieving the goal and establishing the religion of majestic Allah on earth.

5 –Listening and Obedience: In the military, this is known today as discipline. It is expressed by how the member obeys the orders given to him. That is what our religion urges. . . .

6 –Keeping Secrets and Concealing Information: [This secrecy should be used] even with the closest people, for deceiving the enemies is not easy. . . .

7 –Free of Illness: The Military Organization's member must fulfill this important requirement. Allah says, "There is no blame for those who are infirm, or ill, or who have no resources to spend."

8 –Patience: [The member] should have plenty of patience for [enduring] afflictions if he is overcome by the enemies. He should not abandon this great path and sell himself and his religion to the enemies for his freedom. He should be patient in performing the work, even if it lasts a long time.

9 –Tranquility and "Unflappability": [The member] should have a calm personality that allows him to endure psychological traumas such as those involving bloodshed, murder, arrest, imprisonment, and reverse psychological traumas such as killing one or all of his Organization's comrades. [He should be able] to carry out the work.

[Other items described in this section include:]

10 –Intelligence and Insight

11 –Caution and Prudence

12 –Truthfulness and Counsel

13 –Ability to Observe and Analyze

14 –Ability to Act, Change Positions and Conceal Oneself

Fifth Lesson: Means of Communication and Transportation

The Military Organization in any Islamic group can, with its modest capabilities, use the following means: 1. The telephone; 2. Meeting in person; 3. Messenger; 4. Letters; 5. Some modern devices, such as the facsimile and wireless [communication].

Secret Communication is Limited to the Following Types:

1. Common Communication: It is communication between two members of the Organization without being monitored by the security apparatus opposing the Organization. The common communication should be done under a certain cover and after inspecting the surveillance situation [by the enemy].

2. Standby Communication: This replaces common communication when one of the two parties is unable to communication with the other for some reason.

3. Alarm Communication: This is used when the opposing security apparatus discovers an undercover activity or some undercover members. Based

on this communication, the activity is stopped for a while, all matters related to the activity are abandoned, and the Organization's members are hidden from view.

Method of Communication Among Members of the Organization:

1. Communication about undercover activity should be done using a good cover; it should also be quick, explicit, and pertinent. That is, just for talking only.
2. Prior to contacting his members, the commander of the cell should agree with each of them separately (the cell members should never meet all in one place and should not know one another) on a manner and means of communication with each other. Likewise, the chief of the Organization should (use a similar technique) with the branch commanders.
3. A higher-ranking commander determines the type and method of communication with the lower-ranking leaders.

Designating Special Signals Between Those who Meet:

If the two individuals meeting know one another's shape and appearance, it is sufficient to use a single safety sign. [In that case,] the sitting and arriving individuals inform each other that there is no enemy surveillance. The sign may be keys, beads, a newspaper, or a scarf. The two parties would agree on moving it in a special way so as not to attract the attention of those present.

Sixth Lesson: Training

The following security precautions should be taken during the training:

The Place:

The place should have the following specifications:

1. Distance from the populated areas with the availability of living necessities.
2. Availability of medical services during the training.
3. The place should be suitable for the type of training (physical fitness, shooting, tactics).
4. No one except the trainers and trainees should know about the place.
5. The place should have many roads and entrances.
6. The place should be visited at suitable times.

7. Hiding any training traces immediately after the training.

8. Guarding the place during the training.

9. Appropriateness of the existing facilities for the number of training members.

10. Exclusion of anyone who is not connected with the training.

11. Taking all security measures regarding the establishment.

12. Distance of the place from police stations, public establishments, and the eyes of informants.

13. The place should not be situated in such a way that the training and trainees can be seen from another location.

The Trainees:

1. Before proceeding to the training place, all security measures connected with an undercover individual should be taken. Meanwhile, during training at the place, personnel safety should be ensured.

2. Selecting the trainees carefully.

3. The trainees should not know one another.

4. The small size of groups that should be together during the training (7–10 individuals).

5. The trainees should not know the training place.

6. Establishing a training plan for each trainee.

The Trainers:

All measures taken with regard to the commanders apply also to the trainers. Also, the following should be applied:

1. Fewness of the trainers in the training place. Only those conducting the training should be there, in order not to subject the training team to the risk of security exposure.

2. Not revealing the identity of the trainer to the trainees.

3. Keeping a small ratio of trainees to trainer.

4. The training team members should not know one another.

Lesson 9: Security

Assassination is an operation of military means and basic security. . . . Commanders must establish a careful, systematic, and solid security plan to hide the operation from the enemy until the time of its execution, which would minimize the losses in case the executing party is discovered. A tactical plan for the assassination operation must also be established, consisting of the operational factors themselves (members, weapons, hiding places . . .) and factors of the operation (time, place). In this example, we shall explain in detail the part related to the security plan. The part related to operational tactics will be explained in the lesson on special operational tactics.

Security Plan for the Assassination Operation:

The security plan must take into account the following matters:

A. The Commander: The security apparatus should not know his whereabouts and movements. All security measures and arrangements related to members of the Military Organization (soldiers, commanders) apply to him.

B. The Members:

   1) They are elements who are selected from various provinces and are suitable for the operation.

   2) During the selection process, members should not know one another. They should not know the original planners of the operation. In case they do, the commander should be notified. He then should modify the plan.

   3) They should be distributed in small groups (three members) in apartments that are not known except for their proprietors. They should also be given field names.

   4) During the selection process, consider whether their absence from the families and jobs would clearly attract attention. We also apply to them all security measures related to the Organization's individuals (soldiers).

C. Method of Operating:

   1) The matters of arming and financing should not be known by anyone except the commander.

   2) The apartments should not be rented under real names. They (the apartments) should undergo all security measures related to the Military Organization's camps.

   3) Prior to executing an operation, falsified documents should be prepared for the participating individuals.

   4) The documents related to the operation should be hidden in a secure place and burned immediately after the operation, and traces of the fire should be removed.

   5) The means of communication between the operation commander and the participating brothers should be established.

6) Prior to the operation, apartments should be prepared to hide the brothers participating in it. These apartments should not be known except to the commander and his soldiers.

7) Reliable transportation means must be made available. It is essential that prior to the operation, these mans are checked and properly maintained.

D. Interrogation and Investigation: prior to executing an operation, the commander should instruct his soldiers on what to say if they are captured. He should explain that more than once, in order to ensure that they have assimilated it. They should, in turn, explain it back to the commander. The commander should also sit with each of them individually (and go over) the agreed-upon matters that would be brought up during the interrogation.

Assassinations with Poison

We will limit the discussion to poisons that the holy warrior can prepare and use without endangering his health.

Castor beans. The substance ricin, an extract of castor beans, is considered one of the most deadly poisons: 0.035 milligram inhaled or injected in a vein is enough to kill someone. It is a simple operation to extract ricin, and castor beans can be obtained from nurseries throughout the country.

Precatory beans. The herbal poison abrin, extracted from precatory beans, is very similar to ricin. The seeds of this plant are red and black and are used in prayer beads.

Water hemlock. A lethal dose is 3.2 grams. It has a palatable taste and is very similar to parsnip.

Tobacco. There is enough nicotine in three cigarettes to kill a man. If eaten, sixty to seventy milligrams of pure nicotine will kill a person within an hour.

Potato sprout. Both rotten and green, contains solanine.

Dimethyl sulfoxide can be found with horse breeders or veterinarians. Mix poison with this substance, and when the enemy touches it he will die slowly within fifteen minutes to an hour.

Poisoning from eating spoiled food. Since 0.000028 gram will kill a person, this poison is absolutely lethal.

How to prepare spoiled food. Fill a pot with corn and green beans. Put in a small piece of meat and about two spoonfuls of fresh excrement. Pour the water into the pot until there is surface tension at the lip of the pot. Cover the pot tightly. If you do that correctly, there will be no air trapped in the pot. Leave the pot in a dark, moderately warm room for fifteen days. At the end of that period, you will notice a substance on the edge of the pot and a small amount of rottenness. You can make three or four pots at the same time. During the time of the destroyer, Jamal Abdul Nasser, someone who was being severely tortured in prison ate some feces after losing sanity because of the torture. A few hours later he was found dead.

Lesson 11: Espionage

Principles of Muslims Spying on their Enemies.   Spying on the enemy is permitted and it may even be a duty in the case of war between Muslims and others. Winning the battle is dependent on knowing the enemy's secrets, movements, and plans. . . . How can a Muslim spy live among enemies if he maintains his Islamic characteristics? How can he perform his duties to Allah and not want to appear Muslim?

Concerning the issue of clothing and appearance (appearance of a true religion), Ibn Taimia—may Allah have mercy on him—said "If a Muslim is in a combat or godless area, he is not obligated to have a different appearance from those around him. The [Muslim] man may prefer or even be obligated to look like them, provided his action brings a religious benefit to preaching to them, learning their secrets and informing Muslims, preventing harm, or some other beneficial goal."

Resembling the polytheist in religious appearance is a kind of "necessity permits the forbidden" even through they [forbidden acts] are basically prohibited. As for the visible duties, like fasting and praying, he can fast by using any justification not to eat with them [polytheist]. As for prayer, the book (Al-Manhaj Al-Haraki Lissira Al-Nabawiya) quotes Al-Bakhari that "he [the Muslim] may combine the noon and afternoon [prayers] sunset and evening [prayers]. That is based on the fact that the prophet—Allah bless and keep him—combined [prayers] in Madina without fear or hesitation."

Guidelines for Beating and Killing Hostages.   Religious scholars have permitted beating . . . we find permission to interrogate the hostage for the purpose of obtaining information. It is permitted to strike the nonbeliever who has no covenant until he reveals the news, information, and secrets of his people.

The religious scholars have also permitted the killing of a hostage if he insists on withholding information from Muslims. They permitted his killing so that he would not inform his people of what he learned about the Muslim condition, number and secrets.

Information Sources.   Any organization that desires to raise the flag of Islam high and proud, must gather as much information as possible about the enemy. Information has two sources:

Public Source: Using this public source openly and without resorting to illegal means, it is possible to gather at least 80 percent of information about the enemy. The percentage varies depending on the government's policy on freedom of the press and publication. It is possible to gather information through newspapers, magazines, books, periodicals, official publications, and enemy broadcasts. Attention should also be given to the opinion, comments, and jokes of common people. . . . The one gathering information with this public method is not exposed to any danger whatsoever. Any brother can gather information form those aforementioned sources. We cannot label that brother a "Muslim spy" because he does not make any effort to obtain unpublished and covert information.

Secret Sources: It is possible, through these secret and dangerous methods, to obtain the 20 percent of information that is considered secret. The most important of these sources are:

1. Individuals who are recruited as either volunteers or because of other motives

2. Recording and monitoring

3. Photography

4. Interrogation

5. Documents: By burglary or recruitment of personnel

6. Drugging

7. Surveillance

Twelfth Lesson: Espionage (2)—Information-Gathering Using Covert Methods

Information needed through covert means: Information needed to be gathered through covert means is of only two types:

First: Information about government personnel, officers, important personalities, and all matters related to those (residence, work place, times of leaving and returning, wives and children, places visited)

Second: Information about strategic buildings, important establishments, and military bases. Examples are important ministries such as those of Defense and Internal Security, airports, seaports, land border points, embassies, and radio and TV stations

General security measures that should be taken by the person gathering information: During the process of gathering information, whether about governing personalities or establishments, the person doing the gathering must take the following security measures:

1. Performing the exercises to detect surveillance while executing the mission. These exercises are not well defined, but are dependent on the time, place, and the ability to be creative. These exercises include the following:

    a. Walking down a dead-end street and observing who is walking behind you. Beware of traps.

    b. Casually dropping something out of your pocket and observing who will pick it up.

    c. Walking fast then stopping suddenly at a corner and observing who will be affected.

    d. Stopping in front of store windows and observing who is watching you.

    e. Getting on a bus and then getting off after it departs and observing who will be affected.

    f. Agreeing with one of your brothers to look for whoever is watching you.

2. When receiving the gathered information, let the informants travel as far as possible from their place of residence and yours. Let each of them get there using secondary roads, preferably at night.

3. Gather what information you can without emphasizing any particular part. Do not rush or show urgency because your excitement may uncover you and the degree of importance of the information.

4. Avoid anything that reveals your identity quickly. Do not attempt to be too creative or inventive. Remember what Taliran [PH] said to his political emissaries, "Do not be anxious."

5. Move slowly and travel a great distance. The one who is successful in gathering information is the one who is not known or conspicuous.

6. Do not accept events at their face value. Do not overlook a quick friendship or an apparent dispute. Evaluate the importance of events and do not judge them by their appearance.

7. Do not speak vaguely or act mysteriously except when wanting to get a "blabber mouth" to talk about what he knows.

8. Carry personal credentials and know all their contents.

9. Prior to collecting the information, make sure that all necessities related to the mission, especially money, are ready.

10. Study the area where information-gathering takes place carefully: Open and closed streets, residents' customs, ways of dressing, and accent.

11. It is not permitted to carry any weapons during the information-gathering process.

12. Finding a cover prior to gathering the information.

Further, review all security measures concerning members of the Military [Organization] which are covered in prior lessons.

Sample #3. Ayman Al-Zawahiri Targeting Excerpt

The following is an excerpt from Chapter 11 of Ayman al-Zawahiri's book *Knights Under the Prophet's Banner*. The excerpt was published in *al-Sharq al-Awsat* on 12 December 2001. The translation is by FBIS. In its translation note FBIS said, "In the 11th chapter of his memoir, which is considered his 'last will,' al-Zawahiri explores future horizons. It seems that the Egyptian al-Jihad Group leader wrote this chapter shortly before the September 11 events."

Choosing the Targets and Concentrating on the Martyrdom Operations

L. Changing the method of strikes. The mujahid Islamic movement must escalate its methods of strikes and tools of resisting the enemies to keep up with the tremendous increase in the number of its enemies, the quality of their weapons, their destructive powers, their disregard for all taboos, and disrespect for the customs of wars and conflicts.

In this regard, we concentrate on the following:

1. The need to inflict the maximum casualties against the opponent, for this is the language understood by the West, no matter how much time and effort such operations take.

2. The need to concentrate on the method of martyrdom operations as the most successful way of inflicting damage against the opponent and the least costly to the mujahideen in terms of casualties.

3. The targets as well as the type and method of weapons used must be chosen to have an impact on the structure of the enemy and deter it enough to stop its brutality, arrogance, and disregard for all taboos and customs. It must restore the struggle to its real size.

4. To reemphasize what we have already explained, we reiterate that focusing on the domestic [U.S. presence overseas] enemy alone will not be feasible at this stage.

Source: Ben N. Venzke and Aimee Ibrahim, "al-Qaeda Tactic/Target Brief, v1.5" (14 June 2002), available online at http://www.intelcenter.com.

Sample #4. How Can I Train Myself for Jihad

The six-page document—*How Can I Train Myself for Jihad*—advises that "military training is an obligation in Islam upon every sane, male, mature Muslim, whether rich or poor, whether studying or working and whether living in a Muslim or non-Muslim country." It offers tips on various ways to make "suitable preparations for battle" including physical training, martial arts, survival and outdoors training, firearms training, and military training.

quotes from anonymous pamphlet, *How Can I Train Myself for Jihad*, as cited in *Firearms Training for Jihad in America*, a Violence Policy Center report, available online at http://www.vpc.org/studies/jihad.htm.

Sample #5. The Terrorist Handbook, by Gunzenbomz Pyro-Technologies

Available online at http://www.capricorn.org/~akira/home/terror.html and http://isuisse.ifrance.com/emmaf/indterhand.html.

1.0 Introduction

Gunzenbomz Pyro-Technologies, a division of Chaos Industries (CHAOS), is proud to present this first edition of The Terrorist's Handbook. First and foremost, let it be stated that Chaos Industries assumes no responsibilities for any misuse of the information presented in this publication. The purpose of this is to show the many techniques and methods used by those people in this and other countries who employ terror as a means to political and social goals. The techniques herein can be obtained from public libraries, and can usually be carried out by a terrorist with minimal equipment. This makes one all the more frightened, since any lunatic or social deviant could obtain this information, and use it against anyone. The processes and techniques herein SHOULD NOT BE CARRIED OUT UNDER ANY CIRCUMSTANCES!! SERIOUS HARM OR DEATH COULD OCCUR FROM ATTEMPTING TO PERFORM ANY OF THE METHODS IN THIS PUBLICATION. THIS IS MERELY FOR READING ENJOYMENT, AND IS NOT INTENDED FOR ACTUAL USE!!

Gunzenbomz Pyro-Technologies feels that it is important that everyone has some idea of just how easy it is for a terrorist to perform acts of terror; that is the reason for the existence of this publication.

1.1 Table of Contents

2.0 Buying Explosives and Propellants

Almost any city or town of reasonable size has a gun store and a pharmacy. These are two of the places that potential terrorists visit in order to purchase explosive material. All that one has to do is know something about the non-explosive uses of the materials. Black powder, for example, is used in blackpowder firearms. It comes in varying "grades," with each different grade being a slightly different size. The grade of black powder depends on what the calibre of the gun that it is used in; a fine grade of powder could burn too fast in the wrong caliber weapon. The rule is: the smaller the grade, the faster the burn rate of the powder.

2.05 Flash Powder

Flash powder is a mixture of powdered zirconium metal and various oxidizers. It is extremely sensitive to heat or sparks, and should be treated with more care than black powder, with which it should NEVER be mixed. It is sold in small containers which must be mixed and shaken before use. It is very finely powdered, and is available in three speeds: fast, medium, and slow. The fast flash powder is the best for using in explosives or detonators. It burns very rapidly, regardless of confinement or packing, with a hot white "flash," hence its name. It is fairly expensive, costing about $11.00. It is sold in magic shops and theatre supply stores.

2.1 Acquiring Chemicals

The first section deals with getting chemicals legally. This section deals with "procuring" them. The best place to steal chemicals is a college. Many state schools have all of their chemicals out on the shelves in the labs, and more in their chemical stockrooms. Evening is the best time to enter lab buildings, as there are the least number of people in the buildings, and most of the labs will still be unlocked. One simply takes a bookbag, wears a dress shirt and jeans, and tries to resemble a college freshman. If anyone asks what such a person is doing, the thief can simply say that he is looking for the polymer chemistry lab, or some other chemistry-related department other than the one they are in. One can usually find out where the various labs and departments in a building are by calling the university. There are, of course other techniques for getting into labs after hours, such as placing a piece of cardboard in the latch of an unused door, such as a back exit. Then, all one needs to do is come back at a later hour. Also, before this is done, terrorists check for security systems. If one just walks into a lab, even if there is someone there, and walks out the back exit, and slip the cardboard in the latch before the door closes, the person in the lab will never know what happened. It is also a good idea to observe the building that one plans to rob at the time that one plans to rob it several days before the actual theft is done. This is advisable since the would-be thief should know when and if the campus security makes patrols through buildings. Of course, if none of these methods are successful, there is always section 2.11, but as a rule, college campus security is pretty poor, and nobody suspects another person in the building of doing anything wrong, even if they are there at an odd hour.

4.0 Using Explosives

Once a terrorist has made his explosives, the next logical step is to apply them. Explosives have a wide range of uses, from harassment, to vandalism, to murder. NONE OF THE IDEAS PRESENTED HERE ARE EVER TO BE CARRIED OUT, EITHER IN PART OR IN FULL! DOING SO CAN LEAD TO PROSECUTION, FINES, AND IMPRISONMENT!

The first step that a person that would use explosive would take would be to determine how big an explosive device would be needed to do whatever had to be done. Then, he would have to decide what to make his bomb with. He would also have to decide on how he wanted to detonate the device, and determine where the best placement for it would be. Then, it would be necessary to see if the device could be put where he wanted it without it being discovered or moved. Finally, he would actually have to sit down and build his explosive device. These are some of the topics covered in the next section.

Sample #6. Minimanual of the Urban Guerrilla, by Carlos Marighella

The following excerpts are from Carlos Marighella's book *The Liberation of Brazil*, portions of which were widely translated and employed by Latin American and European terrorists, and encouraged physical training and manual skills, as well as the mastery of small arms and explosives. This manual is available online at http://www.marxists.org/archive/marighella-carlos/1969/06/minimanual-urban-guerrilla.

Technical Preparation of the Urban Guerrilla

No one can become an urban guerrilla without paying special attention to technical preparation.

The technical preparation of the urban guerrilla runs from a concern for his physical condition to a knowledge of and apprenticeship in professions and skills of all kinds, particularly manual skills.

The urban guerrilla can have a strong physical constitution only if he trains systematically. He cannot be a good fighter if he has not learned the art of fighting. For that reason, the urban guerrilla must learn and practice the various forms of unarmed fighting, of attack, and of personal defense. Other useful forms of physical preparation are hiking, camping, the practice of survival in the woods, mountain climbing, rowing, swimming, skin diving and training as a frogman, fishing, harpooning, and the hunting of birds and of small and big game.

It is very important to learn how to drive a car, pilot a plane, handle a motor boat and a sailboat, understand mechanics, radio, telephone, electricity and have some knowledge of electronics techniques. It is also important to have a knowledge of topographical information, to be able to determine one's position by instruments or other available resources, to calculate distances, make maps and plans, draw to scale, make timings, and work with an angle protractor, a compass, etc. A knowledge of chemistry, of color combination and of stamp-making, the mastery of the skills of calligraphy and the copying of letters, and other techniques are part of the technical preparation of the urban guerrilla, who is obliged to falsify documents in order to live within a society that he seeks to destroy. In the area of "makeshift" medicine, the urban guerrilla has the special role of being a doctor or understanding medicine, nursing, pharmacology, drugs, basic surgery and emergency first aid.

The basic question in the technical preparation of the urban guerrilla is, nevertheless, to know how to handle weapons such as the submachine gun, revolver, automatic pistol, FAL, various types of shotguns, carbines, mortars, bazookas, etc.

A knowledge of various types of ammunition and explosives is another aspect to consider. Among the explosives, dynamite must be well understood. The use of incendiary bombs, smoke bombs, and other types is also indispensible prior training. To know how to improvise and repair weapons, prepare Molotov cocktails, grenades, mines, homemade destructive devices, how to blow up bridges, tear up and put out of service railroads and railroad cars, these are necessities in the technical preparation of the urban guerrilla that can never be considered unimportant.

The highest level of preparation for the urban guerrilla is the training camp for technical training. But only the guerrilla who has already passed a preliminary examination can go to this school—that is to say, one who has passed the test of fire in revolutionary action, in actual combat against the enemy.

The Urban Guerrilla's Weapons

The urban guerrilla's weapons are light arms, easily obtained, usually captured from the enemy, purchased, or made on the spot. Light weapons have the advantage of fast handling and easy transport. In general, light weapons are characterized as being short-barrelled. This includes many automatic weapons. Automatic and semiautomatic weapons considerably increase the firepower of the urban guerrilla. The disadvantage of this type of weapon, for us, is the difficulty in controlling it, resulting in wasted rounds or a wasteful use of ammunition—corrected for only by a good aim and precision firing. Men who are poorly trained convert automatic weapons into an ammunition drain.

Experience has shown that the basic weapon of the urban guerrilla is the light submachine gun. This weapon, in addition to being efficient and easy to shoot in an urban area, has the advantage of being greatly respected by the enemy. The guerrilla must thoroughly know how to handle the submachine gun, now so popular and indispensible to the Brazilian urban guerrillas.

The ideal submachine gun for the urban guerrilla is the INA .45 caliber. Other types of submachine guns of different calibers can also be used—understanding of course, the problem of ammunition. Thus, it is preferable that the manufacturing capabilities of the urban guerrillas be used for the production of one type of submachine gun, so that the ammunition to be used can be standardized. Each firing group of urban guerrillas must have a submachine gun handled by a good marksman. The other members of the group must be armed with .38 revolvers, our standard weapon. The .32 is also useful for those who want to participate. But the .38 is preferable since its impact usually puts the enemy out of action.

Hand grenades and conventional smoke bombs can also be considered light weapons, with defensive power for cover and withdrawal.

Long-barrelled weapons are more difficult for the urban guerrilla to transport, and they attract much attention because of their size. Among the long-barrelled weapons are the FAL, the Mauser guns or rifles, hunting guns such as the Winchester, and others.

Shotguns can be useful if used at close range and point blank. They are useful even for a poor shot, especially at night when precision isn't much help. A pressure airgun can be useful for training in marksmanship. Bazookas and mortars can also be used in action, but the conditions for using them have to be prepared and the people who use them must be trained.

The urban guerrilla should not attempt to base his actions on the use of heavy weapons, which have major drawbacks in a type of fighting that demands lightweight weapons to insure mobility and speed.

Homemade weapons are often as efficient as the best weapons produced in conventional factories, and even a sawed-off shotgun is a good weapon for the urban guerrilla fighter.

The urban guerrilla's role as a gunsmith has a basic importance. As a gunsmith, he takes care of the weapons, knows how to repair them, and in many cases can set up a small shop for improvising and producing effective small arms.

Experience in metallurgy and on the mechanical lathe are basic skills the urban guerrilla should incorporate into his manufacturing plans for the construction of homemade weapons. This production, and courses in explosives and sabotage, must be organized. The primary materials for practice in these courses must be obtained ahead of time, to prevent an incomplete apprenticeship—that is to say, so as to leave no room for experimentation.

Molotov cocktails, gasoline, homemade contrivances such as catapaults and mortars for firing explosives, grenades made of pipes and cans, smoke bombs, mines, conventional explosives such as dynamite and potassium chlorate, plastic explosives, gelatine capsules, and ammunition of every kind are indispensible to the success of the urban guerrilla's mission.

The methods of obtaining the necessary materials and munitions will be to buy them or to take them by force in expropriation actions specially planned and carried out. The urban guerrillas will be careful not to keep explosives and other materials that can cause accidents around for very long, but will always try to use them immediately on their intended targets.

The urban guerrilla's weapons and his ability to maintain them constitute his firepower. By taking advantage of modern weapons and introducing innovations in his firepower and in the use of certain weapons, the urban guerrilla can improve many of the tactics of urban warfare. An example of this was the innovation made by the Brazilian urban guerrillas when they introduced the use of the submachine gun in their attacks on banks.

When the massive use of uniform submachine guns becomes possible, there will be new changes in urban guerrilla warfare tactics. The firing group that utilizes uniform weapons and corresponding ammunition, with reasonable care for their maintenance, will reach a considerable level of effectiveness.

The urban guerrilla increases his effectiveness as he increases his firepower.

Assaults

Assaults are the armed attacks which we make to expropriate funds, liberate prisoners, capture explosives, submachine guns, and other types of weapons and ammunition. Assaults can take place in broad daylight or at night. Daytime assaults are made when the objective cannot be achieved at any other hour, such as the transport of money by banks, which is not done at night. Night assault is usually the most advantageous for the guerrilla. The ideal is for all assaults to take place at night, when conditions for a surprise attack are most favorable and the darkness facilitates escape and hides the identity of the participants. The urban guerrilla must prepare himself, nevertheless, to act under all conditions, daytime as well as night.

The most vulnerable targets for assaults are the following:

1. credit establishments
2. commercial and industrial enterprises, including plants for the manufacture of weapons and explosives
3. military establishments

4. commissaries and police stations

5. jails

6. government property

7. mass communications media

8. North American firms and properties

9. government vehicles, including military and police vehicles, trucks, armored vehicles, money carriers, trains, ships, and airplanes.

The assaults on businesses use the same tactics, because in every case the buildings represent a fixed target. Assaults on buildings are planned as guerrilla operations, varied according to whether they are against banks, a commercial enterprise, industries, military bases, commissaries, prisons, radio stations, warehouses for foreign firms, etc.

The assault on vehicles—money-carriers, armored vehicles, trains, ships, airplanes—are of another nature, since they are moving targets. The nature of the operation varies according to the situation and the circumstances—that is, whether the vehicle is stationary or moving. Armored cars, including military vehicles, are not immune to mines. Roadblocks, traps, ruses, interception by other vehicles, Molotov cocktails, shooting with heavy weapons, are efficient methods of assaulting vehicles. Heavy vehicles, grounded airplaces and anchored ships can be seized and their crews and guards overcome. Airplanes in flight can be hijacked by guerrilla action or by one person. Ships and trains in motion can be assaulted or captured by guerrilla operations in order to obtain weapons and ammunition or to prevent troop movements.

The Seven Sins of the Urban Guerrilla

Even when the urban guerrilla applies proper tactics and abides by its security rules, he can still be vulnerable to errors. There is no perfect urban guerrilla. The most he can do is make every effort to diminish the margin of error, since he cannot be perfect. One of the means we should use to diminish the possibility of error is to know thoroughly the seven deadly sins of the urban guerrilla and try to avoid them.

The first sin of the guerrilla is inexperience. The urban guerrilla, blinded by this sin, thinks the enemy is stupid, underestimates the enemy's intelligence, thinks everything is easy and, as a result, leaves evidence that can lead to disaster. Because of his inexperience, the urban guerrilla may also overestimate the forces of the enemy, believing them to be stronger than they really are. Allowing himself to be fooled by this presumption, the urban guerrilla becomes intimidated and remains insecure and indecisive, paralyzed and lacking in audacity. The second sin of the urban guerrilla is to boast about the actions he has undertaken and to broadcast them to the four winds. The third sin of the urban guerrilla is vanity. The guerrilla who suffers from this sin tries to solve the problems of the revolution by actions in the city, but without bothering about the beginnings and survival of other guerrillas in other areas. Blinded by success, he winds up organizing an action that he considers decisive and that puts into play the entire resources of the organization. Since we cannot afford to break the guerrilla struggle in the cities while rural guerrilla warfare has not yet erupted, we always run the risk of allowing the enemy to attack us with decisive blows. The fourth sin of the urban guerrilla is to exaggerate his strength and to undertake actions for which he, as yet, lacks sufficient forces and the required infrastructure.

The fifth sin of the urban guerrilla is rash action. The guerrilla who commits this sin loses patience, suffers an attack of nerves, does not wait for anything, and impetuously throws himself into action, suffering untold defeats.

The sixth sin of the urban guerrilla is to attack the enemy when they are most angry. The seventh sin of the urban guerrilla is to fail to plan things, and to act spontaneously.

Other Samples of Terrorism Education in the Public Domain:

The Anarchist Cookbook (the Jolly Roger)
   http://www.anarchist-cookbook.com

   and http://isuisse.ifrance.com/emmaf/anarcook/indanarcook.html

Field Manual for Free Militia (the Free Militia)
   http://www.rickross.com/reference/militia/militia10.html

   and http://www.rickross.com/reference/militia/militia11.html

The Green Book (Sinn Fein/Irish Republican Army)
   http://www.residentgroups.fsnet.co.uk/greenbook.htm

Militia Organizing: Advance Teams (Anonymous/Constitution Society, 1995)
   http://www.constitution.org/mil/org_team.txt

Militia Training: Operation WitWeb (Anonymous/Constitution Society, 1995)
   http://www.constitution.org/mil/witbweb.txt

Reviving the Ready Militia (Anonymous/Constitution Society, 1994)
   http://www.constitution.org/mil/rev_read.txt

Ozymandias Sabotage Handbook, 2-volumes (*Société Anonyme*/The Anonymous Society)
   http://sabotage.org/handbook and http://www.reachoutpub.com/osh

Special Force (Hizballah training video game)
   see http://en.wikipedia.org/wiki/Special_Force for information.

Notes

Preface

1. Albert Bandura, *Social Foundations of Thought and Action: A Social Cognitive Theory* (Englewood Cliffs, NJ: Prentice-Hall, 1986).

2. Albert Bandura et al., 1975.

3. See Martha Brill Olcott and Bakhtiyar Babajanov, "The Terrorist Notebooks," *Foreign Policy* (March–April 2003): 30–40.

4. Ibid.

Chapter 1: Exploring the Training of Terrorists: An Introduction

1. This was the delayed revenge of the Liberation Tigers of Tamil Eelam (LTTE) against Rajiv Gandhi, who had sent the Indian Peacekeeping force to Sri Lanka in 1987 to protect civilians against Tamil militancy. See Ana Carter, "Tamil Tigresses," *Columbia University's Journal of International Affairs* (Spring 1998), online at http://www.columbia.edu/cu/sipa/PUBS/SLANT/SPRING98/article5.html; also see the description of the Liberation Tigers of Tamil Eelam (LTTE) at the South Asian Terrorism Portal, http://www.satp.org/satporgtp/countries/shrilanka/terroristoutfits/Ltte.htm.

2. A vivid, detailed account of this event is available online at http://www.wesleyjohnston.com/users/ireland/past/omagh/main.html; also see the BBC news website at http://news.bbc.co.uk.

3. "16 killed in Pakistan Shooting," *Daily Herald* (Chicago), 29 October 2001, online at http://www.dailyherald.com/special/waronterrorism/story.asp?intID=3719392; and "Pakistani Christians Mourn 16 Killed by Gunmen," *St. Petersburg Times,* 30 October 2001, online at http://www.sptimesrussia.com/archive/times/717/rest/r_5017.htm.

4. See "Women and Suicide Bombing Attacks," http://www.intelligence.org.il/eng/sib/6_04/women.htm.

5. "Police arrest militants planning bomb attack at Catholic Festival," *The Christian Post*, 8 January 2005. Online at http://www.christianpost.com/article/asia/613/section/police.arrest.militants.planning.bomb.attack.at.catholic.festival/1.htm.

6. See U.S. Department of State, *Patterns of Global Terrorism, 1999* (Washington, DC: U.S. Department of State, Coordinator for Terrorism, 2000).

7. Adam Zagorin, "Limousine Terror?" *Time*, 24 January 2005, p. 15.

8. Ibid.

9. Bruce Hoffman, *Inside Terrorism* (New York: Columbia University Press, 1998), p. 203.

10. "Firearms Training for Jihad in America," Violence Policy Center report, online at http://www.vpc.org/studies/jihad.htm.

11. Ibid.

12. Ibid.

13. Quoted from anonymous pamphlet, *How Can I Train Myself for Jihad*, as cited in "Firearms Training for Jihad in America," Violence Policy Center report, online at: http://www.vpc.org/studies/jihad.htm.

14. A. S. Moussaoui, *Zacarias Moussaoui: The Making of a Terrorist* (London: Serpents Tail, 2003), as cited in Michael Taarnby, "Recruitment of Islamist Terrorists in Europe: Trends and Perspectives," Research Report funded by the Danish Ministry of Justice, 14 January 2005, p. 10.

15. Rohan Gunaratna, *Inside Al Qaeda* (New York: Columbia University Press, 2002); Peter L. Bergen, *Holy War, Inc.: Inside the Secret World of Osama bin Laden* (New York: Simon and Schuster, 2001); Marc Sageman, *Understanding Terror Networks* (Philadelphia: University of Pennsylvania Press, 2004); Gilles Kepel, *Jihad: The Trail of Political Islam*, translated by Anthony F. Roberts (Cambridge, MA: Harvard University Press, 2002); and Anonymous, *Through our Enemies' Eyes: Osama bin Laden, Radical Islam, and the Future of America* (Washington, DC: Brassey's, Inc., 2002).

16. "IDF Action in Syria," Israel News Agency, 5 October 2003, available online at http://www.israelnewsagency.com.

17. Boaz Ganor, "Libya and Terrorism," Survey of Arab Affairs: A Periodic Supplement to Jerusalem Letter/Viewpoints 28 (1 June 1992), available online at http://www.ict.org.il/articles/article3.htm.

18. For more on these, please see the chapter by Kumar Ramakrishna in this volume.

19. Maria Ressa, *The Seeds of Terror: An Eyewitness Account of Al-Qaeda's Newest Center of Operations in Southeast Asia* (New York: Free Press, 2003), pp. 133–35.

20. H. H. Tucker, "The IRA in Eire," in Foreign and Commonwealth Office: Republic of Ireland Department: Registered Files (WL Series) 1972–1974, FCO 87–3: British National Archives (1972); see also Brian A. Jackson, "Training for Urban Resistance," in this volume.

21. "French Police Say They Found ETA Training Camp," *Euskal Herreria Journal*, 15 February 2003, online at http://members.freespeech.org/ehj/news/n_conpol_chro01feb.html.

22. Major David E. Smith USMC, "The Training of Terrorist Organizations," CSC Report, 1995, p. 25, available online at http://www.globalsecurity.org/military/report/1995/SDE.htm; Thomas Bedford and Frank Jones, *Sendero Luminoso: Origins, Outlooks and Implications* (Monterey, CA: Naval Postgraduate School, 1986), p. 53.

23. See the chapter by James Aho in Volume 1 of this publication.

24. For example, see Tony Geraghty, *The Irish War: The Hidden Conflict Between the IRA and British Intelligence* (Baltimore, MD: The Johns Hopkins University Press, 2000), p. xxxi.

25. See J. Bowyer Bell, *The IRA, 1968–2000: Analysis of a Secret Army* (London: Frank Cass, 2000); see also David E. Smith, "The Training of Terrorist Organizations."

26. See www.specialforce.net (last accessed 13 November 2004).

27. See Madeleine Gruen's chapter in Volume I of this publication.

28. For example, see Albert Bandura, "Mechanisms of Moral Disengagement," in *Origins of Terrorism: Psychologies, Ideologies, Theologies, States of Mind*, edited by Walter Reich (Baltimore: Woodrow Wilson Center Press, 1998), pp. 161–91; also please see the chapter by Albert Bandura in this volume.

29. For example, see Rex A. Hudson, *Who Becomes a Terrorist and Why: The 1999 Government Report on Profiling Terrorists* (Guilford, CT: The Lyons Press, 2001); and Robert A. Pape, "The Strategic Logic of Suicide Terrorism," *American Political Science Review* 97, no. 3 (August 2003): 343–61.

30. See Ehud Sprinzak, "Fundamentalism, Terrorism, and Democracy: The Case of the Gush Emunim Underground" (paper presented at the Woodrow Wilson Center, Washington, DC, September 1986); Ehud Sprinzak, "The Psychopolitical Formation of Extreme Left Terrorism in a Democracy: The Case of the Weathermen," in *Origins of Terrorism: Psychologies, Ideologies, Theologies, States of Mind*, edited by Walter Reich (Baltimore: Woodrow Wilson Center Press, 1998), pp. 65–85; and Ariel Merrari, "The Readiness to Kill and Die: Suicidal Terrorism in the Middle East," in *Origins of Terrorism: Psychologies, Ideologies, Theologies, State of Mind*, edited by Walter Reich (Baltimore: Woodrow Wilson International Center Press, 1990).

31. Albert Bandura, 1998; also see the chapter by Albert Bandura in this volume.

32. Ibid.

33. Yumi Wijers-Hasegawa, "Aum Chemist Sentenced to Hang," *Japan Times*, 31 January 2004.

34. Albert Bandura, "Mechanisms"; also see the chapter by Albert Bandura in this volume.

35. Jerrold M. Post, "Terrorist Psycho-logic: Terrorist Behavior as a Product of Psychological Forces," in *Origins of Terrorism: Psychologies, Ideologies, Theolo-*

gies, States of Mind, edited by Walter Reich (Baltimore: Woodrow Wilson Center Press, 1998), pp. 25–40.

36. Ibid.

37. For examples, see Gavin Cameron, *Nuclear Terrorism: A Threat Assessment for the 21st Century* (New York: St. Martin's Press, 1999); and Adam Dolnik, "Die and Let Die: Exploring the Links between Suicide Terrorism and Terrorist Use of Chemical, Biological, Radiological, and Nuclear Weapons," *Studies in Conflict and Terrorism* 26, no. 1 (January–February 2003): 17–35.

38. See Marc Galanter, *Cults: Faith, Healing and Coercion*, 2nd edition (New York: Oxford University Press, 1999), pp. 18–33; also see the chapter by Marc Galanter and James Forest in this volume.

39. Dr. Margaret Singer, available online at http://www.factnet.org/coercive mindcontrol.html.

40. Ibid.

41. Ibid.; also see Marc Galanter, *Cults: Faith*.

Chapter 2: "When Hatred Is Bred in the Bone"

1. See for example, Martha Crenshaw, "The Psychology of Terrorism: An Agenda for the 21st Century," *Political Psychology 21* (2000): 405–20; and Clark McCauley and Mary D. Segal, "Terrorist Individuals and Terrorist Groups: The Normal Psychology of Extreme Behavior," in *Terrorism*, edited by Jo Groebel and Jeffrey H. Goldstein (Seville, Spain: Publicaciones de la Universidad de Sevilla [Publications of the University of Seville], 1989), pp. 39–64.

2. The interview material is reported in detail in Jerrold Post, Ehud Sprinzak, and Laurita Denny, "Terrorists in Their Own Words: Interviews with 34 Incarcerated Middle East Terrorist," *Terrorism and Political Violence*, Spring 2003.

3. Muhammed Hafez, *Rationality, Culture and Structure in the Making of Suicide Bombers: A Preliminary Theoretical Synthesis and Illustrative Case Study* (Washington, DC: U.S. Institute of Peace).

4. Ariel Merari, personal communication, November 2003.

5. In the trial during the spring and summer of 2001 in federal court in New York of the al Qaeda bombers of the U.S. embassies in Tanzania and Nairobi, I served as expert witness during the death penalty phase and had the opportunity of spending some 17 hours with Kalfan Khamis Muhammed.

6. For more on al Qaeda's documents, training manuals, and other ideological documents, please see the chapters in Volume 1 by James Forest, Madeleine Gruen, and the chapters in this volume by James Forest, Martha Brill Olcott, and Bakhliyan Babajanov.

7. In 1997, I had the opportunity and challenge of assisting the U.S. Department of Justice as an expert on terrorist psychology at this trial. Portions of the discussion in this section are drawn from Jerrold Post, "Murder in a Political Context: Portrait of an Abu Nidal Terrorist," *Bulletin of the American Academy of Psychiatry and the Law* (Spring 2000).

8. This generational matrix was first presented in "Notes on a Psychodynamic Theory of Terrorist Behavior," *Terrorism: An International Journal* 7, no. 3 (1984): 241–56.

9. Jerrold Post, "Killing in the Name of God: Osama bin Laden and Radical Islam," *Counterproliferation Papers, Future Warfare Series* no. 17 (November 2002), Air University Maxwell Air Force Base, Alabama; a version of this analysis of bin Laden's personality can also be found in the first chapter of Jerrold Post, *Leaders and Their Followers in a Dangerous World: The Psychology of Political Behavior* (Cornell University Press, 2004).

10. Clark McCauley and Mary D. Segal, "Terrorist Individuals and Terrorist Groups," pp. 39–64.

11. A detailed analysis of the role of strategic information operations in countering terrorism is found in J. Post, "Psychological Operations: Principal Weapon in Countering Terrorism," *Joint Force Quarterly* (Fall 2004).

Chapter 3: Training for Terrorism

1. Some sections of this chapter include revised, updated, and expanded material from Albert Bandura, "Role of Mechanisms of Selective Moral Disengagement in Terrorism and Counterterrorism," in *Understanding Terrorism*, edited by Fathali M. Moghaddam and Anthony J. Marsella (Washington, DC: American Psychological Association), pp. 121–50. Copyright © 2004 by the American Psychological Association. Adapted with permission.

2. Albert Bandura, *Social Foundations of Thought and Action: A Social Cognitive Theory* (Englewood Cliffs, NJ: Prentice-Hall, 1986).

3. M. Cherif Bassiouni, "Terrorism, Law Enforcement, and the Mass Media: Perspectives, Problems, Proposals," *The Journal of Criminal Law & Criminology* 72 (1981): 1–51.

4. Albert Bandura, "Mechanisms of Moral Disengagement," in *Origins of Terrorism: Psychologies, Ideologies, Theologies, States of Mind*, edited by Walter Reich (Baltimore, MD: Woodrow Wilson Center Press, 1990), pp. 161–91.

5. Tom Skeyhill, ed., *Sergeant York: His Own Life Story and War Diary* (Garden City, NY: Doubleday, Doran, 1928).

6. Martin Kramer, "The Moral Logic of Hizballah," in *Origins of Terrorism: Psychologies, Ideologies, Theologies, States of Mind*, edited by Walter Reich (Baltimore, MD: Woodrow Wilson Center Press, 1990), pp. 131–57; David C. Rapoport and Yonah Alexander, eds., *The Morality of Terrorism: Religious and Secular Justification* (Elmsford, NY: Pergamon Press, 1982); and Walter Reich, ed., *Origins of Terrorism: Psychologies, Ideologies, Theologies, States of Mind* (Baltimore, MD: Woodrow Wilson Center Press, 1990).

7. See Voltaire quotations online at http://www.quotationspage.com/quote/26816.html.

8. Pope Urban the II's speech calling for the First Crusade, online at http://www.pleasanthill.k12.or.us/Schools/Junior/morton2000/Pat/Pope2.html.

9. Ibid.

10. Julian Borger, "Rhetoric to Arouse the Islamic World," *The Guardian*, 8 October 2001, online at http://www.guardian.co.uk/Print/0,3858,4272496,00.html; and Lynn Ludlow, "Osama Speaks: Inside the Mind of a Terrorist," *San Francisco Chronicle*, 7 October 2001, p. D1.

11. Ibid.

12. Ibid.

13. Ibid.

14. *Los Angeles Times*, 21 November 1995, p. 3.

15. See Paul Hill website, http://www.armyofgod.com/PHillonepage.html.

16. Sandra J. Ball-Rokeach, "The Legitimation of Violence," in *Collective Violence*, edited by J. F. Short Jr. and M. E. Wolfgang (Chicago: Aldine-Atherton, 1972), pp. 100–11. For more recent analysis on this topic, please see the chapters by Brigitte Nacos, Madeleine Gruen and James F. Forest in Volume 1.

17. Muhammed El-Nawawy and Adel Iskandar, *Al-Jazeera: How the Free Arab News Network Scooped the World and Changed the Middle East* (Cambridge, MA: Westview Press, 2002).

18. For more on the use of the Internet by terrorists, please see the chapters by Madeleine Gruen and Gabriel Weimann in Volume 1 of this publication and the chapter by James Forest in this volume.

19. William D. Lutz, "Language, Appearance, and Reality: Doublespeak in 1984," in *The Legacy of Language: A Tribute to Charlton Laird*, edited by P. C. Boardman (Reno, NV: University of Nevada Press, 1987), pp. 103–19.

20. Edward Diener, et al., "Effects of Altered Responsibility, Cognitive Set, and Modeling on Physical Aggression and Deindividuation," *Journal of Personality and Social Psychology* 31 (1975): 328–37.

21. Richard Gambino, "Watergate Lingo: A Language of Non-Responsibility," *Freedom at Issue* no. 22 (November–December 1973): 7–9.

22. Dwight Bolinger, "Intonation and Its Parts," *Language* 58 (1982): 505–33.

23. Richard Gambino, "Watergate Lingo," pp. 15–17.

24. Edward Diener, "Deindividuation: Causes and Consequences," *Social Behavior and Personality* 5 (1977); and Stanley Milgram, *Obedience to Authority: An Experimental View* (New York: Harper and Row, 1974).

25. Harvey A. Tilker, "Socially Responsible Behavior as a Function of Observer Responsibility and Victim Feedback," *Journal of Personality and Social Psychology* 14 (1970): 95–100.

26. Burton C. Andrus, *The Infamous of Nuremberg* (London: Fravin, 1969).

27. Herbert C. Kelman, "Violence without Moral Restraint: Reflections on the Dehumanization of Victims and Victimizers," *Journal of Social Issues* 29 (1973): 25–61.

28. Stanley Milgram, *Obedience to Authority: An Experimental View* (New York: Harper and Row, 1974).

29. Martin Kramer, "Moral Logic."

30. Wim H. J. Meeus and Quinten A. W. Raaijmakers, "Administrative Obedi-

ence: Carrying out Orders to Use Psychological-Administrative Violence," *European Journal of Social Psychology* 16 (1986): 311–24; Stanley Milgram, 1974; and P. C. Powers and Russell G. Geen, "Effects of the Behavior and the Perceived Arousal of a Model on Instrumental Aggression," *Journal of Personality and Social Psychology* 23 (1972): 175–83.

31. Stanley Milgram, *Obedience to Authority*; Harvey A. Tilker, "Socially Responsible Behavior."

32. David M. Mantell and R. Panzarella, "Obedience and Responsibility," *The British Journal of Social and Clinical Psychology* 15 (1976): 239–46.

33. Michael Ignatieff, "The Terrorist as Auteur," *New York Times Magazine*, 14 November 2004, p. 50.

34. Herbert C. Kelman, "Violence without Moral Restraint."

35. Albert Bandura, et al., "Disinhibition of Aggression through Diffusion of Responsibility and Dehumanization of Victims," *Journal of Research in Personality* 9 (1975): 253–69; Edward Diener, "Deindividuation: Causes and Consequences," *Social Behavior and Personality* 5 (1977): 143–56; and Phil G. Zimbardo, "The Human Choice: Individuation, Reason, and Order Versus Deindividuation, Impulse and Chaos," in *Nebraska Symposium on Motivation*, edited by William J. Arnold and David Levine, pp. 237–309 (Lincoln: University of Nebraska Press, 1969).

36. Albert Bandura, "Social Cognitive Theory of Social Referencing," in *Social Referencing and the Social Construction of Reality in Infancy*, edited by Saul Feinman (New York: Plenum, 1992), pp. 175–208.

37. Stanley Milgram, *Obedience to Authority*.

38. Harvey A. Tilker, "Socially Responsible Behavior."

39. Wesley Kilham and Leon Mann, "Level of Destructive Obedience as a Function of Transmitter and Executant Roles in the Milgram Obedience Paradigm," *Journal of Personality and Social Psychology* 29 (1974): 696–702.

40. Bernard Weiner, *An Attributional Theory of Motivation and Emotion* (New York: Springer-Verlag, 1986).

41. Bandura, *Social Foundations*.

42. A full account of this event is provided on the BBC News website at http://news.bbc.co.uk/onthisday/hi/dates/stories/november/8/newsid_515000/2515 113.stm.

43. Melvin J. Lerner and Dale T. Miller, "Just World Research and the Attribution Process: Looking Back and Ahead," *Psychological Bulletin* 85 (1978): 1030–51.

44. Albert Bandura, "Mechanisms of Moral Disengagement," 1990.

45. Mika Haritos-Fatouros, *The Psychological Origins of Institutionalized Torture* (London: Routledge, 2002).

46. Albert Bandura, et al., "Disinhibition of Aggression."

47. Albert Bandura, "Moral Disengagement."

48. Albert Bandura, "The Psychology of Chance Encounters and Life Paths," *American Psychologist* 37 (1982): 747–55.

49. Albert Bandura, *Social Foundations*; Linda Franks and Tom Powers, "Pro-

file of a Terrorist," *Palo Alto Times*, 17 September 1970, pp. 26–28; and Mika Haritos-Fatouros, *Institutionalized Torture*.

50. Albert Bandura, et al., "Disinhibitions of Aggression."

51. Ehud Sprinzak, "Fundamentalism, Terrorism, and Democracy: The Case of the Gush Emunim Underground" (paper presented at the Woodrow Wilson Center, Washington, DC, September 1986); and Ehud Sprinzak, "The Psychopolitical Formation of Extreme Left Terrorism in a Democracy: The Case of the Weathermen," in *Origins of Terrorism: Psychologies, Ideologies, Theologies, States of Mind*, edited by Walter Reich (Baltimore, MD: Woodrow Wilson Center Press, 1990), pp. 65–85.

52. Albert Bandura, *Aggression: A Social Learning Analysis* (Englewood Cliffs, NJ: Prentice-Hall, 1973); and Seymour M. Lipset, "University Students and Politics in Underdeveloped Countries," *Comparative Education Review* 10 (1966): 32–62.

53. Joseph Lelyveld, "All Suicide Bombers are Not Alike," *New York Times Magazine*, 28 October 2001, p. 49.

54. Amy Waldman, "Masters of Suicide Bombing: Tamil Guerrillas of Sri Lanka," *New York Times*, 14 January 2003, p. A1.

Chapter 4: Cults, Charismatic Groups, and Social Systems

1. Portions of this chapter draw from Marc Galanter, *Cults: Faith, Healing and Coercion*, 2nd edition (New York: Oxford University Press, 1999). However, it is not a reproduction of any previously published article or chapter.

2. Sigmund Freud, "Group Psychology and the Analysis of the Ego," in *The Standard Edition of the Complete Psychological Works of Sigmund Freud*, Vol. 18, edited by James Strachey (London: Hogarth, 1955[1921]), p. 16.

3. For example, see the description of Hizb-ut-Tahir's youth recruitment practices (using music, video games, fellowship and religion) in Madeleine Gruen's chapter in Volume 1 of this publication.

4. Reference should be made here to George Herbert Mead, who showed that mind and self are generated in a social process. He posited a "generalized other," namely the organized community or social group that gives the individual a unity of self. See George Herbert Mead, *Mind, Self and Society from the Standpoint of a Social Behaviorist* (Chicago: University of Chicago Press, 1962).

5. Dorwin Cartwright and Alvin Zander, eds. *Group Dynamics: Research and Theory* (Evanston, IL: Row, Peterson, 1962), p. 74.

6. Murray Bowen, *Family Therapy in Clinical Practice* (New York: Jason Aronson, 1978); see also, Lyman Wynne et al., "Pseudomutuality in the Family Relations of Schizophrenics," *Psychiatry* 21 (1958): 205–22.

7. David Reiss, "Varieties of Consensual Experience," *Family Process* 10 (1971): 1–35.

8. A particularly salient example of this described in a study of the Divine Light Mission, a charismatic religious sect founded in 1960 by Sri Hans Ji Maharaj. See Marc Galanter, *Cults: Faith*, pp. 18–33.

9. Sigmund Freud, "Group Psychology," p. 16.

10. For example, this appears to be the case with Abu Musab al-Zarqawi's *Al-Tawhid Wa'al-Jihad* terrorist group in Iraq, as reported in a number of *New York Times* stories throughout 2003 and 2004.

11. James G. Miller, "Living Systems. Basic Concepts," *Behavioral Science* 10 (1965): 193–237.

12. Sigmund Freud, "Group Psychology," p. 16.

13. For example, see the chapter by Evan Kohlman in this volume.

14. For more on charismatic leaders in cult organizations, please see the chapter by Arthur Deikman in this volume.

15. Andrew Pollack, "Japanese Police Find Body of a Lawyer Believed Killed by Cult," *New York Times*, 7 September 1995, p. A15.

16. See U.S. Congress, Senate, Government Affairs Permanent Subcommittee on Investigations, "A Case Study of Aum Shinrikyō," 31 October 1995 Staff Statement, online at http://www.fas.org/irp/congress/1995_rpt/aum/part03.htm; also reported in the *New York Times*, 23 March 1995, p. A14.

17. Murray Sayle, "The Buddha Bites Back," Japan Policy Research Institute Working Paper No. 32 (April 1997), online at http://www.jpri.org/publications/workingpapers/wp32.html, also reported in *New York Times*, 17 May 1995, p. 8.

18. As quoted in the *New York Times*, 4 April 1995, p. 4.

19. Leon Festinger, Henry Riecken, and Stanley Schacter, *When Prophecy Fails* (Minneapolis: University of Minnesota Press, 1956); see also Mike Barkun's chapter in Volume 3 of this publication.

20. Marc Galanter, *Cults: Faith*, pp. 18–33.

21. Sigmund Freud, "Group Psychology," p. 16.

Chapter 5: Psychological Power

1. This chapter draws on material published in Arthur J. Deikman, *Them and Us: Cult Thinking and the Terrorist Threat* (Berkeley, CA: Bay Tree Publications, 2003). It is not a reproduction of any chapter.

2. Margaret Rioch, "All We Like Sheep," in *Group Relations Reader*, edited by Arthur D. Colman and W. Harold Bexton (Sausalito, CA: GREX, 1975), pp. 159–57.

3. Investigative Poetry Group, *The Party: A Chronological Perspective on a Confrontation at a Buddhist Seminary* (Woodstock, NY: Poetry, Crime and Culture Press, 1977), p. 55.

4. Thomas Peters and Robert Waterman Jr., *In Search of Excellence: Lessons from Americas Best-Run Corporations* (New York: Warner Books, 1982), p. 84.

5. In his 1995 bestselling book *The Pursuit of Wow! Every Person's Guide to Topsy-Turvy Times* (London: Macmillan), Tom Peters quotes the industrial psychologist David C. McClelland in paraphrasing the members of a charismatic leader's audience as being "strengthened and uplifted by the experience; they felt more powerful, rather than less powerful or submissive." For more on this topic,

please see David C. McClelland, *Human Motivation* (Cambridge: Cambridge University Press, 1986); see also Mark Greer, "The Science of Savoir Faire," APA Monitor 36, no. 1 (January 2005): p. 28, online at http://www.apa.org/monitor/jan05/savoir.html.

6. For more on cult behavior, please see the chapter by Galanter and Forest in this volume.

7. Harold Geneen (with A. Moscow), *Managing* (Garden City, NY: Doubleday, 1984), p. 144.

8. Peters and Waterman, *In Search of Excellence*, p. 68.

9. Cornelle Meier, interview with the author, 11 June 1986.

10. Rakesh Khurana, *Searching for a Corporate Savior: The Irrational Quest for Charismatic CEOs* (Princeton University Press, 2002).

11. Craig Lampert, "The Cult of the Charismatic CEO," *Harvard Magazine* 105, no. 1 (September/October 2002).

12. Quoted in Flo Conway and Jim Siegelman, *Holy Terror: The Fundamentalist War on America's Freedoms in Religion, Politics, and Our Private Lives* (New York: Dell, 1982), p. 283.

13. James Kavanaugh, *A Modern Priest Looks At His Outdated Church* (New York: Trident Press, 1967), p. 178.

14. Samuel Johnson, "Letter to Lord Chesterfield," 7 April 1775, as cited in James Boswell's *The Life of Johnson*. See James L. Clifford, ed., *Twentieth Century Interpretations of Boswell's Life of Johnson: A Collection of Critical Essays* (Englewood Cliffs, NJ: Prentice-Hall, 1970), p. 615.

15. Rohan Gunaratna, *Inside Al Qaeda: Global Network of Terror* (New York: Columbia University Press, 2002), p.7.

16. Mark Juergensmeyer, *Terror in the Mind of God: the Global Rise of Religious Violence* (Berkeley: University of California Press, 2002), p. 155.

17. Ibid.

18. In this passage, Ruthven is citing Paul Pillar of the Brookings Institute. See Malise Ruthven, *A Fury for God: The Islamic Attack On America* (London: Granta Books, 2003).

19. Daniel Pipes, *Militant Islam Reaches America* (New York: W. W. Norton, 2002), p. 56.

20. Ibid.

21. See Daniel Pipes, "It's Not the Economy, Stupid: What the West Needs to Know about the Rise of Radical Islam," *The Washington Post*, 2 July 1995.

Chapter 6: Teaching Terrorism

1. The following story is explored in great detail in several articles of the Guardian Unlimited website (http://www.guardian.co.uk/bombs), including Jeevan Vasagar, "Deadly Net Terror Websites Easy to Access" (1 July 2000); Nick Hopkins and Sarah Hall, "David Copeland: A Quiet Introvert, Obsessed with Hitler and Bombs" (30 June 2000); and "Nailbomber 'Used Net to Build Bombs'" (5 June 2000).

2. For example, see the Introduction and several chapters in the second and third sections of Volume I.

3. Bruce Hoffman, *Inside Terrorism* (New York: Columbia University Press, 1998), p. 203.

4. Phil Hirschkorn, "Trials Expose Terrorist Training Camps," CNN New York Bureau, 18 July 2001, available online at http://www.cnn.com.

5. Ibid.

6. Debra J. Blanke and Gina M. Wekke, "Distance Education," in J. Forest and K. Kinser, *Higher Education in the United States* (Santa Barbara, CA: ABC-CLIO Press, 2002).

7. See Christopher Dobson and Ronald Payne, *The Terrorists, Their Weapons, Leaders, and Tactics* (New York: Facts on File Publications, 1982), pp. 12–13.

8. See Major David E. Smith USMC, "The Training of Terrorist Organizations," CSC Report, 1995, p. 6, available online at http://www.globalsecurity.org/military/report/1995/SDE.htm.

9. Please see the chapter by Brian Jackson in this volume.

10. See Ibrahim M. Abu-Rabi, *Intellectual Origins of Islamic Resurgence in the Modern Arab World* (Albany: State University of New York Press, 1996).

11. See Anonymous, *Through Our Enemy's Eyes* (Washington, DC: Brasseys, Inc., 2003), p. 274.

12. See Paul Berman, "Al Qaeda's Philosopher: How an Egyptian Islamist Invented the Terrorist Jihad from his Jail Cell," *New York Times Magazine*, 23 March 2003.

13. See the chapter by Brigitte Nacos in Volume 1 of this publication.

14. Please see the chapters by Brigitte Nacos and James Aho in Volume I.

15. For an analysis of this publication, see Stephen Ulph, "A New Journal for Algerian Jihad," *Terrorism Monitor* 2, no. 15 (29 July 2004).

16. Intel report, 2003.

17. Gabriel Weimann, *WWW.Terror.Net—How Modern Terrorism Uses the Internet*, Special Report 116 (United States Institute of Peace, 2004), p. 9, available online at http://www.usip.org.

18. Bruce Hoffman, *Inside Terrorism*, p. 203.

19. See "Leaderless Resistance Strategy Gains Momentum Among Militant White Supremacists" and "Aryan National Congress Focuses on Revolutionary Tactics," *Klanwatch Intelligence Report* no. 74, August 1994, pp. 6–9; also see "Tom Metzger/White Aryan Resistance," on the "Extremism in America" Anti-Defamation League website at http://www.adl.org.

20. For an analysis of this publication, please see the chapter on Christian Militia groups by Combs et al. in this volume. The description of the manual provided in this paragraph draws from this chapter.

21. Ibid.

22. See National Commission on Terrorist Attacks Upon the United States (the 9/11 Commission Report), *The 9/11 Commission Report* (New York: W. W. Norton, 2004), p. 55; also available online at http://www.gpoaccess.gov/911.

23. See Gabriel Weimann, 2005, "Virtual Training Camps," in *Teaching Terror: Knowledge Transfer in the Terrorist World*, edited by James Forest (forthcoming); see also Gabriel Weimann, *WWW.Terror.Net*.

24. Gabriel Weimann, *WWW.Terror.Net*; see also Timothy L. Thomas, "Al Qaeda and the Internet: The Danger of Cyberplanning," *Parameters* (Spring 2003): 115.

25. For more on this topic, please see the chapter by Madeleine Gruen in Volume I of this publication.

26. Ibid.

27. Ibid.; also Gabriel Weimann, "Virtual Training Camps."

28. See www.specialforce.net (last accessed 13 November 2004).

29. At http://www.worldnetdaily.com/news/article.asp?ARTICLE_ID=31323.

30. See the chapter by Madeleine Gruen in Volume I of this publication.

31. For more on this topic, please see the chapter by Brigitte Nacos in Volume I of this publication. See also Cindy Combs, 2005, "The Media as a Showcase for Terrorism," in *Teaching Terror: Knowledge Transfer in the Terrorist World*, edited by James Forest (Boulder, CO: Rowman & Littlefield).

32. Combs.

33. Ibid.

34. Barry Collin, "The Future of Cyberterrorism," *Crime and Justice International* (March 1997): 15–18, cited in Dorothy Denning, "Activism, Hacktivism and Cyberterrorism," in *Networks and Netwars: The Future of Terror, Crime and Militancy*, edited by John Arquilla and David Ronfeldt (Santa Monica: RAND, 1999), p. 281.

35. Timothy L. Thomas, "Al Qaeda and the Internet," p. 112.

36. Mark M. Pollitt, "Cyberterrorism: Fact or Fancy?" *Proceedings of the 20th National Information Systems Security Conference* (October 1997): 285–89, cited in Dorothy Denning, 1999, "Activism, Hacktivism and Cyberterrorism," p. 281.

37. U.S., The White House, *Critical Foundations: Protecting America's Infrastructures*, The Report of the Presidential Commission on Critical Infrastructure Protection (October 1997). Report summary available online at http://www.pccip.org.

38. For more on computer attacking techniques, see Ed Skoudis, *Counter Hack: A Step-by-Step Guide to Computer Attacks and Effective Defenses* (Upper Saddle River, NJ: Prentice Hall, 2002), particularly chapters 7–10; also see David Mandeville, "Hackers, Crackers, and Trojan Horses: A Primer," on the CNN Interactive website (29 March 1999), at http://www.cnn.com/TECH/specials/hacker/primer

39. David Mandeville, "Hackers, Crackers, and Trojan Horses."

40. Dorothy Denning, "Activism, Hacktivism and Cyberterrorism," p. 269.

41. These descriptions are courtesy of David Mandeville, "Hackers, Crackers, and Trojan Horses."

42. U.S. Congress, House, Select Committee on Homeland Security, Subcommittee on Cybersecurity, Science and Research & Development Statement by Daniel G. Wolf, Director of Information Assurance, NSA, 22 July 2003, p. 10

43. John Christensen, "Bracing for Guerilla Warfare in Cyberspace," on the CNN Interactive website (6 April 1999), at http://www.cnn.com/TECH/specials/hackers/cyberterror.

44. Ibid.

45. Steven A. Hildreth, *Cyberwarfare*, a CRS Report for Congress (Washington, DC: Library of Congress, Congressional Research Service, 19 June 2001), p. 15.

46. Ibid., p. 4.

47. See Frank Cilluffo and Paul Byron Pattak, 2004, "Cyber Threats: Ten Issues to Consider," in Russell Howard, Joanne Moore, and James Forest, eds., *Homeland Security and Terrorism* (Guilford, CT: McGraw-Hill, 2005); see also John Christensen, "Bracing for Guerilla Warfare in Cyberspace."

48. John Christensen, "Bracing for Guerilla Warfare in Cyberspace."

49. Jon Swartz, "Cyberterror Impact, Defense under Scrutiny," *USA Today*, 8 August 2004, available online at http://www.usatoday.com/tech/news/2004-08-02-cyber-terror_x.htm.

50. U.S., The White House, *National Strategy for Security Cyberspace*, U.S. GPO, 2002; available online at http://www.whitehouse.gov.

51. For more on this, see Dorothy Denning, "Activism, Hacktivism and Cyber terrorism."

52. A useful reference for steganography can be found at http://www.jjtc.com/Steganography/toolmatrix.htm.

53. U.S. Congress, Senate, Judiciary Subcommittee on Technology, Terrorism and Government Information, 24 February 1998, testimony by Clark L. Staten, cited in Dorothy Denning, "Activism, Hacktivism and Cyberterrorism."

54. See the chapter by Gabriel Weimann in Volume 1 of this publication; The Sheik's *fatwa* was translated and published online at http://www.arabianews.org/english/article.cfm?qid=19&sid=6printme=1 (last accessed August 2004).

55. Timothy L. Thomas, "Al Qaeda and the Internet," p. 118.

56. Ibid., p. 120; see also Yossi Melman, "Virtual Soldiers in a Holy War," *Ha'aretz*, 17 September 2002, http://www.haaretz.com; and Gabriel Weimann, *WWW.terror.net*, p. 11.

57. Patrick S. Tibbetts, "Terrorist Use of the Internet and Related Information Technologies," unpublished paper, School of Advanced Military Studies, Fort Leavenworth, Kansas (June 2002): 7–9, cited in Timothy L. Thomas, "Al Qaeda and the Internet," p. 118.

58. "Citing Al Qaeda Manual, Rumsfeld Re-Emphasizes Web Security," *InsideDefense.com*, http://www.insidedefense.com, 15 January 2003, cited in Timothy L. Thomas, "Al Qaeda and the Internet," p. 118.

Chapter 7: Mediated Terror

1. "Bin Laden Speaks to the American People," *The Washington Post*, 30 October 2004, p. 16.

2. According to "Election Results," CNN.com, retrieved 20 November 2004,

32 percent of Americans who voted in the presidential election believed that the bin Laden tape was "very important," 24 percent "somewhat important," 20 percent "not too important," and 24 percent "not at all important."

3. Daniel J. Watkin, "The Reach of War: Reaction," *New York Times*, 24 June 2004, p. A11.

4. "Purported Bin Laden Tape Endorses Al-Zarqawi," CNN.com, 27 December 2004, accessed 3 January 2005. Bin Laden's tape was first aired on the Arablanguage al-Jazeera television network.

5. *Webster's Ninth New Collegiate Dictionary* (Springfield, MA: Merriam-Webster Inc., 1989), p. 942.

6. Anthony Pratkanis and Elliot Aronson, *Age of Propaganda: The Everyday Use and Abuse of Persuasion* (New York: W. H. Freeman and Company, 1999), p. 9.

7. Ibid., p. 165.

8. Ibid., p. 216.

9. Thomas L. Friedman, "No Mere Terrorist," *New York Times*, 24 March 2002, sect. 4, p. 15.

10. Hamza Hendawi, "Terror Manual Advises on Targets," http://story.news.yahoo.com/news?tmpl=story&u+/ap/20 . . . /afghan_spreading_terror_ (retrieved 11 February 2002).

11. For example, see Andrew Kohut, "Washington 2002: Attitude Adjustment—The 9/11 Effect is Starting to Fade," *Columbia Journalism Review* no. 5 (September–October 2002), online at http://www.cjr.org/issues/2002/5/wash-kohut.asp.

12. "Text: bin Laden statement," http://www.guardian.co.uk./waronterror/story/0,1361,565069,00.html (retrieved 7 April 2002).

13. The statement was posted at http://www.chumba.com/_gospel.htm.

14. "A Spiritual Awakening: Religion in the Media, Dec. 2000–Nov. 2001," study prepared by Douglas Gould & Co. for the Ford Foundation.

15. The quote was taken from the translation of a videotape, presumably made in mid-November 2001 in Afghanistan, available at http://www.washingtonpost.com/wp-srv/nation/specials/attacked/transcripts/binladentext_121301.html (retrieved 7 April 2002).

16. Brigitte L. Nacos, *Mass-Mediated Terrorism* (Lanham, MD: Rowman and Littlefield, 2002), p. 168.

17. For more on this, please see the chapter on Christian militia groups by Cindy Combs in this volume.

18. Lou Michel and Dan Herbeck, *American Terrorist: Timothy McVeigh & the Oklahoma City Bombing* (New York: Regan Books, 2001), p. 299.

19. Richard Bernstein, "Tape, Probably Bin Laden's, Offers Truce to Europe," *New York Times*, 16 April 2004, p. 3.

20. Ibid.

21. Craig Whitlock, "From Bin Laden, Different Style, Same Message," *New York Times*, 25 November 2004, p. A20.

22. Haig was quoted by Brigitte L. Nacos, *Terrorism and the Media* (New York: Columbia University Press, 1994), p. 67.

23. "Iraq Militant Group Posts Video of Mosul Attack," Reuters, 26 December 2004, online at http://www.alertnet.org/thenews/newsdesk/L26687828.htm.

24. Ibid.

25. Nivat is the author of a book titled *Chienne de Guerre: A Woman Reporter Behind the Lines of the War in Chechnya*. She was quoted in Serge Schmemann, "The Chechens' Holy War: How Global Is It?" *New York Times*, 27 October 2002, sect. 4, p. 3.

26. Gabriel Weimann and Conrad Winn, *The Theater of Terror: Mass Media and International Terrorism* (New York: Longman, 1994), pp. 217, 277.

27. Neil MacFarquhar, "Acting on Threat, Saudi Group Kills Captive American," *New York Times*, 19 June 2004, p. 1.

28. Edward Wong, "Video Shows Beheading of Kidnapped British Engineer," *New York Times*, 9 October 2004, p. 6.

29. Ibid.

Chapter 8: Training for Urban Resistance

1. John Horgan and Max Taylor, "The Provisional Irish Republican Army: Command and Functional Structure," *Terrorism and Political Violence* 9 (1997): 1–32.

2. See, for example, Edgar H. Schein, "Organizational Socialization and the Profession of Management," *MIT-Sloan Management Review* 30 (1988): 53–65; Theodore E. Long and Jeffery K. Hadden, "A Reconception of Socialization," *Sociological Theory* 3 (1985): 39–49.

3. C. McAnally, "I Watch as the I.R.A. Blow up a Spiked Border Road," document in Foreign Office: Western Department and Foreign and Commonwealth Office: Western European Department: Registered Files (R and WR Series) 1967–1974, FCO 33-1593/4: British National Archives.

4. Eamon Collins and Mick McGovern, *Killing Rage* (London: Granta Books, 1998), p. 66.

5. J. Bowyer Bell, *The Dynamics of the Armed Struggle* (London: Frank Cass, 1998), p. 137.

6. Eamon Collins and Mick McGovern, *Killing Rage*, p. 66.

7. C. McAnally, "I Watch."

8. Ibid.

9. "Five Days in an IRA Training Camp," *Iris*, November 1983, p. 43.

10. Shane O'Doherty, *The Volunteer: A Former IRA Man's True Story* (London: Fount, 1993), p. 83.

11. Tim Pat Coogan, *The IRA: A History* (Niwot, CO: Roberts Rinehart Publishers, 1993), p. 281.

12. Kevin Boyle and Tom Hadden, *Northern Ireland: The Choice* (London: Penguin Books, 1994), p. 72.

13. Maj. Gen. R. C. Ford, "The Campaign against the IRA: An Assessment of the Current Operational Situation," document in Foreign and Commonwealth Office:

Republic of Ireland Department: Registered Files (WL Series) 1972–1974, FCO 87-2: British National Archives (1972).

14. Tony Geraghty, *The Irish War: The Hidden Conflict Between the IRA and British Intelligence* (Baltimore, MD: The Johns Hopkins University Press, 2000), pp. 31–32.

15. J. Bowyer Bell, *The Secret Army: The IRA*, Revised 3rd ed. (Dublin, Ireland: Poolbeg, 1998), p. 392.

16. H. H. Tucker, "The IRA in Eire," document in Foreign and Commonwealth Office: Republic of Ireland Department: Registered Files (WL Series) 1972–1974, FCO 87-3: British National Archives (1972).

17. Sean O'Callaghan, *The Informer* (London: Corgi Books, 1999), p. 50.

18. C. McAnally, "I Watch."

19. Sean O'Callaghan, *The Informer*, p. 53.

20. "Five Days in an IRA Training Camp," p. 45.

21. Ibid., p. 41.

22. Sean O'Callaghan, *The Informer*, p. 55.

23. C. McAnally, "I Watch."

24. Sean O'Callaghan, *The Informer*, p. 55.

25. Eamon Collins and Mick McGovern, *Killing Rage*, p. 237.

26. "Vietnam Veterans Reported Training IRA Guerrillas," *The Washington Post*, 9 February 1973, p. 12.

27. Toby Harnden, *Bandit Country: The IRA and South Armagh* (London: Coronet Books, LIR, 2000), p. 333.

28. C. McAnally, "I Watch."

29. Tim Pat Coogan, *The IRA*, p. 369; and Eamon Collins and Mick McGovern, *Killing Rage*, p. 66.

30. "Five Days in an IRA Training Camp," p. 39.

31. Maj. Gen. R. C. Ford, "Campaign against the IRA."

32. J. M. Glover, "Northern Ireland Terrorist Trends," London: Ministry of Defense, British Government, 1978.

33. "Five Days in an IRA Training Camp," pp. 39–45.

34. H. H. Tucker, "The IRA in Eire."

35. Sean O'Callaghan, *The Informer*, p. 52.

36. Shane O'Doherty, *The Volunteer*, pp. 85–86.

37. C. McAnally, "I Watch."

38. Toby Harnden, *Bandit Country*, p. 53.

39. Sean O'Callaghan, *The Informer*, p. 151.

40. H. H. Tucker, "The IRA in Eire."

41. Author interviews with law enforcement and former security forces members familiar with the conflict, March 2004, identities withheld by request.

42. Shane O'Doherty, *The Volunteer*, p. 157.

43. Sean O'Callaghan, *The Informer*, pp. 77–78.

44. Toby Harnden, *Bandit Country*, p. 46.

45. Author interviews with law enforcement and former security forces members familiar with the conflict, March 2004, identities withheld by request.

46. Toby Harnden, *Bandit Country*, p. 233; Eamon Collins and Mick McGovern, *Killing Rage*, p. 257.

47. Sean O'Callaghan, *The Informer*, p. 59; Shane O'Doherty, *The Volunteer*, pp. 167–68.

48. Author interviews with law enforcement and former security forces members familiar with the conflict, March 2004, identities withheld by request.

49. H. H. Tucker, "The IRA in Eire."

50. Sean O'Callaghan, *The Informer*, p. 81.

51. Ibid., p. 86.

52. Ibid., pp. 81, 84–85.

53. Ibid., p. 82.

54. "Five Days in an IRA Training Camp," pp. 39–45.

55. Sean O'Callaghan, *The Informer*, p. 52.

56. Ibid., p. 51.

57. Ibid., pp. 144–45.

58. J. Bowyer Bell, *The Gun in Politics: An Analysis of Irish Political Conflict, 1916–1986* (New Brunswick, NJ: Transaction Books, 1987), pp. 53–54.

59. J. M. Glover, "Terrorist Trends."

60. Toby Harnden, *Bandit Country*, pp. 240–42; J. Bowyer Bell, *The Secret Army*, p. 570.

61. Modern training aids and systems, that allow users to build such skills without actual live-fire training, could limit the importance of this constraint for more contemporary groups.

62. J. M. Glover, "Terrorist Trends."

63. C.J.M. Drake, *Terrorists' Target Selection* (New York: St. Martin' Press, 1998), p. 76. Note: Prison time has also been highlighted as a route for transfer of knowledge inside PIRA—prisons acting as "universities of terror"—later in its career as well (Tony Geraghty, *Irish War*, p. xxxi). Although the potential impact of prison venues for transferring certain types of knowledge throughout these organizations is important, it is beyond the scope of the current chapter which focuses on specifically tactical and operational training concerns.

64. Tim Pat Coogan, *The IRA*, p. 330.

65. Sean O'Callaghan, *The Informer*, p. 196.

66. Sean O'Callaghan, *The Informer*, p. 196; Tony Geraghty, *Irish War*, p. 178; and C.J.M. Drake, *Terrorists' Target Selection*, p. 53.

67. H. H. Tucker, "The IRA in Eire."

68. Michael McKinley, "The International Dimensions of Irish Terrorism," in *Terrorism in Ireland*, edited by Y. Alexander and A. O'Day (London: Croomhelm, 1984), p. 17; and J. Bowyer Bell, *The Secret Army*, p. 438.

69. Michael McKinley, "International Dimensions," p. 17.

70. Toby Harnden, *Bandit Country*, pp. 82, 202, 240.

71. John Horgan and Max Taylor, "Provisional Irish Republican Army," p. 14.

72. J. M. Glover, "Terrorist Trends."

73. C.J.M. Drake, "The Provisional IRA: A Case Study," *Terrorism and Political Violence* 3 (1991): 43–60, p. 53.

74. Tim Pat Coogan, *The IRA*, p. 363.

75. Toby Harnden, *Bandit Country*, pp. 240–42; and C.J.M. Drake, "The Provisional IRA: A Case Study," p. 51.

76. Toby Harnden, *Bandit Country*, p. 371. Note: Later, in 2001, an expired chemical battery from a SA-7 missile was found in a field in County Tyrone, though no information is available about how it got there or why (Jane's Terrorism and Insurgency Centre, "JTIC Exclusive: Proliferation of MANPADS and the Threat to Civil Aviation" in Jane's Information Group, 4 February 2003 [Subscription Database], available from http://www.janes.com [cited 14 April 2004]).

77. John Horgan and Max Taylor, "Provisional Irish Republican Army," p. 15.

78. Ibid., pp. 15–17.

79. J. Bowyer Bell, "The Armed Struggle and Underground Intelligence: An Overview," *Studies in Conflict and Terrorism* 17 (1994): 134.

80. Tim Pat Coogan, *The IRA*, p. 413.

81. Ibid., p. 422.

82. Ibid., p. 430.

83. Tony Geraghty, *Irish War*, p. 86.

84. Ibid., p. 83.

85. Ibid., pp. 81–90.

86. Mark Urban, *Big Boys' Rules: The Secret Struggle Against the IRA* (London: Faber & Faber, 1992), p. 115.

87. J. M. Glover, *Terrorist Trends*; Toby Harnden, *Bandit Country*; and Eamon Collins and Mick McGovern, *Killing Rage*, 1998.

88. Toby Harnden, *Bandit Country*, p. 46.

89. Author interviews with law enforcement and former security forces members familiar with the conflict, March 2004, identities withheld by request.

Chapter 9: Teaching New Terrorist Recruits

1. Much of the prose of this chapter is reprinted from Martha Brill Olcott and Bakhtiyar Babajanov, "The Terrorist Notebooks," *Foreign Policy* (March–April 2003): 30–40.

2. For more on the Hizb ut-Tahrir, please see the chapter by Madeleine Gruen in Volume I of this publication.

3. Websites related to the Hizb ut-Tahrir include http://www.hizb-ut-tahrir.org, http://www.khilafah.com.pk, and http://www.hizbuttahrir.org.

Chapter 10: Learning to Die

1. Ariel Merari, "Readiness to Kill and Die: Suicide Terrorism in the Middle East," in *Origins of Terrorism: Psychologies, Ideologies, Theologies, State of Mind*, edited by Walter Reich (Washington, DC: Woodrow Wilson Center Press, 1998), p. 194.

2. Adam Dolnik, "Die and Let Die: Exploring Links between Suicide Terrorism

and Terrorist Use of Chemical, Biological, Radiological, and Nuclear Weapons," *Studies in Conflict and Terrorism* 26, no.1 (January–February 2003): 17–35.

3. Shaul Shay, "Suicide Terrorism in Lebanon," in *Countering Suicide Terrorism* (Herzliya: International Policy Institute for Counter-Terrorism, 2000), p. 130.

4. Rohan Gunaratna, "Suicide Terrorism in Sri Lanka and India," in *Countering Suicide Terrorism*, p. 102.

5. Ehud Sprinzak, "Rational Fanatics," *Foreign Policy* (October 2000).

6. Yael Shahar, *The al-Aqsa Martyrs Brigades: A Political Tool with an Edge* (Herzliya: International Policy Institute for Counter-Terrorism), available at www.ict.org.il (accessed on 26 March 2002).

7. Adam Dolnik, "Die and Let Die," pp. 17–35.

8. Reuven Paz, "The Islamic Legitimacy of Suicide Terrorism," in *Countering Suicide Terrorism*, p. 93.

9. Abu Ruqaiyah, *The Islamic Legitimacy of the "Martyrdom Operations,"* available at http://islam.org.au/articles/16/martyrdom.htm (accessed on 31 October 2001).

10. Dogu Ergil, "Suicide Terrorism in Turkey: The Worker's Party of Kurdistan," in *Countering Suicide Terrorism*, p. 120.

11. Kim Murphy, "Cult of Reluctant Killers," *Los Angeles Times*, 4 February 2004.

12. Yoram Schweitzer, *Suicide Bombings: The Ultimate Weapon?* (Herzliya: International Policy Institute for Counter-Terrorism), available at http://ict.org.il/articles/articledet.cfm?articleid=373 (accessed on 21 November 2001).

13. Mark Jurgensmeyer, *Terror in the Mind of God: The Global Rise of Religious Violence* (Berkeley: University of California Press, 2000), p. 78.

14. Ibid., p. 167.

15. Rohan Gunaratna, "Suicide Terrorism in Sri Lanka and India," in *Countering Suicide Terrorism*.

16. Ariel Merari, "Readiness to Kill and Die: Suicide Terrorism in the Middle East," in *Origins of Terrorism: Psychologies, Ideologies, Theologies, State of Mind*, edited by Walter Reich (Washington, DC: Woodrow Wilson Center Press, 1998).

17. Dogu Ergil, "Suicide Terrorism in Turkey: The Worker's Party of Kurdistan," in *Countering Suicide Terrorism*, p. 120.

18. Barbara Victor, *Army of Roses: Inside the World of Palestinian Women Suicide Bombers* (New York: Rodale Books, 2003).

19. Rohan Gunaratna, "Suicide Terrorism in Sri Lanka and India," in *Countering Suicide Terrorism*.

20. Kim Murphy, "Cult of Reluctant Killers," *Los Angeles Times*, 4 February 2004.

21. Rohan Gunaratna, "Suicide Terrorism: Emerging Global Patterns," *The Colombo Chronicle*, 17 September 2001.

22. Reuven Paz, "Suicide Terrorist Operations in Chechnya: An Escalation of the Islamist Struggle," *Middle East Intelligence Bulletin* 2, no. 6 (2000).

23. Barbara Victor, *Army of Roses: Inside the World of Palestinian Women Suicide Bombers* (New York: Rodale Books, 2003).

24. Yoram Schweitzer, *Suicide Bombings: The Ultimate Weapon?*

25. Edward F. Mickolus, *Transnational Terrorism: A Chronology of Events, 1968–1979* (Westport, CT: Greenwood Press, 1980), p. 593.

26. Adam Dolnik, "Die and Let Die," pp. 17–35.

27. Ibid.

Chapter 11: Terrorist Training Camps of al Qaeda

1. Rohan Gunaratna, "The Post Madrid Face of Al Qaeda," *The Washington Quarterly* 27, no. 3 (Summer 2004): 93. The figure 4000 members comes from al Qaeda detainee debriefs, including the FBI interrogation of Mohommad Mansour Jabarah, a Canadian operative of Kuwaiti-Iraqi origin now in U.S. custody since 2002.

2. Rohan Gunaratna, *Inside Al Qaeda: Global Network of Terror* (New York: Columbia University Press, 2002), p. 73.

3. Rohan Gunaratna and Peter Chalk, *Jane's Counter Terrorism* (Surrey: Jane's Information Group, 2002), p. 22.

4. Judith Miller, "Attacks Take Toll on bin Laden Camps," *New York Times*, 10 October 2001, available at http://rutlandherald.nybor.com/News/Story/35390.html.

5. "Al Qaeda Camp Scared Accused," *Toronto Star*, 20 September 2002; also see "Local Suspects Trained at 9/11 Hijackers' Camp," *The Buffalo News*, 15 September 2002; and "Lackawanna Suspect Takes Plea," *The Buffalo News*, 11 January 2003.

6. "European Terror Suspects Got Al Qaeda Training," CNN, 6 February 2003.

7. "Urgent Quest for Al-Qaeda Chemist's Ricin Stash," *The Straits Times* (Singapore), 7 May 2004.

8. "Ricin Suspect in Al Qaeda Camp," CNN, 10 January 2003.

9. "JI Arrests Have 'Dismantled' Cell: Minister," *The Age*, 18 December 2003.

10. "Bin Laden's Camps Teach Curriculum of Carnage," *USA Today*, 26 November 2001, http://www.usatoday.com/news/sept11/2001/11/26/cover.htm.

11. Rohan Gunaratna and Peter Chalk, *Jane's Counter Terrorism*, p. 24.

12. Ibid., pp. 23–24.

13. Ibid., p. 25.

14. Ibid., p. 23.

15. Chris Brown, "Narratives of Religion, Civilization and Modernity," in Ken Booth and Tim Dunne, eds., *Worlds in Collision: Terror and the Future of Global Order* (New York: Palgrave Macmillan, 2002), p. 293.

16. Timur Kuran, "The Religious Undercurrents of Muslim Economic Grievances," *Social Science Research Council*, available at http://www.ssrc.org/sept11/essays/kuran.htm.

17. Rohan Gunaratna, *Inside Al Qaeda*, pp. 70–76.

18. Rohan Gunaratna and Peter Chalk, *Jane's Counter Terrorism*, p. 21.

19. Ibid., p. 27.

20. Ibid., p. 21.

21. Ibid., p. 25.

22. Ibid., p. 22; also see the chapter by Magnus Ranstorp in this volume.

23. Ibid., p. 27.

24. Ibid., p. 22.

25. "Armies Inc," *The Straits Times*, 8 June 2004.

26. Gabriel Weimann, *WWW.Terror.Net: How Modern Terrorism Uses the Internet*, Special Report 116 (Washington, DC: United States Institute of Peace, 2004); also see Gabriel Weimann's chapter in Volume 1 of this publication.

27. Bruce Hoffman, "Al Qaeda, Trends in Terrorism and Future Potentialities: An Assessment," paper presented at the RAND Center for Middle East Public Policy and Geneva Center for Security Policy, 3rd Annual Conference, *The Middle East After Afghanistan and Iraq* (Geneva, Switzerland, 5 May 2003), pp. 5–8.

28. Available at http://www.justice.gov/ag/trainingmanual.htm.

29. Rohan Gunaratna and Peter Chalk, *Jane's Counter Terrorism*, p. 26.

30. Rohan Gunaratna, *Inside Al Qaeda*, p. 70.

31. "Chaos Lurks in an Abandoned Land: Al Qaeda and the Roots of Terror," *Guardian Newspapers*, 9 August 2002, http://www.buzzle.com/editorials/9-8-2002 -25963.asp?viewPage=3.

32. Rohan Gunaratna, *Inside Al Qaeda*, p. 72.

33. "Inside Bin Laden's Chemical Bunker," *Guardian Unlimited Special Reports*, 17 November 2001, http://www.guardian.co.uk/waronterror/story/0,1361,596415, 00.html.

34. Jack Kelley, "Bin Laden's Camps Teach Curriculum of Carnage," *USA Today*, 26 November 2001, http://www.keepmedia.com/pubs/USATODAY/2001/11/26/ 465425?extID=10026.

35. Tapes Shed New Light on bin Laden's network, CNN, http://www.cnn.com/ 2002/US/08/18/terror.tape.main/index.html and http://www.cnn.com/2002/US/08/ 19/terror.tape.chemical.

36. From the transcriptions done at the International Center for Political Violence and Terrorism Research, Institute of Defense and Strategic Studies, Singapore, from the documents recovered from Afghanistan.

37. For a profile on Ahmed Ressam, see Hal Bernton, Mike Carter, David Heath, and James Neff, "Going to Camp," *Seattle Times*, 24 July 2002.

38. For a profile on Daoud al-'Owhali, see "Life Inside Al Qaeda: A Destructive Devotion," *Los Angeles Times*, 24 September 2001.

39. "Life Inside Al Qaeda: A Destructive Devotion," *Los Angeles Times*, 24 September 2001.

40. "Chaos Lurks in an Abandoned Land," *The Observer*, 8 September 2002, http://observer.guardian.co.uk/afghanistan/story/0,1501,788012,00.html.

41. "Local Suspects Trained at 9/11 Hijackers' Camp; Lackawanna Men Present as Bin Laden Urged Terror," *The Buffalo News*, 15 September 2002, p. A1.

42. Ibid.

43. Ibid.

44. "Bin Laden's Camps Teach Curriculum of Carnage," *USA Today*, http://www.usatoday.com/news/sept11/2001/11/26/cover.htm.

45. Hal Bernton, Mike Carter, David Heath, and James Neff, "Going to Camp."

46. http://www.globalsecurity.org/military/world/afghanistan/zhawar-kili.htm.

47. Intense bombing near Pakistan border, CNN, 14 January 2002.

48. Ibid.

49. From the transcriptions done at the International Center for Political Violence and Terrorism Research, Institute of Defense and Strategic Studies, Singapore, from the documents recovered from Afghanistan.

50. Ibid.

51. Ibid.

52. "Al Qaeda said to revive terror camps, seek 'dirty bomb'," *Washington Times*, 18 December 2002.

53. "Portrait of an Al Qaeda camp," *Christian Science Monitor*, 17 January 2003; also see "Reporters on the Job," *Christian Science Monitor*, 17 January 2003.

54. Daan van der Schriek, "Pankisi's Role in European Terror Plot Remains Unclear," *Eurasia Insight*, 22 January 2003, http://www.eurasianet.org/departments/insight/articles/eav012203a.shtml.

55. Daan van der Schriek, "Pankisi's Role in European Terror Plot Remains Unclear," *Eurasia Insight*, 27 February 2003.

56. "Kurds Face a Second Enemy: Islamic Fighters on Iraq Flank," *New York Times*, 13 January 2003.

57. "Kurds Puzzled by Report of Terror Camp," *New York Times*, 6 February 2003.

58. "Kurds Say Terrorists Make Poison in Zone," *Washington Times*, 13 February 2003.

59. "Intelligence Report: Bin Laden Sought Indonesian Base," CNN, 9 July 2002.

60. "Indonesian al Qaeda Camp on Tape," CNN, 15 October 2002.

61. "Report Charts al Qaeda Operations in Indonesia," CNN, 4 June 2002.

62. According to "Indon Police Uncover Terrorist Training Camps," *Malaysia General News* (7 January 2003), "This is supported by the fact that several of the arrested suspects like Usma, Muhtar Daeng Lau, Suryadi admitted to having received military training and have joined battles in Moro . . . and Afghanistan."

63. "Fifth Terrorist Camp Found in Sulawesi," *Straits Times*, 11 January 2003.

64. "Al-Qa'idah Terrorist Links Reported in Philippines," *BBC Worldwide Monitoring*, 19 September 2002.

65. "Foreign Terrorists not Training in Mindanao Camps—AFP, MILF," *Global News Wire*, 19 September 2002.

66. "Terrorists or not Despite Denials, Their Story Is Sinister," *The New Paper*, 27 December 2002.

67. "Jakarta Requests Philippine Help to Track Down Indonesian Militants in Mindanao," BBC, 23 December 2002.

68. Ibid.

69. Azhar Ghani, "My Eye Opening Trip to Camp Abubakar," *The New Paper*, 28 December 2002.

70. "Cool General in a Hot Seat," *The New Paper*, 28 December 2002.

71. "Philippine 'al Qaeda Camp' Raided," CNN, 5 May 2002.

72. "MILF Camp Overrun; Military Claims Bomb-Making Materials Recovered," *Business World*, 4 November 2002.

73. Bertil Lintner, "Religious Extremism and Nationalism in Bangladesh," http://www.mukto-mona.com/Articles/bertil/religious_extremism4.htm.

74. Bertil Lintner, "Championing Islamist Extremism," http://www.asiapacificms.com/articles/rohingya_al_qaeda/.

75. "Tour by Top al-Qaeda Operative Alleged, Terror Camps in Aussie Bush," *The Mercury*, 3 December 2002.

76. Haji Abdul Qadir, Jalalabad's Governor, cited in "Inside Bin Laden's Chemical Bunker," *The Guardian*, http//www.guardian.co.uk/waronterror/story/0,1361,596415,00.html.

77. "India Identifies Terrorist Training Camps," CNN, 19 September 2001.

78. "Bin Laden's Camps Teach Curriculum of Carnage," *USA Today*, 26 November 2001, http://www.usatoday.com/news/sept11/2001/11/26/cover.htm.

Chapter 12: The Mujahideen of Bosnia

1. Transcript of confiscated Osama bin Laden videotape, December 2001. Transcript commissioned by the U.S. Department of Defense. Transcript and annotations independently prepared by George Michael, translator, Diplomatic Language Services; and Dr. Kassem M. Wahba, Arabic language program coordinator, School of Advanced International Studies, Johns Hopkins University. Released on http://www.cnn.com, 13 December 2001.

2. Azzam Publications, "In the Hearts of Green Birds"; audiocassette tape transliterated by Salman Dhia Al-Deen, http://www.azzam.com.

3. FBI Transcript of conversation involving Omar Ahmad Ali Abdel Rahman, "Muhammad" LNU, and two unidentified males, 20 March 1993; *United States v. Omar Ahmad Ali Abdel Rahman et al*, S3 93 Cr. 181(MBM). Government Exhibit 7057, p. 11.

4. Kathy Evans, "Pakistan Clamps Down on Afghan Mojahedin and Orders Expulsion of Arab Jihad Supporters," *The Guardian* (London), 7 January 1993, p. 7.

5. Tawfig Tabib, "Interview with Sheikh al-Mujahideen Abu Abdel Aziz," *Al-Sirat Al-Mustaqeem*, no. 33 (August 1994).

6. "The Jihad in Bosnia," *Al-Daawah* (Islamabad), Publisher: Shaykh Waseem Ahmed (January 1993).

7. Chuck Sudetic, "Muslims Heed Call to Arms," *New York Times*, 10 November 1992, sect. 1, p. 5.

8. Tom Post with Joel Brand, "Help from the Holy Warriors," *Newsweek*, 5 October 1992.

9. "Bill of Particulars," *United States of America v. Enaam M. Arnaout*, United

States District Court Northern District of Illinois Eastern Division, Case #: 02 CR 892, 3 February 2003, p. 5.

10. Shaykh Abu Abdel Aziz is identified in these documents by his alias Abdulrahman Al-Dosari.

11. "Government's Evidentiary Proffer Supporting the Admissibility of Co-Conspirator Statements," *United States of America v. Enaam M. Arnaout*, 31 January 2003, pp. 24–25.

12. "Bill of Particulars," *United States of America v. Enaam M. Arnaout*, 3 February 2003, p. 5.

13. "Government's Evidentiary Proffer Supporting the Admissibility of Co-Conspirator Statements," *United States of America v. Enaam M. Arnaout*, 31 January 2003, pp. 24–25.

14. Government's Response to Defendant's Position Paper as to Sentencing Factors," *United States of America v. Enaam M. Arnaout*, p. 38.

15. Asla Aydintasbas, "Why They Can't Turn their Backs on the Veil," *The Independent* (London), 28 April 1994, p. 22.

16. Ibid.

17. Azzam Publications, "Abu Muslim al-Turki," http://www.azzam.com.

18. FBI Transcript of conversation between Emad Salem and Siddig Ibrahim Siddig Ali, *United States v. Omar Ahmad Ali Abdel Rahman et al*, S3 93 Cr. 181(MBM). Government Exhibit 641-1T, pp. 19–21.

19. Bryan Brumley, "Bosnian Mujahedeen Will Welcome, Not Threaten, U.S. Soldiers," Associated Press, 4 December 1995.

20. "Issa Abdullah Ali (Bosnia)," *Indigo Publications Intelligence Newsletter*, no. 282, 22 February 1996.

21. Patrick Tracey, "Taking a Powder," *City Paper* (Washington, DC), 29 June 2001.

22. Mark Rice-Oxley, "Islamic Maverick Toying with U.S. Forces in Bosnia: Soldiers," Agence France Presse, 10 February 1996.

23. "NATO Forces Warned of U.S. Extremist in Bosnia," *New York Times*, 23 January 1996.

24. Jean-Louis Bruguiere and Jean-Francois Ricard, "*Requisitoire Definitifaux aux Fins de Non-Lieu. De Non-Lieu partiel. De Requalification. De Renvoi devant le Tribunal Correctionnel, de mantien sous Controle Judiciaiare et de maintien en Detention,*" Cour D'Appel de Paris; Tribunal de Grande Instance de Paris, No. Parquet: P96 253 3901.2, p. 169.

25. Ibid., p. 126.

26. Craig Pyes and Josh Meyer et al., "Bosnia Seen as Hospitable Base and Sanctuary for Terrorists," *Los Angeles Times*, 7 October 2001, p. A1.

27. Lara Marlowe, "Errant Frenchman Became Wanted Criminal after Adopting Bosnian Case as Mujahid," *The Irish Times*, 18 July 1997, p. 8.

28. Emerson Vermaat, "Bin Laden's Terror Networks in Europe," A Mackenzie Institute Occasional Paper, Mackenzie Institute, Toronto, Canada, 26 May 2002.

29. Jean-Louis Bruguiere and Jean-Francois Ricard, "*Requisitoire Definitifaux*

aux Fins de Non-Lieu. De Non-Lieu partiel. De Requalification. De Renvoi devant le Tribunal Correctionnel, de mantien sous Controle Judiciaiare et de maintien en Detention," Cour D'Appel de Paris; Tribunal de Grande Instance de Paris, No. Parquet: P96 253 3901.2, p. 157.

30. Ibid., p. 165.

31. Ibid., p. 157.

32. Ibid.

33. John-Thor Dahlburg, " 'Holy Warriors' Brought Bosnians Ferocity and Zeal," *Los Angeles Times*, 6 August 1996, p. A11.

34. Craig Pyes, "Arrest at U.S. Border Reverberates in France," *New York Times*, 22 December 1999, p. A1.

35. Christophe DeCroix, "Four Suspects Killed in Shootout After Car Bomb Found," *Associated Press*, 29 March 1996.

36. "Belgian Police Overpower Gunman, Free Hostages," Deutsche Presse-Agentur, 29 March 1996.

37. "French Fugitive Takes Belgian Hostages," United Press International, 29 March 1996.

38. Pierre-Yves Glass, "Bandits or Terrorists? Violent Ghetto Gang Seemed a Bit of Both," The Associated Press, 1 April 1996.

39. "French Fugitive Takes Belgian Hostages," United Press International, 29 March 1996.

40. "Belgian Police Overpower Gunman, Free Hostages," Deutsche Presse-Agentur, 29 March 1996.

41. Ibid.

42. "Hostage Drama after Five Killed in Police Raids," Agence France Presse, 29 March 1996.

43. Mary Dejevsky, "Islamic Terror Link to French Siege," *The Independent* (London), 2 April 1996, p. 10.

44. "Hostage Drama after Five Killed in Police Raids," Agence France Presse, 29 March 1996.

45. Mary Dejevsky, "Islamic Terror Link to French Siege," *The Independent* (London), 2 April 1996, p. 10.

46. "Reporter's Transcript of Proceedings," *United States of America v. Ahmed Ressam, aka Benni Noris*, United States District Court for the Western District of Washington, Case #: CR 99-666-JCC, dated 2 April 2001, pp. 9–10.

47. Jean-Louis Bruguiere and Jean-Francois Ricard, *"Requisitoire Definitifaux aux Fins de Non-Lieu. De Non-Lieu partiel. De Requalification. De Renvoi devant le Tribunal Correctionnel, de mantien sous Controle Judiciaiare et de maintien en Detention,"* Cour D'Appel de Paris; Tribunal de Grande Instance de Paris, No. Parquet: P96 253 3901.2, p. 109.

48. John-Thor Dahlburg, " 'Holy Warriors' Brought Bosnians Ferocity and Zeal," *Los Angeles Times*, 6 August 1996, p. A11.

49. Hal Berton et al., "The Terrorist Within; Chapter 5: 'The Terrorist Tracker,' " *Seattle Times*, 23 June–7 July 2002.

50. Cross-examination of Ahmed Ressam, *United States v. Mokhtar Haouari*, United States District Court Southern District of New York, Case: 00CR15, 27 June–6 July 2001, p. 653.

51. Craig Pyes with Josh Meyers and William Rempel, "Bosnia Seen as Hospitable Base and Sanctuary for Terrorists," *Los Angeles Times*, 7 October 2001.

52. Cross-examination of Ahmed Ressam, *United States v. Mokhtar Haouari*, United States District Court Southern District of New York, Case: 00CR15, 27 June–6 July 2001, p. 651; see also Algiers Television, Arabic-language broadcast; 31 August 1993, 1900 GMT.

53. Jean-Louis Bruguiere and Jean-Francois Ricard, *"Requisitoire Definitifaux aux Fins de Non-Lieu. De Non-Lieu partiel. De Requalification. De Renvoi devant le Tribunal Correctionnel, de mantien sous Controle Judiciaiare et de maintien en Detention,"* Cour D'Appel de Paris; Tribunal de Grande Instance de Paris, No. Parquet: P96 253 3901.2, p. 225.

54. Cross-examination of Ahmed Ressam, *United States v. Mokhtar Haouari*, United States District Court Southern District of New York, Case: 00CR15, 27 June–6 July 2001, p. 649.

55. Hal Berton et al., "The Terrorist Within; Chapter 5: 'The Terrorist Tracker,' " *Seattle Times*, 23 June–7 July 2002.

56. Scott Johnson, "Tale of the Wayward Son," *Newsweek*, 8 May 2000, p. 39.

57. Hal Berton et al., "The Terrorist Within; Chapter 6: 'It Takes a Thief,' " *Seattle Times*, 23 June–7 July 2002.

58. "Reporter's Transcript of Proceedings," *United States of America v. Ahmed Ressam, aka Benni Noris*, United States District Court for the Western District of Washington, Case #: CR 99-666-JCC, dated 2 April 2001, pp. 9–10.

59. William Marsden and Nicolas Van Praet, "Mystery Surrounds 'Raouf': Montrealer Seen as Key Link between Local Terror Cells, bin Laden Camps," *Montreal Gazette*, 16 February 2002, p. B1.

60. Christopher Dickey, "Training for Terror: From Credit-Card Fraud to the Art of Disguise, How bin Laden Schools His Recruits in Mayhem," *Newsweek*, 24 September 2002.

61. Cross-examination of Ahmed Ressam, *United States v. Mokhtar Haouari*, United States District Court Southern District of New York, Case: 00CR15, 27 June–6 July 2001, p. 626.

62. Direct Examination of Ahmed Ressam, *United States v. Mokhtar Haouari*, United States District Court Southern District of New York, Case: 00CR15, 27 June–6 July 2001, p. 572.

63. Direct Examination of Abdelghani Meskini, *United States v. Mokhtar Haouari*, United States District Court Southern District of New York, Case: 00CR15, 27 June–6 July 2001, pp. 323–36.

64. Ibid., p. 337.

65. Terence McKenna, "Trail of a Terrorist," Program #2004, Canadian Broadcasting Company (CBC), 25 October 2001.

66. Craig Pyes and Josh Meyer et al., "Bosnia Seen as Hospitable Base and Sanctuary for Terrorists," *Los Angeles Times*, 7 October 2001, p. A1.

67. "Hate Club," *Time*, 5 November 2001, p. 26.

68. For a discussion on the "franchising" of al Qaeda and bin Laden, please see the chapter by Jarret Brachman in Volume I of this publication.

69. Peter Ford, "Islamic Conference Yields Cautious Words, No Action," *Christian Science Monitor*, 4 December 1992, p. 6.

70. "Hate Club," *Time*, 5 November 2001, p. 26.

Chapter 13: Indoctrination Processes

1. *White Paper: The Jemaah Islamiyah Arrests and the Threat of Terrorism* (Singapore: Ministry of Home Affairs, 7 January 2003), pp. 3–4; hereafter Singapore WP.

2. Derwin Pereira, "Jakarta Blast Kills 9, Injures 180," *The Straits Times* (Singapore), 10 September 2004; and "Attack has Imprint of JI's Azahari," *The Straits Times* (Singapore), 10 September 2004.

3. Kumar Ramakrishna and See Seng Tan, "Is Southeast Asia a 'Terrorist Haven?'" in *After Bali: The Threat of Terrorism in Southeast Asia*, edited by Kumar Ramakrishna and See Seng Tan (Singapore: World Scientific/Institute of Defence and Strategic Studies, 2003), pp. 1–2.

4. Greg Fealy, "Islamic Radicalism in Indonesia: The Faltering Revival?" *Southeast Asian Affairs 2004* (Singapore: Institute of Southeast Asian Studies, 2004), p. 111.

5. Martin van Bruinessen, "The Violent Fringes of Indonesia's Radical Islam," http://www.let.uu.nl/~martin.vanbruinessen/personal/publications/violent_fringe.htm (accessed 29 July 2004).

6. Blontank Poer, "Tracking the Roots of Jamaah Islamiyah," *The Jakarta Post*, 8 March 2003.

7. Martin Van Bruinessen, "The Violent Fringes of Indonesia's Radical Islam."

8. "Abu Bakar Bashir: The Malaysian Connection," *Tempo*, 9 November 2002.

9. Ibid.

10. Barbara D. Metcalf, "Traditionalist Islamic Activism: Deoband, Tablighis, and Talibs," Essay based on Institute for the Study of Islam in the Modern World (ISIM) Annual Lecture, Leiden University, 23 November 2001.

11. Daniel Pipes, *Militant Islam Reaches America* (New York and London: W. W. Norton, 2003), p. 8.

12. Barbara Metcalf, "Traditionalist Islamic Activism."

13. Daniel Pipes, *Militant Islam*, p. 8.

14. Ibid., pp. 8–9. For a discussion of moral disengagement, please see Albert Bandura, "Mechanisms of Moral Disengagement," in *Origins of Terrorism: Psychologies, Ideologies, Theologies, States of Mind*, edited by Walter Reich (Cambridge: Cambridge University Press, 1990), pp. 161–91; also see Albert Bandura's chapter in this volume.

15. Tim Behrend, "Reading Past the Myth: Public Teachings of Abu Bakara Ba'asyir," 19 February 2003, available at http://www.arts.auckland.ac.nz/asia/tbehrend/abb-myth.htm (accessed 30 April 2004).

16. Blontank Poer, "Tracking the Roots."

17. John L. Esposito, *Unholy War: Terror in the Name of Islam* (New York: Oxford University Press, 2002), p. 56.

18. Azyumardi Azra, "Bali and Southeast Asian Islam: Debunking the Myths," in *After Bali: The Threat of Terrorism in Southeast Asia*, pp. 46–47.

19. John Esposito, *Unholy War*, p. 53.

20. Ibid., p. 60.

21. This section draws on Tim Behrend, "Reading Past the Myth," and Esposito, *Unholy War*, pp. 52–53.

22. Charles Selengut, *Sacred Fury: Understanding Religious Violence* (Walnut Creek, CA: AltaMira Press, 2003), p. 80.

23. Marc Sageman, *Understanding Terror Networks* (Philadelphia: University of Pennsylvania Press, 2004), p. 16.

24. John Esposito, *Unholy War*, p. 62.

25. Mark Juergensmeyer, *Terror in the Mind of God: The Global Rise of Religious Violence*, updated edition, with a new preface (Berkeley and Los Angeles: University of California Press, 2000), p. 81.

26. Martin Van Bruinessen, "Violent Fringes of Indonesia's Radical Islam."

27. Blontank Poer, "Tracking the Roots."

28. Marc Sageman, *Understanding Terror Networks*, p. 17.

29. See Malise Ruthven, *A Fury for God: The Islamist Attack on America* (London: Granta, 2002), p. 203.

30. Marc Sageman, *Understanding Terror Networks*, p. 18.

31. Tim Behrend, "Reading Past the Myth."

32. Blontank Poer, "Tracking the Roots."

33. Greg Fealy, "Islamic Radicalism," p. 112.

34. Neil J. Kressel, *Mass Hate: The Global Rise of Genocide and Terror*, revised and updated (Boulder, CO: Westview, 2002), p. 211.

35. Willard Gaylin, *Hatred: The Psychological Descent into Violence* (New York: Public Affairs, 2003), p. 24.

36. Ibid., pp. 24–28.

37. Anthony Paul, "Enduring the Other's Other," *The Straits Times* (Singapore), 4 December 2003.

38. Willard Gaylin, *Hatred*, p. 244.

39. Zalman Mohamed Yusof and Mohammad Ishak, "Inside a JI School," *The New Paper on Sunday* (Singapore), 4 January 2004.

40. Singapore WP, p. 16.

41. Mukhlas Interrogation Report, 13 December 2002.

42. Dan Murphy, "How Al Qaeda Lit the Bali Fuse: Part Three," *Christian Science Monitor*, 19 June 2003.

43. Benjamin Beit-Hallahmi and Michael Argyle, *The Psychology of Religious Behavior, Belief and Experience* (London and New York: Routledge, 1997), p. 243.

44. Michael J. Stevens, "The Unanticipated Consequences of Globalization: Contextualizing Terrorism," in *Psychology of Terrorism*, Vol. 3: *Theoretical Under-*

standings and Perspectives, edited by Chris E. Stout (London and Westport, CT: Praeger, 2002), p. 45.

45. Jonathan T. Drummond, "From the Northwest Imperative to Global Jihad: Social Psychological Aspects of the Construction of the Enemy, Political Violence and Terror," in *Psychology of Terrorism*, Vol. 1: *A Public Understanding*, pp. 60, 75.

46. Rush W. Dozier Jr., *Why We Hate: Understanding, Curbing and Eliminating Hate in Ourselves and Our World* (New York: Contemporary Books, 2002), p. 45.

47. Michael J. Stevens, "Unanticipated Consequences," in *Psychology of Terrorism*, Vol. 3, p. 45.

48. Jonathan T. Drummond, "From the Northwest Imperative to Global Jihad," in *Psychology of Terrorism*, Vol. 1, p. 76.

49. Zalman Mohamed Yusof and Mohammad Ishak, "Inside a JI School."

50. Timothy Mapes, "Indonesian School Gives High Marks to Students Embracing Intolerance," *Asian Wall Street Journal*, 2 September 2003.

51. Singapore WP, p. 22.

52. See *Southern Philippines Backgrounder: Terrorism and the Peace Process* (Singapore/Brussels: International Crisis Group Asia Report No. 80, 13 July 2004), pp. 13–17.

53. Albert Bandura, "Mechanisms of Moral Disengagement," in *Origins of Terrorism*, p. 161–91; see also Bandura's chapter in this volume.

54. Ibid., pp. 169–70.

55. *Jemaah Islamiyah in Southeast Asia: Damaged But Still Dangerous* (Jakarta/Brussels: International Crisis Group Asia Report No. 63, 26 August 2003), p. 24.

56. Albert Bandura, "Mechanisms," in *Origins of Terrorism*, pp. 173–81; see also Bandura's chapter in this volume.

57. John Dawson, "The Bali Bombers: What Motivates Death Worship?" *Capitalism Magazine*, 19 October 2003, available at http://www.capmag.com/article.asp?ID=3000 (accessed 1 September 2004).

58. Dan Murphy, "How Al Qaeda Lit the Bali Fuse: Part 2," *Christian Science Monitor*, 18 June 2003.

59. Kumar Ramakrishna, "U.S. Strategy in Southeast Asia: Counter-Terrorist or Counter-Terrorism?" in *After Bali*, pp. 328–29.

Chapter 14: Christian Militia Training

1. Michael Matza, "U.S. Militia Movement Hitting New Highs: Public Anger and Arrests Haven't Deterred Anti Government 'Citizen Soldiers,'" *The Toronto Star*, 13 July 1996.

2. Cindy C. Combs, *Terrorism in the Twenty-First Century*, 3rd edition (Upper Saddle River, NJ: Prentice Hall, 2003); also see the chapter on Christian fundamentalist and militia ideologies by James Aho in Volume I of this publication.

3. Morris Dees and James Corcoran, *Gathering Storm: America's Military Threats* (New York: HarperCollins, 1996).

4. In white supremacist ideology, an Aryan is defined as a Caucasian person of non-Semitic descent, who is regarded as racially superior to members of other races.

5. Cindy C. Combs, *Terrorism in the Twenty-First Century.*

6. Louis Berghoff, "The Militia Movement" (New York: Anti-Defamation League, 2001), online at http://www.adl.org/learn/ext_us/Militia_M.asp?xpicked= 4&item-19.

7. David Lethbridge, "From Mountain Shadow to Estes Park: A Blueprint for Death Squads in North America," 1996, online at http://bethuneinstitute.org/docu ments/shadow.html.

8. For more on dehumanization in the terrorist world, see the chapter on moral disengaged by Albert Bandura in this volume.

9. Cindy C. Combs, *Terrorism in the Twenty-First Century.*

10. Franco Ferracuti and Francesco Bruno, "Italy: A Systems Perspective," in *Aggression in Global Perspective*, edited by A. Goldstein and M. H. Segall (New York: Pergamon Press, 1983).

11. Cindy C. Combs, *Terrorism in the Twenty-First Century.*

12. Louis Berghoff, "Militia Movement."

13. Free Militia, "Section I: Principles Justifying the Arming and Organizing of a Militia," *Field Manual of the Free Militia,* Author, 1994, http://www.rickross.com/ reference/militia/militia10.html.

14. Free Militia, "Section II: Introduction to the Free Militia," *Field Manual of the Free Militia,* Author, 1994, http://www.rickross.com/reference/militia/militia11. html.

15. Abraham H. Foxman (ADL National Director), "The Quiet Retooling of the Militia Movement" (New York: Anti-Defamation League, 7 September 2004), on-line at http://www.adl.org.

Chapter 15: Hizballah Training Camps

1. A phrase coined by U.S. Deputy Secretary of State Richard Armitage, see Daniel Byman, "Should Hezbollah Be Next?" *Foreign Affairs* (November/December 2003).

2. Magnus Ranstorp, "Hizballah's Command Leadership: Its Structure, Decision-Making and Relationship with Iranian Clergy and Institutions," *Terrorism and Political Violence* 6, no.3 (Autumn 1994): 303–39.

3. Magnus Ranstorp, *Hizb'allah in Lebanon: The Politics of the Western Hostage Crisis* (London: Macmillan, 1997).

4. Isabel Kershner, "The Changing Colours of Imad Mughniyah," *Jerusalem Report*, 25 March 2002.

5. Douglas Frantz and Catherine Collins, "The Accountant is a Terrorist," *New York Times Magazine*, 10 November 1996.

6. *The Lebanon Report*, 1993; *al-Majallah*, 15–21 August 1998; and *al-Shira,*

31 August 1998; also see Hala Jaber, *Hezballah: Born with a Vengeance* (New York: Colombia University Press, 1997), and Nizar Hamzeh, *In the Path of Hizbullah* (Syracuse: Syracuse University Press, 2004).

7. *Mideast Mirror*, 16 September 1998.

8. Ed Blanche, "A Bizarre yet Bloody Conflict Drags on in Southern Lebanon," *Jane's Intelligence Review*, 1 October 1997.

9. For the skilful architecture of this process, see Giandomenico Picco, *Man Without a Gun: One Diplomat's Secret Struggle to Free the Hostages, Fight Terrorism, and End a War* (New York: Crown Publishers, 1999).

10. For example, see Rex Hudson, *Terrorist and Organized Crime Groups in the Tri-Border (TBA) of South America*, report prepared by Federal Research Division, Library of Congress (July 2003); and Jeffrey Goldberg, "In the Party of God (parts one and two)," *New Yorker*, 14 October and 21 October 2002.

11. Thomas Sancton, "Iran's State of Terror," *Time*, 11 November 1996.

12. Matthew Levitt, "Hizballah: A Case Study of Global Reach," remarks to a conference on "Post-Modern Terrorism: Trends, Scenarios, and Future Threats," 8 September 2003, at the International Policy Institute for Counter-Terrorism, Herzliya, Israel.

13. Reuters, 27 March 2004.

14. Bill Samii, "Analysis: A Look at Iran's Sponsorship of Terror Groups," *RFE/RL*, 13 January 2005.

15. Kenneth R. Timmerman, *Insight*, 5 January 2004.

16. *Deborah D. Peterson versus The Islamic Republic of Iran*, United States District Court for the District of Columbia, Civil Action No. 01-2094 (RCL), http://www.dcd.uscourts.gov/01-2094.pdf.

17. Yosef Olmert, "Iranian-Syrian Relations: Between Islam and Realpolitik," in *The Iranian Revolution and the Muslim World*, edited by David Menashri (Boulder, CO: Westview Press, 1990).

18. Shimon Shapira, "The Origins of Hizballah," *Jerusalem Quarterly* 46 (Spring 1988): 115–30.

19. For example, Hojatoleslam Ali Yunesi, the cofounder of MOIS, received extensive experience in Palestinian training camps in Lebanon; see *RFE/RL Iran Report* 2, no. 7 (15 February 1999).

20. See Kenneth Katzman, *The Warriors of Islam: Iran's Revolutionary Guard* (Boulder, CO: Westview Press, 1993).

21. Judith Palmer Harik, *Hezbollah: The Changing Face of Terrorism* (London: I. B. Tauris, 2004).

22. *The London Times*, 14 November 1987; and *Independent*, 3 August 1989.

23. See Robert Baer, *See No Evil* (New York: Crown Publishers, 2002); and Nizar Hamzeh, "Islamism in Lebanon: A Guide to the Groups," *Middle East Quarterly* 4, no. 3 (September 1997).

24. *Deborah D. Peterson versus The Islamic Republic of Iran*, United States District Court for the District of Columbia, Civil Action No. 01-2094 (RCL), http://www.dcd.uscourts.gov/01-2094.pdf.

25. Ibid.

26. *Al-Nahar*, 5 June 1985; and *Mideast Mirror*, 14 February 1997.

27. *Al-Manar TV*, 11 November 1999.

28. Nizar Hamzeh, *In the Path of Hizbullah*, p. 72.

29. Ibid., p. 65.

30. See Bob Woodward, *Veil: The Secret Wars of the CIA* (New York: Simon and Schuster, 1987); and David C. Martin and John Walcott, *Best Laid Plans: The Inside Story of America's War Against Terrorism* (New York: HarperCollins, 1989).

31. Nizar Hamzeh, *In the Path of Hizbullah*, p. 74.

32. For details, see Ranstorp, *Hizb'allah in Lebanon*.

33. See description in Con Couglin, *Hostage* (New York: Little, Brown and Company, 1992), pp. 102–6.

34. Sheikh Fadlallah denied this connection; see Martin Kramer, "The Oracle of Hizbullah," in *Spokesmen For the Despised: Fundamentalist Leaders of the Middle East*, edited by R. Scott Appleby (Chicago: Chicago University Press, 1997).

35. Baer, *See No Evil*.

36. *Terry Anderson et al. versus Islamic Republic of Iran*, United States District Court For The District Of Colombia, C.A. No. 99-0698 (TPJ), 22 March 2000.

37. Robert Baer, *See No Evil*.

38. *Kuwait Times*, 28 March 1984.

39. William Buchta, *Iran's Security Sector: An Overview*. Working Paper No. 146 published by the Geneva Centre for the Democratic Control of Armed Forces (DCAF), Geneva 2004.

40. *Le Figaro*, 4 December 1989; *Independent*, 26 April 1988; *Radio Free Lebanon*, 5 July 1990; and *Intelligence Newsletter*, No. 256 (19 January 1995).

41. "Bomb Kills Veteran Hezbollah Guerrilla," *International Herald Tribune*, 20 July 2004.

42. For example, see *Los Angeles Times*, 6 May 2001.

43. For a fascinating insight into this, see Nizar Hamzeh, *In the Path of Hizbullah*, pp. 74–76.

44. Ibid.

45. *Mideast Mirror*, 16 September 1998.

46. Magnus Ranstorp, "The Strategy and Tactics of Hizb'allah's Current 'Lebanonization,'" *Mediterranean Politics* 3, no. 1 (Summer 1998): 103–34.

47. *Jane's Intelligence Review—Pointer*, 1 February 1995; and *New York Times*, 19 July 2000.

48. Haaretz, 10 November 2004.

49. Thomas M. Sanderson, "Transnational Terror and Organized Crime: Blurring the Lines," *SAIS Review* 24, no. 1 (Winter 2004).

50. Douglas Frantz and Catherine Collins, "The Accountant is a Terrorist," *New York Times Magazine*, 10 November 1996; also *Mikdad: Into the Mind of a Terrorist*, film produced by Dan Setton, released in 1998.

51. Berndt George Thamm, *Terrorbasis Deutschland* (Diederichs Eugen, 2004).

52. *Middle East Intelligence Bulletin* 1, no. 9 (September 1999), http://www.ndrtv.de/doku/20040114_fuerallah_smyrek.html.

53. For details of the Shuman case, see http://mfa.gov.il/mfa/go.asp?MFAH0jku0
54. Daniel Sobelman, *New Rules of the Game: Israel and Hizbollah After An Is-raeli Withdrawal From Lebanon,* Memorandum No. 69 (Tel Aviv: Jaffee Center for Strategic Studies, January 2004), pp. 85–86.
55. Daniel Sobelman, "Hizballah Lends Its Services to the Palestinian Intifada," *Jane's Intelligence Review* (November 2001).
56. For background to this kidnapping, see *Haaretz,* 29 October 2004.
57. Jerusalem Report, 22 October 2003.
58. Gary C. Gambill, "Hezbollah's Israeli Operatives," *Middle East Intelligence Bulletin* 4, no. 9 (September 2002).
59. See *Haaretz,* 17 August 2003.
60. Daniel Sobelman, *New Rules.*
61. See *Haaretz,* 27 January 2005.
62. *Haaretz,* 10 September 2002; *CBC News,* 15 March 2004.

Chapter 16: The Human Factor in Insurgency

1. Freddy José Padilla de León, "Terrorism and Subversion: Two Arms and One Single Strategy of Subversion to Destabilize the Country," (Bogotá: Unpublished master's thesis presented to the Faculty of Political Science and International Stud-ies of the Pontifical University, 1994).
2. Eduardo Pizarro, *The FARC 1949–1966. From the Self-defense of Masses to the Combination of all Forms of Struggle* (Bogotá: Tercer Mundo Editores-IEPRI, 1992).
3. Eduardo Pizarro, *Insurgency and Revolution: The Guerrilla in Colombia in a Comparative Perspective* (Bogotá: Tercer Mundo Editores-IEPRI, 1996).
4. Román D. Ortiz, "Insurgent Strategies in the Post Cold War: The Case of the Revolutionary Armed Forces of Colombia," *Studies in Conflict and Terrorism* 25, no. 2 (2002): 127–43.
5. Economic Commission for Latin America, *Statistical Yearbook of Latin America and the Caribbean* (Santiago: CEPAL, 2003).
6. Juan Guillermo Ferro and Uribe Graciela, *The Order of the War. The FARC-EP: Between the Organization and the Policy* (Bogotá: Centro Editorial Javeriano, 2002).
7. A description of the recruitment and role of women in FARC is provided in the chapter by Keith Stanski in Volume 1 of this publication.
8. For more on what has been called "the retributional terrorist," please see the chapter by Raymond Hamden in Volume 1 of this publication.
9. Fernando Reinares, *Terrorism and Antiterrorism* (Barcelona, Spain: Paidos, 1998).
10. Moritz Ackerman, "Marulanda: An Anachronistic Combination between Josef Stalin and Pancho Villa," in *The True Intentions of the FARC,* by Corpora-tion Observatory for La Paz (Bogotá: Intermedio, 1999).
11. Jeremy McDermott, "FARC Gives Notice of an Urban Campaign," *Jane's In-telligence Review* 14, no. 9 (2002): 24–25.

12. For more on this, please see the chapter by Keith Stanski in Volume 1 of this publication.

13. Amnesty International, *Colombia: Marked Bodies, Silenced Crimes: Sexual Violence against Women in the Frame of Armed Conflict* (Madrid: Amnesty International, 2004).

14. For more on topic of charismatic groups and their control over their members, please see the chapter by Marc Galanter and James Forest in this volume.

Chapter 17: Aum Shinrikyō's Chemical Weapons Program

1. This chapter draws in part from a RAND Corporation publication by Brian Jackson et al. entitled *Aptitude for Destruction*, Volume 2: *Case Studies of Organizational Learning in Five Terrorist Groups* (May 2005), available online at www.rand.org/publications/MG/MG332.

2. Different sources translate the titles of the various Aum leaders in different ways. I use the translations employed by Ian Reader, *Religious Violence in Contemporary Japan: The Case of Aum Shinrikyō* (Honolulu: University of Hawaii Press, 2000).

3. For more on charismatic leaders of this type, please see the chapters by Arthur Deikman, Jerrold Post, Marc Galanter, and James Forest in this volume.

4. Ian Reader, *Religious Violence in Contemporary Japan*, p. 97.

5. For a chart depicting the Aum shadow government and the names of the ministers, see D. W. Brackett, *Holy Terror: Armageddon in Tokyo* (New York: Weatherhill, 1996), p. 104.

6. D. W. Brackett, *Holy Terror*, 1996, p. 90.

7. For a listing of Aum companies and facilities, see U.S. Congress, Senate, Committee on Governmental Affairs, Permanent Subcommittee on Investigations, *Global Proliferation of Weapons of Mass Destruction*, Part I (Washington, DC: U.S. Government Printing Office, 1996), pp. 86–87.

8. Haruki Murakami, *Underground: The Tokyo Gas Attack and the Japanese Psyche* (New York: Vintage Books, 2000), p. 250.

9. Ian Reader, *Religious Violence in Contemporary Japan*, p. 53.

10. Ibid., p. 53.

11. Ibid., p. 150.

12. "Day of Judgment: Matsumoto's Aum Cult Grew Rapidly in Late '80s," *The Daily Yomiuri* (Tokyo), 17 February 2004, p. 4.

13. For a chart summarizing Aum's alleged chemical and biological weapons attacks that is drawn from official Japanese sources see David E. Kaplan, "Aum Shinrikyō (1995)," in *Toxic Terror: Assessing Terrorist Use of Chemical and Biological Weapons*, edited by Jonathan B. Tucker (Cambridge, MA: MIT Press, 2000), p. 221.

14. For more on this topic, please see the chapter on moral disengagement by Albert Bandura in this volume.

15. According to Anthony Tu, "About 80 scientists were involved in the manu-

facture of sarin, VX, and other illegal drugs"; see Anthony T. Tu, "Anatomy of Aum Shinrikyō's Organization and Terrorist Attacks," *Archives of Toxicology, Kinetics and Xenobiotic Metabolism* 7, no. 3 (Autumn 1999): 50. Citing Japanese press reports, the Canadian Security Intelligence Service reported that 40 members were involved in the Tokyo subway incident and 15 members "were responsible for building three large chemical plants and laboratories for producing sarin"; see Canadian Security Intelligence Service, *Postscript: Chemical Terrorism in Japan*, 1 November 2000, http://csis-scrs.gc.ca/end/miscdoc/postscr_e.html (accessed 7 July 2004). Another news source reported "some 30 other members . . . put together the steel frame for the sarin plant"; see "Aum Member Says Cult Produced 30 kg of Sarin in '94," *Kyodo News Service*, 26 September 1996.

16. U.S. Congress, Senate, *Global Proliferation of Weapons of Mass Destruction*, p. 57.

17. Ibid.

18. Judge Satoru Hattori quoted in "Cultist the 11th Facing Gallows," *The Asahi Shimbum* (Asahi News Service), 31 January 2004.

19. "Tsuchiya States Faith in Asahara in VX Gas Attack Trial," *Kyodo News Service*, 17 May 1996.

20. "Asahara Wanted Sarin to Have Floral Scent," *The Daily Yomiuri*, 12 March 1996, p. 2.

21. Anthony T. Tu, "Anatomy of Aum Shinrikyō's Organization," p. 77.

22. "White Paper on Police 1996 (Excerpt)," National Police Agency, Government of Japan, Translated and Published by Police Association, March 1997, p. 9. Officials with the Japanese National Police Agency provided this translation to the author in November 2003.

23. "Police Raid 3 More Aum Facilities," *Mainichi Daily News*, 5 April 1995, quoted in Canadian Security Intelligence Service, *Postscript: Chemical Terrorism in Japan*.

24. Anthony T. Tu, "Anatomy of Aum Shinrikyō's Organization," p. 52.

25. "White Paper on Police 1996 (Excerpt)," p. 10.

26. "Aum Member Says Cult Produced 30 kg of Sarin in '94," *Kyodo News Service*, September 26, 1996.

27. Kazuharu Hirano, "The Aum-Shinrikyō Cult and Countermeasures by Japanese Authority: Lessons and Response to Aum-Shinrikyō Affair," paper for FRS Seminar on Non-Conventional Terrorism and the Use of Weapons of Mass Destruction, Paris, France, 12–13 December 2002, p. 5.

28. Haruki Murakami, *Underground*, p. 326.

29. Ian Reader, *Religious Violence in Contemporary Japan*, pp. 208–9.

30. "White Paper on Police 1996 (Excerpt)," p. 12; see also Canadian Security Intelligence Service, *Postscript: Chemical Terrorism in Japan*.

31. Anthony T. Tu, "Anatomy of Aum Shinrikyō's Organization," p. 77.

32. Ibid., p. 51.

33. Author interview with senior official in Japanese National Police Agency, Tokyo, Japan, November 2003.

34. Ian Reader, *Religious Violence in Contemporary Japan*, p. 206.

35. U.S. Congress, Senate, *Global Proliferation of Weapons of Mass Destruction*.

36. Kyle B. Olson, "Aum Shinrikyō: One and Future Threat?" *Emerging Infectious Diseases 5*, no. 4 (July–August 1999): 515.

37. David E. Kaplan and Andrew Marshall, *The Cult at the End of the World: The Incredible Story of Aum* (London: Hutchinson, 1996), p. 106.

38. Canadian Security Intelligence Service, *Postscript: Chemical Terrorism in Japan*.

39. Author interview with senior Japan Defense Agency official, Tokyo, Japan, January 2004.

40. Yliya Papilova and Vladimir Pakin, "Aum Shinrikyō Accuses Oleg Lobov of Selling Sarin: The Russian FSB Does Not Believe the Sectarians' Claims," *Moscow Kommersant-Daily*, 25 April 1997, translated in FBIS (Foreign Broadcast Information Service, operated by the U.S. Central Intelligence Agency), FTS19970521 001577.

41. Ian Reader, *Religious Violence in Contemporary Japan*, pp. 176–77.

42. U.S. Congress, Senate, *Global Proliferation of Weapons of Mass Destruction*, Exhibit 14.b., pp. 610–57.

43. Ibid.

44. See the chapter by Clark McCauley in Volume 3 of this publication.

45. For a thorough discussion of difficulties Aum faced in its effort to develop biological weapons see Milton Leitenberg, "Aum Shinrikyō's Efforts to Produce Biological Weapons: A Case Study in the Serial Propagation of Misinformation," *Terrorism and Political Violence 11*, no. 4 (1999): 149–58.

Chapter 18: Terrorist Training Centers Around the World

1. Phil Hirschkorn, "Trials Expose Terrorist Training Camps," CNN New York Bureau, 18 July 2001, available online at http://www.cnn.com.

2. Ibid.

3. "Al-Qaeda Camps Trained 70,000," BBC News, 4 January 2005, retrieved online at http://news.bbc.co.uk/2/hi/europe/4146969.stm.

4. David E. Smith, *The Training of Terrorist Organizations* (CSC Report, 1995), p. 7; available online at http://www.globalsecurity.org/military/report/1995/SDE.htm.

5. C. J. Chivers and David Rohde, "Turning out Guerillas and Terrorists to Wage a Holy War," *New York Times*, 18 March 2002, p. A1.

6. Ibid.

7. Ibid.

8. Ibid.

9. Nic Robertson, "Tapes Show al Qaeda Trained for Urban Jihad on West," CNN, 20 August 2002, available online at http://www.cnn.com/2002/US/08/20/terror.tape.main.

10. Ibid.

11. John J. Lumpkin, "Bin Laden's Terrorist Training Combined Math, Missiles," Associated Press, 9 October 2001, available online at http://www.globalsecurity.org/org/news/2001/011009-attack02.htm.

12. See [Michael Scheuer]: Anonymous, *Through Our Enemi's Eyes: Osama bin Laden, Radical Islam, and the Future of America* (Washington, DC: Brasseys, Inc., 2003), p. 101.

13. Ibid., pp. 130–31.

14. See, for example, C. J. Chivers and David Rohde, "Turning out Guerillas and Terrorists to Wage a Holy War."

15. Marcia Christoff Kurop, "Al Qaeda's Balkan Links," *Wall Street Journal Europe*, 1 November 2001.

16. "IFOR Soldiers Raid Alleged 'Terrorist Training School'; Iranians Seized," EmergencyNet News Service, citing *ENNFAX Internet Report* 2, no. 47 (16 February 1996).

17. Brian Glyn Williams, "The 'Chechen Arabs': An Introduction to the Real Al Qaeda Terrorists from Chechnya," *Terrorism Monitor* 2, no. 1 (15 January 2004).

18. Saul Shay and Yoram Schweitzer, "The 'Afghan Alumni' Terrorism," 6 November 2000, online at http://www.ict.org.il.

19. Youssef H. Aboul-Enein, "Al-Ikhwan Al-Muslimeen: the Muslim Brotherhood," *Military Review* (July–August, 2003): 26–31.

20. Ibid., p. 28.

21. For more on these, please see the chapter by Kumar Ramakrishna in this volume.

22. Rupert Cornwell, "Iraq now a Terrorist Breeding Ground, Say US Officials," *The Independent*, 15 January 2005, online at http://news.independent.co.uk/world/middle_east/story.jsp?story=601098.

23. See David E. Kaplan and Andrew Marshall, *The Cult at the End of the World*; Amy E. Smithson and Leslie Anne Levy, "Ataxia: The Chemical and Biological Terrorism Threat and the U.S. Response," Report No. 35 (Washington, DC: Henry L. Stimson Center, 2000); and Patrick Bellamy, "Aum Shinrikyō," http://www.crime library.com/terrorists_spies/terrorists/prophet/28.html?sect=22.

24. United Nations, Office of Drugs and Crime, "Terrorism and Weapons of Mass Destruction," online at http://www.unodc.org/unodc/terrorism_weapons_mass_des truction_page002.html (accessed 18 October 2004).

25. Ibid.

26. For example, see "Kashmir Key to Al Qaeda's Strategy Versus US," *Global Policy Forum* (19 June 2002), available online at http://www.globalpolicy.org/wtc/analysis/2002/0619kashmir.htm.

27. Hala Jaber, *Hezbollah, Born with a Vengeance* (New York: Columbia University Press, 1997), p. 12.

28. Ibid., pp. 19–22.

29. Ibid., pp. 22–23.

30. "IDF Action in Syria," *Israel News Agency* (5 October 2003), available online at http://www.israelnewsagency.com.

31. J. Bowyer Bell, *The IRA, 1968–2000: Analysis of a Secret Army* (London: Frank Cass, 2000), p. 184.

32. Boaz Ganor, "Libya and Terrorism," *Survey of Arab Affairs—A Periodic Supplement to Jerusalem Letter/Viewpoints* 28 (1 June 1992), available online at http://www.ict.org.il/articles/article3.htm.

33. Council on Foreign Relations, "Libya," Terrorism: Q&A website, http://cfrterrorism.org/sponsors/libya.html; and Global Security, "Libya" website, http://www.globalsecurity.org/intell/world/libya/facility.htm.

34. J. Bowyer Bell, *The IRA, 1968–2000*, p. 182.

35. H. H. Tucker, "The IRA in Eire," in Foreign and Commonwealth Office: Republic of Ireland Department: Registered Files (WL Series) 1972–1974, FCO 87-3: British National Archives (1972); also see Brian A. Jackson, "Training for Urban Resistance," in this volume.

36. Ibid., pp. 180–85.

37. Ibid., pp. 184–85.

38. David E. Smith, *The Training of Terrorist Organizations*, p. 25.

39. David E. Smith, *The Training of Terrorist Organizations*, p. 25; and Thomas Bedford and Frank Jones, *Sendero Luminoso: Origins, Outlooks and Implications* (Monterey, CA: Naval Postgraduate School, 1986), p. 53.

40. Maria Ressa, *The Seeds of Terror: An Eyewitness Account of Al-Qaeda's Newest Center of Operations in Southeast Asia* (New York: Free Press, 2003), pp. 133–35.

41. Zachary Abuza, *Militant Islam in Southeast Asia: Crucible of Terror* (Boulder, CO: Lynne Rienner, 2003), p. 97.

42. Maria Ressa, *The Seeds of Terror*, p. 110.

43. "Terrorism Questions and Answers," Council on Foreign Relations website, http://www.cfrterrorism.org/havens/somalia.html.

44. Danna Harman, "US Eyes Somali Terror Link," *Christian Science Monitor*, 17 December 2001, online at http://www.csmonitor.com/2001/1217/p6s1-woaf.html; also Defense Secretary Donald Rumsfeld said in January 2001 that "We know there have been training camps there and that they have been active over the years," as reported by Gwen Florio in "Somalis Seek Order in 'Mad Max' Country," *Denver Post*, 24 February 2002, online at http://63.147.64.127/Stories/0,1413,36%257E11614%257E415292,00.html.

45. U.S. Institute of Peace (USIP), *Terrorism in the Horn of Africa*, Report no. 113 (Washington, DC: USIP, January 2004), p. 3.

46. "Attacks on Somalia Openly Discussed," AFROL News (29 November 2001), online at http://www.afrol.com/News2001/som019_war_terrorism.htm.

47. Gwen Florio, "Somalis Seek Order in 'Mad Max' Country."

48. USIP, *Terrorism in the Horn of Africa*, p. 10.

49. See "Terrorist Organizations: Basque Fatherland and Liberty (ETA)," online at http://www.terrorismfiles.org/organisations/basque_fatherland_and_liberty.html.

50. See *Euskadi Ta Askatasuna*, online at http://www.ict.org.il/inter_ter/orgdet.cfm?orgid=8 and "A Blow to Basque Terrorism," *Profiles in Terror* (12 December 2003), online at http://www.profilesinterror.com/updates/2003_12_07_archive.html.

51. "French Police Say They Found ETA Training Camp," *Euskal Herreria Journal* (15 February 2003), online at http://members.freespeech.org/ehj/news/n_conpol_chro01feb.html.

52. Rohan Gunaratna, *Sri Lanka's Ethnic Crisis and National Security* (Colombo: South Asian Network on Conflict Research, 1998).

53. Manoj Joshi, "On the Razor's Edge: The Liberation Tigers of Tamil Eelam," *Studies in Conflict and Terrorism* 19, no. 1 (January–March 1996): 19–42.

54. Alan Feur, "Jihad, Inc.: The Bin Laden Network of Companies Exporting Terror," *New York Times* (13 February 2001), as cited in [Michael Scheuer], *Through Our Enemies' Eyes*, p. 126.

55. USIP, *Terrorism in the Horn of Africa.*

56. See Hala Jaber, *Hezbollah*, pp. 12–22.

57. Office of the Coordinator for Counterterrorism, U.S. Department of State Publication no. 10136, *Patterns of Global Terrorism*, 1993, online at http://www.hri.org/USSD-Terror/93/statespon.html; www.fas.org; www.mipt.org.

58. "IDF Action in Syria," Israel News Agency, 5 October 2003, available online at http://www.israelnewsagency.com.

59. Ely Karmon, "Islamic Terrorist Activities in Turkey in the 1990s," *Terrorism and Political Violence* 10, no. 4 (Winter 1998): 101–21.

60. Ibid.

61. Ely Karmon, "Terrorism in Turkey: An Analysis of the Principal Players" (International Policy Institute for Counterterrorism, 1999), available online at http://www.ict.org.il/articles/articledet.cfm?articleid=74.

62. See James Aho, "Christian Fundamentalism and Militia Movements in the United States," in Volume I of this publication.

63. See the chapter by James Aho in Volume I of this publication.

64. Ibid.

65. For more on the history of this region, see Ahmad Rashid, *Jihad: The Rise of Militant Islam in Central Asia* (New Haven: Yale University Press, 2002).

66. Center for Nonproliferation Studies, Monterey Institute of International Studies, Special Section: Terrorist Attacks on America, "Islamic Movement of Uzbekistan," http://cns.miis.edu/research/wtc01/imu.htm.

67. Sources for this paragraph on Yemen include Evgenii Novikov, "The Soviet Roots of Islamic Militancy in Yemen," *Terrorism Monitor* 2, no. 7 (8 April 2004), online at http://www.jamestown.org; and "Terrorism Questions and Answers," Council on Foreign Relations website http://www.cfrterrorism.org/havens/yemen.html.

68. Evgenii Novikov, "The Soviet Roots of Islamic Militancy in Yemen," *Terrorism Monitor* 2(7) (8 April 2004), online at http://www.jamestown.org.

69. "Terrorism Questions and Answers," Council on Foreign Relations website http://www.cfrterrorism.org/havens/yemen.html.

70. J. Boyer Bell, *The IRA: 1968–2000*, p. 181.

Select Bibliography and Resources for Further Reading

Abduvakhitovm, Abdujabbar A. "The Jadid Movement and its Impact on Contemporary Central Asia." In *Central Asia*. Edited by Hafeez Malik. New York: St. Martin's Press, 1994.

Abu-Rabi, Ibrahim M. *Intellectual Origins of Islamic Resurgence in the Modern Arab World.* Albany: State University of New York Press, 1996.

Abuza, Zachary. *Militant Islam in Southeast Asia: Crucible of Terror.* Boulder, CO: Lynne Rienner, 2003.

Ackerman, Moritz. "Marulanda: An Anachronistic Combination between Josef Stalin and Pancho Villa." In *The True Intentions of the FARC.* Corporation Observatory for La Paz. Bogotá: Intermedio, 1999.

Amnesty International. *Colombia: Marked Bodies, Silenced Crimes: Sexual Violence against Women in the Context of Armed Conflict.* Madrid: Amnesty International, 2004.

Anonymous. "Militia Organizing: Advance Teams." Constitution Society, 1995. Online at http://www.constitution.org/mil/org_team.txt.

Anonymous. "Militia Training: Operation WitWeb." Constitution Society, 1995. Online at http://www.constitution.org/mil/witweb.txt.

Anonymous. "Reviving the Ready Militia." Constitution Society, 1994. Online at: http://www.constitution.org/mil/rev_read.txt.

Anonymous. *Through our Enemies' Eyes: Osama bin Laden, Radical Islam, and the Future of America.* Washington, DC: Brassey's, Inc., 2002.

Ball-Rokeach, Sandra J. "The Legitimation of Violence." In *Collective Violence.* Edited by J. F. Short Jr. and M. E. Wolfgang, pp. 100–11. Chicago: Aldine-Atherton, 1972.

Bandura, Albert. "Mechanisms of Moral Disengagement." In *Origins of Terrorism: Psychologies, Ideologies, Theologies, States of Mind.* Edited by Walter Reich. Baltimore, MD: Woodrow Wilson Center Press, 1998.

Bandura, Albert. "Moral Disengagement in the Perpetration of Inhumanities." *Personality and Social Psychology Review* 3 (1999): 193–209.

Bandura, Albert. "Role of Selective Moral Disengagement in Terrorism and Counterterrorism." In *Understanding Terrorism*. Edited by Fathali M. Moghaddam and Anthony J. Marsella, pp. 121–50. Washington, DC: American Psychological Association, 2004.

Bandura, Albert. *Social Foundations of Thought and Action: A Social Cognitive Theory*. Englewood Cliffs, NJ: Prentice-Hall, 1986.

Bandura, Albert, et al. "Disinhibition of Aggression through Diffusion of Responsibility and Dehumanization of Victims." *Journal of Research in Personality* 9 (1975): 253–69.

Bedford, Thomas, and Frank Jones. *Sendero Luminoso: Origins, Outlooks and Implications*. Monterey, CA: Naval Postgraduate School, 1986.

Beit-Hallahmi, Benjamin, and Michael Argyle. *The Psychology of Religious Behaviour, Belief and Experience*. London and New York: Routledge, 1997.

Bell, J. Bowyer. "The Armed Struggle and Underground Intelligence: An Overview." *Studies in Conflict and Terrorism* 17 (1994): 115–50.

Bell, J. Bowyer. *The Dynamics of the Armed Struggle*. London: Frank Cass, 1998.

Bell, J. Bowyer. *The Gun in Politics: An Analysis of Irish Political Conflict, 1916–1986*. New Brunswick, NJ: Transaction Books, 1987.

Bell, J. Bowyer. *The IRA, 1968–2000: Analysis of a Secret Army*. London: Frank Cass, 2000.

Bell, J. Bowyer. *The Secret Army: The IRA*. Revised 3rd ed. Dublin, Ireland: Poolbeg, 1998.

Bergen, Peter L. *Holy War, Inc.: Inside the Secret World of Osama bin Laden*. New York: Simon and Schuster, 2001.

Berlet, Chip. "Millennium Shoot Out: Armed and Dangerous, the Far Right Builds Barricades for a Spiritual Tsunami." *Toward Freedom* (December 1999).

Berman, Paul. "Al Qaeda's Philosopher: How an Egyptian Islamist Invented the Terrorist Jihad from his Jail Cell." *New York Times Magazine*. 23 March 2003.

Bourdeaux, Michael. *The International Politics of Eurasia*. Volume 3. *The Politics of Religion in Russia and the New States of Eurasia*. Armonk, NY: M. E. Sharpe, 1995.

Bowen, Murray. *Family Therapy in Clinical Practice*. New York: Jason Aronson, 1978.

Boyle, Kevin, and Tom Hadden. *Northern Ireland: The Choice*. London: Penguin Books, 1994.

Brackett, D. W. *Holy Terror: Armageddon in Tokyo*. New York: Weatherhill, 1996.

Brown, Chris. "Narratives of Religion, Civilization and Modernity." In *Worlds in Collision: Terror and the Future of Global Order*. Edited by Ken Booth and Tim Dunne. New York: Palgrave Macmillan, 2002.

Cameron, Gavin. *Nuclear Terrorism: A Threat Assessment for the 21st Century*. New York: St. Martin's Press, 1999.

Cartwright, Dorwin, and Alvin Zander, eds. *Group Dynamics: Research and Theory.* Evanston, IL: Row, Peterson, 1962.

Christensen, John. "Bracing for Guerilla Warfare in Cyberspace." CNN Interactive website (April 6, 1999): http://www.cnn.com/TECH/specials/hackers/cyberterror.

Cilluffo, Frank, and Paul Byron Pattak. "Cyber Threats: Ten Issues to Consider." In *Homeland Security and Terrorism.* Edited by Russell Howard, Joanne Moore, and James Forest. Guilford, CT: McGraw-Hill, 2005.

Collins, Eamon, and Mick McGovern. *Killing Rage.* London: Granta Books, 1997.

Combs, Cindy C. *Terrorism in the Twenty-First Century.* 3rd ed. Upper Saddle River, NJ: Prentice-Hall, 2003.

Conway, Flo, and Jim Siegelman. *Holy Terror: The Fundamentalist War.* Dell Books: New York, 1982.

Coogan, Tim Pat. *The IRA: A History.* Niwot, CO: Roberts Rinehart Publishers, 1993.

Crenshaw, Martha. "The Psychology of Terrorism: An Agenda for the 21st Century." *Political Psychology* 21 (2000).

Dees, Morris, and James Corcoran. *Gathering Storm: America's Military Threats.* New York: HarperCollins, 1996.

Deikman, Arthur J. *Them and Us: Cult Thinking and the Terrorist Threat.* Berkeley, CA: Bay Tree Publications, 2003.

Denning, Dorothy. "Activism, Hacktivism and Cyberterrorism." In *Networks and Netwars: The Future of Terror, Crime and Militancy.* Edited by John Arquilla and David Ronfeldt. Santa Monica, CA: RAND, 2001.

Dobson, Christopher, and Ronald Payne. *The Terrorists, Their Weapons, Leaders, and Tactics.* New York: Facts on File Publications, 1982.

Dolnik, Adam. "Die and Let Die: Exploring Links between Suicide Terrorism and Terrorist Use of Chemical, Biological, Radiological, and Nuclear Weapons." *Studies in Conflict and Terrorism* 26, no. 1 (January–February 2003): 17–35.

Doskoch, Peter. "The Mind of the Militias." *Psychology Today* (July/August 1995).

Dozier, Rush W., Jr. *Why We Hate: Understanding, Curbing and Eliminating Hate in Ourselves and Our World.* New York: Contemporary Books, 2002.

Drake, C.J.M. "The Provisional IRA: A Case Study," *Terrorism and Political Violence* 3, no. 2 (1991): 43–60.

Drake, C.J.M. *Terrorists' Target Selection.* New York: St. Martin's Press, 1998.

Economic Commission for Latin America. *Statistical Yearbook of Latin America and the Caribbean.* Santiago: CEPAL, 2003.

El-Nawawy, Mohammed, and Adel Iskandar. *Al-Jazeera: How the Free Arab News Network Scooped the World and Changed the Middle East.* Cambridge, MA: Westview Press, 2002.

Ergil, Dogu. "Suicide Terrorism in Turkey: The Worker's Party of Kurdistan." In *Countering Suicide Terrorism.* Herzliya: International Policy Institute for Counter-Terrorism, 2000.

Esposito, John L. *Unholy War: Terror in the Name of Islam*. New York: Oxford University Press, 2002.

Ferracuti, Franco, and Francesco Bruno. "Italy: A Systems Perspective." In *Aggression in Global Perspective*. Edited by A. Goldstein and M. H. Segall. New York: Pergamon Press, 1983.

Ferro, Juan Guillermo, and Uribe Graciela. *The Order of the War. The FARC-EP: Between the Organization and the Policy*. Bogotá: Centro Editorial Javeriano, 2002.

Festinger, Leon, Henry Riecken, and Stanley Schacter. *When Prophecy Fails*. Minneapolis: University of Minnesota Press, 1956.

"Five Days in an IRA Training Camp." *Iris* (November 1983): 39–45.

Foreign and Commonwealth Office: Republic of Ireland Department. 1972. Maj. Gen. R.C. Ford—"The Campaign against the IRA: An Assessment of the Current Operational Situation." FCO 87–2: British National Archives.

Foreign and Commonwealth Office: Republic of Ireland Department: Registered Files (WL Series) 1972–1974. H. H. Tucker. "The IRA in Eire." FCO 87–3: British National Archives, 1972.

Foreign Office: Western Department and Foreign and Commonwealth Office: Western European Department: Registered Files (R and WR Series) 1967–1974. Clipping: "I Watch as the I.R.A. Blow up a Spiked Border Road," by C. McAnally. FCO 33–1593/4: British National Archives.

Foxman, Abraham H. "The Militia Movement Today." New York: Anti-Defamation League, 2004. Online at http://www.adl.org/learn/ext_us/Militia_M.asp?xpicked=4&item=19.

Foxman, Abraham H. "The Quiet Retooling of the Militia Movement." New York: Anti-Defamation League, 7 September 2004. Online at http://www.adl.org.

Freud, Sigmund. "Group Psychology and the Analysis of the Ego." In *The Standard Edition of the Complete Psychological Works of Sigmund Freud*. Vol. 18. Edited and translated by James Strachey. London: Hogarth, 1955 [1921].

Galanter, Marc. *Cults: Faith, Healing and Coercion*. 2nd ed. New York: Oxford University Press, 1999.

Gambill, Gary C. "Hezbollah's Israeli Operatives," *Middle East Intelligence Bulletin* 4, no. 9 (September 2002).

Gaylin, Willard. *Hatred: The Psychological Descent into Violence*. New York: Public Affairs, 2003.

Geraghty, Tony. *The Irish War: The Hidden Conflict Between the IRA and British Intelligence*. Baltimore, MD: The Johns Hopkins University Press, 2000.

Glover, J. M. *Northern Ireland Terrorist Trends*. London: Ministry of Defense, British Government, 1978.

Gunaratna, Rohan. *Inside Al Qaeda: Global Network of Terror*. New York: Columbia University Press, 2002.

Gunaratna, Rohan. "The Post-Madrid Face of Al Qaeda." *The Washington Quarterly* 27, no. 3 (Summer 2004).

Gunaratna, Rohan. *Sri Lanka's Ethnic Crisis and National Security.* Colombo: South Asian Network on Conflict Research, 1998.

Gunaratna, Rohan. "Suicide Terrorism in Sri Lanka and India." In *Countering Suicide Terrorism.* Herzliya: International Policy Institute for Counter-Terrorism, 2000.

Hamzeh, Nizar. *In the Path of Hizbullah.* Syracuse, NY: Syracuse University Press, 2004.

Harik, Judith Palmer. *Hezbollah: The Changing Face of Terrorism.* London: I. B. Tauris, 2004.

Haritos-Fatouros, Mika. *The Psychological Origins of Institutionalized Torture.* London: Routledge, 2002.

Harnden, Toby. *Bandit Country: The IRA and South Armagh.* London: Coronet Books, LIR, 2000.

Hildreth, Steven A. *Cyberwarfare: A CRS Report for Congress.* Washington, DC: Library of Congress, Congressional Research Service, 19 June 2001.

Hoffman, Bruce. *Inside Terrorism.* New York: Columbia University Press, 1998.

Horgan, John, and Max Taylor. "The Provisional Irish Republican Army: Command and Functional Structure." *Terrorism and Political Violence* 9, no. 3 (1997): 1–32.

Hudson, Rex A. *Who Becomes a Terrorist and Why: The 1999 Government Report on Profiling Terrorists.* Guilford, CT: The Lyons Press, 2001.

International Crisis Group. *Jemaah Islamiyah in Southeast Asia: Damaged But Still Dangerous.* Jakarta/Brussels: International Crisis Group Asia Report No. 63, 26 August 2003.

Jaber, Hala. "Inside the World of Palestinian Suicide Bombers." *Sunday Times.* 24 March 2002. Available at http://www.sunday-times.co.uk/article/0,,178 -245592,00.html (accessed on 9 April 2002) (access requires registration).

Jaber, Hala. *Hezbollah: Born with a Vengeance.* New York: Columbia University Press, 1997.

Jane's Terrorism and Insurgency Centre. *JTIC Exclusive: Proliferation of MAN PADS and the Threat to Civil Aviation* [Subscription Database]. Jane's Information Group, 4 February 2003 [cited 14 April 2004]. Available from http://www.janes.com.

Jorisch, Avi. "Al-Manar: Hizballah TV, 24/7." *The Middle East Quarterly* 11 (Winter 2004).

Joshi, Manoj. "On the Razor's Edge: The Liberation Tigers of Tamil Eelam." *Studies in Conflict and Terrorism* 19, no. 1 (January–March 1996).

Juergensmeyer, Mark. *Terror in the Mind of God: The Global Rise of Religious Violence.* Berkeley: University of California Press, 2000.

Kaplan, David E. "Aum Shinrikyō (1995)." In *Toxic Terror: Assessing Terrorist Use of Chemical and Biological Weapons.* Edited by Jonathan B. Tucker. Cambridge, MA: MIT Press, 2000.

Kaplan, David E., and Andrew Marshall. *The Cult at the End of the World: The Incredible Story of Aum.* London: Hutchinson, 1996.

Katzman, Kenneth. *The Warriors of Islam: Iran's Revolutionary Guard*. Boulder, CO: Westview Press, 1993.

Kelman, Herbert C. "Violence without Moral Restraint: Reflections on the Dehumanization of Victims and Victimizers." *Journal of Social Issues* 29 (1973): 25–61.

Kepel, Gilles. *Jihad: The Trail of Political Islam*. Translated by Anthony F. Roberts. Cambridge, MA: Harvard University Press, 2002.

Kohlmann, Evan. *Al Qaeda's Jihad in Europe: The Afghan-Bosnian Network*. Oxford: Berg Publishers, 2004.

Kramer, Joel, and Diana Alstad. *The Guru Papers: Masks of Authoritarian Power*. Berkeley, CA: North Atlantic Books; London: Frog Ltd., 1993.

Kramer, Martin. "The Moral Logic of Hizballah." In *Origins of Terrorism: Psychologies, Ideologies, Theologies, States of Mind*. Edited by Walter Reich, pp. 131–57. Cambridge: Cambridge University Press, 1990.

Kramer, Martin. "The Oracle of Hizballah." In *Spokesmen For the Despised: Fundamentalist Leaders of the Middle East*. Edited by R. Scott Appleby. Chicago: Chicago University Press, 1997.

Kressel, Neil J. *Mass Hate: The Global Rise of Genocide and Terror*. Revised and updated. Boulder, CO: Westview, 2002.

Laqueur, Walter. "Reflections on Eradication of Terrorism." In *International Terrorism*. Edited by Charles Kegley Jr. New York: St. Martin's Press, 1990.

Leitenberg, Milton. "Aum Shinrikyō's Efforts to Produce Biological Weapons: A Case Study in the Serial Propagation of Misinformation." *Terrorism and Political Violence* 11, no. 4, (1999): 149–58.

Lethbridge, David. "From Mountain Shadow to Estes Park: A Blueprint for Death Squads in North America." Bethune Institute, 1996. Online at http://bethune institute.org/documents/shadow.html.

Long, Theodore E., and Jeffery K. Hadden. "A Reconception of Socialization." *Sociological Theory* 3, no. 1 (1985): 39–49.

Lutz, William D. "Language, Appearance, and Reality: Doublespeak in 1984." In *The Legacy of Language: A Tribute to Charlton Laird*. Edited by P. C. Boardman, pp. 103–19. Reno: University of Nevada Press, 1987.

Mandeville, David. "Hackers, Crackers, and Trojan Horses: A Primer." CNN Interactive website (29 March 1999), http://www.cnn.com/TECH/specials/ hacker/primer.

Mashberg, Tom. "Veil Lifts on New Deadly Breed of Suicide Terrorist," *Boston Herald*, 30 September 2001.

Matza, Michael. "U.S. Militia Movement Hitting New Highs: Public Anger and Arrests Haven't Deterred Anti Government 'Citizen Soldiers.'" *Toronto Star*. 13 July 1996.

McCauley, Clark. "Psychological Issues in Understanding Terrorism and the Response to Terrorism." In *Psychology of Terrorism*. Vol. 3. *Theoretical Understandings and Perspectives*. Edited by Christopher Stout, pp. 3–30. Westport, CT: Praeger, 2002.

McCauley, Clark, and Mary D. Segal. "Terrorist Individuals and Terrorist Groups: The Normal Psychology of Extreme Behavior." In *Terrorism*. Edited by Jo Groebel and Jeffrey H. Goldstein, pp. 39–64. Sevilla, Spain: Publicaciones de la Universidad de Sevilla (Publications of the University of Seville), 1989.

McDermott, Jeremy. "FARC Gives Notice of an Urban Campaign." *Jane's Intelligence Review* 14, no. 9 (2002): 24–25.

McKinley, Michael. "The International Dimensions of Irish Terrorism." In *Terrorism in Ireland*. Edited by Y. Alexander and A. O'Day. London: Croomhelm, 1984.

Mead, George Herbert. *Mind, Self and Society from the Standpoint of a Social Behaviorist*. Chicago: University of Chicago Press, 1962.

Merari, Ariel. "Readiness to Kill and Die: Suicide Terrorism in the Middle East." In *Origins of Terrorism: Psychologies, Ideologies, Theologies, State of Mind*. Edited by Walter Reich. Baltimore, MD: Woodrow Wilson Center Press, 1998.

Mickolus, Edward F. *Transnational Terrorism: A Chronology of Events, 1968–1979*. Westport, CT: Greenwood Press, 1980.

Milgram, Stanley. *Obedience to Authority: An Experimental View*. New York: Harper and Row, 1974.

Miller, James G. "Living Systems. Basic Concepts." *Behavioral Science* 10 (1965): 193–237.

Murakami, Haruki. *Underground: The Tokyo Gas Attack and the Japanese Psyche*. New York: Vintage Books, 2000.

Murphy, Kim. "Cult of Reluctant Killers." *Los Angeles Times*. 4 February 2004.

Nacos, Brigitte L. *Mass-Mediated Terrorism*. Lanham, MD: Rowman and Littlefield, 2002.

Nacos, Brigitte L. *Terrorism and the Media: From the Iran Hostage Crisis to the World Trade Center Bombing*. New York: Columbia University Press, 1994.

National Commission on Terrorists Attacks Upon the United States (the 9/11 Commission). *The 9/11 Commission Report*. New York: W. W. Norton, 2004. Available online at http://www.gpoaccess.gov/911.

O'Callaghan, Sean. *The Informer*. London: Corgi Books, 1999.

O'Doherty, Shane. *The Volunteer: A Former IRA Man's True Story*. London: Fount, 1993.

Olcott, Martha B. "Central Asia's Political Crisis." In *Russia's Muslim Frontiers*. Edited by Dale F. Eickelman. Indianapolis: Indiana University Press, 1993.

Olcott, Martha Brill, and Bakhtiyar Babajanov. "The Terrorist Notebooks." *Foreign Policy* (March–April 2003): 30–40.

Olmert, Yosef. "Iranian-Syrian Relations: Between Islam and Realpolitik." In *The Iranian Revolution and the Muslim World*. Edited by David Menashri. Boulder, CO: Westview Press, 1990.

Olson, Kyle B. "Aum Shinrikyō: One and Future Threat?" *Emerging Infectious Diseases* 5, no. 4 (July–August 1999).

Ortiz, Román D. "Insurgent Strategies in the Post Cold War: The Case of the Revolutionary Armed Forces of Colombia." *Studies in Conflict and Terrorism* 25, no. 2 (2002): 127–43.

Padilla de León, Freddy José. "Terrorism and Subversion: Two Arms and One Single Strategy of Subversion to Destabilize the Country." Bogotá: unpublished master's thesis presented to the Faculty of Political Science and International Studies of the Pontifical University, 1994.

Pape, Robert A. "The Strategic Logic of Suicide Terrorism." *American Political Science Review* 97, no. 3 (August 2003): 343–61.

Paz, Reuven. "The Islamic Legitimacy of Suicide Terrorism." In *Countering Suicide Terrorism*. Herzliya: International Policy Institute for Counter-Terrorism, 2000.

Paz, Reuven. "Suicide Terrorist Operations in Chechnya: An Escalation of the Islamist Struggle." *Middle East Intelligence Bulletin* 2, no. 6 (2000).

Paz, Reuven. *Tangled Web: International Networking of the Islamist Struggle.* Washington, DC: The Washington Institute for Near East Policy, 2002.

Phillips, Howard, ed. *Field Manual of the Free Militia.* Free Militia, 1994. Online at: http://www.rickross.com/reference/militia/militia11.html.

Pipes, Daniel. *Militant Islam Reaches America.* New York and London: W. W. Norton, 2003.

Pipes, Daniel. "The Scourge of Suicide Terrorism." *The National Interest* (Summer 1986).

Pizarro, Eduardo. *The FARC 1949–1966. From the Self-Defense of Masses to the Combination of all Forms of Struggle.* Bogotá: Tercer Mundo Editores-IEPRI, 1992.

Pizarro, Eduardo. *Insurgency and Revolution: The Guerrilla in Colombia in a Comparative Perspective.* Bogotá: Tercer Mundo Editores-IEPRI, 1996.

Polesky, Joelie E. "The Rise of Private Militia: A First and Second Amendment Analysis of the Right to Organize and the Right to Train." *University of Pennsylvania Law Review* (April 1996).

Post, Jerrold M. *Leaders and Their Followers in a Dangerous World: The Psychology of Political Behavior.* Cornell University Press, 2004.

Post, Jerrold M. "Psychological Operations: Principal Weapon in Countering Terrorism." *Joint Force Quarterly* 35 (Fall 2004).

Post, Jerrold M. "Terrorist Psycho-logic: Terrorist Behavior as a Product of Psychological Forces." In *Origins of Terrorism: Psychologies, Ideologies, Theologies, States of Mind.* Edited by Walter Reich, pp. 25–40. Baltimore, MD: Woodrow Wilson Center Press, 1998.

Post, Jerrold M., Ehud Sprinzak, and Laurita M. Denny. "Terrorists in Their Own Words: Interviews with 34 Incarcerated Middle East Terrorist." *Terrorism and Political Violence* 15, no. 1 (Spring 2003).

Pratkanis, Anthony, and Elliott Aronson. *Age of Propaganda: The Everyday Use and Abuse of Persuasion.* New York: W. H. Freeman and Company, 1999.

Ramakrishna, Kumar, and See Seng Tan, eds. *After Bali: The Threat of Terrorism in Southeast Asia.* Singapore: World Scientific/Institute of Defence and Strategic Studies, 2003.

Ranstorp, Magnus. "Hizballah's Command Leadership: Its Structure, Decision-

Making and Relationship with Iranian Clergy and Institutions." *Terrorism and Political Violence* 6, no. 3 (Autumn 1994): 303–39.

Ranstorp, Magnus. *Hizb'allah in Lebanon: The Politics of the Western Hostage Crisis.* London: Macmillan, 1997.

Ranstorp, Magnus. "The Strategy and Tactics of Hizb'allah's Current 'Lebanonization.'" *Mediterranean Politics* 3, no. 1 (Summer 1998): 103–34.

Rapoport, David C., and Yonah Alexander, eds. *The Morality of Terrorism: Religious and Secular Justification.* Elmsford, NY: Pergamon Press, 1982.

Rashid, Ahmad. *Jihad: The Rise of Militant Islam in Central Asia.* New Haven: Yale University Press, 2002.

Reader, Ian. *Religious Violence in Contemporary Japan: The Case of Aum Shinrikyō.* Honolulu: University of Hawaii Press, 2000.

Reich, Walter, ed. *Origins of Terrorism: Psychologies, Ideologies, Theologies, States of Mind.* Baltimore, MD: Woodrow Wilson Center Press, 1990.

Reinares, Fernando. *Terrorism and Antiterrorism.* Barcelona, Spain: Paidos, 1998.

Reiss, David. "Varieties of Consensual Experience." *Family Process* 10 (1971): 1–35.

Ressa, Maria. *The Seeds of Terror: An Eyewitness Account of Al Qaeda's Newest Center of Operations in Southeast Asia.* New York: Free Press, 2003.

Roy, Olivier. *The Foreign Policy of the Central Asian Islamic Renaissance Party.* New York: Council on Foreign Relations, 2000.

Roy, Olivier. *The New Central Asia: The Creation of Nations.* New York: New York University Press, 1994.

Rumer, Boris. *Central Asia: A Gathering Storm?* New York: M. E. Sharpe, 2002.

Ruqaiyah, Abu. "The Islamic Legitimacy of the 'Martyrdom Operation.'" Available at http://islam.org.au/articles/16/martyrdom.htm (accessed on 31 October 2001).

Ruthven, Malise. *A Fury for God: The Islamic Attack On America.* London: Granta Books, 2003.

Sageman, Marc. *Understanding Terror Networks.* Philadelphia: University of Pennsylvania Press, 2004.

Schbley, Ayla. "Religious Terrorism, the Media, and International Islamization Terrorism: Justifying the Unjustifiable." *Studies in Conflict & Terrorism* 27, no. 3 (May–June 2004).

Schein, Edgar H. "Organizational Socialization and the Profession of Management." *MIT-Sloan Management Review* 30, no. 1 (1988): 53–65.

Schweitzer, Yoram. "Suicide Bombings: The Ultimate Weapon?" Herzliya: International Policy Institute for Counter-Terrorism. Available at http://ict.org.il/articles/articledet.cfm?articleid=373 (accessed on 21 November 2001).

Schweitzer, Yoram. "Suicide Terrorism: Development and Main Characteristics." Herzliya: International Policy Institute for Counter-Terrorism, 2000. Available at http://ict.org.il/articles/articledet.cfm?articleid=112.

Selengut, Charles. *Sacred Fury: Understanding Religious Violence.* Walnut Creek, CA: AltaMira Press, 2003.

Shahar, Yael. "The Al-Aqsa Martyrs Brigades: A Political Tool with an Edge." Herzliya: International Policy Institute for Counter-Terrorism. Available at www.ict.org.il (accessed on 26 March 2002).

Shay, Shaul. "Suicide Terrorism in Lebanon." In *Countering Suicide Terrorism*. Herzliya: International Policy Institute for Counter-Terrorism, 2000.

Skeyhill, Tom, ed. *Sergeant York: His Own Life Story and War Diary*. Garden City, NY: Doubleday, Doran, 1928.

Skoudis, Ed. *Counter Hack: A Step-by-Step Guide to Computer Attacks and Effective Defenses*. Upper Saddle River, NJ: Prentice Hall, 2002.

Sloan, Stephen, and Sean Anderson. *Historical Dictionary of Terrorism*. 2nd ed. London: The Scarecrow Press, 2002.

Smithson, Amy E., and Leslie Anne Levy. "Ataxia: The Chemical and Biological Terrorism Threat and the U.S. Response." Report No. 35. Washington, DC: Henry L. Stimson Center, 2000.

Sobelman, Daniel. "Hizballah Lends Its Services to the Palestinian Intifada." *Jane's Intelligence Review* (November 2001).

Sobelman, Daniel. *New Rules of the Game: Israel and Hizbollah After An Israeli Withdrawal From Lebanon*. Memorandum No. 69. Tel Aviv: Jaffee Center for Strategic Studies, January 2004.

Sprinzak, Ehud. "The Psychopolitical Formation of Extreme Left Terrorism in a Democracy: The Case of the Weathermen." In *Origins of Terrorism: Psychologies, Ideologies, Theologies, States of Mind*. Edited by Walter Reich, pp. 65–85. Baltimore: Woodrow Wilson Center Press, 1998.

Sprinzak, Ehud. "Rational Fanatics." *Foreign Policy* 120 (October 2000): 66–73.

Taarnby, Michael. "Recruitment of Islamist Terrorists in Europe: Trends and Perspectives." Center for Cultural Research (University of Aarhus, Denmark) on behalf of the Danish Ministry of Justice. 14 January 2005.

Thomas, Timothy L. "Al Qaeda and the Internet: The Danger of Cyberplanning." *Parameters* (Spring 2003): 118.

Tu, Anthony T. "Anatomy of Aum Shinrikyō's Organization and Terrorist Attacks with Chemical and Biological Weapons." *Archives of Toxicology, Kinetics and Xenobiotic Metabolism* 7, no. 3 (Autumn 1999).

U.S. Congress. House Committee on Financial Services Subcommittee on Oversight and Investigations. 11 March 2003. "Progress Since 9/11: The Effectiveness of U.S. Anti-Terrorist Financing Efforts: Arabian Gulf Financial Sponsorship of Al Qaeda via U.S.-Based Banks, Corporations and Charities." Testimony of Matthew Epstein with Evan Kohlmann. http://financialservices.house.gov/media/pdf/031103me.pdf.

U.S. Department of State. *Patterns of Global Terrorism* 2002. Department of State Publication 11038. Washington, DC: Office of the Secretary of State, Office of the Coordinator for Counterterrorism. Available online at http://www.state.gov/s/ct/rls/pgtrpt/.

U.S. The White House. *National Strategy for Security Cyberspace*. U.S. GPO, 2002. Available online at http://www.whitehouse.gov.

United States Institute of Peace. *Terrorism in the Horn of Africa: Special Report 113*. Washington, DC: United States Institute of Peace, 2004.

Urban, Mark. *Big Boys' Rules: The Secret Struggle Against the IRA*. London: Faber and Faber, 1992.

Victor, Barbara. *Army of Roses: Inside the World of Palestinian Women Suicide Bombers*. New York: Rodale Books, 2003.

Weimann, Gabriel. *WWW.Terror.Net—How Modern Terrorism Uses the Internet*. Special Report 116. Washington, DC: United States Institute of Peace, 2004. Available online at http://www.usip.org.

Weimann, Gabriel, and Conrad Winn. *The Theater of Terror: Mass Media and International Terrorism*. New York: Longman, 1994.

Weiner, Bernard. *An Attributional Theory of Motivation and Emotion*. New York: Springer-Verlag, 1986.

Weir, Fred. "Chechen Rebels Go Kamikaze." *Christian Science Monitor*. 6 July 2000.

Wiebes, Cees. *Intelligence and the War in Bosnia, 1992–1995*. Amsterdam: Netherlands Institute for War Documentation, 2002. Hamburg and London: LIT Verlag, 2003. Piscataway, NJ: Transaction, 2003.

Wright, Robin. *Sacred Rage: The Wrath of Militant Islam*. New York: Simon & Schuster, 2001.

Wynne, Lyman C., et al. "Pseudomutuality in the Family Relations of Schizophrenics." *Psychiatry* 21 (1958): 205–22.

Index

About the Editor and Contributors

JAMES J. F. FOREST, Ph.D., is Director of Terrorism Studies and Assistant Professor of Political Science at the U.S. Military Academy, where he teaches undergraduate courses in a range of subjects and directs research initiatives for the Combating Terrorism Center. Recent publications include *Homeland Security and Terrorism* (with Russell Howard and Joanne Moore, 2005), *Teaching Terror: Knowledge Transfer in the Terrorist World* (2005), a 200-page *Annotated Bibliography of Terrorism and Counterterrorism* (2004), available online at the Center's website (http://ctc.usma. edu), and *Terrorism and Oil in the New Gulf* (with Matt Sousa, forthcoming). His research has also appeared in the *Cambridge Review of International Affairs*, the *Journal of Political Science Education*, and the *Encyclopedia of Intelligence and Counterintelligence* (2005). Dr. Forest received his graduate degrees from Stanford University and Boston College and undergraduate degrees from Georgetown University and De Anza College.

ARABINDA ACHARYA, Ph.D., is an Associate Research Fellow and Manager of Strategic Projects at the International Center for Political Violence and Terrorism Research at the Institute of Defense and Strategic Studies. He is also the Research Coordinator for the Centre for Peace and Development Studies, India. His area of research includes conflict, political violence and human security. His published works have appeared in journals such as *Asian Defense and Diplomacy* (Kuala Lumpur), *The Georgetown Journal of International Affairs*, *Harvard Asia Quarterly*, *Pacific Affairs and Contemporary Southeast Asia*, and *Asia Pacific Review*.

BAKHTIYAR BABAJANOV is a Senior Research Fellow at the Institute of Oriental Studies of the Academic of Sciences of Uzbekistan. He has researched and written extensively on Islamic groups and the activities of the Hizb ut-Tahrir movement in Uzbekistan, including two chapters in *Islam in the Post-Soviet Newly Independent States: The View from Within*, edited by Aleksei Malashenko and Martha Brill Olcott (2001).

ALBERT BANDURA, Ph.D., is David Starr Jordan Professor of Social Sciences in Psychology at Stanford University. He has been elected to the presidency of the American Psychological Association and Western Psychological Association, and to the honorary presidency of the Canadian Psychological Association, the American Academy of Arts and Sciences, and the Institute of Medicine of the National Academy of Sciences. His published works include *Social Foundations of Thought and Action: A Social Cognitive Theory* (1986) and numerous other books, book chapters, journal articles, and conference presentations.

CINDY C. COMBS, Ph.D., is a Professor in the Department of Political Science at the University of North Carolina at Charlotte, where she teaches courses on security policy, terrorism, political violence, and international law. Combs is author of the bestseller *Terrorism in the Twenty-First Century*, 4th edition (2004) and co-author of *Encyclopedia of Terrorism* (2002). She also directs the university's Model United Nations program. She earned her Ph.D. in political science from George Washington University and master's and bachelor's degrees from Appalachian State University.

ELIZABETH A. COMBS is a student in the Department of Political Science at the University of North Carolina at Charlotte, where she conducts research on security policy, terrorism, political violence, and international law.

ARTHUR J. DEIKMAN, M.D., is Clinical Professor in the Department of Psychiatry at the University of California, San Francisco. He has written about mysticism, consciousness, service, and cult psychology in everyday life. Dr. Deikman is the author of several articles, reports, and books, including *The Wrong Way Home: Uncovering the Patterns of Cult Behavior in American Society* (1994) and *Them and Us: Cult Thinking and the Terrorist Threat* (2003).

ADAM DOLNIK is a Research Associate and Manager of Training at the International Center for Political Violence and Terrorism Research (ICPVTR) at the Institute of Defense and Strategic Studies in Singapore. He has worked as a researcher at the WMD Terrorism Research Program at the Monterey Institute of International Studies and at the United Nations Terrorism Prevention Branch in Vienna. His research has been published in a number of books and journals, including *Terrorism and Political Violence, Studies in Conflict and Terrorism, International Negotiation: Journal of Theory and Practice, Perspectives: Central European Review of International Affairs,* and *Yaderny Kontrol.*

MARC GALANTER, M.D., is Professor of Psychiatry at New York University and Director of NYU's Division of Alcoholism and Drug Abuse at its World Health Organization Collaborating Center and its Center for Spiritual Recovery from Mental Illness and Addiction. He has served as President of the Association for Medical Education and Research in Substance Abuse, the American Academy of Addiction Psychiatry, and the American Society of Addiction Medicine. He has published over 250 articles, chapters, and books, including *Cults: Faith, Healing and Coercion* (2nd edition 1999) and *Spirituality and Psychiatry at the Crossroads* (in press), and is editor of the journal *Substance Abuse.*

ROHAN GUNARATNA, Ph.D., is head of the International Centre for Political Violence and Terrorism Research at the Institute of Defense and Strategic Studies in Singapore. He is also a Senior Fellow at the Combating Terrorism Center at the U.S. Military Academy at West Point, and an Honorary Fellow at the International Policy Institute for Counter Terrorism in Israel. He is the author of over 100 papers and reports on terrorism as well as eight books—including the international best-seller *Inside Al Qaeda: Global Network of Terror* (2002).

BRIAN A. JACKSON, Ph.D., is an Associate Physical Scientist in RAND's Science and Technology Policy Institute. He has authored numerous reports, books, articles, and conference papers on terrorism, and his current and research activities include an ongoing project on personal protective technology for emergency responders and an examination of the adoption of new technologies by terrorist groups.

EVAN KOHLMANN, Ph.D., is an international terrorism consultant based in Washington, DC. He has served as an expert witness on al Qaeda and Osama bin Laden in post-9/11 federal terrorism trials held in the United States. His articles have appeared in the *New York Post*, FoxNews.com, and the *National Review*, and he is frequently interviewed as a terrorist expert in the major media, including NBC, CNN, and Fox news programs.

LYDIA MARSH is a student in the Department of Political Science at the University of North Carolina at Charlotte, where she conducts research on security policy, terrorism, political violence, and international law.

BRIGITTE L. NACOS, Ph.D., a long-time U.S. correspondent for publications in Germany, is an Adjunct Professor of Political Science at Columbia University. Her published works include *Terrorism and the Media: From the Iran Hostage Crisis to the World Trade Center Bombing* (1994) and *Mass-Mediated Terrorism: The Central Role of the Media in Terrorism and Counterterrorism* (2002).

MARTHA BRILL OLCOTT, Ph.D., is a senior associate at the Carnegie Endowment for International Peace, in Washington, DC, and co-director of the program on ethnic relations at the Carnegie Moscow Center. Dr. Olcott is professor emerita at Colgate University. She is the author of several books including *Kazakhstan: Unfulfilled Promise* (2002) and the forthcoming *Central Asia's Second Chance*.

ROMÁN D. ORTIZ, Ph.D., is Professor and Researcher at the Department of Political Science, School of Social Sciences at Los Andes University (Bogotá), where he focuses on the analysis of political violence and terrorism phenomena in Latin America. He has previously taught and researched these topics at Spanish academic institutions such as the General Gutiérrez Mellado Institute and the Ortega y Gasset Institute. Included in his most recent publications is the paper "President Alvaro Uribe's Counterinsurgency Strategy: Formula for Victory or Recipe for a Crisis?" published by the Elcano Institute in Madrid.

JOHN V. PARACHINI, Ph.D., is a policy analyst at RAND in Virginia, and has directed a variety of projects on the propensity of terrorists to acquire chemical, biological, radiological, and nuclear weapons. His recent publications include *Combating Terrorism: The 9/11 Commission Recommendations and the National Strategies* (2004), *Homeland Security: A Compendium of Public and Private Organizations' Policy Recommendations* (2003), *Combating Terrorism: Assessing the Threat of Biological Terrorism* (2001), and *Anthrax Attacks, Biological Terrorism and Preventive Responses* (2001).

JERROLD M. POST, Ph.D., is Professor of Psychiatry, Political Psychology, and International Affairs and Director of the Political Psychology Program at the George Washington University. He came to GWU after a twenty-one-year career with the Central Intelligence Agency, where he was founding director of the Center for the Analysis of Personality and Political Behavior. He has been conducting research and publishing on the psychology of terrorism since the late 1970s.

KUMAR RAMAKRISHNA, Ph.D., is Assistant Professor and Head of Studies at the Institute of Defense and Strategic Studies, Nanyang Technological University, Singapore. His current research interests include propaganda theory and practice; history of strategic thought; and counterterrorism. His published works include *Emergency Propaganda: The Winning of Malayan Hearts and Minds, 1948–1958* (2002), *The New Terrorism: Anatomy, Trends and Counter-Strategies* (2003) and *After Bali: The Threat of Terrorism in Southeast Asia* (2004).

MAGNUS RANSTORP, Ph.D., is the research director of the Center for Asymmetric Threat Studies at the Swedish National Defence College in Stockholm. He will be heading a major funding research project on Strategic Terrorism Threats within Europe, including the issue of radicalization and recruitment of jihadi extremists. He is the author of *Hizb'allah in Lebanon: The Politics of the Western Hostage Crisis* (1997) and numerous articles and monographs on terrorism and counterterrorism. He is a member of the International Editorial Advisory Board of *Studies in Conflict and Terrorism*, and is internationally recognized as a leading expert on Hizballah, Hamas, al Qaeda, and other militant Islamic movements. In 2003, he was invited to testify before 9/11 Commission in the first hearing, "The Attackers, Intelligence and Counterterrorism Policy."